Making History New

Making History New

MODERNISM AND HISTORICAL NARRATIVE

Seamus O'Malley

OXFORD
UNIVERSITY PRESS

OXFORD

UNIVERSITY PRESS

Oxford University Press is a department of the University of Oxford.
It furthers the University's objective of excellence in research, scholarship,
and education by publishing worldwide.

Oxford   New York
Auckland   Cape Town   Dar es Salaam   Hong Kong   Karachi
Kuala Lumpur   Madrid   Melbourne   Mexico City   Nairobi
New Delhi   Shanghai   Taipei   Toronto

With offices in
Argentina   Austria   Brazil   Chile   Czech Republic   France   Greece
Guatemala   Hungary   Italy   Japan   Poland   Portugal   Singapore
South Korea   Switzerland   Thailand   Turkey   Ukraine   Vietnam

Oxford is a registered trade mark of Oxford University Press
in the UK and certain other countries.

Published in the United States of America by
Oxford University Press
198 Madison Avenue, New York, NY 10016

Library of Congress Cataloging-in-Publication Data
O'Malley, Seamus.
Making history new : modernism and historical narrative / Seamus O'Malley.
p.   cm.
Includes bibliographical references and index.
ISBN 978–0–19–936423–7
1. Modernism (Literature)—England.   2. Historical fiction, English—History and criticism.
3. Narration (Rhetoric)—History—20th century.   I. Title.
PR478.M6O63 2015
820.9'112—dc23

2014015666

1   3   5   7   9   8   6   4   2

Printed in the United States of America on acid-free paper

To Em, my best friend

"There is everything, or Everything, the great undifferentiated past, all of it, which is not history, but just stuff. . . . From that, you make history, which is never what *was* there, once upon a time."

—CAROLYN STEEDMAN, *DUST: THE ARCHIVE AND CULTURAL HISTORY*

"But if there are no stories, what end can there be, or what beginning? Life is not susceptible perhaps to the treatment we give it when we try to tell it."

—VIRGINIA WOOLF, *THE WAVES*

{ CONTENTS }

Preface   ix
History and the Holocaust Test   ix
Chapter Summaries   xvi
Acknowledgments   xxi

Introduction   1
I Know God, I Know My Heart: The Presuppositions of Nineteenth-Century
    History   11
Ellipses in Modernist Narratology   17
James and Conrad's Senses of the Past   22
Ford and the "Devil of Theorizing"   27
The Myths of High Modernism: Eliot, Pound, Lewis   33
Paul Ricoeur's Narratology of History   40

1. Joseph Conrad and the Necessity of History in *Nostromo*   48
"In the Thick of History"   51
The Necessary Failure of History   55
The Miracle of Histories   63
Vanishing Traces: *Under Western Eyes*   67
Nostromo and the Historical Novel   68

2. Rewriting and Repetition in *The Good Soldier*   71
The Unity of Style   71
Avoidance and Repetition   74
His-story (Dowell's, That Is)   80
Revisionary Fictions   84
Repetition and the Field of History   88

3. Returning, Remembering, and Forgetting in *The Return
of the Soldier*   92
West's Modernist Pastoral   92
History Through the Pastoral   102
History and Forgetting   109

4. The Rememoration of *Some Do Not . . .* (*Parade's End*, Volume 1)   118
No Enemy and the Wartime Failure of Impressionism   118
Some Do Not . . . : Ford's Rewriting of West's Pastoral   123
Modernism and the "Memory Crisis"   129
Amnesia and the Severance of Social Identity   134
"Epic Forgetting": The Necessity of History, the Necessity of Forgetting   138

5. **The Impossible Necessity of** *Black Lamb and Grey Falcon*   147
   West's Historical Novel   147
   Memory and Forgetting   151
   History's Impossibilities   154
   Nonsense and Supersense   156
   Modernism at War   161
   The Horror of History   170
   History's Strange Necessities   177

Conclusion: History after the Holocaust   180

Notes   193
Works Cited   247
Index   263

History and the Holocaust Test

The radical epistemology of postmodern historical theory enters a highly charged social space when faced with what Lubomír Doležel calls "the Holocaust test."[1] When confronted with humanity's greatest crime, doubting the validity of historical representation comes dangerously close to doubting the Holocaust itself. A 1989 conference "History, Event, and Discourse" saw a bracing debate between Hayden White, the most daring of poststructural theorists of historiography, and Carlo Ginzburg, an experimenter in historical form who is more traditional on issues of historical truths. The conference led to the collection *Probing the Limits of Representation: Nazism and the "Final Solution"* (1992), edited by Saul Friedländer.[2] Friedländer, in his introduction, voices a wariness at White's historical relativism, but also acknowledges the paucity of inherited historiographical forms to depict the Holocaust in any true sense, a point shared by nearly all the contributors to the volume.[3] The Holocaust is, in Friedländer's terms, an "event at the limits," as traditional methods of depiction fail to live up to the scale of horror. Instead, historians struggling to write about the Holocaust are faced with the dual challenge of representing the unrepresentable while simultaneously obeying an ethical imperative to remember and recreate the past in language. As Michael S. Roth writes in *Memory, Trauma, and History* (2012), historical trauma "cannot be contained in representation, but it is 'too big to fail'—too important to be left out of an attempt to make sense of the past at either the individual or collective level."[4] Any historian working with an "event at the limit" must confront this aporia of necessity and impossibility.

This study will examine how Joseph Conrad, Ford Madox Ford, and Rebecca West anticipated these debates in their own experiments with the historical novel and works of narrative history. These three modernist British writers struggled with representations of history in much the same way that subsequent historians would after the Holocaust—skeptical of narrative's abilities to represent historical objects, but simultaneously driven by the need to narrate past human experience. What separates this constellation of writers from other canonical modernists, and makes them so valuable for a study of modernism and the writing of history, is their adherence and dedication to narrative. If "to write a poem after Auschwitz is barbaric," as Adorno famously stated, is it equally barbaric to craft narratives? Can storytelling do justice to history? As the philosopher Paul Ricoeur remarked on Holocaust histories, "one either counts the cadavers or one tells the story of the victims."[5]

Conrad, Ford, and West had also grappled with this crisis of historical form. What both frustrated and fascinated these three writers about historical writing was an issue central to modernism itself, the gap between subjects and their representations. In 1962 West wrote a discursive essay titled "The Event and Its Image." Touching on issues of empire, epistemology, and Joseph Conrad ("Conrad, whose nobility was just too fierce for saintliness"), West formulated a theory of writing and knowledge that had been latent in much of her work after the Second World War:[6]

> Not everything that happens to us is an experience. It is an event. But an experience is an event which affects one so that it tests one, and one tests it. It calls on one to take account of it, to pass a judgement on it, to modify one's philosophy in the light of the added knowledge it has brought one. Then, if it retains its importance after it has been scrutinized in this way, by the head, by the heart, one incorporates an image of the event into one's mind; and should one be an imaginative writer one can afterwards project it into the visible world as a poem, a novel, a short story, a play.[7]

She might have added, "a history." In this essay West ponders the means by which the past becomes knowledge or understanding, especially via written texts. Telling stories are how we process the past, whether it is through composing a lyric poem, talking to a therapist, or writing a work of history. Events are continually occurring; experience is rare and hard-fought. The discipline of history faces the gargantuan task of taking human events and turning them into experiences, narrating the past in an attempt at understanding.

West was a personal witness to many of the events of the twentieth century that we have collectively attempted to absorb as experiences. She lived through history. But the term "history" can also refer to the narratives we tell and write about the past, and in this more textual sense she was present at one of the key moments of history, the postwar Nuremberg Trials. These trials, for which West wrote articles for the *Daily Telegraph* and *The New Yorker*—eventually published as *A Train of Powder* (1955)—were one of the first public instances of the events of the Holocaust becoming an experience. Lyndsey Stonebridge opens her work *The Judicial Imagination: Writing after Nuremberg* (2011) with West because West "allows us to catch a glimpse, as it were, of what it meant to respond to genocide in the pre-history of the era of the witness," a description that could equally be applied to Conrad's witnessing of the reach of European empires, or Ford's witnessing the Western Front during the First World War.[8] As Margaret Stetz writes of the trials, "Rebecca West proved an important figure. She had not only an immediate impact upon how British newspaper readers saw the trials at their conclusion, but also an ongoing influence in forming the events into the stuff of political and social history."[9] At Nuremberg, West was an observer of the moment when history became histories, when the past was transformed into narratives of the past. And, while not present at the events of the Holocaust, she has shaped how we perceive them.

Throughout the trial, West's writerly voice constantly moves through the past, the atrocities of the Nazis; the present, the trial and its surrounding culture; and especially the future, what she terms "the service rendered to history by the Nuremberg trial":

> This was immense. Many thousands of documents from enemy archives were submitted by the prosecution, and as they could be challenged by the defence their authenticity was guaranteed; and the witnesses annotated them and had to prove their annotations under cross-examination. Though they are not now easily accessible to the general reader, they are there for the student; and the lawyers had to act with a haste that was all to the good. The historians would have taken them to their studies, shut the doors, and dealt with them at the slow pace of scholarship, and scholarly prejudices and obsessions would have struck deep roots and grown a quickset hedge about the facts before the work was done.[10]

Here West is both acknowledging the limitations and biases of historical writing, while also making the case for the utter necessity of historical testament so that future historians can deal with the traces and narratives of the past to craft new histories. Trials of this kind serve at least two purposes, one legal, the other historical. Legally, punishments have to be issued, judgments made. But the trial is also necessary for documentary purposes, especially in a case like Nuremberg, where the guilt of the accused was solidly established even before the trial had begun, and no one doubted the greater ramifications of the legal proceedings of a small handful of men: the trial was in the service of history more than law.

West had covered another trial, for *The New Yorker* in 1945, of William Joyce, the infamous traitor "Lord Haw-Haw." Joyce had daily broadcasted pro-Nazi propaganda into Great Britain, so again his guilt was clear to all (the trial only hinged on technicalities dealing with his ambiguous national origin). From this trial, West generalized that the law was "the solution by a community of one of its temporal problems": "To make laws is a human instinct which arises as soon as food and shelter have been ensured, among all peoples, everywhere. . . . But neither they nor any other society could define exactly what they were doing when they were making that agreement and ordaining those penalties."[11] Laws are hastily made and hastily enforced, at least in comparison to the slower rhythms of the discipline of history, and West stressed the service that the Joyce trial provided for future historians: "I was encouraged to make a book about these people by an eminent lawyer who was concerned because the shortage of newsprint due to the war meant that these trials were either not reported or were reported too briefly for the public to gain any real information regarding a significant tendency."[12] West had to make sure that a reliable record was left behind, so she could not trust the mechanics of the law nor the daily narratives of print journalism. She had first encountered this challenge before the war, in composing her masterpiece *Black Lamb and Grey Falcon* (1941). Concerning the trial of the Serbian assassins of Franz Ferdinand in 1914, she wrote that

> [t]here were naturally no English or French correspondents at that time; and there were apparently no American journalists. None could follow Serbo-Croat, so they took their material from German colleagues. The most dramatic event of our time was thus completely hidden from us at the time when it most affected us; and it has only been gradually and partially revealed.[13]

For the West of the late 1930s, this was no academic issue, as she traveled to Yugoslavia believing, accurately, that a Nazi invasion of the country was inevitable, and that she had to take an "inventory of a country down to its last vest-button."[14] The death of Franz Ferdinand, which was such a catalyst to the atrocities of the twentieth century, were still only "partially revealed," and West's efforts before and after the war were to ensure that the major events of her lifetime would be fully exposed. Only then could events become experience.

The subjects of West's musings on the role of the law and the field of history have become central topics for theorists of history. In his analysis of twentieth-century show trials, *The Judge and the Historian* (1991, English translation 1999), Carlo Ginzburg compares the roles of historian and judge and concludes that "the notions of evidence and truth are . . . an integral part of the profession of historian."[15] Both judge and historian must evaluate the testimony of witnesses and draw conclusions, but Paul Ricoeur in *Memory, History, Forgetting* (2004) argues that Ginzburg does not adequately consider where the two roles diverge. Most obviously, the subjects of a trial are allowed cross-examination that the subjects of history are denied. But more important, for Ricoeur, is what happens after the judge pronounces or the historian concludes. The former's ruling is usually carried and never reversed; the historian's conclusions are "submitted to the critique of the corporation of historians and to the critique of the enlightened public, and the work subjected to an unending process of revision, which makes the writing of history a perpetual rewriting. This openness to rewriting marks the difference between a provisional historical judgment and a definitive judicial judgment."[16] Legal judgments are final. But history repeats itself, not in the sense of events reoccurring, but by the constant return of historians to events of the past to reanalyze and renarrate them. For Ricoeur, "[t]he circles that the judge closes after having cautiously opened them, the historian pries open again."[17] In her trial reportings, West dramatizes how history is continually being reprised, retold, re-visioned, revised, represented.[18]

History revisions in order to understand, in order to turn events into experiences. Stonebridge argues that

> [u]nderstanding what turns a trial from a legal event into a historical experience is a—if not the—key question for war crime and genocide trials. To transform reason into aesthetics is to demand not only that justice is done, but also that it is felt to be done by a community of witnesses, victims, perpetrators and bystanders.[19]

Ideally, genocide trials serve such a double purpose, but toward the end of the Nuremberg proceedings West lamented that it "was one of the events which do not become an experience."[20] Observing the state of German culture after the war, she worried that the full implications of the trials had not sunk in, that, as Stonebridge explains, there was "a quietly menacing sense that something is still missing."[21] For Debra Rae Cohen, West stressed "the impossibility of completely 'reading' Nuremberg," and West's anxiety, shared by many, was that history would always remain opaque and inaccessible, which, in the context of postwar Europe, made justice for the Nazis' victims increasingly unobtainable.[22] In a sense, she was right as to the opacity of history, as West was one of the many participants and observers at Nuremberg who could not see the magnitude of the damage done to the Jewish population of Europe, and that Jews were targeted for systematic destruction in a manner not even in keeping with the most barbaric forms of warfare.[23] Thus the events were recalcitrant to experience in more ways than West could even acknowledge. West believed that the event of the war had not been absorbed into experience by the German people; what she did not yet see is how the event of the Holocaust had to become an experience for the entire world.

West's inability to perceive the full horrors of the Nazi regime was shared by many (although not all) Western observers. What separates her writings from that of her contemporaries is her concern with the crisis of historical narrative itself, which she insisted does not live up to the task of historical remembering. Cohen argues that "West both depicts Nuremberg's historic challenge and acts it out on the level of form. Yet this depiction is itself a divided one."[24] West voices her frustrations, not just at postwar Germany, but at the very process of historical transmittal and representation:

> But destiny cares nothing about the orderly presentation of its material. Drunken with an exhilaration often hard to understand, it likes to hold its cornucopia upside down and wave it while its contents drop anywhere they like over time and space. Brave are our human attempts to counteract this sluttish habit . . . brave the men who, in making the Nuremberg trial, tried to force a huge and sprawling historical event to become comprehensible. It is only by making such efforts that we survive.[25]

This passage encapsulates West's attitudes toward historical writing: it is impossible to faithfully record and understand the past, but such brave attempts are absolutely necessary for humanity's survival. We must never forget what it is impossible to adequately remember. While West may not have perceived the Holocaust at Nuremberg, she intuited the historiographical process and dramatized both the means by which events would someday become experiences, as well as the myriad challenges that such a process entails.

West's perceptions of the workings of historical memory and narrative did not free her from her own limitations, as critics have justifiably found fault with her handling of Nuremberg, but that in itself evidences the repetitive nature of the historiographical process.[26] Later historians of Nuremberg have gotten it more right via their revisions. Her coverage of the Nuremberg trials, which analyzed the traces left by the war, is now a trace in histories of genocide trial reportings in histories like that by Stonebridge. History repeats; it never rests.

Thus any historian who wants to both narrate the past, but also maintain an awareness of the contingent nature of such narrations, must struggle with the formal mechanics of historical presentation. Sometimes orthodox forms will not suffice. This book will look at some of those unorthodox experiments launched under the umbrella of literary modernism, but subsequent attempts at new ways of writing history can be found in written histories, documentaries, art installations, and performances. One major instance is the United States Holocaust Memorial Museum, located in Washington, D.C., which has chosen to represent the Holocaust to its visitors employing narrative, although not in a linear, "realist" fashion. Established in 1993, the Museum calls itself "a living memorial to the Holocaust": a combination of display museum, research library, and community resource center. The curative choices in the display museum are one reaction to the twentieth century's historiographical crisis, and hopefully the following brief analysis of it will be useful in understanding both the methods, but especially the stakes, of experimental historiography. As Jeffrey Karl Ochsner notes, in the display rooms of the Museum "the narrative is primary; the objects, including historical photographs and films as well as artifacts, are in fact seen as evidence offered to sustain and validate the narrative."[27] Despite the powerful challenges to narrative launched by mid-century structuralist historians, as well as the repeated difficulties encountered by narrative historians on the subject of the Holocaust, the Museum has opted for narrative and storytelling as their primary organizing principle. However, Ochsner notes, this presents "a particular problem": objects have been uplifted from their original context and inserted into a narrative chosen by the curative historian, and thus "the appropriation of the objects by the museum cannot avoid separating us from the real experiences of the Holocaust itself."[28] This problem of selection is not unique to a physical presentation of a narrative, as even textual narratives must be made out of selections and appropriations. Ochsner concludes, however: "[o]n the other hand, without the Holocaust Museum the memory of the history of the Holocaust might be lost."[29]

History's necessity and impossibility has always and will always taunt historians and writers, but the Museum's specific narrative choices attempt to ameliorate the "problem" that Ochsner notes. The Museum employs narrative, but not just *a* narrative. Visitors do not get a linear story; instead, they are randomly given individual identity cards of Holocaust victims as they enter the museum, and are encouraged to try to comprehend what is happening, not just through a twenty-first-century visitor's perspective, but also through the perspective of the assigned identity. As you proceed through the museum, you read further information in your identity card as your identity's fate becomes further revealed. Thus no two visits to the museum will be quite the same: on my visit I was a male university student from eastern Germany; my wife was a schoolgirl from Poland. Multiple perspectives are built into the museum experience, as there are thousands of possible ways to experience it.

The display rooms themselves fracture into multiple narratives. While one's walk through the museum generally follows a chronological format, there are many shifts in levels of history. We are given the macro-history: the rise of the Nazis, Germany's military advances, the emergence of the Final Solution, the Allies' victories. Although these proceed in a linear fashion, they are interrupted by micro-histories of specific individuals, mostly victims, whose artifacts we experience with striking immediacy, allowing us an uncomfortably intimate access to the lives whose collective experience makes up the history of the war. This rapid shift across levels was one of the signature features of Rebecca West's *Black Lamb and Grey Falcon*, as she also alternated between large- and small-scale narratives in her depiction of Balkan history.

The Holocaust Museum is just one instance of a historical perspective that struggles to live up the ethical task of historical remembering while also acknowledging the paucity of received historical forms. Late-twentieth-century efforts to enforce justice around issues of genocide evidence the necessity of histories, and the historian Elazar Barkan writes of the "centrality of historical memory in contemporary political conflict evident all around us."[30] In regard to the Turkish genocide of Armenians during and after the Great War, Barkan concludes that this "is an intense case that exemplifies the ascendancy of demands for historical redress and acknowledgment in international politics. It testifies not only to the growing role of human rights in political debates, but also to the public awareness that historical identity is central to shaping relations between states and peoples."[31] In cases like Armenia or the former Yugoslavia, Barkan stresses the need for "shared narratives" across communities that are "unlikely to be linear or monovocal and will most likely have distinct registers. There may be meta-agreement and a variety of interpretations about the local and the specifics."[32] Such projects are daunting, not just because of the vast volume and array of research methods required, but also because of the pressure it puts on narrative form. Again, West had to confront similar obstacles during her personal tour through the Balkans in *Black Lamb,* depicting a region whose very name has become synonymous with chaotic fragmentation. But West embeds the challenge in the narrative itself, as her constant shifting of levels allows us to see how histories are constructed, exposing the story as a story, while also fulfilling the very human need to have events from the past related to us as stories themselves. West was facing a situation as urgent as that of postwar redress, which was the threat of the annihilation of Balkan collective memory as Germany was preparing to invade. West's *Black Lamb* is, I will argue, one major culmination of modernist historiography, the late and most robust manifestation of a process that began at the turn of the century when writers, especially Joseph Conrad and Ford Madox Ford, were questioning the legitimacy of inherited historiographical forms, and yet were simultaneously driven by ethical imperatives to remember.

Chapter Summaries

In my Introduction I explore some of the reigning narratives regarding modernism, the historical novel, and historical narrative generally. For some critics the modernist historical novel is simply an impossibility. Criticism of the postmodern historical novel, in particular, has been eager to cast modernism as averse to the narration of history in order to argue for postmodernism's privileged access to historiographical form. For other critics the historical novel is regarded as solely a nineteenth-century phenomenon, but the genre actually continued into the twentieth century and even played a key role in the emergence of British literary modernism.

The modernist era inherited a perplexing array of historical discourses. The powerful and diverse achievements of nineteenth-century German historiography, especially via the work of Ranke, Hegel, and Dilthey, shared one major assumption: that history was accessible to human intelligence. A heavy degree of learning, labor, and Absolute Spirit might be necessary to unlock its secrets, but their faith in the task of the historian never wavered. As the twentieth century emerged through the more skeptical notions of Nietzsche, Freud, and Bergson, historiographical assumptions began to be scrutinized to an unprecedented degree, and this came in tandem with the revolutions to poetic and fictional form that we associate with modernism. But if the practices of history were being questioned, its pressing needs only intensified. As Foucault charted in *The Order of Things* (1966), the nineteenth century felt that it needed the discipline of history to restore a sense of order to reality that the process of secularization was threatening to undermine.

It is my contention that many modernist writers, especially Joseph Conrad, Ford Madox Ford, and Rebecca West, responded to these challenges by using the form of the historical novel and historical narrative to explore such pressing issues, but above all to question the very process of historiography itself: How do events from the past become written historical narratives? How does history turn into histories? In this Introduction I look briefly at Henry James, Virginia Woolf, Ford, Conrad, Ezra Pound, T. S. Eliot, W. B. Yeats, and Wyndham Lewis to survey the heterogeneity of textual and aesthetic approaches of the modernist period. Pound and Eliot, especially, have been taken to be representative of modernism's relationship to history, especially their choice of non-narrative forms. Pound's *The Cantos*—his "poem including history"— includes dense networks of historical signifiers, advancing a specific speculative philosophy of history that precludes any attempt at historical narrative, rendering the concept of the modernist historical novel implausible. *The Cantos* contain the idea and signs of history—history as a concept. By the middle cantos, however, they are not *histories*: they do not attempt to narrate history, but rather include references to past events, which is quite a different thing. History is "included" in the same way as foreign languages and allusions to other literary texts are included. The fragmented poem by no means "escapes from history," as the old Lukacian argument went, but it does resist narrative as a means of depicting such history.

Wyndham Lewis was eager to see this aspect of Pound's work: while critical of Pound in the twenties, he shared with the poet a hostility to narrative that Lewis laid out in *Time and Western Man* (1927). Eliot, likewise, aggressively rejected narrative and instead looked to the synchronic ordering of myth to give meaning to time. Rather than retreating from history altogether, the writings of Eliot and Pound actually presage the structuralist and poststructuralist critiques of historical narratives, and provide models of poetic and visual modes of historiography that have strong affinities with the structuralist, synchronic works of history by writers such as Fernand Braudel and Jacques Le Goff. But not every modern followed this path, just as not every historian rejected diachrony and narrative, and the poetic fragmented images of Pound and Eliot are only one method of trying to "include history." We can shift the way we think about modernism's relationship to history by considering the constellation of Conrad, Ford, and West.

Finally, the theoretical underpinning of my study will be the work of Paul Ricoeur, whose formal investigations of history I summarize at the end of the Introduction. In his two major works on historical form, *Time and Narrative* (1983) and *Memory, History, Forgetting* (2004), Ricoeur elucidated the interactions between history and fiction, between memory and narrative, and, especially pertinent for any study of Ford and West, the complex role of forgetting in the writing of history.

Chapter 1, "Joseph Conrad and the Necessity of History in *Nostromo*," argues that the historical novel was crucial to the formation of English modernism. Conrad's *Nostromo* (1904), a novel set in the fictional Latin American country of Castaguana, depicts a nativist uprising and its effects on the multiracial town of Sulaco. The novel raises troubling questions of empire, nationhood, and race, but Conrad's text is also engrossed with history as a form: the text constantly alludes to works of history within its own narrative, most strikingly a text written by one of the characters called *Fifty Years of Misrule*. Comparing this fictional historical text with the historical fiction that we are reading prompts us to ponder the many similarities between the various forms. Poststructuralist critics have fastened on *Nostromo's* slippages between history and fiction as a means by which the authority of historical discourse is undermined. However, Conrad also stresses the need for historical texts, especially with the journalist Martin Decoud. In one scene Decoud writes letters to his sister overseas, recounting recent political upheavals. He is writing by candlelight in a café, and the very act of textual production seems to ward off the darkness outside that is described in such threatening terms. Much later, Decoud dies by his own hand, in solitude, leaving behind only a bloody smear—a parody of a written historical testament. *Nostromo* suggests that the tragedy in such cases is not so much the death of a solitary individual but rather the inability to bequeath an historical text to posterity, possibly responding to Herodotus's defense of his history, composed "so that human achievements may not become forgotten in time." Despite Conrad's famously despairing judgments of the possibilities of communication in *Heart of Darkness* and *Lord Jim*, in *Nostromo* he highlights the human need for histories to maintain historical continuity and ward off the darkness of textual oblivion.

Thus the modernist historical novel was present in, and an essential part of, modernism's emergence as a cultural phenomenon. Ford Madox Ford's *The Good Soldier*, the masterpiece of narrative self-consciousness, can also be taken as a historical novel, depicting the upper crust of Europe on the brink of war. Ford's novel goes further than just historical reconstruction, however, and I am more drawn to how it dramatizes the process of historical narration. Formally, the novel offers a dissenting vision of historical circularity, as I argue in Chapter 2, "Rewriting and Repetition in *The Good Soldier*." Critics of modernism and history have been drawn to the Viconian cycles in Joyce or the spirals of Yeats, suggesting a modernist concern with circularity and return. But for Ford, history is circular not in the mystical or speculative sense in which seminal occurrences or forces are repeated throughout time; rather, our own attempts to retell the past in language—the forms of history—are themselves destined to cyclical revision. In *The Good Soldier*, key events, like the quartet's trip to Marburg or the suicide of Florence Dowell, appear several times throughout the narrative. But this recurrence is not due to some cosmic shape of history, but rather to the more ordinary workings of memory and narrative, as Dowell keeps returning to the most intense periods of his past in an effort to better understand them. We can analogize such a process to historiographical practices, which continually retell moments from the past like the French Revolution or the Holocaust, each time hoping to improve on previous tellings. For my purposes, I read Ford's novel as theorizing the entire field of history, circular in its endless repetition of narrations.

Rebecca West's first novel *The Return of the Soldier* (1919) pursues this interest in nonlinear histories. The historical novel was very much a male-dominated genre, for the most part excluding women as essential to the foundations and workings of the European nation-state. But in West's hands the genre becomes a means of interrogating inherited notions of patriarchy, power, and social class, while also working through the paradox of West's position as a feminist writer, still disenfranchised by her nation, qualifiedly launching a defense of the war effort against Germany. Her first novel is thus an exploration of some of the most pressing political issues of the war era, and I will investigate how and why the historical novel was called upon to negotiate these concerns in Chapter 3, "Returning, Remembering, and Forgetting in *The Return of the Soldier.*" However, her deceptively simply text contains even more layers of complexity that relate to memory, history, and forgetting. The mode in which West chose to write her novel was the pastoral, as we are never directly presented with trench warfare, and West exploits the pastoral trope of presence via absence. As far back as Virgil, the pastoral mode depicts idyllic moments from shepherds' lives in order to signal other, often more violent, discourses. The setting of this Big House novel rarely strays from Baldry Estate, and yet the protagonist's absence of memories continually suggests a traumatic and shattering war. Analogously, Baldry's memories of war are never present, but this amnesia only draws the war in closer to himself and those around him. Baldry's amnesia is also the novel's meditation on the role of forgetting in narrative history. Baldry expresses a Nietzschean desire to escape from the oppressive burden of history, while the text simultaneously alerts us to the sobering need for memory and remembrance. However, Baldry's forgetting, paradoxically, preserves the traumatic nature of the war in a way that any fully informed account could not, as amnesia becomes the depository of historical experience.

Chapter 4, "The Rememoration of *Some Do Not . . .*," turns to the first volume of Ford's *Parade's End* (1924–1928). This epic story of the Great War and its effect on English society has been praised for its handling of historical materials, and criticism has only begun to unearth what is so revolutionary in these works, and what makes them so highly relevant to our own period. But many features of Rebecca West's first novel conspicuously reappear in *Some Do Not . . .* (1924), and I argue that Ford deliberately lifted his story and many methods (and his hero's name) from West's work: in both novels, a wealthy, landed, shell-shocked soldier named Christopher suffers from a bad marriage and seeks comfort in a warmer and wiser lover. These two works are early engagements with the formulation of shell-shock as a medical condition, yet are simultaneously theorizings of modernist historical practices. Both heroes do not have access to their war memories: the only depictions of war are secondhand. For West and Ford, language cannot directly name historical objects (hence their critique of what is sometimes called "historical realism," the default mode of orthodox history). Instead, history and historical events must be "thought round," to use the words of Ford's protagonist.

For Ford, himself a witness to the Battle of the Somme, narrating his war experience was partly self-therapeutic. But he also saw himself as occupying a unique social role: "I wanted the novelist to in fact appear in his really proud position as historian of his own time."[33] In Ricoeur's words, history must "live up to the task of memory," and Ford and West utilized modernist techniques to that end. Ford was writing of a war he had seen; West, in 1938, began writing of the war to come. Chapter 5, "The Impossible Necessity of *Black Lamb and Grey Falcon*," advances West's work (1941) as a monument to modernist historiography. Her immersion in the formative years of modernism, I argue, makes itself felt in her epic work, a sprawling travel tour of the Balkans on the eve of the Second World War. West's text defies genre categorization, but we might dub it a novel, because of its fictionalization of many aspects of her journeys, but more pressingly, in the full Bakhtinian sense it devours multiple discourses, resulting in a multi-hybrid form incorporating history, fiction, travel, art appreciation, and ethnology. The style of *Black Lamb* is both compellingly authoritative and highly subjective. It continually frets about its own form, wondering, like Conrad's Marlow, if its story is having any effect on its reader, or if communication is just an impossible ideal. For West, the stakes are tremendous, as in 1938, the book's setting, the Third Reich was poised to invade and dismantle Yugoslavia, which for West's 1941 readers was already an accomplished fact. Her work was a call to intervention against fascism, and it is striking to see modernist techniques, that for the most part were limited to literary circles of the European capitals, adopted for a text meant to galvanize several empires into action against the Nazi menace. West's ethical imperative to act led her to fictionalize major segments of her historical journey, raising troubling questions about the relationship between narrative and fact, personal memory and collective, and the duty we owe to the past compared with that of the future.

I conclude with a brief overview of the current state of "creative history," noting when contemporary historians either borrow or seem influenced by modernist techniques. My contention is that modernist novels are fecund sites for historians striving for new forms of narrative.

{ ACKNOWLEDGMENTS }

Since parts of this book began as seminar essays from as far back as 2003, I have had over a decade of help and support. I would first like to thank Brendan O'Neil at Oxford University Press for his kind efforts. Thanks also to Oxford's anonymous readers who helped make this book better.

Hunter College's English M.A. is still the best deal in town, and I would especially like to acknowledge Cristina Alfar's warmth and guidance. At the CUNY Graduate Center, I benefited from a roster of challenging scholars, such as Ammiel Alcalay, Sandi Cooper, Mario DiGangi, Steven Kruger, and Alan Vardy. Robert Reid-Pharr's writing seminar tricked me into beginning my dissertation, so I never had to face a blank screen. I blush to think of what might have seen print without the bracing critiques of Nico Israel and Talia Schaffer.

While the writing support group of Lizzie Harris McCormick, Laurel Harris, and Caroline Zoe Krzakowski provided academic critique, I am equally grateful for the friendships that emerged.

Critics often reflect their subjects, and the Ford Madox Ford community enjoys animated discussions over long French dinners. Max Saunders has made Ford scholarship so exciting and relevant, both through his foundational biography and steady generosity. Sara Haslam has given me support, advice, and a valuable friendship. Paul Skinner was the first to ever edit my work into print. Thanks also to Jason Andrew, John Attridge, Alexendra Becquet, Isabelle Brasme, Ashley Chantler, Laura Colombino, Andrew Frayn, Meg Hammond, Rob Hawkes, Paul Lewis, Gene Moore, Alan Munton, Martin Stannard, Karolyn Steffens, Nathan Waddell, and Joseph Wiesenfarth.

I would also like to thank all the Rebecca West scholars who helped shape my material, especially Debra Rae Cohen, Phyllis Lassner, and Bernard Schweizer.

Thanks also to Christopher GoGwilt for advice on Conrad, and Jesse Cleary-Budge for translations from German.

I am grateful for the postdoctoral fellowship at New York University that enabled me to get through some late phases of the book. Special thanks to Patrick Deer and Peter Nicholls.

My colleagues at Stern College for Women are all that an academic could ever wish for, so thanks to Joy Ladin, Matt Miller, Nora Nachumi, Ann Peters, Linda Shires, and Marnin Young.

Grateful acknowledgement is made to the Division of Rare and Manuscript Collections at the Carl A. Kroch Library at Cornell University, as well as the Beinecke Rare Book and Manuscript Library at Yale University.

The way that Jane Marcus puts her feminism into daily practice is an inspiration for me, and I try, in my professional role and as a father of a daughter, to live up to her ideals.

For mentoring me through all the facets of my career, and continually finding ways to challenge and spur me to look beyond the obvious, I will always be grateful to Richard Kaye. He is my model of the curious and engaged scholar.

Loving thanks to Mom, Dad, Deirdre, Maire, and Grenye, for providing love and safety, but also for always provoking new ways of thinking.

My daughter Corinna and my son Hugo have made me a new kind of happy. Fernanda Garcia's loving care makes me rest easy during the day when I'm away from them.

Finally, I would like to thank Emily for her love, but words are not adequate.

Portions of Chapter 2 and 4 originally appeared in *Ford Madox Ford's Literary Contacts* (2007) and *The Edwardian Ford Madox Ford* (2013), both published by Rodopi.

Making History New

Introduction

In an 1876 review of *Middlemarch* Henry James rhetorically asked, "If we write novels so, how shall we write History?"[1] James was struck not only by George Eliot's multilayered staging of rural English society in a moment of transformation, but also by the shared affinities between narrative fiction and narrative history. Over a century later, contemporary theorists term orthodox histories "realist" because of the intersecting narrative tropes and techniques. But what if historians—rather than employing a "realist" style—instead tried to write like late-period Henry James? Or James Joyce, or Gertrude Stein? How, then, would they write history?

Two more rhetorical questions, posed by two contemporary theorists, might help stage the issues at stake in this study. The first question is from Fredric Jameson, who, in a review of Peter Weiss's historical novel *The Aesthetics of Resistance* (1975), asks, "Why should some genuinely historical representation of daily life in a given crisis not be achievable?"[2] The second is from an essay by Carlo Ginzburg, "Microhistory: Two or Three Things That I Know about It":

> Granted, the figure of the omniscient historian-narrator, who unravels the slightest details of an event or the hidden motivations that inspire the behavior of individuals, social groups, or states, has gradually established itself. But it is only one of the many possibilities, as the readers of Marcel Proust, Virginia Woolf, and Robert Musil know, or should know. . . . Thus, the hypotheses, the doubts, the uncertainties became part of the narration; the search for truth became part of the exposition of the (necessarily incomplete) truth attained. Could the result still be defined as "narrative history"? For a reader with the slightest familiarity with twentieth-century fiction, the reply was obviously yes.[3]

Reductively put, Jameson asks why there are no modernist historical novels, and Ginzburg asks if historians can learn anything from the methods of the moderns. As Ginzburg suggests, a possible solution to the search for a more radical approach to historical narrative can be found in the work of the moderns themselves, and I would go further and argue that modernist historical novelists provide both efforts at modernist history as well as potential models for creative historiographical form. Twentieth-century works of history have mostly either adhered to nineteenth-century conventions of narrative realism, or, more radically, have abandoned narrative altogether (most notably by the *Annales* School).[4] It may be, however, that the modernist historical novel—responding to what Jameson would dub the "given crisis" of modernity—provides a different and potentially productive model for narrative history.

Besides intervening in the scholarship of modernism and history, I would like to address this work to historians who are continually looking for new forms with which to write history, addressing Ginzburg's question as to whether modernism holds any potential as a formal model. Many creative historians in the latter half of the twentieth century have self-consciously distanced themselves from orthodox historical writing (despite entrenched opposition to experiments and "theory" in the field of history).[5] Classics of "microhistory," that is, history that analyzes small-scale subjects for larger forces, like Ginzburg's *The Cheese and the Worms* (1976) and Natalie Zemon Davis's *The Return of Martin Guerre* (1983), are examples of the movement away from historical narratives as neutral transmitters of historical events.[6] Ginzburg, possibly taking his cue from Proust or Joyce, writes of *The Cheese and the Worms* that it "does not restrict itself to the reconstruction of an individual event; it narrates it."[7] In an oft-cited 1979 article in the journal *Past and Present*, Lawrence Stone observed the growing dependence on narrative in the field of history: "More and more of the 'new historians' are now trying to discover what was going on inside people's heads in the past, and what it was like to live in the past, questions which inevitably lead back to the use of narrative."[8] Since then, writers like Evelyn Juers, Peter Englund, Sven Lindqvist, Ryszard Kapuściński, Alexander Kluge, Simon Schama, and Jonathan Spence, to name only a few, have been providing alternative narrative models to counter orthodox historical forms.

A study of modernism can enrich this burgeoning field of creative history because of the means by which modernism had interrogated historical narrative and its formal assumptions. The field of history is constantly looking for new topics and subjects. But history also needs new forms, and historians might benefit from examining early twentieth-century historical fiction, specifically the group of texts that I will often refer to as "modernist historiography."[9] My goal is to deepen our understanding of how modernism relates to a genre both popular and invested in historical ideas. New Modernist Studies professes an interest in both history and mass culture, and the historical novel can put productive pressure on how we theorize both modernism and the textual nature of history.

Yet this potential model inevitably raises the question as to which novels qualify as "historical." In one sense, the term "historical novel" is redundant, as fiction, unlike many other forms, usually depends upon historical specificity. As Irving Howe put it, "In a novel there is no 'once upon a time. . . .' There is London in the 1840s, Moscow in the 1950s. The clock rules."[10] We need then to formulate what delineates the historical novel. Ford Madox Ford, in his dedicatory letter to his historical novel *No More Parades* (1925), wrote that "[a]ll novels are historical, but all novels do not deal with such events as get on to the pages of history."[11] This might once have been a satisfying definition: the historical novel is one whose subjects can be found in works of history. But the twentieth century has seen a shift away from research on world leaders and moments of rapid change, and now more quotidian topics are commonly explored by historians. Previously the novel had a near-monopoly on daily life; now history is also drawn to the everyday.

Further problems of defining the genre emerge in its most canonical study, Georg Lukács's *The Historical Novel* (1937). Lukács spends little time defining his parameters, dismissing many novels that take place in the past where history is "treated as mere costumery."[12] Although he does not often use the term, these historical costume-dramas might best be dubbed "historical romance." However, his strong definition, that the historical novel "is precisely historical, that is, [contains a] derivation of the individuality of characters from the historical peculiarity of their age," does not take us much further: it is hard to imagine Isabel Archer in any age save her own, but if *A Portrait of a Lady* is a historical novel then the genre becomes synonymous with the novel itself. If Lukács's rich engagement with historical novels and their role in European intellectual history threatens to be undercut by a lack of specificity as to what marks a novel as "historical," then I fear that my own project may be open to the same charge, and the reader and I might diverge as to which works of modernism qualify. Identifying the historical novel as simply one that takes place in the past has never been acceptable: most works of fiction use some form of past verb tenses, so even works set in current settings seem to have happened some time ago. Some might especially query my inclusion of *The Return of the Soldier*, which depicts West's contemporary world of the end of the Great War. We should remember, however, that in the founding text of scientific history, *The History of the Peloponnesian War* (c. 495 BCE), Thucydides asserted that he only used information "from certainty, where I myself was a spectator, or from the most exact information I have been able to collect from others," a practice that might well describe West's adaption of media and film depicting trench warfare.[13] To see a distant past as "historical" and more recent times as "current events" usually assumes that the former needs serious analysis, while the latter simply needs good reporting. But the modernists, as we shall see, were too skeptical of subjective witnessing for that distinction to hold.

The modernist historical novel, then, might not be simply any "modernist" novel written between 1900 and 1945 that takes place in the past. Rather, we might qualify the genre as one for which history is not just a setting but a concept and a process—not just a particular specificity of time and space but a more invested engagement with what T. S. Eliot called "the pastness of the past," even when that past is a recent one. The works I consider are always as equally invested in history as a narrative project as they are as a subject or setting. Many have historians as characters, signaling a self-interrogation of the discourse of history (shifting the focus from history as referent to history as narrative); or, conversely, they have characters suffering from faulty memory or amnesia, employing the absence of memories to signal the presence of the past, thus questioning the very foundations of the historical discipline. Readers still might quibble with my selections, but we should be mindful that works of modernism present a unique challenge for classification of any type. Early reviewers were stymied by some of the more radical experiments by Joyce or Woolf, many declaring that *Ulysses* and *The Waves* were not novels at all. The modernist historical novel might sometimes operate with the same degree of initial unrecognizability.

While the modernist historical novel may resist easy definition, any exhaustive effort to identify and analyze members of the genre, using any set of parameters, would fill several volumes. Despite the paucity of criticism on the subject, prominent examples abound from the modernist era. Robert Graves's *I, Claudius* (1934) has served as the genre's twentieth-century prototype, always popular and much imitated. Sylvia Townsend Warner wrote many historical novels, including *Summer Will Show* (1936) and *After the Death of Don Juan* (1938). Mary Butts concluded her career as a novelist with the Alexander the Great novel *The Macedonian* (1933) and *Scenes from the Life of Cleopatra* (1935). Virginia Woolf's *Jacob's Room* (1921), *Mrs. Dalloway* (1924), and *To the Lighthouse* (1927) could be read as a historical trilogy of the postwar era; less controversially, her novel *The Years* (1937) self-consciously dramatizes specific moments in recent British history. (I will turn briefly to *Orlando* [1928] and *Between the Acts* [1940] as well.) While I am looking primarily at the work of Joseph Conrad (*Nostromo*), Ford Madox Ford (*The Fifth Queen, The Good Soldier, Parade's End*) and Rebecca West (*The Return of the Soldier, Black Lamb and Grey Falcon*), even among their works I have had to exclude Conrad's *The Rover* (1923) and *Suspense* (1925); Ford's *The "Half Moon"* (1909), *Ladies Whose Bright Eyes* (1913), *The Young Lovell* (1914), and *A Little Less Than Gods* (1928); and West's *The Birds Fall Down* (1966) and her unfinished *Saga of the Century*, which included *The Fountain Overflows* (1958) and the posthumous *That Real Night* (1987) and *Cousin Rosamund* (1987). If we look beyond the British novel we can include American examples like Stephen Crane's *Red Badge of Courage* (1895); William Carlos Williams's *In the American Grain* (1925); H. D.'s *Palimpsest* (1926); Willa Cather's *Death Comes for the*

Archbishop (1927); and William Faulkner's *Absalom, Absalom!* (1936), to name only a prominent few.

Many critics of the historical novel presume that the modernist historical novel is either an idiosyncrasy or simply does not exist. Studies of the historical novel usually race through, or sometimes even skip over, the modernist period, hastily assuming that modernism's concern with subjectivity, fragmentation, and alienation would dampen its practitioners' ability, or even desire, to narrate a historical period or event. Instead, postmodern fiction writers have drawn critical attention, but we too hastily assume historical fiction to be solely a postmodern concern.[14] I would like to demonstrate not simply how much of both critical theory and fictional developments were anticipated by the moderns, but more urgently to mark out a modernist historiography in its own uniqueness. In studies of historical fiction, this blurring between the modern and postmodern has usually worked to modernism's disadvantage, and we lose the exceptional nature of the modernist contribution to fictional historiography. For example, Elisabeth Wesseling, in *Writing History as a Prophet: Postmodernist Innovations of the Historical Novel* (1991), nicely describes "the philosophical dismantling of the historical heritage" that was central to postmodern historical theory and historical fiction.[15] After the assault on historical orthodoxy by critics like Hayden White, novelists like Rushdie or Márquez had become fit topics for historiographical research.[16] But Wesseling's own "history" of the historical novel sees some periods as more central than others:

> If we now ask ourselves when writers began to develop an alternative for the classical model in order to express an awareness of the fact that the meaning and intelligibility of history could not be taken for granted anymore, I would suggest that this phenomenon only came about after World War II, with postmodernist innovations of the historical novel. We may therefore locate the tertiary phase in the diachronic development of the historical novel in this period.[17]

She rushes through the modernist period with quick notes on Woolf and Conrad, seeing modernism as trying to either transcend or escape from history.[18]

I would argue that even perceptive critics like Wesseling miss key attempts by modernists to narrate history because modernism had been defined as a mode of writing that resists such a project.[19] But the past two decades of modernist studies have shown just how invested modernism was in "history," in all the senses of the term. At the same time, the excitement of the postmodern has faded and is no longer seen as so radical or different from what preceded it. Michael North has recently written that "[s]ince postmodernism defined itself in large part by its greater eclecticism and stylistic openness, it required as foil a modernism as exclusive as possible. Thus, the rivalry between postmodernism and modernism was read back into history, quite openly, as an antipathy between modernism and mass culture."[20] North's point on mass culture is equally valid for a critique of any form of criticism that would use historical awareness to distinguish between the modern and postmodern.[21] In this work I would like to assert modernism's role in what critics like Wesseling and Linda Hutcheon assume to be uniquely a postmodern interest.

I thus want to adjust this lineage and reinscribe modernism into the historical novel's own history. Studies of the historical novel usually work in two parts, first charting the nineteenth-century novel and its relationship to nation, and then the postcolonial/postmodern experiments in deconstruction and the interrogation of national identities. Perry Anderson, in his recent account, concurs with Jameson that "modernism proper, because of its commitment to the primacy of immediate perception, appears to have been constitutively incapable of generating the totalising retrospect that defines a true historical novel."[22] My problem with such narratives is the elision of the intervening years, as these accounts of the "postmodern return" of the historical novel redact 50 years of literary history. The notion that the historical novel had disappeared before the Second World War has more to do with critical trends than with fictional practices. The historical novel never left.

The case of Virginia Woolf's *Orlando* is illustrative, as it is sometime mentioned as the sole modernist historical novel: Anderson refers to it as "the only work that defies Jameson's judgment that a modernist historical novel would be impossible," but quickly qualifies it as "occupy[ing] a niche in the development of the genre."[23] Jerome DeGroot, in *The Historical Novel* (2010), writes that in Woolf's hands, "[h]istorical fiction has become something which can be formally undermined by someone seeking to reorder the novel form itself. *Orlando* breaks the historical novel apart by demonstrating that its cleaving to realistic narrative, to the 'truth' of explication, might be somehow flawed and aesthetically problematic," and that any further attempts at modernist historical fiction was unthinkable.[24] *Orlando* certainly is fictional history: a history of England from the Elizabethan age to the present; a history of women; a history of sexuality. But critics may focus on *Orlando*, not because of what it offers for history, but for what it refuses. Its playful tone has been used to prove that the moderns could not take history seriously; its elements of fantasy that history and the social world were held in low regard; and its *roman à clef* genre that the moderns were more concerned with the personal than the historical. Avrom Fleishman ominously detects a "hint of a profoundly ahistorical view—*plus ça change, plus c'est la même chose.*"[25] While these are not fair readings of the depths of *Orlando*, it is important that we understand the use to which this novel has been put in histories of the historical novel. Woolf's achievements in the genre have simultaneously impaired criticism's ability to read them as such.[26]

The New Critical assumption that modernist works flee from history is long gone.[27] However, certain residual prejudices remain regarding the historical novels of the modern era, which await the attention given to nineteenth-century and postmodern manifestations. At first, postmodern theorists, despite their radical differences from the New Critics, shared the latter's view of modernism's relationship to history, as first-wave deconstructionists generally approached texts synchronically. Subsequently New Historicism and, more recently, New Modernist Studies have aggressively resituated modernism into historical frameworks. More than just contextual analyses, these methodologies focused on the textual nature of history, often juxtaposing primary documents with a literary text. Generally the assumption behind such critical practices is that the fictional texts under review *are* history, and that all modernist texts are equally viable for analysis because of what they have to offer to explorations of literature and history. In this view, all history is textual and every text is history. The resulting critical article or book emerges as a history itself, but as Rita Felski argues in *Uses of Literature* (2010), the text "is being diagnosed rather than heard," that is, the text is used as a trace or document for the New Historian's own narrative, his or her own history.[28] My goal is not necessarily to dispute the overall validity of this practice, because its results have been so productive, and in fact much of its methods inform my analysis. What I would like to do is parse the meaning of the term "history," shifting attention toward modernist texts that more self-consciously see themselves as histories. Hopefully this will let us "hear," in Felski's phrasing, what modernist histories are saying.

Reading texts "as histories" rather than "as history" avoids the too-simple usage of the term. Sometimes critics assume—too hastily—that the discipline of history will always trail any modification to the epistemological objects of historiography, either mirroring or transparently giving access to notions of what history is, and that a study of forms and literary structure will give access to the "philosophy of history" underlying a work. This is not always the case, and the writers under consideration were skeptical about the relationship between history as discourse and its epistemological objects, which are also, misleadingly, called "history." Central to my analysis is the use, and misuse, of the term "history," which is beguiling in its apparent simplicity. As Hegel noted, the term "denotes the actual events (in Latin, *historiam res gestae*) as well as the narration of the events (in Latin, *historiam rerum gestarum*)."[29] We might add a third definition, which is the academic or intellectual field from which texts are generated about the past. Unlike most other fields, history is saddled with a name that can mean many things. The field of history produces histories. And these histories are about history, not the field but the collective human experience of the past. So history produces histories about history.[30] Michel de Certeau notes that "[h]istoriography (that is, 'history' and 'writing') bears within its own name the paradox—almost an oxymoron—of a relation established between two antinomic terms, between the real and discourse. Its task is one of connecting them and, at the point where this link cannot be imagined, of working *as if* the two were being joined."[31] This blurring of the uses of the term—the *"as if"*—does not just make for semantic mistakes, but rather obfuscates the role of writing in the construction of histories. As de Certeau notes, "usually we are all too likely to erase the verb (or their productive act) to give more weight to the complement (the fruits of their labors)."[32]

Darien Shanske has usefully dubbed this process "isomorphism," of which we should continually be wary, as it can lead to vagueness when we discuss literature and history.[33] Many critics who write about the modernists' relationship to history are performing *speculative* philosophizing of history, focusing on history's signifieds: what Lukács described as "history as a process, of history as the concrete precondition of the present," and synonymous with "actual events," *Geschichte*, forces of history, and generally "History with a big H."[34] Throughout this work I will try to keep such definitions of history from falling into their linguistic and aesthetic representations, not only for heuristic purposes, but because I believe that a distrust of the isomorphic process is what animates the works of the modernist historians. I will try to use "historiography" to refer to the critical theory and practice of writing history, and "history" to refer to the myriad conceptual objects (events, personages, etc.) that can be called such.

The speculative philosophies of history of Joseph Conrad, Ford Madox Ford, and Rebecca West, while interesting, do not have much in common and are not the focus of this book. Put baldly, Conrad merged a nostalgic British grand syllogism with his own romantic Polish nationalism.[35] Ford believed, like many English thinkers of his time, both in the inevitability of progress and the inevitability of decline.[36] West was a suffragette and socialist who eventually decided that Western society needed a strong ruler to guide its citizenry.[37] My summaries do not, of course, do any justice to their ideas, but their philosophies of history are not their main contribution to a conversation on historical form, and their experiments in form and style were accompanied by widely divergent political and social conclusions. While it is true that form is never neutral, neither is it ever predictive of a writer's beliefs or perspectives. I want to investigate, then, how these three writers intuited the challenge that English literary modernism, to which they were central, posed to the writing of history, and what it meant for the epistemological certainty that their generation inherited.

When critics discuss modernism and history they usually focus on speculative philosophies of history. For example, Louise Blakeney Williams in *Modernism and the Ideology of History: Literature, Politics, and the Past* (2002) analyzes issues of progress, linearity, and politics in the work of several modernists. Criticism of this sort addresses mostly the signified of history—history's shape, meaning, or causality—rather than the narratologies of history with which these modernists struggled. When critics do address historical narratives, they generally do so to support a point about the history-as-content that they see in the works of the modernist writers, and usually assume a literary-historical isomorphism. When Williams argues that in *A Vision* Yeats writes cyclically because he believes that history happens in cycles, she is correct, but we should not assume that every writer believes in this historical transparency. Yeats's *A Vision* is a theory of history. But despite its complex web of ideas and dense prose, its narratological assumptions are devastatingly simple: since history is cyclical, write cyclically. As intricate as the resulting text may be, both conceptually and textually, it is based on the notion that writing should reflect its referent, that there is a correspondence between historical narrative and historical object. Yeats, like any empirical historian, believed that histories should be transparent and reflect the workings of the historical signified—he just happens to have a theory of history that most historians would find unorthodox or untenable (not to mention unempirical).

Writers like Conrad, Ford, and West have a different relationship to the writing of history: they are concerned not so much with the trajectory of historical forces as with the process of the writing of history, and, unlike Yeats, want to force apart the narrative of history from its referent, destroying the illusion of transparency. Thus, keeping the semiotic levels of "history" apart is key to my thesis. Such an effort encourages critical attention to the nuances of the term. Moreover, the prying apart of history and its narratives was at the heart of these writers' experiments in historical narrative.

Another ambition of this work is to show how invested in historical form literary modernism was from its very beginnings. Conrad, Ford, and West occupy differing places of prominence in the current modernist canon, but all three were essential to the production and proliferation of modernism. Conrad is often acknowledged as the English language's first modernist, having crafted novels and stories that question their own construction and that doubt our ability to communicate experiences through language. What I am terming his "modernist historical novels," especially *Nostromo* (1904), appeared well before what we think of as the "high modernist" novels of Joyce or Woolf, or the canonical poetry of Eliot and Pound. Rebecca West's role in modernism has only recently been rediscovered, as her reviews from the *New Statesman* from the twenties show her championing the work of Lawrence, Woolf, and Joyce, urging a generation of readers to discover what was New.[38] Her own fiction from the period, especially *The Return of the Soldier* (1919), reveals her immersion in these literary experiments; she returned to them in her masterpiece *Black Lamb and Grey Falcon*, a partly fictionalized, historically immersed travel tour of Yugoslavia.

Ford Madox Ford was present at modernism's many births. He collaborated with Conrad; he provided mentorship to Ezra Pound; his *English Review* in 1909 provided a forum for writers like Hardy and Conrad and the very first pieces by D. H. Lawrence and Wyndham Lewis; and his *transatlantic review* in 1923 did the same for Ernest Hemingway, Gertrude Stein, and William Carlos Williams.[39] Ford wrote many historical fictions, both traditional and experimental. He also wrote several works of history: the mostly orthodox *The Cinque Ports* (1900) and *History of Our Own Times* (posthumously published in 1988), and the more impressionist *Provence* (1935) and *The Great Trade Route* (1937). More than any other modernist, he was preoccupied—near obsessed—with historiography. Ford's oeuvre has three crucial aspects that lend themselves to my project: the first is a hyper-awareness of the contingent nature of narrative, best seen in *The Good Soldier* (1915), whose narrator keeps repeating the same story over and over in slightly altered form. The result is a profound self-consciousness about the difficulties inherent in any narration. The second is his desire to write history through fiction, whether it is from previous epochs, as in his Tudor-era *Fifth Queen Trilogy* (1905–1908), or the history of his own time in *Parade's End* (1924–1928).

The third is Ford's impressionism, which, in Conrad's famous phrase, strives "to make you *see*." An impressionist will not call an object a "house" but rather "a parallelogram of black and brown" that eventually can be recognized as a house. For Ford the real is always interpreted. As Jesse Matz has argued in *Literary Impressionism and Modernist Aesthetics* (2001), impressionist techniques incorporate interpretation much more than has been assumed by literary critics, as impressionist texts do not simply pass on empirical data. So it is with history, as historical objects are always filtered through interpretations and then narrated by the historian. Just as with Monet's haystacks, multiple narratives can be written about one historical object with equal—and thus troubling—validity.

Ford's theory of how to write history is perhaps the most compelling part of his historical output. He does not start from a theory of what history is and then work backward to the writing; instead he has a theory of writing that applies to both fiction and history—best outlined in his book *Joseph Conrad: A Personal Remembrance* (1924)—and he believes that the same skepticism, impersonality, and sense of experimentation that goes into the writing of modernist fiction should also be applied to the writing of history. This approach does not make for historical accuracy—certainly, Ford did not think such a thing was attainable—and professional historians have had as much patience with his histories as many listeners did with his tall tales. But more crucially, we must state at the outset that modernist practices do not grant the creative historian privileged access to the past. No formal paradigm, modernist or otherwise, can escape ideological limitations: Ford's brilliant formulations of historical narratology do not prevent his prejudices and cultural biases from shaping his work. Similarly, Conrad's powerful skepticism does not save him from ethnic stereotyping, and West's multilayered dramatizations of historical processes fail to weaken either her antipathy to Muslim Slavs or her sympathy for British imperialism. These writers are united not by what they see in the past, nor any measurable degree of success in depicting that past, but how they formulate the process of representing the past in language.

Modernism is often credited with the formal discoveries that have led to poststructural theories of history, but rarely are works of literary modernism viewed as precursors to postmodern histories. However, I would hesitate to suggest that the modernist experimenters had much of an impact on twentieth-century professional historians: Carlo Ginzburg's question about historical form needed to be posed because of the lack of influence of modernism on the discipline of history. What I do suggest is that modernist historiography was a dynamic force in its own right, regardless of its eventual reworkings in postmodern theory, and that we can turn to it for formal models of historiography. Modernism has not been incidental to the history of historical fiction, and neither was history incidental to the formation of modernism. The struggle to depict history in language was central to many of the radical insights of the modernist period.

I Know God, I Know My Heart: The Presuppositions of Nineteenth-Century History

The fact that history always seeks new forms—and that history has a history of its own—is elementary but needs continual reminding, and one unavoidable aspect of Western historiography is the sometimes indistinguishable nature of fiction and history. Fiction writers have been writing "histories" since Homer, and "Homer, Shakespeare, Balzac, Tolstoy" might invoke the Western canon, but it is also a list of writers who wrote fictional accounts of historical events. Any overview of history must grapple with how radically different previous eras have thought about histories, and how there was no essential difference between "story" and "history" for the ancient Greeks. In *What Was History?: The Art of History in Early Modern Europe* (2007), Anthony Grafton explains how the ancients produced *artes poeticae* but not *artes historicae*. Their theories of art, poetry, and rhetoric assumed an inclusion of verse or drama that depicted a historical past. It was not until the Italian Renaissance that there was an emergence of *artes historicae*, with the dialogue *Actius* by Giovanni Gioviano Pontano in 1499. This text marked the slow divergence of history and literature, but it was not until the nineteenth century and the hegemony of professional historians that we might regard their separation as complete.

What unites fiction and history, both then and now, is narrative, a point that became a source of embarrassment for mid-century structuralist critics, who urged a move toward methods of writing history that depended less on techniques inherited from the telling of stories (leading to a reliance on statistics, geographical analyses, etc.). But John Burrow, in *A History of Histories* (2008), writes that "[t]he impulse to write history has nourished much effective narrative, and narrative—above all in Homer—was one of the sources of history as a genre. It would be a strange paradox if narrative and history turned out to be incompatible."[40] In fact, recent scholarship has asked if narrative is not just a cultural touchstone but a biological one as well: Brian Boyd's *On the Origin of Stories: Evolution, Cognition and Fiction* (2009) argues that "narrative reflects our mode of understanding events, which appears largely—but with crucial exceptions—to be a generally mammalian mode of understanding. The many culturally local conventions of human behavior and explanation tend to be adjustable parameters within common cognitive systems."[41] The persistence of narrative in the field of history, then, may be due not to the intransigence of anti-structuralist historians but rather a very human need for the ordering of past events in story form.[42]

The structuralist critique of narrative history shares much in common with a conflict within literary modernism regarding the depiction of history, and later in this Introduction I will turn to the works of Eliot and Pound for examples of non-narrative modernist historiography. But I would first like to address another topic that is much debated in historical modernist criticism, and that is the idea of progress, decline, and circularity in modernism's philosophy of history. A teleological view of history—as Mr. Deasy puts it in *Ulysses*, that "all human history moves towards one great goal"—was by no means universal in the decades before the war.[43] To be sure, teleology had its powerful proponents: in England, "whig"-style views of constitutional progress; in Germany, a Hegelian belief in history as the slow steady expression of Spirit; in France, the Enlightenment dream of societies based increasingly on reason and logic; and in the United States, the notion of "manifest destiny."[44] But these were by no means uncontested views. In England, "the factory of the world" that emerged in the nineteenth century seemed to many not so much an advance in civilization, but, to critics like Matthew Arnold, a decline from the pan-fluted age of Greek antiquity, or, as Tennyson put it in *Idylls of the King*, Arthur's "realm / Reels back into the beast." While both a conservative Hegelian and radical Marxist would see industrialism as a necessary phase toward something higher, Arnold and Tennyson—or even the socialist William Morris—recoiled and hoped for the return of Hellenic or medieval values.

The situation was similar in Enlightenment Germany, where Kant in his *Contest of Faculties* doubted that history inevitably improved over time.[45] The godfather of modern "scientific" history, Leopold von Ranke, argued directly against Hegel's teleological philosophy of history, stating that "every epoch is equally close to God." He complained in his essay "History and Philosophy"

(1830) that "[o]ne of the ideas which is continually repeated in the philosophies of history is the irrefutable proposition that mankind is involved in an uninterrupted progress, a steady development of its own perfection."[46] Ranke pointed to the "Dark Ages" as an example of a time when history reversed the march of progress.

Not only were there no hegemonic views regarding progress and decline before the war, but the Edwardian Age was not as optimistic regarding its future as is casually assumed. George Dangerfield's three-headed hydra of suffragism, Irish nationalism, and labor unrest from *The Strange Death of Liberal England* (1935) presents a picture of Edwardian England on the verge of disaster, the soothing images of high tea and lawn tennis disturbed by suffragist protest and labor stoppages.[47] Meanwhile, in France, decadent writers like Joris Karl Huysmans, as well as their conservative critics like Max Nordau, saw history moving entropically toward degeneracy, not improvement. Modernism inherits this struggle: the young Thomas Mann worked these ideas into his first novel, *Buddenbrooks* (1905), and in *The Magic Mountain* (1924) embodies them in the cynic Leo Naphta, who battles against the progressive humanism of Lodovico Settembrini. The tension between utopia and decay in modernism is most strikingly felt in the rapid shift from the pastoral idealism of D. H. Lawrence's *The Rainbow* (1915) to the nihilism of *Women in Love* (1917). Alongside all these works are the circular theories that emerge from Yeats's *A Vision* and Joyce's *Finnegans Wake* (1939), both of which depict history not moving backward or forward but rather in spirals or Viconian cycles.[48]

Both the nineteenth and early twentieth centuries, then, are marked by a variety of approaches to the nature of history's trajectory. What distinguishes the two eras might be the epistemological certainty of the nineteenth century regarding history and its uses, and its transformation into skepticism and suspicion as the new century progressed. As Foucault argues in *The Order of Things*, the nineteenth century saw a shift from a faith in systems to a faith in history.[49] For example, Darwin's *Origin of the Species* (1859) posited that we can learn about organisms by looking at their diachronic development, instead of simply looking at their synchronic makeup, or how they fit into a larger ordering system. Similarly, Hegel argued that the development of world history is proof of a living Spirit, and that Spirit can only be revealed in history. While Ranke disagreed with Hegel's teleology, he did believe that history, more than any other discipline, has the power to reveal the design of the universe. In his essay "The Great Powers" (1833) he explains,

World history does not present such an accidental tumult, conflict, and succession of dates and peoples as appears at first sight. Nor is the often dubious advancement of civilization its only significance. There are forces, and indeed spiritual, creative forces, life itself, and there are moral energies whose development we can see. We cannot define them or put them into abstractions but they can be glimpsed and perceived. We can develop a sympathy for their existence. They unfold, capture the world, and express themselves in the greatest variety of forms; contend with, contain, and conquer one another. In their interaction and succession, in their life, their decline or resurrection, which then encompasses an ever greater fullness, higher significance, and wider extent, lies the secret of world history.[50]

Ranke may have doubted the progressive nature of history, but he did contend that history was no "accident." Here the scientific historian's views of history border on the mystical, as Ranke believes that historiography can reveal "life itself" and the "moral energies" that animate humankind.[51] In "On the Relation of and Distinction Between History and Politics" (1831) he writes,

> History leads us to unspeakable sweetness and refreshment at every place. For what could be more pleasant and more welcome to human understanding than to become aware of the inner core of events, of their deepest mysteries; or to observe in one nation or another how men's enterprises begin, increase in power, rise, and decline? Or gradually to attain a knowledge, either directly through a justified intuition or indirectly through a sharpeyed, thorough recognition, of those things in which each human age excelled, or sought or strove to attain and achieved? For this is likewise a part of divine knowledge. This is what we seek with the help of history to attain; history is motivated wholly by this effort.[52]

Ranke's train of thought is not far from Hegel's belief that, since we can discern the marks of God in plants and animals, "then why not also in world history?": "The divine wisdom, i.e. Reason, is one and the same on the large scale and on the small, and we must not consider God to be too weak to apply His wisdom on a large scale."[53] This faith in historiography, rather than faith in history per se—that is, a belief in the power of historiography to reveal truths larger than the mere chronology of human events—unites Hegel and Ranke, and also unites them with British Victorian sages like Carlyle and Arnold.

Hegel not only suggested that history inevitably progresses, but also asserted that history is understandable to human intelligence. Like any object, it is not a sealed away Kantian in-itself perceived only as phenomena, but rather is accessible to human consciousness through dialectical thought. Most nineteenth-century historians shared, on some level, this assumption, believing that history is accessible to our thinking and that writing successfully names history's objects. (Even Vico, seemingly the enemy of Hegelian progressivism, trusted in history's powers.[54]) Hegel famously said that the Owl of Minerva flies only at dusk, suggesting that the disciplines of history and philosophy comprehend historical truths in hindsight, but he never doubted the eventual emergence of this comprehension.

It is this historio-epistemological certainty, more than notions of progress or decline, that the modern era questioned. But there was another side to nineteenth-century historiography, one that descended from Hegel and Ranke but that shifted the focus from historical objects to the more subjective recording and narrating of them. In Germany, Wilhelm Dilthey asked, in the manner of Kant, "How is history possible?" and "Are there *a priori* conditions for the study of history?" Dilthey's answer to his query was that history is the product of human nature, and that we are uniquely conditioned to study history because it is also a study of ourselves. Unlike a study of the natural sciences, in the field of history humans are studying humanity, bonded by the shared a priori condition of our intrinsic being. For Dilthey, the historian is able to imagine himself from the perspective of historical subjects, and he termed this process the "transposition of self," the "rediscovery of the I in the thou."

Dilthey staged a debate in his work between the objective and subjective views of the process of historiography at the same time that F. H. Bradley was investigating similar problems with his first essay, "The Presuppositions of Critical History" (1874).[55] (Bradley is central to English modernism because of Eliot's interest in him: Eliot wrote his doctoral dissertation on Bradley and also includes some of his writings in a footnote to *The Waste Land*.) Bradley, like Dilthey, wanted to overcome the division between objectivism and subjectivism in the recordings of history, and in his formulation the historian himself (history still regarded as a male preserve) becomes the place in which this contradiction is resolved: "The historian, as he is, is the real criterion; the ideal criterion (if such an antithesis can be pardoned) is the historian as he ought to be. And the historian who is true to the present *is* the historian as he ought to be."[56] A historian who is in accord with his culture's perspectives and mores is the ideal vehicle for relating the objects of history. What Bradley assumes, first, is a radical separation between historian and history:

> the mass of historical material is no longer one with ourselves, is not any more carried about in and with us as a part of the substance which we feel to be natural to us, but has, as a possession, been separated from the mind, and is held apart from and over against it as an object which presents a problem for the intelligence.[57]

For Bradley there is no history that is not mediated by the historian. This separation between historical objects and subjective recorder marks a shift away from Hegel's or Ranke's approach to historiography, and we might see a strong affinity between Dilthey and Bradley and the subsequent modernist suspicion of the discipline of history. However, for Dilthey and Bradley this separation between subject and object is overcome by the identification between historian and historical subject: while historical objects are based on witnesses from the past—who themselves have their own subjectivities and limitations—the historian's consciousness is *not* based on others' testimony, and is thus a reliable instrument with which to perceive and narrate history. The historian's own consciousness, for Dilthey, is "a self-conscious unity," and "regarding its matter as from the outside demands from it the same oneness, that intelligible unity which, as the world of an intelligence, it is to have and virtually has."[58] Thus a unified consciousness demands of historical objects the same adherence to unity and consistency that consciousness itself possesses. For Bradley, as long as the unified consciousness of the historian is true to itself and its own time, it is uniquely positioned to make conclusions regarding the historical objects it comes across, and "from that basis we will order our world."[59]

Bradley's strategy for resolving the subject/object gap rests upon a romantic presupposition that the next generation would not share.[60] As Rousseau asserted in the "history of my soul," *The Confessions*, "I know my own heart and understand my fellow man."[61] Bradley shares this confidence in his capability for self-knowledge. But a key term for Bradley regarding consciousness is "unified," a modifier that the age of Freud and cubism would no longer accept. As Dr. Monygham says of the self in *Nostromo*, "[it] is the last thing a man ought to be sure of," and Rebecca West writes in *Black Lamb and Grey Falcon*, "if people are severed one from another by misapprehension of fact and temperamental differences, so they are alien from reality by confusions connected with the instruments which are all they have to guide them to it. The mind is its own enemy."[62] As the twentieth century began, the human psyche was increasingly formulated as a set of warring forces that never achieve any stable unity. For the modernists generally, self-knowledge becomes suspect and no basis for a reliable mechanism of historiography: access to the self is conceived as an arduous task, not an assumed condition. As Oscar Wilde quipped, "only the shallow know themselves."

Thus both major schools of nineteenth-century historiography presented visions of the process of history that would be unworkable for the moderns, who neither believed in history's ability to show us God or The Absolute, as Ranke and Hegel thought, nor could accept Dilthey and Bradley's belief in the ideal historian. The modernist writers I am analyzing were suspicious of the ability of consciousness and writing to transcend the barriers between the self and history-as-object.[63] (We might see the work of the modernists as a return to Kantian skepticism, were it not for their equally skeptical views of the a priori human faculties of reason.) And, while it is difficult to find one trait that unites all of the works we have come to dub modernist, most moderns had a distrust of traditional modes of narrative.[64] What makes the case of modernist historiography so compelling, however, is how their works soldiered through this crisis and continued to tell historical stories that were not just criticisms of historical narrative, but also new examples of it. While a writer like Conrad continually expressed his doubts over the narratability of human experience, historical or otherwise, he also continually returned to storytelling, struggling to find new forms with which to overcome the barriers he so clearly perceived.

Ellipses in Modernist Narratology

The moderns were thus in a unique position in regard to the writing of history. They distrusted the ability of the field of history to reveal anything beyond itself; they distrusted the role of the historian; and they distrusted the main vehicle, narrative, through which history is usually told. But what they did share with the nineteenth century is the burden of history, by which I mean not the oppressive weight of the past but rather the overwhelming need to relate it in language. Foucault asserts that in the nineteenth century the field of history took on unprecedented importance because of the need for a chronological ordering of human existence, part of the new, secularized need for placing one's self and one's era in a historical context. But if literary modernism begins to question the means of historical representation, what would satisfy this still-pressing need for histories?

Strategies varied and we may talk of modernist historiographies only in the plural. Eliot's and Pound's aesthetics have been hegemonic in studies of modernist historical form, and I will look more closely at them later in this Introduction. Another strategy was silence and ellipsis. Given the frequency of fragmentation and narrative gaps in modernist writing, critics like Hayden White and Fredric Jameson have sometimes branded modernism as anti-narrative, fueling assumptions about the relationship between modernism and history, as well as the neglect of the modernist historical novel. In Chapter 1 I argue for Conrad's *Nostromo* as a founding text in a modernist constellation of historical narrative, but I pause here to analyze some of that novel's narratological strategies, because all of the texts I will explore employ ellipsis to some degree.

In *Nostromo*, key events are often not directly imparted to the reader. Instead, most of the action transpires between chapters. We never witness many events central to the Monterist Revolution, the driving plot events of the novel: Nostromo's epic ride across Castaguana, for example, has already happened as Part III, Chapter 10 begins. What we witness in each chapter is the fallout, or the impressions that the event has made on the characters. We should term this manner of narration "impressionist," but in a way that goes beyond just a description of the presentation of empirical impressions. The narrative style of *Nostromo* shares much with Conrad's depictions of objects and people from his earlier works, as in *Heart of Darkness* when Marlow states that "bundles of acute angles sat with their legs drawn up."[65] In such an instance the reader's consciousness might not immediately realize that Marlow is describing human beings, since these starving African men are not named but visually illustrated. Ian Watt has termed this technique "delayed decoding," "since it combines the forward temporal progression of the mind, as it receives messages from the outside world, with the much slower reflexive process of making out their meaning."[66] The reader's "decoding" of the image of African men is thus "delayed" for an instant before we realize what is being depicted.[67] This mode is a form of visual defamiliarization, what Jameson has eloquently called "the transition from the naïve naming of the outside world in realism to the presentation of the image" that marks the passage from realism to modernism.[68] This impressionist style was announced by Conrad's famous preface to *The Nigger of the "Narcissus,"* in which he stated that the goal of literature should be "to make you see."[69]

Nostromo incorporates this impressionist device on the level of plot, not just visual description. We are no longer encouraged just "to see," but also to do something more. As chapters begin, an event, instead of an object, is described, but our attempts to decode it are delayed as we read the impressions being processed by the characters. In *Lord Jim*, Jim's jump off the *Patna* is ellipsed, and then, of course, obsessively returned to, although we are never given the central event itself. In *Nostromo*, Conrad takes this model of narrating the event and applies it horizontally across a series of events. Note the difference from the earlier *Heart of Darkness*, in which events often occur in "real time" (although recounted). We can witness, from 1899 to 1904, a modification of the visual impressionism of the earlier work into the more historiographical mode of *Nostromo*, where the impressionist style depicts, obliquely, historical or social events from the past. In this historical novel, visual experience is under suspicion, and so events will not be directly depicted. Instead, gaps and absences will narrate the story/history.

Avrom Fleishman writes that "*Nostromo* marks a new movement in English historical fiction by taking as its object of imitation not only a historical period but the experience of historical time itself," as we get in the novel not only a diachronic depiction of the fictional Castaguana but also a synchronic meditation on how time and history unfold.[70] Conrad relies heavily on what Gerard Genette has termed "narrative stasis," a mode of narrative in which plot time is not advancing but the narrative continues to describe objects or thoughts. Genette's *Narrative Discourse* (1980) uses Proust's work as its central text, and his analyses are useful in studying Conrad, West, or Ford. For Genette, texts have various "speeds" that we can measure. We can count the number of pages per "story time" hour or year. The more pages—narrative time, or space—per hour or year, the slower the narrative. Proust's pace can thus be measured: if a three-hour dinner party takes two hundred pages, we can scientifically deduce that Proust is a slow read. But rarely do texts have only one speed. Instead, they vary, according to Genette, using one of four modes of temporal organization that modulate the relationship between "story time"—what happens on the level of plot—with "narrative time"—what is actually being described on the page of the text:

1. *summary*: narrative duration is reduced, and events are summarized; large amounts of story time can be covered in a short amount of narrative time;
2. *dramatic scene*: narrative and story time are nearly equal; events unfold as they are described;
3. *narrative stasis*: the story has stopped but the narrator keeps describing things, usually scenery or characters;
4. *ellipsis*: story time covered by zero amount of narration; an event may have occurred but it has been skipped over by the narration and we only learn of the events retrospectively.[71]

In Proust's work, according to Genette, there is not much use of *summary* and *narrative stasis*. Instead, we get *dramatic scenes* that go on for hundreds of pages even though they only cover one evening, and then *ellipsis*, in which years may pass without a single word of narrative.

Nostromo relies less than *À la recherche* on *dramatic scenes* and more on *narrative stasis*. Literary impressionism leans heavily on this mode—when Ford later wrote in *Joseph Conrad: A Remembrance* that "[w]e . . . must not narrate but render impressions," he is describing this dynamic.[72] But most important, Conrad also employs *ellipsis* between each chapter: plot time has continued but there is no narrative time dedicated to describing those events. Events "occur" in the white space between chapters.

History is thus what is "ellipsed" and occluded from the narrative of *Nostromo*. But rather than seeing this contraction as *the* modernist aversion to narrating history, I contend that these ellipses are *a* modernist attempt at actually narrating history, one that differs from the fragmentation and mythical typologies of Eliot and Pound (and that, importantly, predates any of their published work—Conrad was not simply "applying" an already established modernist aesthetic to a historical novel, but rather was using a historical novel to further a new way of writing). "History" is not directly depicted in the novel in the traditional manner, but the novel is still concerned with concepts that written "histories" deal with: causation, motivation, fallout, and so on. Just because Nostromo's ride—"the famous ride to Cayta, sir. An historical event, sir!"—is ellipsed does not mean that it is not central to the story.[73]

Some critics see the novel's elliptical style as an attempt to avoid history altogether: Jameson argues that "Conrad's stylistic practice can be grasped as a symbolic act which, seizing on the Real in all of its reified resistance, at one and the same time projects a unique sensorium of its own, a libidinal resonance no doubt historically determinate, yet whose ultimate ambiguity lies in its attempt to stand beyond history."[74] Jameson recognizes these ellipses: "This central event [of the Monterist revolution] is therefore present/absent in the most classic Derridean fashion, present only in its initial absence, absent when it is supposed to be most intensely present."[75] But unlike Genette, Jameson deems them non-narrative:

> the impossibility of envisioning such change, on the nature of genuine History, the historical Event which marks a decisive shift from one state of things (fallen nature) to another (genuine society), not as an event that can be narrated, but rather as an aporia around which the narrative must turn, never fully incorporating it into its own structure. . . . History is by its thoroughgoing demonstration of the impossibility of narrating this unthinkable dimension of collective reality, systematically undermining the individual categories of storytelling in order to project, beyond the stories it must continue to tell, the concept of a process beyond storytelling.[76]

Jameson marks the gaps and occlusions, but concludes that Conrad is trying to use them as a means of escaping "genuine History." Hayden White, drawing on Jameson, makes a similar argument in his essay "The Modernist Event":

> Modernist literary practice effectively explodes the notion of those characters who had formerly served as the subjects of stories or at least as representatives of possible perspectives on the events of the story; and it resists the temptation to emplot events and the actions of the characters so as to produce the meaning-effect derived from demonstrating how one's end may be contained in one's beginning. Modernism thereby effects what Fredric Jameson calls the derealization of the event itself.[77]

White suggests that modernism does not "emplot" events, and he thus might read *Nostromo's* ellipses as "antinarrative." In *The Content and the Form*, White considered "disemplotment, after the manner of modernist, antinarrativist writers" and concludes that "the very notion of a modernist historiography, modeled on the modernist, antinarrativist novel, would be in Ricoeur's estimation a contradiction in terms."[78]

Jameson's and White's conclusions, however, are not the only ones to be drawn from Conrad's ellipses. Michael Sayeau provides clarity in *Against the Event: The Everyday and the Evolution of Modernist Narrative* (2013) by arguing that works like those of Conrad employ a "anti-evental structure," whereby a text like *Heart of Darkness* or *Nostromo* will "deploy anti-evental narration in order to turn their stories subtly but significantly 'untellable' in the narratological sense."[79] The result is still narrative, even if the event itself is under scrutiny as a possible site of representation, and given the decoupling of events from history by *les Annalistes*, we cannot so easily conclude that an "anti-evental" aesthetic is automatically an anti-historical one. Furthermore, using

Genette's schema, we can interpret narrative silences as an essential part of the narrative, not a retreat from it. As Beverley Southgate notes in *Postmodernism in History: Fear or Freedom?* (2003), "it might be that narrative disruptions—breaks in narrative and gaps in history—could represent what happened more convincingly than that even flow that seems to take everything so comfortably and comfortingly into its embrace."[80] We can thus imagine historical fiction that is both modernist and meeting Ricoeur's standards for history; and with the works of Conrad, Ford, and West we have abundant examples. Modernist narrative practices, since Henry James at least, had sought, via avoidance and ellipses, to *intensify* the event, not obliterate it. For Jameson and White, any ellipsis is an escape from narrative and is thus "beyond storytelling," but they too quickly equate "depicting" or "envisioning" with "narrating."[81] For Conrad, events are unrepresentable in any direct form, but by his very act of narration he maintains a tentative faith in the powers of human representation. Faced with the impossibility of depicting the Monterist Revolution, Conrad turns deeper into narrative itself, exploring the power of its ellipses and lacunae to signal that which is incapable of direct depiction. Conrad does not trust appearances in any naïve sense, but his impressionist techniques imply that our senses are all we have, and we must make do with their faulty mechanisms.

We might take the concluding scenes of Woolf's *Between the Acts*, her posthumously published last novel, as dramatizing some of the dynamics of ellipses and how they can animate a historical novel. Like *Orlando, Between the Acts* is partly a history of England from the Elizabethan era to Woolf's own time. In the novel, Miss la Trobe has written a pageant of English history—strange, fragmented, and oblique, but still recognizably a narrative. She is the modernist historical novelist, shifting the focus of history, downplaying many of the "great deeds" of the historical record in order to register the marginal and ignored. However, toward the end of the pageant—the weather had been fine so the day was spent outdoors—a sudden burst of rain scatters the actors and audience:

Then once more, in the uproar which by this time has passed quite beyond control, behold Miss Whatshername behind the tree summoned from the bushes—or was it THEY who broke away—Queen Bess; Queen Anne; and the girl in the Mall; and the Age of Reason; and Budge the policeman. Here they came. And the Pilgrims. And the lovers. And the grandfather's clock. And the old man with a beard. They all appeared. What's more, each declaimed some phrase or fragment from their parts. . . . *I am not* (said one) *in my perfect mind* . . . Another, *Reason am I* . . . *And I? I'm the old top hat. . . . Home is the hunter, home from the hill* . . . *Home? Where the miner sweats, and the maiden faith is rudely strumpeted. . . . Sweet and low; sweet and low, wind of the western sea* . . . *Is that a dagger that I see before me?* . . .

The owl hoots and the ivy mocks tap-tap-tapping on the pane. . . . Lady I love till I die, leave thy chamber and come . . . Where the worm weaves its winding sheet . . . I'd be a butterfly. I'd be a butterfly. . . . In thy will is our peace. . . . Here, Papa, take your book and read aloud. . . . Hark, hark, the dogs do bark and the beggars . . .[82]

Historical figures and forces disperse in random directions, with no apparent design or intention. A fragmented narrative of history becomes a heap of broken images, analogous to the parable of Walter Benjamin's Angel of History.[83] Traditional historical narrative, then, seems too broken a tool to live up to the ethical and political imperative to bring the past into the present to effect social change, and the brackets of *To the Lighthouse*, the intricate discursions of *Three Guineas*, and the rained-out pageant play of *Between the Acts* are Woolf's violent assault on historical norms and assumptions, both ideological and narratological. Like Conrad, Ford, and West, Woolf never abandons narrative altogether, but in works like *Between the Acts* she launches such a critique of it as to almost render it unusable, scattering its actors and blasting its roles to bits. This may partly explain why she is often used as both the example of modernist history, and also the proof of its impossibility.

Modernist histories often narrate by absence, but that is still a form of narration. We do not have to read the modernists as recoiling from the narrating of history, or as solely incorporating history into mythical systems and speculative philosophies of history, but instead may see them as using more oblique but still penetrating historiographical methods to render historical objects. With *Parade's End*, Ford literally (and obsessively) uses ellipses— three or four dots—to narrate, to signal to the reader what is left out. In West's *The Return of the Soldier*, an entire war is occluded, and yet most readers would agree that the war is simultaneously, hauntingly, very present. Modernist historical fictions, possibly drawing from *Nostromo's* difficult lessons, do narrate history, but stay true to the most radical technical and aesthetic innovations of their time.[84]

James and Conrad's Senses of the Past

As I mentioned, many of the works I will consider contain an active historian. In 1900 Henry James began a novel that he would never finish, *A Sense of the Past*, featuring the young American historian Ralph Pendrel. It is the rare James text that takes place further back in time than the "visitable past" of social memory. The plot, however, begins contemporaneously, with Pendrel deeply in love with the beautiful Aurora Coyne. Coyne partly returns his affections, but makes clear that she needs "men who've been through something."[85] Pendrel, alas, has not. He has only written about the deeds of others.

Pendrel is an ambitious scholar, however, dissatisfied with prevailing modes of historiography: "What he wanted himself was the very smell of that simple mixture of things that had so long served; he wanted the very tick of the old stopped clocks. . . . He wanted the unimaginable accidents, the little notes of truth for which the common lens of history, however the scowling muse might bury her nose, was not sufficiently fine."[86] Pendrel is searching for a historical form or method that would convey the truths of the past in all their fullness, something the "common lens" of orthodox history does not permit. As Coyne gently wards off his romantic advances, she makes sure to remind him of his love for the past that, she suspects, is stronger than his love for her:

> You said it was the thing in life you desired most to arrive at, and that wher- ever you had found it—even where it was supposed to be most vivid and inspired—it had struck you as deplorably lacking intensity. At the intensity required, as you said, by any proper respect for itself, you proposed if pos- sible yourself to arrive—art, research, curiosity, passion, the historic pas- sion, as you called it, helping you. From that moment . . . I saw. The sense of the past *is* your sense.[87]

For Pendrel—and possibly for James as well—historical research is only one component of the historiographical process. Aesthetics and "intensity" play equal, if not superior roles.

Pendrel travels to England—"over there" is the only proper place to study history, unlike the adolescent United States, which "denies the old at every turn"—to visit an ancestral house.[88] During his walk through the manor he is magically transported back through time. (Both Ford Madox Ford and Re- becca West would also write time-travel novels: Ford with *Ladies Whose Bright Eyes* and West with her unfinished "Time Flies."[89]) This accident should be for Pendrel a wish fulfilled, as instead of having to settle for textual recreations of the past, he is now able to encounter it unmediated. But one of the first things he comes across in this past world is a portrait of an ancestor, bearing his same name, and with a strikingly similar appearance:

> He was staring at the answer to the riddle that had been his obsession, but this answer was a wonder of wonders. The young man above the mantel, the young man brown-haired, pale, erect, with the high-collared dark blue coat, the young man revealed, responsible, conscious, quite shining out of the darkness, presented him the face he had prayed to reward his vigil; but the face—miracle of miracles, yes—confounded him as his own.[90]

What Pendrel encounters, in his journey into the past, is only himself, or at best a reproduction or projection of himself. Furthermore, after Pendrel trav- els back in time he alters the flow of history, leaving the past different from how he first encountered it. The obvious critique is that the historian is more present in the field of history than is the past itself; when Pendrel returns to

his present, he has discovered nothing but his own presence and his own influence on the past.[91]

Pendrel reports his strange findings to the American ambassador, and the
latter's question to Pendrel—"You're sure . . . that you know which of you is
which?"—echoes many of the critiques of the historian's role throughout the
twentieth century.[92] Theorists of history have accused orthodoxy of pretend-
ing that the past was as an objective, autonomous realm; instead, such critique asserts, the past is a contemporary concern, a projection of the historian that more closely resembled him or herself than it does any traces of
previous eras.

James put the novel aside for over a decade. He eventually returned to it
during the Great War as a distraction from world events, and that act itself
contains some of the paradoxes and ambiguities of history: James clearly
knew he was living through "history," the years of the Great War falling
under Claude Lévi-Strauss's definition of a "hot chronology." It is to a history,
however, that he would turn for escape.[93] (We will see that Ford's characters
in *The Good Soldier*, another wartime text, turn to histories for solace from
the present.) James left *A Sense of the Past* unfinished, and it was published
posthumously in 1917. His literary descendents, however, were equally drawn
to the issues raised by narrative history. If the subjectivity of the historian was
a central topic in historical debates, a second was the affinities between historical narrative and fictional ones. Historians have had to defend their methods against this charge, while the task—or opportunity—for novelists has
been more ambiguous.[94] In his essay "Henry James: An Appreciation,"
Conrad states that

> [f]iction is history, human history, or it is nothing. But it is also more than
> that; it stands on firmer ground, being based on the reality of forms and the
> observation of social phenomena, whereas history is based on documents,
> and the reading of print and handwriting—on second-hand impression.
> Thus fiction is nearer truth. But let that pass. A historian may be an artist
> too, and a novelist is a historian, the preserver, the keeper, the expounder,
> of human experience.[95]

Conrad anticipates Hayden White in seeing the similarity between fictional
and historical narratives. For Conrad, the only thing that can distinguish fiction and history is that the latter is based on documents (a point that White
does not cede). Conrad here desires to defend fiction by comparing it with
history, first equating the two, then drawing them apart, then finally bringing
them back together. His phrase "reality of forms" is maddeningly Conradian,
as is the idea that history is "second-hand impression," implying that fiction
is a "first-hand impression." But if fiction is impressionism first-hand, what is
it an impression of? Possibly something personal and subjective, and this
seems to take us further away from history and collective human experience.

How then is fiction history? In the obvious sense, any novel is a sort of history of its time, but, more probingly, Conrad was attuned to the shared language, tropes and vocabulary of the two forms. In his short story "The Tale" (written 1915, published posthumously 1925), he creates a fictional world in which there are historical events and fictional events. The story, based on correspondence with Ford during the First World War, uses a similar frame as *Heart of Darkness* but also has a narrative twist that sharpens Conrad's interrogations of the field of history.[96] A woman in the story asks a man to tell "a tale not of this world." By that, she does not mean the supernatural: "I mean another—some other—world. In the universe—not in heaven."[97] The man begins to tell his tale in a dimly lit room, and as in *Heart of Darkness*, a figure narrates a story in the dark, highlighting the ability of words to construct images and events— to make something where before there was nothing.

The story is of a commanding officer in the British navy who comes across a cargo ship while patrolling the seas. The ship is from a neutral country, but the officer suspects espionage on the part of the captain, "a Northman." The officer boards the ship to investigate and interrogate the captain: "All the time the Northman was speaking the commanding officer had been aware of an inward voice, a grave murmur in the depth of his very own self, telling another tale, as if on purpose to keep alive in him his indignation and his anger with that baseness of greed or of mere outlook which lies often at the root of simple ideas."[98] The officer, like any historian, is trying to get at the correct "story" as to what has happened. He has to "read" or research traces of espionage: altered logs, contraband cargo, strange routes through the water. His task is made difficult by the competing stories that assert themselves—what he keeps encountering is yet "another tale." Eventually the commanding officer orders the captain to get moving, but the fog is so thick that the Northern captain protests, saying he is not sure where he is and fears moving until the fog clears. The officer is insistent, so the neutral ship moves off, only to crash against the rocks. The tale-teller then states, "So he had spoken the truth. He did not know where he was. But it proves nothing. Nothing either way. It may have been the only truth in all his story."[99]

On one level we have the classic Conradian meditation on the difficulty of ascertaining the truth from any situation—the difficulty of producing an accurate narrative through the fog of facts. But the narrator, at the concluding twist, reveals himself to have been the commanding officer: "Yes, I gave that course to him. It seemed to me a supreme test. . . . I don't know whether I have done stern retribution—or murder."[100] Thus, the tale is revealed to have been his own true one: his story is history, at least within the fictional frame of the story. With this device, the story gains critical purchase on how histories get crafted, as throughout we have in our minds two "worlds": the world of the woman and man, which we know to be fictional but take as the "real" world as we read; and the "other world" of the narrated tale, which we believe to be fictional not just for us but for the couple. The two frames collapse, evincing how easy it originally was to bifurcate this fictional world into real and imagined. Within the story, what was fictional is revealed to be historical, in that it "really" happened. The entirety is still fiction for us, but as a meditation on historiography "The Tale" shows how seamlessly one mode of writing can slip into another, because fiction and history share so many of the same techniques and tropes: "the tale" in "The Tale" could be both the story at sea or the story of the narrator's confession. (And while the term "tale" could be a neutral synonym of "story," it might carry the implication of an untruth, intending to make us question the veracity of the narrator's claims, just as he questions the Northman.) All the narrator has to do is shift person from third to first and the entire tale changes from the fictional "something I can imagine" to what Paul Ricoeur formulated as "what I would have witnessed had I been there," which marks historical discourse.

Conrad experiments further with the slippage between history and fiction in his "Author's Note" to *Nostromo*, in which he states:

> My principal authority for the history of Costaguana is, of course, my venerated friend, the late Don Jose Avellanos, Minister to the Courts of England and Spain, etc., etc., in his impartial and eloquent "History of Fifty Years of Misrule." That work was never published—the reader will discover why—and I am in fact the only person in the world possessed of its contents. I have mastered them in not a few hours of earnest meditation, and I hope that my accuracy will be trusted. In justice to myself, and to allay the fears of prospective readers, I beg to point out that the few historical allusions are never dragged in for the sake of parading my unique erudition, but that each of them is closely related to actuality; either throwing a light on the nature of current events or affecting directly the fortunes of the people of whom I speak.[101]

Nostromo is usually not credited with the complex framing devices that mark *Heart of Darkness* or *Lord Jim*, but here in Conrad's note we see that this work of historical fiction is fictionally based on a work of history that is fictional but that also appears as a "real" text in the novel written by one of the characters. And when Conrad writes this "Author's Note"—added in 1917—he is writing as a fictional version of the established author Joseph Conrad, not some unnamed writer. (Later in the note he makes references to *Typhoon* and *Mirror of the Sea*.[102]) His posing as "Joseph Conrad" further erodes the distinction between history and fiction, although, as I will argue in Chapter 1, he sees the forms as having vastly different social prerogatives and functions. Despite the similarities between the two genres, differences exist, although these cannot be ascertained from the text alone.

Ford and the "Devil of Theorizing"

Early on in James's *The Sense of the Past*, we learn that the protagonist Ralph Pendrel had written a precocious text titled "An Essay in Aid of the Reading of History." This fictional essay, of which we are only given a few snippets, bears a ghostly resemblance to another unpublished Edwardian text, Ford Madox Ford's essay "Creative History and the Historic Sense," and we might take this latter text as a founding, if highly problematic, document in modernist historiography. Ford had just completed *The Cinque Ports* (1900), a history of the medieval Five Ports, which were "in England a little group of commonwealths quite independent of the general government of the kingdom" and that were "outside the pyramid of the Norman feudal system."[103] *The Cinque Ports* is a work of orthodox history, for the most part like many other works published at the time. Ford does, however, in his introduction make one caveat: the book is "aimed not at accuracy but at suggestiveness!"[104] Just how valuable an inaccurate history might be is something that would interest Ford throughout his career. Can a history be more than just the transmitting of historical data or analysis? As we have seen, classical or Renaissance historians would have found this question puzzling, as the conveying of historical facts was not always the first priority of historical discourse. But such an attitude would be anathema for the new empirical schools with which Ford felt he was competing.[105]

Ford's essay, written in 1904, pushes these concerns in more radical directions. It reviews various historical works, but it is also a creative manifesto for writing history. Concurrently, Ford was reading the manuscript of *Nostromo* and was beginning *The Fifth Queen*, his series of historical novels about the reign of Henry VIII, and was thus preoccupied with the interactions of history and fiction. He writes that a historian should be "impersonal," and we might at first assume that Ford is arguing for objective historical empiricism, urging historians away from the self-absorption of a Ralph Pendrel. He laments that "the English public does not want impartial history. It asks for ethical points of view, ethical 'leads'; just as it can not understand 'the use' of impersonal fiction. Consequently only the political tract 'pays' & we have phenomena like the histories of Hume, Macaulay & Froude."[106] While this may still seem an argument in favor of empirical methods (and here Hume is evoked as a Tory historian, not empirical philosopher), the mention of "impersonal fiction," in which Ford clearly alludes to Flaubert, and, by extension, his and Conrad's own work, should alert us to the problems with this term. Ford does not equate the "impersonal," when it comes to the writing of history, with "objective." Objectivity is problematic for Ford: "the writing of impersonal history is a difficult matter, because the suppression of self is difficult. Yet in spite of the fact that the reading public does not want impartial writing & of the race habit of regarding History as polemics we have a powerful & industrious school of 'scientific' historians, a comparatively new growth in England."[107] In a sense this problem is built into the proto-modernist aesthetic of Flaubert, who argued for impersonality in fiction while at the same time stating "Emma Bovary, c'est moi." Ford—and modernism—inherits this conflict, seeing impersonality as the ideal but objectivity as unattainable.

Equally important is Ford's attack on the "powerful & industrious school of 'scientific' historians." John Attridge argues that the scientific tradition against which Ford and Conrad were rebelling was not the empiricism of the Victorians but more specifically the Edwardian drive toward specialization, and Attridge tracks the rise of the professional in British culture before the war alongside the highly defensive literary response. Specialization emerged in the nineteenth century, as "the late-Victorian rise of the research ideal in English historiography [marked] a shift . . . from the generalist man of letters to the research academic."[108] As suspicious as Ford was of the Victorian sages, he was equally suspicious of latter generations of historians who eschewed the grand rhetoric of Carlyle in favor of more research-based methods.[109] Conrad expressed similar doubts in *A Personal Record* (1908): "And what is a novel if not a conviction of our fellow-men's existence strong enough to take upon itself a form of imagined life clearer than reality and whose accumulated verisimilitude of selected episodes puts to shame the pride of documentary history."[110] Or, as he more succinctly puts it in *Lord Jim*, "They wanted facts. Facts! They demanded facts from him, as if facts could explain anything!"[111] Writers like James, Stevenson, Conrad, and Ford continually highlighted the similarities between fiction and history—James wrote in the "Art of Fiction" that "as the picture is reality, so the novel is history," and Ezra Pound, despite his differences from these other writers (which I will elucidate in the next section), was part of the new wave of reaction against professional history, as evidenced by his essay "I Gather the Limbs of Osiris," which argues for new approaches to depictions of the past.[112]

Note, however, that both kinds of modern history—the "scientific" and the "cultural modernist"—were Making It New. The term "modernist historiography" is bound to cause confusion because of its different meaning in the field of history, where it is sometimes even synonymous with realism.[113] Modernism as a concept was applied retrospectively to the arts and culture, but modernism in historiography was conceptualized even later, after the arrival of postmodern theory, which necessitated a term to describe what came before the postmodern but after the Victorian. So, for example, Michael Bentley's *Modernizing England's Past: English Historiography in the Age of Modernism, 1870–1970* (2005) explores an English historiography that he terms "modernist" but that has little in common with Picasso, Proust, or Bauhaus.[114] Bentley characterizes the philosophy of these modernist historians as a positivist one that critiqued the prevailing "whig" theory of history: "The whigs and all other forms of apprentice-historical scholarship had 'distorted' the 'truth' of the matter by becoming emotionally involved with their story and by insisting that history had to be a story in the first place. Modernized history did not do this or, if it did, that was because it had fallen into the hands of a bad historian whose 'interpretation' of 'the facts' was 'biased.'"[115] The methods of "modernist" historians like Frederic William Maitland and T. F. Tout were more strenuous and self-limiting than the whigs: "Modernists came to believe that imagination weakened history by permitting speculation. They wanted their arguments to compel acceptance through their sheer force of evidence and depth of footnotes, as though a modernized history had no need for rhetoric."[116] One might force a kinship between these "modernist historians" and, say, Pound's or Amy Lowell's Imagism. However, the similarities end there: as Ford was quick to appreciate, cultural modernists assigned a much higher value to the imagination than did the professional historians.[117]

Ford reacts against this type of "modernist historiography," finding fault with both the "Scientific Historian as well as the Polemical. And these things tend to destroy the sense of proportion which is really the Historic Sense."[118] That last beguiling, Jamesian term is for Ford what is necessary to write good history, and is what both the sages and scientists lacked.[119] To achieve the "Historic Sense," the historian must somehow be neither polemical nor objective, must be impersonal but also "suggestive." In his essay Ford does not offer a productive course through these contradictions; his creative experiments were the means to resolving these conflicts on a different register. The critique he makes of historiography out of this contradiction is important, as he goes on to argue that any historian, even a scientific one, is faced with these dilemmas, and that in the writing of history the writerly aspect of the process takes over: "But as soon as they have begun to write—as soon as they have begun that projection of materials which is Creative History—they have, according to their own earlier ideals, slipped down hill and they confess that it is impossible to write without 'points of view.'"[120] As a disciple of James, this last phrase is a charged one: for Ford the problem is not intention but the basic act of writing history, which he believes cannot escape from the conventions of narrative and perspective. A historian researches in the archive, but "the moment he emerges from these retreats it is his duty to be a creative artist"; and "as soon as your historian has gathered his materials together the devil of theorizing enters into him."[121] It is not just that every historian has a subjectivity and limited perspective, a point on which most historians would agree. Ford's insight is that any work of history involves some sort of theory, and that theory is always to some degree aesthetic and thus creative.[122] History is then returned to fiction: "Thus we have the pendulum shewn in its swing back toward the Historical Novel. It is in fact quite possible to be impersonal in research; it is frankly impossible as soon as it comes to projection."[123] The historical novel would fail the test of empiricism, but for Ford, every work of history slips "down hill" toward fiction regardless of aspirations toward objectivity, so one may as well embrace the fictive nature of the entire enterprise with a self-conscious historical novel, fully aware of the challenges facing any narrative historian.

For Ford, such a work was *The Fifth Queen*, a trilogy of novels comprising *The Fifth Queen* (1906), *Privy Seal* (1907), and *The Fifth Queen Crowned* (1908). They center around Katharine Howard, Henry VIII's fifth wife, who desires to see the restoration of the Catholic Church but is in the end beheaded for her supposed sexual infidelities to the king. It hearkens back to Shakespeare's histories and anticipates works such as Hilary Mantel's *Wolf Hall* (2009) and *Bring Up the Bodies* (2012). What is most striking in his trilogy is Ford's prose, as in this representative passage:

> In the shadow of the high walls, and some in the moonlight, the serving-men held their parliament. They discoursed of these things, and some said that it was a great pity that T. Culpepper was come to Court. For he was an idle braggart, and where he was disorder grew, and that was a pity, since the Queen had made the Court orderly, and servants were little beaten. But some said that like sire was like child, and that great disorders there were in the Court, but quiet ones, and the Queen the centre. But these were mostly the cleaners of dishes and the women that swept rooms and spread new rushes.[124]

The vocabulary and syntax are chosen to evoke the Tudor era, and, while the novel was a critical success, some of Ford's contemporaries bemoaned this choice of language. An *Academy* reviewer of the first volume deplored the use of "'Wardour Street English,' from that well-known Soho thoroughfare where antiques and, more especially, sham antiques were to be found in such abundance."[125] And if all Ford had to offer was "sham" history, then we might safely pass over such an experiment. However, it is Ford's use of imagery in the novel that establishes a means of dramatizing history—both events from the past and our conceptions of them—as well as a critique of inherited forms of fictional history-writing. Paul Wiley writes that *The Fifth Queen* trilogy "establishes the pattern for nearly all of Ford's later historical novels in its interweaving of art, morals, and diplomacy in a unified impression of a selected period."[126] The "unified impression" is an apt phrase, and relates not just to language but also Ford's choice of imagery. *The Fifth Queen* is strikingly visual, and Joseph Weisenfarth argues that "[i]n an important sense representation (Holbein's work) here becomes (in the absence of the extensive printed and photographic records available from later periods) the primary stuff of the fictional account, the reality to which a realist or naturalist author would refer."[127] Despite the inevitable comparisons to Walter Scott, Ford weaves together such a tight assemblage of language and images that we are hard pressed to find either predecessors or successors. Wiley suggests a comparison with Flaubert's *Salammbô*, but the less overwrought "La Légende de Saint Julien l'Hospitalier"—which Ford once referred to as "incomparable history"—may be the closer in form.[128] In this tale of St. Julien, Flaubert's style is surfaced and austere, and at the end of the story we find out why: "Et voilà l'histoire de saint Julien l'Hospitalier, telle à peu près qu'on la trouve, sur un vitrail d'église, dans mon pays" ["And that is the story of St. Julien the Hospitaler, more or less as you find it, on a stained-glass window of a church in my town."] The story is in the style of stained glass, just as *The Fifth Queen* is in the style of Hans Holbein. Both texts are representations of representations— "telle à peu près qu'on la trouve"—and thus not "realistic," which is why Ford's novels stand out against the backdrop of what Woolf would later dub the "materialist" writers of the Edwardian era.

The Fifth Queen moves past a literary mode that valued verisimilitude and into one that meditates on the mimetic process, and despite its archaisms, the trilogy never pretends to be a window onto the past, but rather a representation of what has been used to represent the past, or a re-representation. It values reflection over transparency. *The Fifth Queen* is re-visionary history, re-presenting us with images and visions of the past, and this is what ultimately separates Ford from Scott and the nineteenth-century historical novel, and marks one defining element of a modernist historical novel.[129] By re-presenting historical documents and period paintings, Ford highlights the reconstructed nature of any history and takes part in the process of historiography that Ricoeur notes as being "writing through and through," in which any sort of historical representation enters into a textual chain, as it is not just the writing of *The Fifth Queen* that is "history," but also the original writing of the documents that Ford consulted in the archive, and the pictorial "writing," of tapestries and court paintings, that all inform Ford's aesthetic.[130] In this sense, Ford's trilogy is a rewriting, in the sense that any work of history is a rewrite or revision of previous texts. This is a concern that would occupy Ford throughout his career—if you write over 80 volumes, some of them are bound to be rewrites of other books, both yours and other writers'—and that would inform the fragmented style of *The Good Soldier*. Ford's career of rewriting is intimately tied to his modernist historiography, one that sees any work of history as both a new, creative work but also one that is bound to previous texts. Rewriting is central to modernism—Eliot with the grail legends, Joyce rewriting *The Odyssey*—and Ford's rewriting in *The Fifth Queen* establishes another key paradigm for the modernist historical novel.

Joseph Conrad, however, saw *The Fifth Queen* not as the beginning of a new tradition but as the culmination of an old one. After reading proofs of the final volume, he wrote to Ford on February 20, 1908: "There is not a single false note, not a jar, hardly ever a pause. It is a great harmony. How fine—how very fine! It is in fact—the whole cycle—a most noble conception. Last night when I closed the proofs for the first time I asked myself whether this was not the Swan song of Historical Romance." Then he wrote to John Galsworthy on the same day: "Ford's last Fifth Queen novel is amazing. The whole cycle is a noble conception—the Swan Song of Historical Romance—and frankly I am glad to have heard it."[131] The second letter, while repeating some key phrases, is double-edged: his compliments to Ford are still strong, and yet he is "glad" to have heard the death-knell of the historical romance. (Conrad could not know that his own last years would be spent working on historical fictions.)

Conrad's words mark two simultaneous processes in the formation of the historical genre. He makes no distinction between historical fiction and "Historical Romance," and in fact the two terms were mostly synonymous at the turn of the century. Jonathan Nield's popular *A Guide to the Best Historical Novels* (1911, editions published until 1925) uses the two terms interchangeably, as does Ernest Baker in *A Guide to Historical Fiction* (1914).[132] (Conrad and Ford were well acquainted with the term via their collaborative novel *Romance* (1903), set in the Caribbean in the early nineteenth century.) Over time, however, common usage has distinguished historical romance from historical fiction, roughly along the same lines that the genre of romance was distinguished from the realist novel.[133] Nield's and Baker's compendiums testify to the popularity of the genre in the modern period, and although usually associated with the previous century, the twentieth century opened with an unprecedented output of historical novels.[134] However, this is also the period when the historical novel began to be estranged from "serious" literature, and Baker, also the author of *A Guide to the Best Fiction* (1913), distinguishes his two projects, "the standard of selection in the one being determined by literary considerations, and in the other by the extent to which a story illustrates any given period of history."[135] Here we see the splitting of the "historical" from "literary" fiction, as Baker argues that "the two works do not really overlap, their aims being widely different." The modern era thus saw the tripartite division of historical romance, historical fiction, and literary fiction.

Henry James voiced the growing suspicion of historical genres in a letter to Sarah Orne Jewett in 1901, writing that "[t]he 'historic' novel is, for me . . . condemned to a fatal cheapness," and that the attempt at rendering historical facts is simply "humbug."[136] Virginia Woolf has the narrator of her short story "A Mark on the Wall" complain, "But how dull this is, this historical fiction! It doesn't interest me at all." Cheap or dull, the genre suffered under the critical modern gaze, as even historical fiction writers like Conrad and Woolf attacked it. The classification itself became a sort of negative judgment, and thus works like *Nostromo* are not read by critics as historical fiction, despite the tangential presence of figures like Garibaldi and Bolivar, although Baker had included it his catalog of historical fiction.[137] It was the "High Moderns," however, who were most suspicious of historical narrative of any sort, and their aesthetic has served as a blanket representation for modernism's relationship to history.

The Myths of High Modernism: Eliot, Pound, Lewis

If so much of modernism both anticipates postmodern historical theory, and provides models for the writings of postmodern history, why have criticism and theory been so slow to acknowledge the modernist historical novel, and modernism's contribution to historiographical theory? The slighting of modernist historiography may have to do with modernism's anti-narrativist reputation, which is reductive at best, but as Ginzburg pointed out, orthodox historians have indeed been averse to modernist experimentation. One further reason for modernism's historiographical reputation has been the prominence of Pound, Eliot, and Yeats in modernist criticism. On a basic level, it is too presumptive to take the work of poets to speak for a modernist corpus where prose was equally prominent, but I would argue that there are more complex issues at play in the neglect of modernist historical fiction. These poets' approaches to history, while diverse, share many techniques and practices—namely, fragmentation, the use of myth, and synchrony—and these practices have been allowed to speak for the entire modernist canon, especially regarding its relationship to historiography. For obvious reasons, I oppose such a sweeping reading of modernism that transfers the assumptions of the high modernist poets onto the entire literary field. However, an exploration of these assumptions is in order, as the modernist poets were as equally drawn to historical subjects as were prose experimenters like Woolf and Conrad.

I am not considering the charge against the high moderns for being "ahistorical": Yeats was steeped in Irish history, and Ezra Pound called an epic poem "a poem including history," intending his *The Cantos* to be such a poem. And no generation of critics has ignored their reliance on historical resources. Rather, the critical issue, in Pound's case, has been his usage of the term "history." It is not that he is abusing the term, but rather using it in a way that marks out a specific relationship between modernism and history, one that often precludes attempts at historical narrative, rendering the concept of the modernist historical novel implausible. And while we might expect lyric poets to gravitate toward non-narrative forms, Eliot and Pound had verse narrative models in Dante and Browning (both experimenters themselves in verse histories).

Thus the slighting of narrative was a conscious choice, and not simply a question of genre. A clear instance of how Pound desired to move history away from narrative is in what David Ten Eyck in *Ezra Pound's Adams Cantos* (2012) has recently termed the "documentary method," a technique that dates back to the Malatesta Cantos (VIII–XI) but that achieve full flowering in the Adams Cantos (LXII–LXXI).[138] Throughout the 1930s, Pound was extolling the role of editors in assembling historical documents out of the vastness of archives: Ten Eyck writes that "he was increasingly willing to describe editorial activity in terms of a struggle to master a range of documentary material through strength of will."[139] Pound greatly admired editors, as they pruned down archival material to make historical documents coherent and accessible. Pound's prioritizing of editing results in a deprioritization of narrative: "The belief in such editorial intelligence stands behind Pound's confidence that a series of juxtaposed, source-based fragments can serve as the basis for understanding an entire historical complex," a role that narrative had traditionally occupied.[140]

Thus Pound incorporates history into modernist texts—it is "included"—but never as a narrative-based organizing principle. In this sense, Pound's aesthetic aligns with the structuralist vision of writing histories, eschewing narrative in favor of other methods of textual production; or with Walter Benjamin's dream of constructing a historical narrative based only on quotations. It is not the case, then, that Eliot, Pound, and Yeats were "less historical" or even less interested in history than their contemporaries. "History" is indeed one prominent element of *The Cantos*, which references Chinese dynasties, Provençal kings, and early colonial America, often with specific references to dates or documents. Note these examples from the first Canto:

> And the King o'Ragona, Alphonse le roy d'Aragon
> was the next nail in our coffin[141]

> And thou shalt not, Firenze 1766, and thou shalt not
> sequestrate for debt any farm implement
> nor any yoke ox nor
> any peasant while he works with the same[142]

> Yeou taught men to break branches
> Seu Gin set up the stage and taught barter,
> taught the knotting of chords
> Fou Hi taught men to grow barley
> 2837 ante Christum[143]

Canto IX and XXXI even include excerpts from letters and other historical documents from Lunarda da Palla and Thomas Jefferson. Likewise, Eliot's poetry also "includes history" in the form of "broken images" from the past: "To Carthage then I came" from *The Waste Land* tells the story of St. Augustine; "A Cooking Egg" describes historical personas he will meet in heaven: "I shall not want Society in Heaven, / Lucretia Borgia shall be my Bride." Yeats "includes" both Irish myth and Irish history, and poems like "September 1913" and "Easter 1916," with their specific dates, unequivocally announce their historical nature.

James Longenbach, in *The Modernist Poetics of History: Pound, Eliot, and the Sense of the Past* (1987), analyzes the works of these three poets and argues that they were actually trying to initiate a poetics that was deeply invested in historiography. Longenbach's study is so valuable, not just for his appreciation of poetic forms, but for his insistence on parsing the various meanings of "history" (a parsing I would like to extend to the modernist novelists). Longenbach argues that the modernist poets define themselves against the prevailing positivist modes of history: "for Pound, the historian who borrows the tools of positivism is powerless to understand the past; but the historian who is endowed with the magical powers of the artist may penetrate its mysteries."[144] Pound's suspicion of positivism is bound up in his aesthetics of allusion and fragmentation, and in his essay "I Gather the Limbs of Osiris," he complains that "[i]n every art I can think of we are dammed and clogged by the mimetic."[145] Pound articulates the basic distrust of both positivist history and literary realism that many of his contemporaries shared. The revolt against the former, not surprisingly, brought about a revolt against the latter: the high modernists were in self-conscious rebellion against historiographical orthodoxies, and their use of historical fragments was their means of distinguishing themselves from professional historians, especially German philology.[146]

Pound's methods have generally been the ones associated with literary modernism. The allusions and historical references that populate *The Cantos* should quickly dispel the Lukacian accusation of history aversion. However, for Pound, history was not narratable. Pound believed that his fragmented poetry, rather than historical narratives, could bring the past back to life, and could answer Dilthey's call for "lived history." Longenbach argues that *The Cantos* gradually move away from historical narrative into a more synchronic, fragmented approach to history that becomes Pound's signature style, and likewise Ten Eyck writes of the middle cantos that "the documentary transcription of source-based material now carries a far greater bulk of the poetic burden" than the earlier Malatesta or Venetian ones, and that by the Adams Cantos "[n]arrative commentary is extremely limited."[147] (We may see this movement as analogous to twentieth-century historiography's movement away from narrative in the form of the *Annales* School.) For the first three of Pound's Cantos, history is personalized, as Longenbach writes: "the imagination is in the service of the historical sense ... for Pound, all ages are contemporaneous in the mind of the visionary."[148] Thus in Canto I: "I sat to keep off the impetuous impotent dead, / Till I should hear Tiresias."[149] Pound, like Eliot in *The Waste Land*, uses Tiresias as an omniscient figure, capable of seeing through both time and space. But by Canto VIII, Pound's strategy has shifted, and he lets the "facts" speak more for themselves:

SIGIMUNDUS PANDOLPHUS DE MALATESTIS
In campo Illus. Domini Venetorum die 7
aprilis 1449 contra Cremonam
. . . . . and because the aforesaid most illustrious
Duke of Milan
Is content and wills the aforesaid Lord Sigismundo
Go into the service of the most magnificent commune
of the Florentines[150]

Dates, names, and documents are included without any interpretation, either by the narrator or another character in the poem. Tiresias no longer comments on the fragments that he witnesses, and meaning is dependent largely on context and juxtaposition. There is an argument—it is hard to imagine Pound without one—but he has consciously withheld any narrative voice attached to it. The fragments are left unnarrated. Thus, within Pound's poem we see the ambivalent place that narrative begins to occupy in modernist historiography, and we can even read the progression of his epic poem as analogous to the drift away from narrative that structuralist theory would instigate.[151]

The Cantos still "contain history," but now the sense of the term has shifted. Gibbon's *The Fall of the Roman Empire*, we might say, contains "a history," one historical narrative, but *The Cantos* "contain history," not just one single history. They contain the idea and signs of history as a concept, but by the middle cantos they are not *histories*: they do not attempt to narrate history, but rather to include references to past events. History is "included" in the same way as foreign languages and allusions to other literary texts are included. The fragmented poem escapes, not from history, but from narrative. Tim Armstrong, in *Modernism: A Cultural History* (2008), observes something similar in the work of the modernist lyricists: "the historical recovery in Yeats, Pound and Eliot is selective, a fetishization of particular moments and sites. . . . The result is histories particularly isolated from any dynamic context . . . or offered up simply as reified artworks, detached from their context."[152] But Armstrong continues: "In this, the modernists differ markedly from their Victorian forebears." Although Armstrong is correct as far as the High Modernist poets go, his latter statement does not fit so neatly with the group of modernist writers I am exploring. I hope my shift in focus will complicate modernism's relationship to history so that we will not speak so broadly about "the modernists" and history.

The mature Pound's theories of writing history remain mostly unarticulated, as his important essays on historiography were written before his transformative experiments in the later Cantos. We might turn to Wyndham Lewis's critique of Pound in *Time and Western Man* (1927) for an ungenerous, although productive theorization of "high" modernist historiography. Lewis

keenly recognized many of the qualities that Longenbach highlights in
Pound's poetry, as Lewis formulated, in prose, the distrust of historical narratives that we see in the poetry of his canonical friends, the "Men of 1914."
Lewis's work is thus useful in theorizing what makes Conrad, Woolf, Ford,
and West distinct from the high moderns.

Lewis targets Pound's belief that all times exist at once, and derisively
quotes from Pound's *Spirit of Romance*: "It is dawn at Jerusalem while mid-
night hovers over the Pillars of Hercules. All ages are contemporaneous. It is
B.C., let us say, in Morocco. The Middle Ages are in Russia."[153] Later Lewis
writes that Pound seems to believe he "has really walked with Sophocles
beside the Aegean; he has *seen* the Florence of Cavalcanti; there is almost nowhere in the Past that he has not visited; he has been a great *time-trotter*, as we
could describe this new kind of tourist."[154] Lewis indeed saw Pound as an
existential historian, in the Dilthean sense, although coming from Lewis this
was no compliment. Besides Pound, Lewis's book attacks Joyce, Stein, Speng-
ler, and above all Bergson, whose philosophy Lewis believed to have infected
not only the arts but science as well (i.e., Einstein's theory of relativity). Bergson opposed *durée*, the time that we feel, which is variable and not linear or
rational, to the scientific or social partitioning of time, and Lewis's critique
was that Bergson's emphasis on time, instead of space, led to an overestima-
tion of the ephemeral and fleeting nature of sensation.[155] Lewis writes:

> The less reality you attach to time as a unity, the less you are able instinc-
> tively to abstract it; the more important, concrete, individual, or personal
> time becomes. . . . It is the same as in disbelief of the reality of life: the more
> absolute this disbelief is, as a formulated doctrine, the more the *sensation*
> of life (which we all experience impartially, whatever our philosophy) will
> assume a unique importance.[156]

Lewis advocates a shift in prioritization toward space, and his critique becomes increasingly based on genre. Arguing that music, which depends so
much on time, is a mere "emotional object," Lewis elevates sculpture, which
is spatial and thus an "intellectual object."[157] With music, or any representative of time-philosophy, one is only

> the series of your temporal repetitions; you are no longer a centralized self,
> but a spun-out, strung-along series . . . an *object*, too, always in the making,
> who *are* your states. So you are a *history*: there must be no Present for you.
> You are an historical object, since your mental or time-life has been as it
> were objectified. The valuable advantages of being a "subject" will perhaps
> scarcely be understood by the race of *historical objects* that may be expected
> to ensue.[158]

On the one hand, Lewis may here be critiquing the passivity of any philosophy or art that makes the individual so historically determined. (Lewis may

also be channeling Nietzsche's essays on history and forgetting, which I will address in Chapter 3 in relation to Rebecca West.) In this sense "history" implies being trapped in the past, which mitigates one's power over the present.[159] (In an odd way this conclusion dovetails with Lukács's idea of how the working class, now an object of history, can become its subject—a dovetailing both writers would find objectionable.)

But Lewis also means "history" as in the stories of what happened, as in "a history." Lewis's chapter "History as the Specific Art of the Time School" takes aim at the field of historiography: "If music is the art most appropriate to the world-view of the time-philosopher, then history is certainly the form in literature that must be above all others congenial to him. For the 'time' view *is* the historical view *par excellence*."[160] Even more than Bergsonian philosophy, or music, historical narratives are dependent upon time—Lewis quotes Thomas Mann's "time is the medium of narration"—and thus partake in the devaluation of space.[161] So although Lewis heavily critiques Pound, Lewis agreed with his fellow "Man of 1914" that narration was not equipped to deal with the past and must be depicted in other ways. (Despite these objections, Lewis did continue to write narrative fiction for the rest of his life, often quite successfully, and actually some of the best moments of, say, *The Revenge for Love* (1937) are when he is experimenting with time and consciousness.)

For both Lewis and Pound, in distinct but related ways, narrative was a false imposition of order on the flux of life, be it the past or present. Lewis may have disbelieved that the flux was important, and Pound may have thought narrative too linear to grapple with existence, but neither saw much use for narrative as a means to order the past.[162] Lewis, more than any other writer, articulates a distrust of historical narratives as a viable way of organizing temporal existence in language.[163]

The validity of Lewis's specific critiques of narrative history are less important than his slighting of the entire genre of historical writing, since such a categorical dismissal indicates one strain of modernist reaction against historiography (a strain that has been allowed to speak for the whole). Fragmentation was a common technique for the modernist poets, but at the same time they were frustrated with leaving fragments fragmented, as Ten Eyck articulates: "It is in the nature of historical documents . . . to offer a fragmented narrative surface," but "their tendency toward narrative fragmentation must be overcome by a contrary force, which will work to bind them into a coherent artistic vision."[164] The case of T. S. Eliot demonstrates this most clearly. His musings on history share affinities to Pound's, but were instead filtered through F. H. Bradley, who argued that the problem facing historiography was the false distinction between data and interpretation, and, as we have seen, he insisted that the individual historian was the ideal conduit for the past to enter the present. Longenbach writes, "For Eliot, all knowledge is relative, and 'meaning' is necessarily the function of an interpretive strategy."[165]

But all interpretations are relative to their own systems: "then the critic with the most *whole* and *ordered* system can assay interpretations that approach the absolute." The goal is then to construct the proper synchronic system that does the interpreting for you: "Eliot believes that if we can 'somehow' expand our point of view into a 'system' wide and coherent enough to encompass the whole truth, then our interpretations would be absolutely true."[166] Synchrony, not diachrony, would produce a satisfying order to knowledge.

Longenbach traces the development of Eliot's creation of these systems. The early poems present us with lonely, isolated figures like J. Alfred Prufrock or Gerontion, who have no historical consciousness or awareness. Their monologues express these characters' points of view, and their musings are not integrated into any system: they are left as fragments. *The Waste Land* also features similar figures, such as the typist or Phlebus, who are fragments from various times and places. But for Longenbach *The Waste Land* contains "so many individual consciousnesses unified that the voice intoning the poem often *seems* to be the voice of history itself, an expression of the 'entire past' woven into the texture of the present."[167] Eliot had thus arrived at a totalizing system that kept his lonely fragmented figures somehow united across time and space: Tiresias, "though blind . . . can see" the entire poem and the system behind it. His vision is transhistorical. But instead of Bradley's Hegelian notion of a such a transhistorical Absolute Spirit, Eliot posits the accumulation of different and differing points of view that combine within the system, and "it is finally not rational process but an irrational *faith* in the possibility of wholeness that makes Eliot's world cohere."[168] The result is a system and a structure. Unsurprisingly, myth became increasingly prominent in Eliot's work as a means to bind fragments into meaningful wholes.[169]

It is undeniably true that many modernist writers turned to myth to give some sort of meaning and unity to their fragmented visions of the world.[170] Walter Benjamin, while not drawn to myth per se, continually experimented with synchronous methods of writing history, as in his parable of the Angelus of Novus: moving forward in time but facing the past, the Angel is witness to the accumulation of violence and destruction that history has wrought. The result is an accumulation of fragments and signifiers of history, and Benjamin's vision of history finds a strong echo in the works of the high moderns.

For Conrad, Ford, and West, however, history requires narrating (and Conrad launches an early and aggressive critique of myth in *Nostromo*, as I will argue in Chapter 1). For these writers, language approaches history like a satellite approaching a planet, trapped in its orbit but never reaching ground. Language surrounds historical objects like the mists in Marlow's tales, never relaying the kernel of truth. The resultant narrative, however, does not exist to invalidate depictions of the past, but rather to stage the difficulties in the historical process itself. The modernist historians keep a distance between historical objects and the language used to depict them, but again we should not see this distance as an aversion but rather a recognition of the need for such oblique strategies in the narration of history. The historical novels and narratives of Conrad, Ford, and West can shift the way we think about modernism's relationship to history, and we should see the poetic fragmented images of Pound and Eliot as only one method of trying to "include history." The modernist historical novel provides a means to complicate our notions of how modernism confronts or absorbs history in all of its forms.

Paul Ricoeur's Narratology of History

There have thus been a variety of aesthetic strategies for wrestling with the multifaceted concept of history, and there has been an equally broad set of theoretical ways of "doing history" in literary criticism. Consider the example of Conrad's ellipses in *Nostromo*. Looking narratologically at such a plot device and its ramifications for history, which is my intention, is not equivalent to how Pierre Macherey would see "history" as what is unconsciously "left out" of any text, such as Jane Austen "leaving out" the lives of domestic servants.[171] Nor am I focused on how ellipses might demonstrate Adorno's "negative dialectic," whereby the very density and opacity of the text signals ("negatively") a society driven by utility and exchange.[172] Nor is my goal to see a modernist text like Conrad's through the lens of Heideggerian "historicity," how time is lived and experienced. These historical approaches do not even exhaust the categories of "historical" literary analysis, and such a variety of methodologies demonstrates the need for clarity in deploying the multifaceted term "history."[173] In this book I would like, instead, to read my chosen texts as works of historical narratives. With *Nostromo*, and the other works I will consider, the text signals that which it is not depicting, and spurs the reader to work backward into what has been elided. I believe this is the key difference between looking for history *in* a text, which we can do to any text (Jameson's "Always historicize!"), and seeing a text *as* a work of narrative history or historical fiction.

To uncover what is so unique about modernist historiography I have turned to the writings of Paul Ricoeur, the philosopher who has most assiduously investigated the relationships between narrative, history, and memory. Ricoeur's work models the kind of historical analysis that is necessary in dealing with modernism's formal interrogation of narrative. With his philosophy as a critical lens, we can see how Conrad, Ford, and West exploited modernism's narratological experiments to explore the process by which collective human experience becomes historical narrative.

Ricoeur responds to the skepticism of critical theory that has cast doubt on the validity of narrative in the field of history, writing extensively on the necessity of narrative to any understanding of historical processes, both in his multivolume *Time and Narrative* (1983) and his last major work before his death, *Memory, History, Forgetting* (2004), where he insists that, even though it was "almost as though structuralism had given historiography a perfidious kiss of death," in truth any kind of history, including structuralist analyses, involves time on some level.[174] Since I am looking at how Conrad, Ford, and West chose not to abandon narrative in depictions of the past, Ricoeur's works are essential in guiding us through their experiments.

Ricoeur opens *Time and Narrative* with two questions: How does a new, unspoken thing—meaning or truth—"[spring] up in language" through the narrative process?[175] How does a story bring together disparate elements and somehow manage to create a meaning that goes beyond the story, signaling a concept that is often not explicitly named in the narrative? For Ricoeur, the answer is narrative's ability to manipulate time, a force that is beyond our logical understanding yet deeply informs our ability to know and experience the world. Narrative helps us make sense of "our confused, unformed, and at the limit mute temporal experience."[176]

For both history and modernist fiction, time is an element in need of rigorous theorization. In Part IV, Ricoeur announces that he will analyze historiography and narratology, but then asks if he should also include "the phenomenology of time-consciousness."[177] Such a category is akin to Dilthey's "existential history" or Heidegger's "historicity"—history as it is experienced, and not as it has been recounted. Convincingly conveying historicity is a challenge faced by any writer depicting the past (and especially the historical novelist). Ricoeur examines how poetry or fiction tries to "solve" the aporia between what we call "time" and how we perceive time. What we *call* time is what Ricoeur refers to as "cosmic time": time as infinitely progressing both forward and backward, arbitrarily divisible into seconds or hours. How *we* perceive time is akin to Bergson's *durée*, and is the kind of time dramatized by Virginia Woolf in *Mrs. Dalloway* or Proust in *À la recherche du temps perdu*. Art and narrative can help us make sense between these two times, and Ricoeur shows how in *Mrs. Dalloway*, Big Ben announces the chronological, cosmic time, while the narrative encourages us to focus on how the characters relate to this social marking. He explains that "the variations in this relation, depending on the character and the occasion, themselves constitute the fictive temporal experience that the narrative constructs with such extreme care in order to be convincing to the reader."[178] Chronological time "is the same" for all the characters in the technical, cosmic sense, but they experience it all differently: "Only fiction, precisely, can explore and bring to language this divorce between worldviews and their irreconcilable perspectives on time, a divorce that undermines public time."[179]

But what about history? What methods does it use to solve the distance between the perception and reality of time? History, unlike most fiction, relies on documents that it then reconstructs as a narrative.[180] But it is a very specific kind of narrative: history responds to the aporias of time by elaborating a "third time"—between lived time and "cosmic time"—which is simply "historic time."[181] Instead of measuring time in felt minutes or years, history can measure time in terms of climate eras or ruling dynasties, socially constructed ways of conceiving time. Phenomenological depictions of time like Bergson's or Woolf's cannot say what a week feels like, as much as they can accurately evoke feelings of lived time. History, on the other hand, has created "reflective instruments" that narrow the gap between lived time and universal time: calendars, generations, and documents act as bridges between the present and the past. These bridges exist physically in the present—you can look at them in museums or archives, and librarians might even let you touch them—but are "traces" of the past and so represent a temporal world that is not our own.[182]

For Ricoeur, these "traces" link the present with the past and also mediate between cosmic time and lived time. Historians respect documents, or an archive of documents, because they believe that through those documents history has left a "trace." History is "a knowledge by traces": "a passed past [it's passed by and gone] that nevertheless remains preserved in its vestiges."[183] So it has both gone away and stayed put. This paradox allows us to think in two kinds of time at once: the trace reflects a "hybrid time." It is phenomenological in that the trace was once *in time*, and can be "felt" like it was in living time, but it is from the past, so is "history," a marker on an outdated calendar.[184] Thus the trace "refigures time by constructing the junction brought about by the overlapping of the existential and the empirical."[185] Traces and documents are the way in which history, unlike fiction, bridges two kinds of time. As in the Holocaust Museum, historical traces are physically present but signal an absent past, however imperfectly.

Ricoeur concludes his great work by bringing history and fiction back together. History and fiction borrow from each other's "intentionalities," as on a simple level, the historian has to use his or her imagination to create narratives of history.[186] The historian is also an artist. But more important, the "imaginary" plays a role in history because of the way in which readers experience works of history. To "read" a calendar date from the past is to *interpret*: we read times or dates that are assigned to *imagined* presents. If we read January 5, 1943, we can imagine living in that moment; it is an "imaginable present," though in the past. Thus the place of imagination in historiography lies just as much in the reader as in the historian, and both history and fiction are in a sense "imaginary narratives." When we "read" traces of history, lived time is reinscribed into the present via our imagination—history "comes to life." The past becomes not something that "has happened" but rather is "what I would have witnessed had I been there."[187] History is thus conditional and imaginary, even as it is based on facts. For Hayden White, it was the historian whose imagination was most at work in history; for Ricoeur, the reader is also involved in the "imaginary" process of history.

Such an insight leads Ricoeur to ponder *how* writers of history achieve this readerly response: historians "render" and "depict" events, employing fictional devices, or more specifically devices from narrative that the modern age has divided into "historical" and "fictional." It should come as no surprise that great historians learn from great fiction writers. But Ricoeur sees the reverse as also true: novelists write a story "as if" it took place in the "as if past." The common usage of the past tense in fiction sets the temporal scene for the narrative: the "facts" of the story are "past facts for the narrative voice":

> If this hypothesis stands up, we can say that fiction is quasi-historical, just as much as history is quasi-fictive. History is quasi-fictive once the quasi-presence of events placed "before the eyes of" the reader by a lively narrative supplements through its intuitiveness, its vividness, the elusive character of the pastness of the past, which is illustrated by the paradoxes of standing-for. Fictional narrative is quasi-historical to the extent that the unreal events that it relates are past facts for the narrative voice that addresses itself to the reader. It is in this that they resemble past events and that fiction resembles history.[188]

We are used to hearing that history is like fiction, and so much of postmodern historical theory revolves around that notion. Here, however, Ricoeur shows how fiction equally borrows from history, and I believe that this insight can drastically shape the way we read works of fiction, historical fiction, and especially self-conscious works of modernist historical fiction. In the works I examine, there is often a fictional historical text embedded in the main narrative—that is, a work of history within the fictional world of the novel that is "historical" for the characters themselves, just as we saw with Conrad's "The Tale." These embedded narratives work with such dexterity because of the shared language and "intentionalities" of narration fiction and narrative history.

Time is thus central to both fiction and history, and despite the structuralist assault on historical narrative, the latter has proved a resilient mode with which to depict the past, possibly answering some sort of human need for temporal stories. When Ricoeur writes of the Holocaust that "one either counts the cadavers or one tells the story of the victims," both tasks would be considered "writing history." While the former might be a structuralist analysis of the Holocaust, relying on statistics, the latter employs the devices of fiction. But note the ethical dimension to the writing of history: for Ricoeur, history has to "live up to the task of memory" in cases like the Holocaust, as we have an obligation to "never forget." To do this, history often has to shed some of its positivist tendencies and embrace fiction instead. Such an imperative is traceable back to Herodotus, who in the first paragraph of his narrative states that he writes "so that human achievements may not become forgotten in time."[189] Despite all its transmutations, we still expect history to fulfill this ethical, societal role of collective remembering that Herodotus first formulated. I would argue that Conrad, Ford, and West attempted to "live up" to the task of historical memory through their experiments in both historical fiction and factual-based histories. An ethical imperative motivates many of their historical experiments, an imperative that emerges from their experience of twentieth-century history (even when the twentieth century is not their chosen subject).

But what about the modernist poets, or the works of James Joyce? Although Pound and Eliot were often trying to imagine moments from the past—Dilthey's "existential history"—they generally eschewed historical narratives in favor of mythical narratives, or non-narrative mythical typologies. Approaching history, they jettisoned historical narrative. Instead of "living up to the task of memory," Eliot opted for organizational structures that devalued the memory of secular humankind and tried to find something beyond human history.[190] Joyce, by contrast, historically dated *Ulysses*, but, as his title suggests, still looked to something beyond human history to give sense to June 16, 1904. The calendar time is not enough; there must be a myth superimposed on time to rescue it from meaninglessness, the meaninglessness of a day.[191]

Myth has played such an important role in modernist criticism, but we should be clear as to how myth relates to both fiction and history. In *The Sense of an Ending* (1967), Frank Kermode explores the difference between the mythical lies told by the Nazis, and the "lies" told by Shakespeare when he created fictional characters for the stage. For Kermode, fiction is aware of its own fictionality. Although fiction asks the reader to suspend disbelief, it does so with an awareness of this suspension. Once we finish *Hamlet*, we return to our world and are aware that Ophelia did not die because she never really lived. Myth, on the other hand, is a lie that thinks it is true. It does not encourage a return to disbelief after the curtain closes or the last page is turned. Myth is a "degenerate fiction" that has lost its self-consciousness:

> Fictions can degenerate into myths whenever they are not consciously held to be fictive. In this case anti-semitism is a degenerate fiction, a myth; and *Lear* is a fiction. Myth operates within the diagrams of ritual, which presupposes total and adequate explanations of things as they are and were; it is a sequence of radically unchangeable gestures. Fictions are for finding things out, and they change as the needs of sense-making change. Myths are the agents of stability, fictions the agents of change. Myths call for absolute, fictions for conditional assent.[192]

Fictions, unlike myths, are aware of their own contingent natures, and this is where modernist works become so valuable as staging-grounds for myth, history, and fiction: in their hyper-awareness of their own contingency, they dramatize their own problematics. However, this very self-awareness forced Eliot and Yeats into using myth to recover a sense of meaning, but Conrad, Ford, and West—aggressively critical of myth—did not respond in the same way. Using Ricoeur's and Kermode's analyses, I believe that the version of modernism advanced by Conrad, Ford, and West is central to unlocking some of the mysteries of historical narrative, since they were dissatisfied with inherited forms of narrative but worked through these challenges to forge new methods of historical storytelling.

Ricoeur even makes the argument that modernist experimentation is the style that most intimately depicts the mechanics of historiography. In his history of the novel, he notes that early forms, as practiced by Defoe or Richardson, prized the imitation of reality. For the earliest English novelists, mimesis was imitation, and language was referential. By the mid-nineteenth century, novelists realized that such techniques were not adequate, and that "artificial" plot devices were necessary. Thus the history of the realist novel is, on the one hand, a revolutionary attempt at new forms to render life "realistically," that is, with a high degree of verisimilitude; on the other, an increased awareness of the *formality* of such an enterprise. Ricoeur concludes that "[t]his is why the call for verisimilitude could not long hide the fact that verisimilitude is not just resemblance to truth but also a semblance of truth."[193] Realist novelists discovered that we need formal structures to tell truths.[194] Ricoeur argues that the golden age of the realist novel was the result of a balance between an ambition toward reproducing reality as we see it, and a realization that techniques and conventions are always necessary in this process. Realism was never naïve mimesis, and Dickens was aware of the contingent nature of narrative. However, he did allow his readership to at least pretend for 500 pages that such contingency did not exist.[195] The modernists were not so generous and never allowed their readers a moment's rest; they force us to focus on the constructedness of any narrative.

Today, mainstream history reads more like realism than it does any other mode, but Ricoeur argues that the realist novel may not be the best example of fiction being like history: "the true mimesis of action is to be found in the works of art least concerned with reflecting their epoch. Imitation, in the usual sense of the term, is here the unparalleled enemy of mimesis. It is precisely when a work of art breaks with this sort of verisimilitude that it displays its true mimetic function."[196] So modernism, while appearing to be most stylistically distant from what we commonly think of as a historical mode of writing, may actually possess an aesthetic that ushers it closest to actual processes of the construction of history. If history is a nightmare from which modernism is trying to awake, this may be because of their mutual but uncomfortable closeness, the nightmare of uncanny self-recognition.[197]

Ricoeur's interests in history and narrative culminated in his final work, *Memory, History, Forgetting*, where he synthesizes two millennia of writings on history, mostly to address the dynamic of how memories becomes histories, and the various roles that forgetting plays in history. He explores numerous aspects of history: passive versus active memory, the difference between a *search for* memory and the *evocation of* memory. He also includes an ethical analysis of memory—"it is justice that turns memory into a project"—that will become important in how some of the texts I deal with treat their own ethical obligations to witness moments of history, dramatizing both the difficulties and necessities of the transformation of memory into history.[198] Finally, Ricoeur explores the treatment of forgetting in philosophy and history. Forgetting is usually depicted as the enemy of history and memory, but Ricoeur argues for a kind of forgetting that is healthy and constructive, and since two of the texts I am dealing with, West's *Return of the Soldier* and Ford's *Parade's End*, depict protagonists suffering from amnesia, Ricoeur's treatment of forgetting can grant new insights into their work.

Key to all of this is the role of narrative, which links Ricoeur's two works, and in both he urges a more nuanced reading of narrative in the field of history than has been allowed by both traditionalists and poststructuralists.[199] Hayden White had depicted the historiographical process as one by which historians, using various types of narrative, approach an archive and organize data in various ways that will shape interpretation and meaning. But Ricoeur stresses that the act of writing is present in the process even before the historian arrives on the scene, usually before the historian is even born, in the form of archives, which are usually *written* transmissions of memory into text. So writing does not just appear at the last moment to shape information:

> Writing, in effect, is the threshold of language that historical knowing has already crossed, in distancing itself from memory to undertake the threefold adventure of archival research, explanation, and representation. History is writing from one end to another.[200]

From a history's origins, either in oral testimonies, census-takings, or the tabulating of statistics, writing plays a role, even prior to any act of narration. (This is why structuralist history, while eschewing narrative, still feels comfortable with consulting narratives themselves, such as diaries or newspaper articles, as documentary evidence.) Ricoeur stresses that narrative history is a form of history uniquely aware of the textual and time-bound nature of the entire process: "representation as narration does not simply turn naively toward things that happened. The narrative form as such interposes its complexity and its opacity on what I like to call the referential impulse of the historical narrative."[201] For the purposes of my project, insights like these can illuminate the work of writers who, operating from within the emergence and eventual hegemony of literary modernism, exploit modernism's self-awareness and contingency in an effort to write forms of history that highlight, instead of evade, their own problematics.

Despite his argument that modernist works are akin to the textual process of historiography, Ricoeur actually warns against turning to modernism as a formal model:

> [w]e are not forbidden an ongoing search for a way to fill the gap between the representative capacity of discourse and what the event demands, even while guarding ourselves against nourishing an illusion in favor of those styles of writing Hayden White calls "modernist," parallel to the one he condemns on the side of the realist tradition.[202]

Both Ricoeur and White feel uneasy about employing modernism for a telling of history, but Carlo Ginzburg's question that opened this introduction may serve as an invitation from the field of history to explore how modernism treats the historical process, and ultimately what a modernist history would look like. I would argue that modernist works *can* be models for historical narrative. The constellation of Conrad, Ford, and West initiated a genealogy that might now include working historians like Ginzburg, Natalie Zemon Davis, David Kertzer, Barbara Duden, Robert Rosenstone, Simon Schama, and Peter Englund. These creative historians, like their modernist fictional predecessors, are fully aware of the debates surrounding historical narrative but have chosen to fashion new methods of narrative historiography.

My hope is that a study of the historical fictions of Joseph Conrad, Ford Madox Ford, and Rebecca West will reinscribe the modern era into histories both of the historical novel and of history itself. In *Figural Realism*, Hayden White acknowledges that

> modernism appears less as a rejection of the realist project and a denial of history than as an anticipation of a new form of historical reality, a reality that included among its supposedly unimaginable, unthinkable, and unspeakable aspects: the phenomena of Hitler, the Final Solution, total war, nuclear contamination . . . a profound sense of the incapacity of our sciences to explain, let alone control or contain these; and a growing awareness of the incapacity of our traditional modes of representation even to describe them adequately.[203]

Modernism bequeathed to the twentieth century a variety of ways of depicting its own violent era, as well as historiography's own "incapacities." My hope is that modernist historiography is both appreciated in its own right, as well as recognized as a possible resource in the constant struggle for new historical forms.

Joseph Conrad and the Necessity of History
in *Nostromo*

Histories of modernist literature, especially those of English-language modernism, often begin with Joseph Conrad, and his novel *Nostromo* (1904) evidences a fascination with history, both as narrative and referent, that was
present in literary modernism from its origins. We might dub *Nostromo* a
"historical novel" because it takes place before and away from its time and
place of composition—it is "in history." Although the settings and characters
are all fictional, the nation of Costaguana is clearly coded as South American,
and several of the characters served with historical figures like Garibaldi and
Bolivar.[1]

In the novel a revolution by the disaffected General Montero forces the
English silver baron Charles Gould to find someone to whom to entrust
some valuable silver. He turns to Nostromo, a sort of folk hero in the town
of Sulaco. Nostromo sets off to hide the precious cargo with Martin
Decoud, a journalist who had been sending articles to Europe about the
uprising and who is becoming a trusted figure within the new, separatist
region of the Occidental Republic of Sulaco. Their boat sinks during their
flight, and Decoud ends up moored on a small island, eventually killing
himself out of loneliness and despair. Nostromo returns, saying the silver
has been lost, but in truth he is selling it to get rich. He is shot at the end
by a supporter who mistakes him for a thief, an unheroic ending for a
false hero.

Readers have often found *Nostromo* to be an unfulfilling mixture of Conrad's personal, introspective style with his more social and political mode of
narration. A 1905 unsigned review from the *Daily Telegraph* is representative:
"He has many of the qualities which go to the making of a great novelist;
ideas, character, situations throng so thickly round him that he is unable to
cope with them. He has extraordinary vigour of conception, his canvas is immense, and yet it is overcrowded. . . . He has almost a touch of genius, yet not

enough of that divine spark."[2] Hardly any reviews were wholly negative, as early critics always found something to praise about the novel. Virginia Woolf, in a *TLS* review for the second edition of the novel (1918), wrote that:

> there results a crowding and suffocating superabundance which makes "Nostromo" one of those rare and magnificent wrecks over which the critics shake their heads, hesitating between "failure" and "astonishing," unable to determine why it is that so much skill and beauty are powerless to flat the fabric into the main stream of active and enduring existence. The demon which attends Mr. Conrad's genius is the demon of languor, of monotony, of an inertness such as we see in the quiescence of the caged tiger. In "Nostromo" the tiger broods superb, supine, but almost completely immobile.[3]

The decades of criticism that followed tended to support these early responses to the novel, as *Heart of Darkness* and *Lord Jim* made up the bulk of Conrad criticism, with *Nostromo* often benignly ignored. But some of the very qualities that made the novel difficult for earlier readers have attracted poststructural, postcolonial, and new historicist readings, and it has become more of a central text in Conrad studies.

Nostromo is just one of Conrad's many historical novels. Toward the end of his life, especially, he was drawn to Napoleonic Europe with *The Rover* (1923) and the posthumous *Suspense* (1925), but he had also crafted shorter pieces like "The Duel" (1908) and "Prince Roman" (1911). *Nostromo* is unique in Conrad's marshaling of his challenging narrative techniques to narrate both historical events and the recording of those events. His other historical fiction, although later in Conrad's career, feels more nineteenth century, but with *Nostromo* Conrad pushes the boundaries of the form of the historical novel, and as a result it bears little resemblance to the works of Scott or Balzac.

Conrad explores the bifurcated nature of the term "history," cautioning us to not be deceived by its isomorphic nature. (The epigraph from Shakespeare's *King John*, "a history" about historical figures, alerts us to the history/histories slippage.) Central to the text's handling of history and histories is Decoud, because while Nostromo (in Italian, "our man") wants to *be history*, Decoud (the decoder) wants to *write histories*. Decoud writes to his sister that Nostromo "seems to have a particular talent for being on the spot whenever there is something picturesque to be done" and "has a peculiar talent when anything striking to the imagination has to be done."[4] In these passages, we see both Decoud's actions as historian and Nostromo's urge to be remembered as historical: our two characters dramatize the two semantic sides of history.[5] As a journalist, Decoud has been sending out brief articles to the international press: "I wrote out the cable myself. We have no Reuter's agency man here."[6] He also writes longer letters to his sister informing her about the political situation in Costaguana, and from these letters we observe that he is deeply steeped in European history.[7] In both efforts at textual production, Decoud shapes the events of the recent past into some sort of narrative: if he is not a historian in every sense, he is at least trying to leave a reliable trace with which a historian might some day craft a history, to enter into Ricoeur's "endless" textual chain of historiography that continually mines the textual traces of the past. Pamela Demory writes of scenes like this that "Conrad comments on the problem of the relationship between history and the past, between the historical narrative and history, between, in effect, historiography as signifier and event as signified and, in doing so, critiques both the traditional nineteenth-century notion of history and the nineteenth-century realist novel."[8] As with Rebecca West and Ford Madox Ford in their fictionalization of the Great War, Decoud acts as a Thucydides of the Monterist Revolution, a witness to events and a transformer of history into histories.

Decoud's writerly nature has attracted poststructuralist readings. Deconstructive and New Historicist analyses, while debunking the New Critical assumptions of Conrad's aversion to history, have instead postulated that Conrad voices a bleak skepticism regarding our ability to narrate the past. Pamela Demory writes that "the 'history' of the ideal historian as related in this novel turns out to be impossible, and it is in the very impossibility of his position that the novel makes its most telling comment on the meaning of history."[9] Similarly, Daphna Erdinast-Vulcan, in "Nostromo and the Writing of History," believes the novel to be "a perfect fictional historiography—perfect in that it thematizes and enacts the failure of historiography," and that rather than trying to evade the inevitable, as Jameson argues, it makes multiple attempts at grasping historical events—only to see that project continually frustrated.[10] And Christophe Robin notes:

> this can be read as an early anticipation of modernist or even postmodernist suspicion of historical discourse, as the realization that history is, like fiction, a discourse, an ideological reorganization of events to make sense of the past. . . . When Conrad questions historical discourse through its fictionalization, he simultaneously reassesses the ontological criteria that underlie the historical narrative. He thereby lays the foundation of a narrative reflexivity that will soon be a defining criterion of modernism and postmodernism and that will contaminate all discourses, including historical discourses.[11]

These readings celebrate the deconstructive power of Nostromo—its power to "contaminate," its ability to see history as "impossible"—but do not see Conrad finding anything salvageable or redemptive in the discourse of historiography.[12] My argument is that Conrad—in keeping with what I have termed "modernist historiography"—simultaneously says that one can't go on narrating history, and then goes on narrating history. While the novel may tempt us to focus on the *failures* of writing history, it also maintains the necessity of historical narratives, and through the successes and failures of Decoud launches a tentative defense of history as a discipline.

"In the Thick of History"

I will begin my analysis of *Nostromo* by looking at one long passage in which the manuscript is in Ford Madox Ford's hand. Ford either wrote the section himself (to help Conrad meet his serial deadline) or merely acted as Conrad's amanuensis: if he did not give birth to this section, he was at the very least its midwife, which, as I will argue throughout, is a fitting role for the modern writer most preoccupied by history and its forms.[13] I have also begun this chapter with the section in Ford's hand because I want to highlight the possible moment at which an English modernist historiography became not just one author (or possibly just one text), but instead a genealogy.

The section of the novel in Ford's handwriting is saturated with historiographical self-awareness. The Monterist revolution has just begun, and the remnants of the European "Blanco" party in Sulaco are deciding what course of action to take. Martin Decoud tells Antonia, his lover: "No, but just imagine our forefathers in morions and corselets drawn up outside this gate, and a band of adventurers just landed from their ships in the harbour there. Thieves, of course. Speculators, too. Their expeditions, each one, were the speculations of grave and reverend persons in England. That is history, as that absurd sailor Mitchell is always saying."[14] The last reference is to Captain Mitchell, the English seaman in charge of shipping in the area, who continually announces the arrival of a new chapter of history. Decoud, by contrast, has a more nuanced understanding of the historical process, and asks Antonia to "imagine" the scene he describes. History, here, is not simply "what happened," but rather what we all imagine to have happened, or possibly the very process of imaginative reconstruction in the Bradlean sense. His disparaging remark at the end, "That is history," operates on the surface as an indictment against the official history of a glorious independence movement that was actually, Decoud knows, nothing but the scurrilous actions of thieves and speculators. Decoud feels compelled to relate such insight because of what the official history tells, which is that these "grave and reverend persons" from Europe civilized the natives of Costaguana.[15] But the "that" in "that is history" can refer to both the events and also the narrative about those events. Decoud—and Conrad—urge us to distinguish between history's signifier and signified, and note how easily they collapse into isomorphism, blurring narrative and referent. There is a gap between "what happened" and what we imaginatively reconstruct, and yet we use the same term—"history"—to signal both concepts.

Nostromo is so rich for a study of modernist historiography because not only is it historical fiction, but embedded in it are multiple works of fictional history.[16] Don Jose Avellanos, Antonia's father and an elder statesman of Sulaco, has written a "manuscript of a historical work" on Costaguana entitled *Fifty Years of Misrule*. Avellanos thinks that "at present . . . it was not prudent (even if it were possible) 'to give it to the world'" because of the political turmoil gripping Costaguana.[17] But later in the passage, we learn that for Captain Mitchell, "[a]lmost every event out of the usual daily course 'marked an epoch' for him or else was 'history,'" and as events unfold he is "feeling more and more in the thick of history."[18] Avellanos and Mitchell, just like Decoud and Nostromo, represent the narrative and referent side, respectively, of the sign "history." Ursula Lord, in *Solitude versus Solidarity in the Novels of Joseph Conrad* (1998), argues that Don Jose, Captain Mitchell, and Decoud are all historians: Mitchell represents "the allied and anxious good will of the material interests of civilization," that is, imperialism; Don Jose, through his historical work, the "passionate plea for . . . peace and prosperity"; and Decoud a nihilist reading of past historical events.[19] Thus within *Nostromo* are not just one but at least three works of history that try to make sense of past events.[20] Far from trying to escape from history, Conrad piles it on thick: Demory writes that "this is a novel not so much about a particular period in history, real or imagined, as it is about history itself—the process, what it consists of, how it becomes a story, how it is constructed."[21] We might say that *Nostromo* is "in historiography" as much as it is "in history," attuned to, and dramatizing, the process by which events become narratives.

Part of this awareness stems from its portrayals of political power and its relationship to what version of events get told. Mitchell's most assertive act as historian is when he gives tours throughout the town toward the end of the novel. A typical moment of this tour:

> "All the great world of Sulaco here, sir." Captain Mitchell bowed right and left with no end of formality; then with animation, "Doña Emilia, Mrs. Gould's carriage. Look. Always white mules. The kindest, most gracious woman the sun ever shone upon. A great position, sir. A great position. First lady in Sulaco—far before the President's wife. And worthy of it."[22]

Edward Said, in *Beginnings: Intention and Method* (1975), describes Mitchell's tour as "well-intentioned propaganda," and remarks that "propagandistic descriptions of monuments, as Nietzsche once observed, provide one with the most insufficient and inaccurate sort of history."[23] Mitchell's tour is grossly inaccurate, most blatantly when he praises Nostromo and states that "He has done for Separation as much as anybody else, and . . . has got less than many others by it."[24] The obvious irony is that Nostromo is hoarding the lost silver, so has "got" more than anyone involved out of the events. Said notes that characters in *Nostromo* believe that "the past, given only ordinary attention and no official recording, [was] somehow unthinkable and without sufficient authority," and they are thus in need of histories to make sense of their past.[25] All of these various histories are necessary; otherwise the past is just a random accumulation of facts and data.

Whenever a work of history is present, that means there must be some sort of conflicting view of events: Hayden White, in his essay "The Value of Narrativity in the Representation of Reality" (1980), argues that narrative history—as opposed to annals or chronicles—depends upon a rich social world in which events from the past are fought over: "in order to qualify as historical, an event must be susceptible to at least two narrations of its occurrence. Unless at least two versions of the same set of events can be imagined, there is no reason for the historian to take upon himself the authority of giving the true account of what really happened."[26] Annals and chronicles record events; histories *compete* for an interpretation of them. *Nostromo* dramatizes this need for histories, as each "historian" in the novel has a different take on the events of the conflict. If each character were in agreement about what the past was all about, there would be no need for histories—town records would suffice. But as it stands, a mere chronicle of events would be absurd, as events cannot "speak for themselves." But if the events themselves are not speaking, who is? Or, more important, for whom does the historian speak? As Nietzsche recognized, history—the telling of history—inescapably involves issues of power, so White's "competition" usually has a victor. In *Nostromo*, Captain Mitchell is the dubious spokesperson for the victorious parties of the war, suggesting a skeptical attitude on the novel's part toward written (or oral) works of history.[27]

Conrad's project, however, is valuable not just for its critique of power. The historical monopoly of the new Occidental Republic of Sulaco is only one byproduct of the process of narrating the past. The self-consciousness of *Nostromo* turns our attention to the histories embedded in it, forcing an awareness of how history, and not just fiction, can never be a transparent window onto the past. Such an insight was implicit in Conrad's earlier impressionist works, and we can read *Nostromo* as a further development of some of the narratological experiments of a novel like *Lord Jim*. In Michael Valdez Moses's persuasive reading in *The Novel and the Globalization of Culture* (1995), modernity is "posthistorical" in the Hegelian sense of having nowhere left to go, human freedom already having been established as a universal goal, so much so that even dictatorships pay lip service to it. However, this posthistorical condition gives rise for a longing for what Moses terms a "premodern world" when historical developments were still possible, and such desires inform the structure of *Lord Jim*:[28]

The achronicity of the narrative suits a posthistorical consciousness that can no longer conceive of any further linear movement in history . . . . And yet, despite Conrad's stunning employment of these formal devices, he abandons them in the latter half of his work. Conrad's response to the impasse of modernity, at least in *Lord Jim*, is to return to a world in which history is not yet completed, a land where fundamental political issues are not settled and in which premodernist narrative forms—romance, epic, tragedy—still possess verisimilitude.[29]

If we choose to read *Lord Jim* as a historical novel, the bifurcation that frustrates readers like Jameson takes on a more critical purchase, as the modernist techniques of the first, "posthistorical" half spur the desire for "premodernity" and its accompanying forms of either romance or realist historical fiction.

In *Nostromo* such unevenness is distributed equally, an appropriate formal gesture given the combined and uneven development of Costaguanan society. Running through *Nostromo*, despite its density and tortuous narrative devices—Woolf's "languor"—is a rather nimble switching between fictional and historical narrative modes. When Avellanos realizes that he is a personal witness to an important historical moment, "Vague plans of another historical work, wherein all the devotions to the regeneration of the country he loved would be enshrined for the reverent worship of posterity, flitted through his mind."[30] This reverie suggests that the novel we are reading is "another historical work" about the revolution—although, to be sure, not one that is enshrining or reverential—thus pointing beyond the text to *Nostromo* as a published work by the "real" Joseph Conrad. The "Author's Note" of the novel functions like "The Tale," establishing a fictional world but then distinguishing between history and fiction within it. *Nostromo* shares with "The Tale" this urge to include histories and fictions within its own historical-fictional world, although its treatment of this dynamic is more nuanced, as we are not expected to take the historical texts as accurately depicting the past, but rather are encouraged to be suspicious of the official record of events.

Several of the characters beyond our narrator have read *Fifty Years of Misrule*: Decoud advises Antonia to read it, although he himself seems to take it with a heavy dose of skepticism.[31] Later, when Decoud recounts his arrival at the meeting at which Don Jose is planning surrender, he states:

Whatever happens, [Don Jose] will not survive. The deception is too great for a man of his age; and hasn't he seen the sheets of "Fifty Years of Misrule," which we have begun printing on the presses of the Porvenir, littering the Plaza, floating in the gutters, fired out as wads for trabucos loaded with handfuls of type, blown in the wind, trampled in the mud? I have seen pages floating upon the very waters of the harbour. It would be unreasonable to expect him to survive. It would be cruel.[32]

At this point Don Jose is no longer the fervent believer in the ideas to which his history subscribes, and subsequently critics have read *Nostromo* as highlighting the distance between political ideals and stark reality. Ursula Lord interprets the scene with Don Jose's disillusionment: "[i]dealism, however admirable Conrad finds it, is invariably incapable of being sustained by action."[33] This is certainly true, and is a recurring theme in many of Conrad's works, especially *Lord Jim*. But the novel is also about the distance between historical events and the narratives recounting them; note the formal difference between this constant switching from "fictional" to "historical," as opposed to *Lord Jim*'s more stark incompatibility of pre- and posthistoricism. Don Jose dreams of writing a second work of history to celebrate Decoud and Captain Mitchell, but instead we get *Nostromo* by our unnamed narrator, passed on by a fictional Joseph Conrad, which tells of the less exalted reality of this historical moment. The fate of *Fifty Years* is itself key to this dynamic, as Decoud is printing the work to spur separation, and so this work of history must be powerful and incendiary; yet it is "littering the Plaza, floating in the gutters . . . trampled in the mud." On the one hand, histories should have this power to transform society, and yet they are also so easily used and degraded. The fictional historical text of *Fifty Years of Misrule* moves through our historical fictional text of *Nostromo* to highlight the ease with which one type of writing can bleed into the other. As in "The Tale," the ability of any writer to shift back and forth from history to fiction is so facile because of their shared language and resources. In his "Henry James" essay, Conrad seemed to align fiction and history to argue for the former's importance; in *Nostromo* he is more inclined to do so to raise suspicions about the latter. However, I will argue that he simultaneously views historiography as necessary to the human condition, despite the difficulties and limitations of the discourse.

The Necessary Failure of History

While Conrad may demonstrate the affinities between history and fiction, he also retains for history a separate role. As Wittgenstein might put it, to know the difference between history and fiction we must look to their functions. This is Lubomír Doležel's injunction in *Possible Worlds of Fiction and History* (2010): "Relocating the problem of the relationship between fiction and history from the level of discourse to the level of world means asking whether the possible worlds of history and fiction are identical in their function and global structure or show some marked differences in these respects."[34] Such an approach acknowledges the shared language and resources of fiction and history, but also points to their divergent functions in society. In this light, deconstructive approaches like those of Hayden White might suffer from formalist excess. In *Nostromo*, history takes on a social necessity that is in productive tension with Conrad's skepticism regarding communication and epistemology, and it is this sense of necessity, I will argue, that critics have left out in their accounts of Conrad and history.

Conrad's relationship to history can be clarified when we compare him to the next generation of modernists, many of whom employed myth as either an organizational principle or ideal. Conrad depicts the myth-making of the character of Nostromo, but is always critical of this process, using his title character to expose the hollowness of myth, and not using myth to expose the hollowness of modernity, as W. B. Yeats and T. S. Eliot would do. In the "Author's Note" he writes that Nostromo "is still of the People, their undoubted Great Man—with a private history of his own."[35] Against the creation of popular myth, the narrator states that he will set out to reveal the true "history" behind it. For all of Conrad's suspicions of historiography, the text implies that only narrative history can rescue meaning and value from obfuscating myth (and, as the quote suggests, that "Great Men" versions of history are to a degree mythical). Why else go "behind" the public façade of Nostromo? To do so implies a privileging of a mode of narration that can uncover some sort of truth. As Frank Kermode notes, "Myths call for absolute, fictions for conditional assent."[36] Myths think that they are true absolutely, while fiction is aware of its own constructed ontology. Poststructuralist criticism has persuasively argued how powerfully the novel deconstructs myth and historical discourse, but has slighted the fact that it achieves all this through another form of narrative, through Decoud's writings.

As the novel opens, we hear of Nostromo before we actually encounter him. Signora Teresa laments, "'Oh! Gian' Battista, why art thou not here? Oh! why art thou not here?' She was not then invoking the saint himself, but calling on Nostromo, whose patron he was."[37] Teresa is not invoking a saint, but the nearest thing she knows to one, as she believes that only Nostromo can save them from the raging violence. Captain Mitchell brags to his superiors about Nostromo's status: "Fifty per cent. of that murdering mob and professional bandits from the Campo, sir, but there wasn't one that hadn't heard of Nostromo. As to the town *leperos*, sir, the sight of his black whiskers and white teeth was enough for them. They quailed before him, sir. That's what the force of character will do."[38] Nostromo's "character" within the world of the novel is a mythical, powerful force, one that Mitchell and Gould realize they can exploit for their own ends. But for Conrad, "character" in the narratological sense is exactly what has to be unearthed through the telling of the story, and the result will be to weaken the myth (at least for the reader), not reinforce it.

In the earlier parts of the novel the narrative voice seems to join in this myth-making: Nostromo is "now dismounted and in the checked shirt and red sash of a Mediterranean sailor, bawling orders from the end of the jetty in a stentorian voice. A fellow in a thousand!"[39] With hindsight this is ironic, given what we eventually know about the supposedly great Nostromo. But at this point the narration is still describing Nostromo from the outside, from the town's collective perspective: "The hand on the mare's neck trembled suddenly. She dropped her head before all the eyes in the wide circle formed round the generous, the terrible, the inconstant Capataz de Cargadores."[40] Similarly: "The circle had broken up, and the lordly Capataz de Cargadores, the indispensable man, the tired and trusty Nostromo, the Mediterranean sailor come ashore casually to try his luck in Costaguana, rode slowly towards the harbor."[41] The piled-on adjectives and rhetorical overkill hint that we should be suspicious of such mythologizing, but the narrative is nevertheless focalized through the town itself, as "come ashore" indicates the position to which Nostromo has emerged. Although the narrator is often omniscient, the novel withholds this omniscience until later, and lets the impressions of the town speak in the earlier chapters.

The deconstruction of Nostromo's myth begins with Decoud. Like the narrator, he begins by speaking in the rhetoric of the town when describing Nostromo: "Behold the illustrious Capataz de Cargadores . . . coming in all his splendour after his work is done. The next great man of Sulaco after Don Carlos Gould."[42] We soon learn, as we do with the narrative at large, that this rhetoric is ironic. Decoud knows that Nostromo is really out to make money, and shrewdly states that "I suppose he looks upon his prestige as a sort of investment."[43] He goes on to state that he knows of Nostromo's legend but has a hard time believing it: "I have heard no end of tales of his strength, his audacity, his fidelity. No end of fine things. H'm! incorruptible? It is indeed a name of honour for the Capataz de Cargadores of Sulaco. Incorruptible! Fine, but vague." The repeated term "incorruptible" forcibly foreshadows Nostromo's eventual corruption from the "lost" silver.[44]

Decoud's suspicions mark the beginning of the turn of the narrative against the myth of Nostromo. Woolf was unsatisfied with this dynamic in her review:

> his characters have the rare quality of erring upon the side of largeness. The gestures with which they move upon his wide stage are uniformly noble, and the phrases lavished upon them are beautiful enough to be carved for ever upon the pedestals of statues. But when critics speak of the "failure" of "Nostromo" it is probable that they refer to something inanimate and stationary in the human figures which chills our warmest sympathies.[45]

Woolf narrows in on the dynamic of Nostromo's characterization, but this "failure" is one of the novel's successes, as it exposes Nostromo's hollowness, "chilling" our enthusiasm for this "Great Man." Nostromo loses much of his mythic status for the reader as he and Decoud head off with the silver, and the narration becomes increasingly internal, less from the perspective of the town. The novel from this point shifts away from public discourse into a more subjective type of language that we associate with Marlow's narratives from *Heart of Darkness* and *Lord Jim*. This is not an arbitrary narrative decision: it is the presence of the townspeople that informs the mythical mode, and once they recede into the distance Nostromo loses his mythic hold on the reader.

During the operation we learn that Nostromo has normal doubts and fears and is no superman. But what is more interesting is how, for the town, his legend continues to grow after the mission, and as the novel comes to a close there is a growing disconnect between the public Nostromo and the private one whose "history" we have learned. As Captain Mitchell gives his tour of the town, the story of Nostromo's ride becomes legendary:

> In the Construction Camp at the railhead, he obtained a horse, arms, some clothing, and started alone on that marvelous ride—four hundred miles in six days, through a disturbed country, ending by the feat of passing through the Monterist lines outside Cayta. The history of that ride, sir, would make a most exciting book. He carried all our lives in his pocket. Devotion, courage, fidelity, intelligence were not enough. Of course, he was perfectly fearless and incorruptible. But a man was wanted who would know how to succeed. He was that man, sir.[46]

This is similar rhetoric and vocabulary to what we have seen in the earlier parts of the novel, but now the reader knows the truth behind the mythic characterization (and that the "exciting book" is not the one we are reading—the ride, like much of the action in *Nostromo*, is ellipsed). What was formerly foreshadowing becomes full-blown dramatic irony, and we are now on guard against such rhetoric. Mitchell also relates a conversation he had with Nostromo: "I begged him not to think any more about the silver, and he smiled. A smile that went to my heart, sir. 'It was no mistake,' I told him. 'It was a fatality. A thing that could not be helped.' '*Si, si!*' he said, and turned away. I thought it best to leave him alone for a bit to get over it. Sir, it took him years really, to get over it."[47] Since the reader knows that Nostromo was lying during this conversation, the mythic status of Nostromo becomes a target for the novel's cynical deconstruction of it. The myth is socially powerful and yet clearly empty, and again note Conrad's distinction from Yeats and Eliot, who would see more social and aesthetic potential for mythical forms. For Conrad, it is myth itself that makes Nostromo such a hollow man.

Decoud intuited Nostromo's motive to be purely monetary, but this does not exhaust Nostromo's motivations, as he is also driven by a desire to be remembered. Signora Teresa, no longer believing Nostromo to be saintlike, tells him that "[t]hey have turned your head with their praises. . . . They have been paying you with words. Your folly shall betray you into poverty, misery, starvation. The very *leperos* shall laugh at you—the great Capataz."[48] Her predictions are of course correct, as Nostromo begins to believe that he might be able to live up to the public praise he constantly receives. After he receives his mission, he states that "they shall learn I am just the man they take me for."[49] This deceptively simple statement indicates two things: first, that he is aware of the distance between what they think he is and what he really is, and second, that he is going to have to work to be worthy of that status. But it also shows how much Nostromo *desires* to be worthy of it, just as much as he desires compensation. He says of this mission that "[i]t shall be talked about when the little children are grown up and the grown men are old."[50] Nostromo wants to *be* history, the next in the line of Great Men. He may have begun his career as a legend cynically, trying to angle it for wealth, but by the time he receives his mission he has been fooled by his own myth.[51] Nostromo's epiphany relates to his own vanity:

> His vanity was infinitely and naively greedy, but his conceptions were limited. Afterwards his success in the work he found on shore enlarged them in the direction of personal magnificence. This sailor led a public life in his sphere. It became necessary to him. It was the very breath of his nostrils. And who can say that it was not genuine distinction? It was genuine because it was based on something that was in him—his overweening vanity, which Decoud alone . . . had taken the trouble to find out. Each man must have some temperamental sense by which to discover himself. With Nostromo it was vanity of an artless sort. Without it he would have been nothing.[52]

Nostromo's vanity is the converse of the town's mythologizing of him. The myth is "genuine" because the town's estimation of him matches what he thinks of himself, but without that myth he is "nothing." The character development of Nostromo throughout the novel is more of an emptying than a fleshing-out: as he gains subjectivity he loses everything else, as we subsequently encounter only his vanity and his desire to be perceived as a legend.[53] This may be the "chill" that Woolf detected, as we come to realize that there is nothing to warm us in the heart of Nostromo.[54]

But in a sense there is an eventual deepening to Nostromo's character, which is his growing awareness of such vanity. As he remembers his "last act he had performed on Sulaco," giving a coin to a poor old woman, he sees that this action was in keeping with his legend. But his main act in the novel is to hoard money, not distribute it: the mission to hide the silver that is supposed to make him even more legendary is a lonelier enterprise, with no recognition from anyone. His decision to steal the silver is made once he realizes that there will be no public record of his deeds on the water. For Nostromo, any deed not recorded may well have not been performed in the first place: "The necessity of living concealed somehow, for God knows how long, which assailed him on his return to consciousness, made everything that had gone before for years appear vain and foolish, like a flattering dream come suddenly to an end."[55] Nostromo's deepening is the shift from the meaning of the word "vanity," as it transforms from meaning "self-absorbed" to meaning "futile." He now sees the emptiness of the myth that he let the town, and eventually himself, believe. Any sort of fullness to Nostromo's character depends, paradoxically, upon this sense of his own emptiness: "with no intellectual existence or moral strain to carry on his individuality, unscathed, over the abyss left by the collapse of his vanity; for even that had been simply sensuous and picturesque, and could not exist apart from outward show."[56] Nostromo is redeemed from his own vanity by this painful epiphany of such vanity, and he is saved from the power of myth because he realizes its illusionary nature. By the time the separatist project has completed, Nostromo cynically trusts only physical, as opposed to social, capital: "[h]is courage, his magnificence, his leisure, his work, everything was as before, only everything was a sham. But the treasure was real. He clung to it with a more tenacious, mental grip."[57] The town's myths no longer hold any attraction for him.[58]

Conrad pits Nostromo's history against the town's myths, highlighting the gap between the two and the falsity of a kind of history. For all of Conrad's uneasiness with histories, he sees it here as a necessary corrective to delusional and dangerous mythologizing.[59] Historiography may be problematic, as poststructuralism has continually argued, and Conrad himself intuited, but the response of modernist historiography is not a blanket despair, but rather the seeking out of new methods. As untrustworthy as our main narrator might be, he is surely a more reliable guide to this fictional world than Captain Mitchell or Don Jose Avellanos. If history were "impossible," there would be no difference in validity, in the fictional world of the novel, between Mitchell's account of Nostromo and the one that we read for ourselves.

Poststructuralism has generally found versions of itself in Conrad, but if we map out more accurately a modernist version of historiography—one poised between the Enlightenment and its postmodern dissenters—we can see that it may have many affinities with and may anticipate subsequent types of histories, but ultimately it remains its own mode of writing history. Decoud serves as Conrad's embodiment of the problematics of modernist narration and historiography, but also as its hero. *Nostromo* often stages Decoud's act of writing against a background of darkness. Decoud writes his letter to his sister in Viola's Café, and during a brief pause from his work he looks out the window: "Decoud was met by a darkness so impenetrable that he could see neither the mountains nor the town, nor yet the buildings near the harbour; and there was not a sound, as if the tremendous obscurity of the Placid Gulf, spreading from the waters over the land, had made it dumb as well as blind."[60] Decoud seems to be gazing into a heart of darkness. This makes him think that

[i]n the most skeptical heart there lurks at such moments, when the chances of existence are involved, a desire to leave a correct impression of the feelings, like a light by which the action may be seen when personality is gone,

gone where no light of investigation can ever reach the truth which every death takes out of the world. Therefore, instead of looking for something to eat, or trying to snatch an hour or so of sleep, Decoud was filling the pages of a large pocket-book with a letter to his sister.[61]

Against the creeping darkness outside there is the act of writing by candle-light, the "light" of the historical document that will be his impressions of his experience. The act of writing itself is not necessarily therapeutic (as it will be for John Dowell in *The Good Soldier*); instead, it is more important that the texts will be read by a sympathetic reader. Conrad stresses, not the act of writing itself, but the notion that Decoud's text will someday, "when personality is gone," be read and Decoud brought back to life, at least in a textual sense. It is just this extinction of personality that Derrida insists, in "Signature Event Context," is essential to understanding language, as any sort of meaningful communication presupposes absence: first, Decoud's sister is absent from De-coud's environs, which necessitates the act of writing instead of speaking; second, for Decoud's writings to have any larger significance, they must be intelligible after his death, or in Derrida's terms, "my future disappearance."[62] Writing is "a progressive extenuation of presence," the keeping-present of ideas.[63] "All writing, therefore, in order to be what it is, must be able to function in the radical absence of every empirically determined addressee in general."[64] Unlike a private code, Decoud's letter must be legible to others besides his sister to have any social significance.

But for Derrida the letter breaks away from its author and enters the world as a series of floating signifiers. A Derridean reading will thus focus on De-coud's eventual failure as historian, both as fraternal correspondent and chronicler of the revolution. In the café scene, as soon as Decoud finishes writing, he feels the horror creep over him again: "With the writing of the last line there came upon Decoud a moment of sudden and complete oblivion."[65] Soon after, he and Nostromo embark on their mission with their silver into the dark waters, and from this point on Decoud leaves no historical traces behind him, the light of history snuffed out: "[t]he Capataz, extending his hand, put out the candle suddenly. It was as if his companion had destroyed, by a single touch, the world of affairs, of loves, of revolution."[66] The candle from the café writing scene reappears here, the last artificial light Decoud will ever see. Just as Nostromo has no public witnesses to his "picturesque" great-ness in the dark, Decoud no longer has a means of communication with the outside world—neither with his time nor those to come.

As the pair sets out, reality seems to fade away as the darkness Decoud had witnessed from the café has now completely engulfed them:

> When [Nostromo's] voice ceased, the enormous stillness, without light or sound, seemed to affect Decoud's senses like a powerful drug. He didn't

even know at times whether he were asleep or awake. Like a man lost in slumber, he heard nothing, he saw nothing. Even his hand held before his face did not exist for his eyes. The change from the agitation, the passions and the dangers, from the sights and sounds of the shore, was so complete that it would have resembled death had it not been for the survival of his thoughts. In this foretaste of eternal peace they floated vivid and light, like unearthly clear dreams of earthly things that may haunt the souls freed by death from the misty atmosphere of regrets and hopes. Decoud shook himself, shuddered a bit, though the air that drifted past him was warm. He had the strangest sensation of his soul having just returned into his body from the circumambient darkness in which land, sea, sky, the mountains, and the rocks were as if they had not been.[67]

Once enmeshed in this darkness, Decoud's physical reality recedes and he is left only with his disembodied thoughts. He is a pure Cartesian ego, certain only of his ability to think. Nostromo to him is now just a voice, much like Kurtz was for Marlow and Marlow was to his fellow passengers. He is out of touch not only with his surroundings but also his own past: "All his active sensations and feelings as far back as he could remember seemed to him the maddest of dreams. Even his passionate devotion to Antonia into which he had worked himself up out of the depths of his scepticism had lost all appearance of reality."[68] As Decoud becomes cut off from his own personal history, the social world in turn loses track of Decoud: no one ever learns of his fate.

After Nostromo drops him off on the island with the silver, Decoud commits suicide, and we are told that he died of "solitude, the enemy known but to few on this earth, and whom only the simplest of us are fit to withstand."[69] When Nostromo returns much later, he tries to reconstruct what happened on the island, but can only conclude that "[h]e will never come back to explain."[70] By killing himself, Decoud "disappeared without a trace" except for a smattering of blood.[71] Decoud was unable to leave a trace behind and thus was unable to become part of history—not in Nostromo's mythical sense of becoming a legend, nor in Don Jose's sense of being part of a nationalist project, nor in Captain Mitchell's vision of material progress, but rather in the sense of textual continuity that historical documents and traces can provide us. Decoud left behind no markings except the blood smear, a parody of a written record, or a macabre example of Derrida's concept of the signature, which "implies the actual or empirical nonpresence of the signer. But, it will be said, it also marks and retains his having-been present in a past now, which will remain a future now, and therefore in a now in general, in the transcendental form of newness (*maintenance*)."[72] The blood of Decoud signifies, parodically, both his presence in the past, and his future state of extinction in that past.

The Miracle of Histories

Usually we are encouraged, especially in poststructural criticism, to read in Conrad's works a vacillation between a lack of faith in basic communication—which the criticism applauds—and a retrograde, sometimes even reactionary belief in some sort of meaning beyond words, or as Paul Armstrong puts it, the "conflict between suspicion and faith—suspicion about the contingency of the codes and interpretations we live by, but faith in them nonetheless because we cannot do without them."[73] Erdinast-Vulcan reads Decoud's suicide in this light: "Having surrendered to the skeptical relativistic outlook, he ends up by being stranded, both literally and figuratively, without a foothold in an indifferent, senseless universe. Conrad is well aware, as evidenced in Decoud's suicide, of man's need for a stable frame of reference, for a belief in some Absolute. He cannot afford to loosen his hold on all 'saving illusions' as his character had done."[74] As in much criticism of Conrad, we are here offered two options, a "senseless universe" or "some Absolute." The Derridean distrust of absolutes subsequently leads many critics to valorize Conrad's sense of a senseless universe. Marlow's "[w]e live as we dream—alone" and more explicitly his narration from *Lord Jim* are often evoked to support this:

> It is when we try to grapple with another man's intimate need that we perceive how incomprehensible, wavering, and misty are the beings that share with us the sight of the stars and the warmth of the sun. It is as if loneliness were a hard and absolute condition of existence; the envelope of flesh and blood on which our eyes are fixed melts before the outstretched hand, and there remains only the capricious, unconsolable, and elusive spirit that no eye can follow, no hand can grasp.[75]

No critical account of Conrad's project should ignore such dire pronouncements as to the possibilities of communication, especially the emphasis on the "hard and absolute condition of existence." But the fate of Decoud, in a negative fashion, might actually demonstrate Conrad's belief in the necessity for and possibilities of human communication, especially writing. And this is not necessarily a willed return to premodern values or anything so regressive: there may be other options in a Conradian universe.

The tragedy of Decoud is not so much his death as his loneliness, both in his last hours and after his death, as no one can make contact with any trace he may have left behind. Captain Mitchell says of Nostromo that he was "[a]bsolutely making history," but it is Decoud who is the real historian.[76] Decoud's suicide, then, does not evidence some existential inability to communicate but rather a specific historical situation in which human speech or writing may have averted this tragedy—not saved his life, but at least preserved it textually. Decoud's letters to his sister survive in the fictional world of the novel, and will provide valuable resources to future historians of Costaguana. The fate of Decoud himself, by contrast, falls into oblivion. Communication may be difficult, as the novel stresses, but a lack of it is the real tragedy. As George Levine writes of Conrad in *The Realistic Imagination* (1981), "[w]hat gives dignity to mankind is not withdrawal and detachment from the illusions of consciousness, but engagement in them."[77] Despite the limits of our ability to communicate experience that Marlow voices to his fellow passengers, *Nostromo* urges us toward a recognition of the utter necessity of such efforts, not in an absolutist sense, but rather with a recognition of a hierarchy of values of narratives.

Some histories, then, are just better than others. Had Decoud survived, or at least left behind a textual trace of events, the hegemonic power of Captain Mitchell's propagandistic historical tours might be loosened. Decoud's failure could be read not as universally representative of the human condition but rather as a warning against "withdrawal," one that suggests some redemptive and successful ability on our part to communicate. Paul Ricoeur's early works on language, such as *Interpretation Theory: Discourse and the Surplus of Meaning* (1976)—often at odds with the playful/bleak conclusions of poststructural theory—stress the positive side of communication, what he actually refers to as a "miracle," and we could use his theories as a countermove to the pessimism of the poststructural, which may help us find other modes of narratology and epistemology in Conrad's works. For Ricoeur, communication is always *with* someone else, even if that someone else is an unintended reader in a distant land in a distant future. Unlike thinkers such as Habermas, Ricoeur argues that language is not about communicating *experience* per se—we experience like we dream, alone—but rather the *meaning* left behind from the experience that can be transferred: "This something is not the experience as experienced, but its meaning. Here is the miracle. The experience as experienced, as lived, remains private, but its sense, its meaning, becomes public. Communication in this way is the overcoming of the radical non-communicability of the lived experience as lived."[78] Experience still remains stubborn in its inability to be related, but meaning is not so shackled to the contingent. This is because—and here is Ricoeur's central response to Derrida's notion of "writing orphaned"—language as intention, as problematic as it may be, is always met by the intention of the hearer/reader, who "intends" to understand the speaker/writer: the writer's "intention implies the intention of being recognized, therefore the intention of the other's intention."[79] Ricoeur fosters Derrida's orphans, and thus "language is itself the process by which private experience is made public."[80] When Decoud writes the letter to his sister, he intends to convey his experience, and we can only deduce that she will try to understand this experience as best she can. The very act of letter-writing is a socially accepted form in which there is a writer and reader, a sender and addressee, a mutual relationship of intention. This wards off the darkness, even if only for a brief time, or as Ricoeur writes, as if from within *Nostromo* itself: "the solitude of life is for a moment, anyway, illuminated by the common light of discourse."[81] Future historians, toiling away by candlelight over Decoud's letters, will be better equipped to write their own histories of Costaguana's events, thanks to the "miracle" of the written word.

Decoud's suicide is the opposite case, as his last act is one of despair and not communication. No miracle occurs, not because of the incommunicability of existence or anything so grand, but rather because Decoud is deprived of the very human tools, language and writing, by which we usually connect with others. While it may seem ironic that Decoud ends his life in the full glare of the sun, Conrad had already established a link between the strange sunlight of Sulaco—the sun rises late because it must crest the Huguerota mountain—and history in its non-textual sense. For example, as Giorgio Viola watches violent events unfold in Sulaco, he cannot understand their import:

> In a speckless sky the sun hung clear and blinding. Knots of men ran head-long; others made a stand; and the irregular rattle of firearms came rippling to his ears in the fiery, still air. Horsemen galloped towards each other, wheeled round together, separated at speed. Giorgio saw one fall, rider and horse disappearing as if they had galloped into a chasm and the movements of the animated scene were like the peripeties of a violent game played upon the plain by dwarfs mounted and on foot, yelling with tiny throats, under the mountain that seemed a colossal embodiment of silence. Never before had Giorgio seen this bit of plain so full of active life; his gaze could not take in all its details at once.[82]

The "speckless" sunlight makes it difficult for Viola to make any sense of what he is witnessing. History unfolds before his eyes as utter chaos, and all his experience in the Garibaldi campaigns cannot help him sort out the disorder of political events. (Earlier, contemplating his hung portrait of Garibaldi, "a thread of strong sunshine cut it perpendicularly."[83]) He is suffering from too much history, as it were, and it is the more controlled, artificial, and selective light of Decoud's café candle that signals an ability to sort through human existence and put it into some sense of order or textual shape. In other words, Decoud is the one character who can, at least momentarily, navigate between the blinding glare and the blinding darkness, between the chaos of the past and the irreversibility of oblivion. Such navigation—indicated by the candle and pen—is what Decoud is deprived of in his solitude, and on his last day he witnesses a display of sun equally blinding to Viola's: "[a]fter a clear daybreak the sun appeared splendidly above the peaks of the range. The great gulf burst into a glitter all around the boat; and in this glory of merciless solitude the silence appeared before him, stretched taut like a dark, thin string."[84] The tragedy for Decoud is not that he has somehow escaped from history: history assaults him with all its deadly force and full stare. It is rather that history is shaping him more than he is shaping history. Without pen and paper, without his candle, he is cut off from the textual chain of history that allows humanity to debate meaning and causation.

This stress on the necessity of communication appears through much of Conrad's work, even his most bleak. Michael Levenson, in *Modernism and the Fate of Individuality: Character and Novelistic Form from Conrad to Woolf* (1991), analyzes *Heart of Darkness* and points out that, as much as Marlow lies to Kurtz's Intended, and as much as he seems to distrust human language, he does narrate his experience on the *Nellie* to both his listeners and, by narrative extension, to the reader. Marlow often interrupts his narrative, worrying that this attempt at storytelling is not truly communicating. But, Levenson argues, making too much of this anxiety ignores the fact that Kurtz has managed to communicate with Marlow: "Although Marlow must remain locked within his cage, he can speak (perhaps to no one) of hearing (or perhaps imagining) a cry from another cage, and he thus creates an image of how understanding would occur, if only understanding *could* occur."[85] As terrifying as the disembodied voices are, coming from Kurtz and Marlow through the darkness, they are having an effect: terror is actually a mark of success when it comes to communication. The fact that Kurtz has managed to convey something at all to Marlow should give us pause before we give in completely to Marlow's pessimism regarding language and communication. We may watch him doubt his ability to tell stories, "[b]ut standing outside this world, *we* can know them; we know that a man rattling his cage has rattled the cage of another."[86] So it is with Decoud: he dies of despair from solitude, believing, like Marlow, that he will never be able to communicate with another. But we readers do get to witness Decoud's last days, due to the "miracle" of Conrad's composition. The isolation of the island slowly drives Decoud insane, and he even comes to believe "that Antonia could not possibly have ever loved a being so impalpable as himself."[87] Having lost connection with other human beings, and having lost the ability to tell his story or leave an intelligible trace behind, Decoud has lost his own self and his own history. History, for Decoud—and possibly Conrad—is not the nightmare. History, or histories, are the only things that save us from the nightmare of oblivion, the engulfing darkness. The "immense indifference of things" can only be countered by acts of writing and the narration of histories, a willed entry into the textual chain of history. *Nostromo* does not highlight the failure of historiography, rather it dramatizes both its difficulties and its necessity.

Vanishing Traces: *Under Western Eyes*

What makes *Nostromo* such a forceful initiation of the modernist historical novel is its awareness of the constructed nature of history, with a simultaneous awareness of the human need for such narratives. It might seem odd, with a novel that depicts torture and murder during a political upheaval, to argue that Conrad wants more history in the world, not less. But again, the term "history" can mislead us: what might be needed are more *histories* to light us through the darkness of *history*. The novel's insights might appear clearer when contrasted with the attitudes that inform the later *Under Western Eyes* (1911). That novel shares many qualities with *Nostromo*: they both could be classified as "political thrillers" (as would *The Secret Agent* [1907]); both have a protagonist who is surrounded by people who idealize him, while he knows himself to be no hero; both novels take a cynical attitude toward revolutionary activity, and seem suspicious that all such work will produce any real political change. Formally, both employ sudden time-shifts and ellipses, and are based on fictional found documents, as the narrator of *Under Western Eyes* has access to Razumov's actions and mental state because of the diary he has left behind. Razumov, like Decoud, needs to communicate with the outside world: "The universal aspiration with all its profound and melancholy meaning assailed heavily Razumov, who, amongst eighty millions of his kith and kin, had no heart to which he could open himself. . . . No human being could bear a steady view of moral solitude without going mad."[88] For both figures, writing, especially by candlelight, is a means by which to overcome this solitude, this darkness: "It calmed [Razumov]—it reconciled him to his existence. He sat there scribbling by the light of a solitary candle."[89] And once again, the narrative highlights the problematics of such activity: the narrator of *Under Western Eyes* warns us that "because of the imperfection of language there is always something ungracious (and even disgraceful) in the exhibition of naked truth."[90]

Despite these formal and thematic similarities, *Under Western Eyes* lacks the preoccupation with history in the full sense that *Nostromo* holds. When characters speak of "history" in *Under Western Eyes* they usually mean the forces of progress or revolution, as when Razumov leaves his "manifesto" for the police to find, in which he desires "History not Theory."[91] History for these characters is never about the recording of events or political forces. As conspirators or spies they are obsessed with history's opposite, with covering their tracks, leaving no trace behind. Written documents get destroyed, witnesses get killed, evidence goes missing, the single solitary candle snuffed out.

Interestingly, when Conrad added his "Author's Note" in 1920 to this novel, he began by stating that "[i]t must be admitted that by the mere force of circumstances *Under Western Eyes* has become already a sort of historical novel dealing with the past."[92] The "circumstances" of course were the actual Russian Revolution of two years previous. Conrad seems to be using "historical" here almost as a pejorative, implying that his novel may have become "outdated," as he wrote to Andre Gide in 1918: "I think that the Russian revolution has made my Western Eyes look terribly outdated."[93] In the "Author's Note" he can only "venture to hope that it has not lost all its interest" because it still depicts the psychology of the Russian mind, which supposedly has not dated. But I would argue that it is not historical events that make the novel less relevant to any discussion of historiography than *Nostromo* (which, concerning a fictional country, is in less direct danger of being upstaged by real-world activity). *Nostromo* theorizes the workings of the narrative of history in a way that Conrad would never attempt again on such a scale, despite his continual return to the genre of the historical novel. *Under Western Eyes* is, in a sense, *Nostromo* rewritten in a real historical setting but simultaneously emptied of history. Conrad's aversion to the Russian empire partly informs this attitude: in his essay "Autocracy and War" (1905), he wrote, "Russian autocracy succeeded to nothing; it had no historical past and it cannot hope for a historical future. It can only end."[94] But Conrad's personal distrust of Russia, or his own ideological limitations in the handling of revolutionary circles, are not what prevent *Under Western Eyes* from serving as a model of historical narrative. (Many professional historians suffered from the same limitations; this does not mean that they did not write histories.) After *Nostromo*, Conrad's preoccupation with how history gets recorded had waned, and for the remainder of his writing life his historical interests were more concerned with topic and era than with representational methods. Instead of facing the complexity of history in all its senses, works like *Under Western Eyes*, "Prince Roman," *The Rover*, or *Suspense* investigate history as a setting, not as a textual process.

Nostromo and the Historical Novel

Taking an overview of Conrad's historical work, we see a heavy emphasis on Napoleonic Europe; with *Under Western Eyes*, a distrustful regard for Russia; and with "Prince Roman," a desire to confront Poland's troubled history. Such topical gravitations seem in keeping with Conrad's Polish upbringing and Francophila, but the setting of *Nostromo* is harder to explain. Conrad set many of his novels and stories in areas he had visited, but never with the curious mixture of national fictionality and historical specificity that we find in *Nostromo*. J. H. Stape writes that Conrad "hacked out 'Nostromo' from books, his memories of the Caribbean, and his brief glimpse of the South American coast in 1876"—hardly a robust basis on which to write his longest work.[95]

The geopolitical nature of *Nostromo* partly draws on the breakaway and establishment of Panama in 1903 and the interventionist role of the United

States. Such aggressive American moves would later characterize the new, in-direct form of imperialism that came to dominate as the century progressed (and that would stand in stark contrast to the blatant and direct rule of King Leopold in the Congo). Costaguana and Sulaco are fictionally coded, how-ever, unlike "off-stage" figures like Garibaldi. Old Viola, an "austere republi-can" "often called simply 'the Garibaldino' (as Mohammedans are called after their prophet)," "had been one of Garibaldi's Immortal Thousand in the con-quest of Sicily."[96] Viola is the strong link to Europe's tangled history of nation-alist revolutions: Richard Niland notes that the name of Viola's café, "L'Albergo d'Italia Una," serves as "another signpost of the importance of nineteenth-century nationalism."[97] Garibaldi was for Viola "an immortal hero! This was your liberty; it gave you not only life, but immortality as well!"[98] By contrast, "the name of Cavour—the arch intriguer sold to kings and tyrants—could be heard involved in imprecations against the China girls, cooking in general, and the brute of a country where he was reduced to live for the love of liberty that traitor had strangled."[99] Garibaldi's later failures were, to Viola, "a catas-trophe that had instilled into him a gloomy doubt of ever being able to under-stand the ways of Divine justice."[100] Not merely a living anachronism, Viola is a character almost completely depicted in relationship to his experience in the Italian independence campaigns, which Conrad relates with great detail.[101] Niland links Viola with Conrad's own Polish patriotism and his "broad historical support for national independence movements, particularly those opposing the empires that controlled Poland."[102] But Viola might also link to the Italian novelist Alessandro Manzoni and his novel *The Betrothed* (1827), a salient example of what Lukács called the "classical form" of the his-torical novel. *The Betrothed* played a central role in constructing the "imagi-nary community" of the Italian nation, and is representative of how the his-torical novel generally was so essential to nineteenth-century European political thought. With *Nostromo*, however, the "gloomy doubt" that plagues Viola informs the narrative as well, and the novel stages the Sulacan revolt as a belated, and jaded version of the revolutions of 1848 (which, as Marx fa-mously wrote, were already farcical repetitions themselves). Conrad had no illusions as to the mixed nature of political ambitions in revolutionary situa-tions: in "Autocracy and War" he wrote of the French Revolution that the "parentage of that great social and political upheaval was intellectual, the idea was elevated: but it is the fate of any idea to lose its royal form and power, to lose its 'virtue' the moment it descends from its solitary throne to work its will among the people."[103] Still, Conrad's portrait of Viola is an admiring one, even if he sees his radical ideas as doomed and only now embodied in bogus heroes like Nostromo. The difficult ironies of the novel are partly the result of this intricate negotiation with the inherited form of the historical novel, whose ideological underpinnings Conrad cannot share, but whose aspira-tions for national independence strike deep chords in his Polish past.

Belated, displaced, ironic, fragmented, impressionistic: with *Nostromo*, Conrad bequeathed one model of the modernist historical novel before modernism as we usually define it had even emerged. Conrad took great pains over its composition, pains shared by his general readership: one early reviewer warned that "many readers will never survive it."[104] The novel's recalcitrance is the result of a complex series of maneuvers on Conrad's part with history, historical form, and changing political realities. While not immediately appreciated, *Nostromo* is a trove of methods and techniques whose influence has been widespread, especially for those modern writers drawn to issues of historical representation.[105] Ford Madox Ford knew *Nostromo* intimately, and references to Conrad occur in Rebecca West's oeuvre throughout her career. With these three writers we can see how modernism, from its beginnings to its endings, took an interest in history not just in the sense of political events or the shaping forces of the past, but also in how the events from collective human experience get formed into narratives. Making history new, they struggled through the seemingly impossible, yet urgently necessary task of living up to social memory.

Rewriting and Repetition in *The Good Soldier*

The Unity of Style

Ford Madox Ford found both financial and critical success with *The Fifth Queen*. Throughout the decade he continued to apply its formula to a number of historical novels, with middling levels of success: *The Half Moon* (1909), *A Portrait* (1910), and *The Young Lovell* (1913). The books continued to sell, and he wrote to J. B. Pinker in 1910 that "I suppose I shall have to stick to historical novels for the Constable Contract . . . though I hate writing them," and critics, both then and now, note a drop in the quality of these works.[1] Ford himself looked back disparagingly at this Edwardian output after the war. In his book on Conrad (1924) he describes this kind of novel as "nothing more than a *tour de force*, a fake more or less genuine in inspiration and workmanship, but none the less a fake."[2] By that time he had written *The Good Soldier* and was already at work on *Parade's End*, so partly this is a "High Modernist" looking back at his more traditionalist work with disdain. But he may have also realized an inherent problem in the form that he had perfected with *The Fifth Queen* and then applied by rote to his other historical novels.

Each subsequent historical novel after *The Fifth Queen* takes place in a different historical period and is depicted with a different linguistic style, one that attempts to somehow "capture" the era. Here is a passage from *The Half Moon*, which takes place during the discovery of the New World:

> Nevertheless, he did not consider that death or forfeiture were very near him, and it behoved a proper man not to take death early and unnaturally into his account, but to lay his plans for the future so that, if he died in the three-scores, he might leave to his heirs a goodly name and heritage. For this he wished to see the New World, so that he might know what merchandises he should best send thither and what he must commission his agents there buy for him of the savages.[3]

The language is not contemporaneous, nor is it the pictorial style of *The Fifth Queen*. Instead, as might be appropriate for a novel of sea exploration taking place in 1609, it is speculative, peppered with language that Ford usually avoided like "behoved" and "thither." The Georgian-era (George I, that is) *A Portrait* uses language that could be found in Gibbon or Joseph Addison:

> Mr. Roland had not seen this house nor his brother in the last six years, for his uncle would neither let the younger son come down from Town nor the elder go up to it. The uncle having attempted to drive his coach up the steps of St. Paul's whilst the Te Deum Service was being held after the battle of Wagenau, and having been forcibly prevented by William the Third's order and by William the Third's Bodyguard—the uncle having arrived at the conclusion that this was his right as Lord of the Courts-Baron of Winterbourne, of Bassett, of Pitt Minima, and of Cheveril St. Francis. The most learned jurists have since denied this claim, which was revived by his nephew, the present Mr. Bettesworth, the decision being that the right which was granted by Henry the Third had been to ride one horse and lead three up the steps of the Church of St. Paul in the village of Ludger.[4]

The language here, as befits the eighteenth century, is light, precise, and qualified. Finally, here is the late-mediaeval *Young Lovell* (1913):

> Their mother, who was a proud Dacre with the proudest of them, flushed vicious red. She said that her daughters were naughty jades, and if their husbands had not three times each been beggared by Scots raiders they might have had leave to talk so. But, being what they were, it would be better if they closed their mouths over one who had paid all his ransoms, whether to the Scots or on the bloody field of Kenchie's Burn, with swordblows solely. She had paid one thousand marks to artificers of Brussels for stuffs to deck that hall and the street of the township where it led from the chapel whence her fair, brave son should come; so that banners and carpets hung from the windows, the outer galleries, stairways and the roofs where they were low. And she wished she had spent ten thousand on her son who had won booty enough to pay all she had laid out on him and her daughters' husbands' ransoms besides—after the day of Kenchie's Burn.[5]

While not the language of the Tudor court, Ford's prose still conjures up feudal rhythms and cadence.[6] Max Saunders writes that "[i]t is in the sustaining of a strange and compelling style of the past that his force makes itself felt in his historical fiction," and indeed one aim of these linguistic styles is to emphasize what T. S. Eliot called "the pastness of the past."[7] Robert Green notes that such styles indicate that the time of the novels "was fundamentally different from the inchoate present."[8] But this unifying role of language, which Ford exploited in *The Fifth Queen* to great success, reifies the past as it tries to find one manner in which a time period can be depicted.[9] While Ford may use characters as contrasting social "types" in Lukács's sense, there is no internal conflict of style or language: any contradiction in society, be it of class, religion, or nation, gets frozen via a series of tableaus that confer an organic wholeness to a given era. And while *The Fifth Queen* may depict what for Ford was a key "turning point" in history—the transition from feudal to modern— even that novel seems less interested, on the level of style, with the turning and more interested in how to capture the moment into a series of static, solid images.[10]

With these romances, written between 1904 and 1914, Ford continually attempts to impose a sense of aesthetic unity on the historical era he depicts, flattening out any sense of conflict or dynamism. His early works owe more to Pre-Raphaelism—in its day a major challenge to pictorial realism, eschewing verisimilitude in favor of idealized figures and flat surface areas—than to his friend Conrad or any other early modernist experiment.[11] We might even detect a running strain of Hegelian idealism in Ford's early historical novels. Hegel writes in his *Philosophy of History* (1837) that

> [i]t is the temporal whole that constitutes one being, the Spirit of one people. To it belong the individual citizens: each individual is the child of his people, and likewise the child of his time. . . . No one is left behind by his time, nor can he overstep it. The spiritual entity is his very own, and he is its representative.[12]

Ford often adopted this kind of language, titling one of his books *The Spirit of the People* (1907) and stating in the Preface to *Ancient Lights* (1911) that "I don't really deal in facts, I have for facts a most profound contempt. I try to give you what I see to be the spirit of an age, of a town, of a movement. This can not be done with facts."[13] Despite the social conflicts depicted in the historical novels, their static aesthetic reflects a belief in "the temporal whole" of an era. Hegel wrote that "only *this* philosophy and only *this* art can exist in *this* state," and Ford in his early work seems to be searching for the appropriate stylistic "*this*" with which to craft his novels.[14] *The Fifth Queen* uses this style to re-present representation of the past, to show history as a constant rewriting. But with the subsequent, lesser novels he simply picks a style and methodically executes it throughout the work to give some sort of historical flavor. To see each era as organic and self-sustained guarantees that the depiction of the era will be oversimplified, and that any manner of change or transformation, no matter how explicitly depicted, will be frozen with language into an ahistorical ideal.[15]

Where does this approach to modernity fit in the canons of modernism? We usually associate modernism with fragmentation, but our definitions also include Brancusi's sculptures and Bauhaus architecture, the minimalist paintings of Kasimir Malevich and Ellsworth Kelly. We could make an argument that Ford's better early works are part of this side of the modernist spectrum.

But what is fascinating is how Ford ends up at the other, fragmented end; how he works through this period of "wholeness" and ends up in pieces later on with *The Good Soldier*.[16] Saunders notes in his essay "From Pre-Raphaelism to Impressionism" that "his turn towards Impressionism coincides with his turn away from the historical novel" and that "as he was moving away from Pre-Raphaelism and toward Impressionism . . . it was precisely the historical novel that became the most productive site of his aesthetic self-examination, because it was there that a struggle between the Pre-Raphaelite and the Impressionist was taking place."[17] The result was *The Good Soldier*, a novel that, more than any other of the modern period, questioned the fundamentals of narrative and history.

Avoidance and Repetition

The Good Soldier presents an enticing challenge for any historicizing critical approach. A text both fragmented and tightly woven, it seems, at least at first glance, to be hermetically sealed against historical forces, allowing only the smallest seepages of social change or unrest to seep through. Two couples, one American, one English and Irish, meet at a spa for weak hearts in Germany, and immediately become close. The narrator, John Dowell, is unaware that his wife Florence is having an affair with Edward Ashburnham, the titular English good soldier. Edward is only Florence's latest in a long line of extramarital affairs, and as Dowell recounts the last ten years of his life he slowly realizes the full extent of his wife's infidelities. Early criticism of the novel was attracted to the text's formal qualities, reading it as a work that challenged the basic narratological premises of the novel as developed by the Victorian realists, but criticism of the past decade has found that the novel intensely confronts history in several ways. Rob Doggett explores the relationship between the novel's interrogation of epistemology and Ireland's status within the British Empire;[18] Karen A. Hoffmann traces how masculinity is defined in imperial terms;[19] Sarah Henstra looks at the performative nature of late-imperial Englishness;[20] Carey J. Mickalites sees the workings of capitalism in the unstable yet object-like characters;[21] and Evelyn Cobley reads the novel alongside the emerging discourses of industrial efficiency.[22]

While recent criticism has thus explored how history works through the novel, we should be equally interested in how *works* of history work through the novel. References to historians of all sorts abound in *The Good Soldier*, including Jean Froissart, John Addington Symonds, Leopold von Ranke, and Elizabeth Penrose (the best-selling "Mrs. Markham"). History is where the characters in *The Good Soldier* escape as they flee direct engagement with their private lives, turning to these authors for brief solace. While the narcissistic narrative of John Dowell might lead us to believe that the novel is a deep exploration of subjectivity, and a recoiling from historical forces, most of the action of the novel involves evasion and retreat from interiority. It is to history, works of history, that Dowell and the other characters turn for relief.

This obsession on the part of the characters with history as a discipline points to another level of historical engagement in the text, and I would like to broaden the formal scope of the earlier criticism and see *The Good Soldier* as a work that questions not just fictional narrative but historical narrative as well. Ford's experiments concern not just the basic elements of the novel— characters, point of view—but also aspects of writing that histories depend on, such as chronology, verification, causation, and meaning. If *The Good Soldier* asks if it is possible to narrate what we're not sure has happened, then this has serious implications for the field of history and the composition of historical narratives.[23] The text calls attention to the isomorphic nature of the term "history," as it is both signifier and signified, the past and our record of it. However, at the same time that the novel critiques historiography so intensely, the characters use history as place of refuge from their wrecked personal lives, fleeing to works of history as distractions from facing up to their own dark truths. Thus while history is being interrogated as a discipline, it is also, paradoxically, offered as a very human and necessary means for coping with the ravages of modern life. Ford extends Conrad's explorations of history from *Lord Jim*, as Michael Valdez Moses notes that Jim "hopes to return to the heroic possibilities of a bygone era, to find once again an arena in which personal courage and political action become historically meaningful."[24] Jim has much greater success than the characters that populate *The Good Soldier*, finding an actual holdout from modernity in Patusan. Ford's figures must settle for narratives about the premodern world—histories, not history—to effect their "discontent with posthistorical modernity."[25]

Dowell's narrative method itself shares affinities with the rhythms of the discipline of history. He keeps returning to key moments in his life, renarrating them in an effort to learn more about his past; the field of history also continually returns to significant events in an effort to retell their stories. Ford keeps history and histories in complex tension, dramatizing the problematic transformation of one into the other. *The Good Soldier* is thus uniquely positioned in modernism as staging the simultaneous constitution and disjunction between history and its narratives.

Any attempt at historical literary criticism with *The Good Soldier* must grapple with the already theorized nature of history in this text. Whatever historical text or texts we bring to bear on the novel—histories of imperialism, histories of gender formulations, and so on—Ford's text reveals them as narratives that are as problematic and unstable as Dowell's own. Although it may capture a specific culture and moment in time—the upper crust of prewar Edwardian England on the brink of disaster—history in *The Good Soldier* is felt just as strongly as a discipline, as the characters, especially

Dowell, use the field of history to work out, or escape from, their own personal problems.

Before the rise of New Historicism and New Modernist Studies, modernist works were sometimes read as texts that resisted history. For example, in *A Genealogy of Modernism* (1984), Michael Levenson notes in canonical modernism "a retreat to the surer, if more modest, zone of the self" away from the public sphere or social world.[26] But Florence and Edward are not the inward-looking types: their gaze is continually directed at a romantic Other. More important, what may appear as Dowell's solipsistic venture in his personal story is actually marked by repeated efforts to avoid the telling of the story, and to dwell on historical accounts of the past instead. Ford's novel is very much a work of avoidance: Florence and Edward must avoid getting caught in their affairs, and getting caught in the lie of their heart conditions; Leonora must avoid any type of scene with Edward, while also avoiding any breach of Catholic doctrine; for Dowell, his confounding ignorance in the face of the copious evidence regarding Florence's infidelities is in some sense a willed avoidance. One way for the characters to avoid the truth is to turn to histories. Far from being a nightmare from which the characters try to awake, history is a daydream, a means of escape from a horrifying present. History is something to escape *into*: "Even when [Edward] was twenty-two he would pass hours reading one of Scott's novels or the Chronicles of Froissart."[27] When the Catholic Nancy panics after discovering that people she knew got divorced, she takes solace in history: "She felt a sudden safeness descend upon her and for an hour or so her mind was at rest. It seemed to her idiotic to not have remembered Henry VIII and the basis upon which Protestantism rests. She almost laughed at herself."[28] History is what frees the characters from their nightmarish presents.

Dowell as narrator often turns to historical tales when he is about to relate something painful or sensitive to the reader. After he confesses his utter loneliness, he then asks us to "Consider the lamentable history of Peire Vidal," the Provençal troubadour.[29] As we shall see later, Dowell's relationship to Vidal is crucial narratologically, but psychologically the "consideration" of Vidal allows Dowell a mental respite from contemplating his own solitude. This consideration points to another avoidance, this one Florence's: Vidal reminds him of Provence, which in turn reminds him of a trip they both took through southern France. He describes Florence

with the faraway look in her eyes—which wasn't however in the least romantic—I meant that she didn't look as if she were seeing poetic dreams, or looking through you, for she hardly ever did look at you!—holding up one hand as if she wished to silence any objection—or any comment for the matter of that—she would talk. She would talk about William the Silent, about Gustave the Loquacious, about Paris frocks, about how the poor dressed in 1337, about Fantin Latour, about the Paris-Lyon-Mediterranée train-de-luxe.[30]

Florence avoids Dowell in several ways in this scene: her "faraway look" signals either the historical epochs she recounts, or her affair with Edward—anywhere except the present with her husband. She also literally avoids Dowell's gaze, as she "hardly ever did look at you." Florence's chattering—another form of avoidance—covers many topics, but history dominates them. Nor are the references arbitrary, as Florence herself is both "silent" like William regarding her affairs and "loquacious" like Gustave regarding long-dead historical figures. History gives Florence something to talk about besides her infidelity to Dowell, and for Dowell it is something to listen to rather than face the truth of their relationship. (It is appropriate that Dowell and Florence met at the then-popular Browning Teas, regular gatherings to celebrate the poet who specialized in the historical dramatic monologue.) Dowell soon reveals that he even encouraged Florence in her interest in history as a way of avoiding certain subjects:

> For do you understand my whole attentions, my whole endeavours were to keep poor dear Florence on to topics like the finds at Cnossos and the mental spirituality of Walter Pater. I had to keep her at it, you understand, or she might die. [. . .] For twelve years I had to watch every word that any person uttered in any conversation and I had to head it off what the English call "things"—off love, poetry, crime, religion and the rest of it.[31]

One safe area of discussion, apparently, is the field of history, and it is through history that Dowell avoids "things" and that Florence avoids Dowell.

By the time Dowell is writing his text, he knows that Florence's heart condition is faked. For most narrators, this early moment in the narrative would be a good time to let us in on this important piece of information, but Dowell instead digresses back to Peire Vidal. Once he finishes his story he returns to describing Florence, but the question of the heart condition has passed, and Dowell has successfully avoiding telling us the truth, his narrative stream winding around the rock of truth. First-time readers come away from this chapter with more knowledge of Vidal than Florence, as even between Dowell and his "silent imaginary listener" there is a redirection into historical narratives.

Avoidance is not necessarily escapism, however, nor is avoidance in *The Good Soldier* necessarily nostalgic. Criticism of Ford often touches on nostalgia, especially around *The Fifth Queen*.[32] But rather than using his work to express nostalgia, I believe that Ford uses it to stage nostalgia, which gives the works more of a critical purchase. In *The Fifth Queen*, Katharine's tragedy may not be that she has been born too late in history—she is Catholic in the increasingly Protestant England—but rather that she is constantly mistaking her own time period and constantly misreading historical texts. In *The Fifth Queen*, as in *The Good Soldier*, many of the characters are obsessed with history, especially the idealist Katharine. Early in the novels, she is "thinking upon the heroes of Plutarch, [and] she found the present times despicable."[33] Many chapters later, the spy Thockmorton seems to offer a reply: "But these are not the days of Plutarch. . . . And I doubt the days of Plutarch never were. . . . I would ask you how many broken treaties, how many deeds of treachery, went to the making of the Roman state, since Sinon a traitor brought about the fall of Troy, since Aeneas betrayed Queen Dido and brought the Romans into Italy."[34] Such a riposte is the counterpoint of the text: Katharine espouses idealism via ancient works of history, and the more modern characters rebuke her for her idealism by critiquing the existence of her idealized past. Toward the end of the trilogy, Katharine is discussing politics with her friend Cicely Eliott, and laments the era into which she was born: "In the day of Caesar it was simple to do well. . . . But still I think that these be degenerate days." Cicely replies, "Oh, Queen of dreams and fancies . . . I am very certain that in the days of your noble Romans it was as it is now. Tell me, if you can, that in all your readings of hic and hoc you lit not upon such basenesses? . . . I have seen the like in the plays of Plautus that here have been played at Court." Katharine weakly replies that "the days of Plautus were days degenerated and fallen already from the ancient nobleness."[35] Cicely's response sums up the text's attitude toward nostalgia: "You should have Queened it before Goodman Adam fell. . . . If you go back before Plautus, go back all the way."[36]

The Fifth Queen provides nothing to be nostalgic for, although it does depict nostalgic figures, yearning for ancient Greece and Rome. If Ford's Edwardian readers feel nostalgic for the Tudor court, such longings can stretch indefinitely into the past, as the Tudors pine for antiquity, and the ancient Romans can pine for the days of democratic Athens, who pine for the lost days of Arcady, and so on. Cicely's rebuke to "go back all the way" to Adam and Eve is the text's critique of the nostalgia it stages.[37] *The Fifth Queen* portrays Katharine's nostalgic avoidance critically, but we are sympathetic to her desire to escape her immediate surroundings. For Ford, avoidance and nostalgia are always about the present, and in his novels avoidance can be a form of coded communication. In *The Good Soldier* Florence often talks with her lover Edward about history: "I have heard her lecture Teddy Ashburnham by the hour on the difference between a Frans Hals and a Wouwerman and why Pre-Mycenaic statues were cubical with knobs at the top."[38] Florence uses historical topics to safely talk with Edward in public and avoid suspicion. The most extended scene in this regard is their trip to "M------" to see Martin Luther's signed document of protest. (Another avoidance: Ford ellipses the name of the town of "Marburg," even though the location of Luther's document would be readily accessible, even common knowledge to many readers.)

The trip is Florence's idea, ostensibly because "it was part of the cure to make an excursion three or four times a week," but Dowell notes, with a double meaning that readers might not catch the first time through, that "Florence, of course, had a motive of her own. She was at that time engaged in educating Captain Ashburnham—oh, of course, quite pour le bon motif!"[39] The motif, of course, ce n'est pas bon, as the "educating" is mostly a pretense for their sexual activity. But if the field of history is Florence's means of gaining access to Edward, for Leonora history is a way to win her husband back:

> Leonora herself always struck me as being remarkably well educated. At any rate she knew beforehand all that Florence had to tell her. Perhaps she got it up out of Baedeker before Florence was up in the morning. I don't mean to say that you would ever have known that Leonora knew anything, but if Florence started to tell us how Ludwig the Courageous wanted to have three wives at once—in which he differed from Henry VIII who wanted them one after the other, and this caused a good deal of trouble—if Florence started to tell us this, Leonora would just nod her head in a way that quite pleasantly rattled my poor wife.[40]

Leonora can always match Florence's historical knowledge, possibly signaling to Edward that he shouldn't need Florence and that Leonora is still a willing and available wife. Again, the historical reference is not arbitrary, as Ludwig the Courageous and Henry VIII are Edward-type figures who demanded more than one partner. History is how Leonora communicates to Florence that she knows about the affair: the phrase "she knew beforehand all that Florence had to tell her" does not just refer to historical facts, but to Edward's infidelity. Leonora's stoic display of historical knowledge communicates to Florence that she is aware of the affair, and to Edward that it need not continue. Is Florence aware of this? Does she know that Leonora knows? "She used to exclaim: 'Well if you knew it [the historical story], why haven't you told it all already to Captain Ashburnham? I'm sure he finds it interesting!'"[41] This could be an aggressive move on Florence's part, challenging her rival in her ability to tell "interesting" historical tales, all as code for sexual conduct. (Florence feels the need for this because of her insecurity regarding Edward: "It really worried poor Florence that she couldn't, in matters of culture, ever get the better of Leonora."[42]) Because of the ideological straightjacket that Edwardian upper society imposes upon its members, they must resort to other discourses like historical discussions to express emotions. If history is what is forcing them to be so upright and evasive—that is, the history of the European landed caste and its social rules and obligations—history as a discipline or discourse is what allows them a coded means to evade and avoid such rules.

The novel aggressively stages this interest in the historiographical process. While the characters are all avid readers of history, in a sense Florence and

Dowell are historians themselves. Florence performs background research and investigates primary sources to construct her narrative at Marburg, and Dowell is, on a very basic level, trying to fashion the events of the past into a coherent narrative. Critics writing on this novel have sometimes used the term "history" to describe Dowell's text: Grover Smith writes that "*The Good Soldier* incorporates three histories finally: the one which Dowell has ignorantly lived through, the one which Dowell impressionistically constructs, and the one which really happened."[43] Smith argues that we will never get the third history, and are only left with the first two. In this sense, the "real" history remains silent and all we get are two histories: the history of Dowell's ignorance and the history of Dowell's writing.

I would argue that this missing history—what "really happened"—broadens the critique of the novel to include all narrative, not just novelistic form, and that Ford's experiment has ramifications for historiography and how we theorize history as a narrative. Dowell tells us as much about what he incorrectly presumed was going on as about what he thinks really happened. These presumptions—what people thought, often mistakenly, about their historical situation—are now seen as just as important by historians as what "really happened." Carlo Ginzburg's microhistory masterpiece *The Cheese and the Worms* (1980), in which the quirky misreadings of scholastic doctrine by the humble miller Menocchio give important insights into sixteenth century Italy, evidences how the field of history has widened its scope to include perceptions of events, not just the facts of the events themselves. Traditional orthodox history may say that an earthquake happened on this date; twentieth-century schools of history, especially those of the French *histoire des mentalités*, studied what people thought of that earthquake, what they thought its causes were, who they blamed, what they thought they should do to prevent another one.[44] *The Good Soldier* anticipates this mode by foregrounding Dowell's incorrect presumptions. However, we as readers are initially drawn into this state of ignorance, not by watching Dowell's ignorance from afar like we do Othello's, but rather sharing in it. First-time readers will assume for many pages that Florence has a real heart problem, for example. Like Dowell, we are fooled by convention and Florence's manipulations. Although the novel is saturated in irony, it is not dramatic irony: since Dowell is our only source for information, we're never in on the jokes and contradictions until a second read-through.

His-story (Dowell's, That Is)

Such radical critiques of narrative historiography may at first seem to clash with the ostensible content of *The Good Soldier*. Reading a story about rich people sleeping around as questioning the very foundation of history may seem trivial, but the novel anticipates this reaction: "Someone has said that the death of a mouse from cancer is the whole sack of Rome by the Goths, and I swear to you that the breaking-up of our little four-square coterie was such another unthinkable event."[45] Dowell is constantly trying to broaden, hyperbolically, the scope of the story beyond his immediate circumstances, so that the fate of his friends have relevance and resonance to equal that of Gibbon or Ranke. Much of Dowell's inflations are due to his own neuroses, as we shall see, but I would first argue that they are the result of the novel's ambitions beyond simply presenting "A Tale of Passion." The sadness of his story may not ultimately concern the tragic fates of the characters, but rather the inability to discover stable truths. Dowell laments,

> there is nothing to guide us. And if everything is so nebulous about a matter so elementary as the morals of sex, what is there it guide us in the more subtle morality of all other personal contacts, associations, and activities? Or are we meant to act on impulse alone? It is all a darkness.[46]

Ultimately it is not just "morality" that is under question in this novel, but also epistemology, narratology, and mnemonics. Furthermore, the novel demonstrates how the radical questioning of these categories has drastic consequences for the writing of histories, as much as it does for novels.

The most extended critique of writing is through Dowell himself. As narrator, he is trying to construct a narrative based on what happened, so he is trying to write a history in the broad sense in which we often use that word. From the first sentence he begins, like many historians, by obfuscating his own role in the telling of the tale: "This is the saddest story I have ever heard."[47] By implying that the story is something he has been told, rather than lived through, Dowell attempts to distance himself from the events he is trying to record. From the beginning, he tries to remove himself from the narrative, but with every subsequent sentence we see how futile this effort is. This act of removal, so obviously problematic in this instance, highlights the process by which the historian traditionally effaces his or her own subjectivity and strives to be a neutral transmitter of data and analysis, resulting in the authoritative tone that some critics even refer to as "realist" because of the traits it shares with the third-person omniscience of literary realism. The modernism of *The Good Soldier*—its stress on the limits of subjectivity and its critique of narrative omniscience—demonstrates how difficult, if not impossible, narrative impartiality truly is.[48]

Furthermore, the word "story" in the first sentence is as problematic as the word "heard." What happened throughout eight years of Dowell's life was not a "story" but rather events that Dowell is fashioning into a story. The story is *his* story, not only because he was a major character in the events but because he is the only one who gets to shape these events into a narrative. Florence and Edward and any other character would surely tell it differently (and we should recall Hayden White's argument that chronicles do not suffice when social interpretations of the past are in conflict: histories emerge out of the struggle for power). By calling "what happened" a "story," Dowell implies that he is simply passing along this information, instead of manipulating it in various ways. This was White's central critique of orthodox historiography in *Metahistory: The Historical Imagination in Nineteenth-Century Europe* (1973): a story is never "already there" for the historian to simply pluck from the stream of time and pass on to the reader. Instead, the historian "arranges the events in the chronicle into a hierarchy of significance by assigning events different functions as story elements in such a way as to disclose the formal coherence of a whole set of events considered as a comprehensible process with a discerning beginning, middle, and end."[49] For White, the result is a story, as much as any work of fiction is a story. The facts of such a story may have really occurred, but the means by which the events are recounted share the same formal qualities as fiction. (We might here introduce a third generic category of autobiography, which is the form that Dowell's narrative most closely resembles and which is usually offered much more leeway when it comes to fictionalizing techniques. White would insist, however, that even orthodox works of history are as driven by storytelling as fiction or autobiography.)

The text highlights this tension between facts and narrative after Dowell tells the story of Peire Vidal. Vidal is madly in love with the queen La Louve but she does not return his feelings, so he sets off for Jerusalem "to redeem the Holy Sepulcher."[50] He returns and "fell all over the Lady's bed." Dowell finishes with "Anyhow, that is all that came of it. Isn't that a story?" Dowell is not being facetious: he really does not know if what he has just narrated counts as a story or not. He has told us what happened to Vidal, but this not does necessarily qualify Dowell's words as a story. It may just be a chronicle. This indicates a distinction between a narrative and "what happened"—a distinction that informs much of the larger issues that *The Good Soldier* complicates. With the Vidal passage, Dowell is sure of the events but not of the narrative structures necessary to convey those events. Dowell, in his own befuddled way, recognizes the difference between a narrative's signifier and signified, and statements like "Isn't that a story?" serve to widen the gap between the two semiotic levels, forcing upon the reader a realization of the constructed nature of the narrative he or she is reading.

Earlier, after recounting some of his travels, Dowell had asked, "Is all this a digression or isn't it a digression?"[51] To answer the question, one would need to know what exactly the story was, and this means being aware of a hierarchy of values assigned to each fact. Historians do not just pass on whatever facts they come across: they organize them into narratives, with some facts regarded as more essential than others to the telling of the story. So if the story in *The Good Soldier* is "what happened" to our quartet of characters, then Dowell's ramblings are a digression, since they do not have any relevance to the love quadrangle under consideration. But if the story is Dowell's reconstruction of events in his narrative, then this is not a digression at all, but rather an essential part of Dowell's journey. In either case, the narrative shapes the value assigned to facts or events; the facts do not have a priori values that can simply be recounted.

Finally, the "this" in the first sentence of the novel must also be questioned. Dowell later states that he "shall just imagine myself for a fortnight or so at one side of the fireplace of a country cottage, with a sympathetic soul opposite me. And I shall go on talking, in a low voice while the sea sounds in the distance and overhead the great black flood of wind polishes the bright stars."[52] Dowell is not actually relating a story—he is writing one—but he will pretend that there is a listener. So does "this" in the first line refer to what Dowell is writing, years after the event, or to the constructed narrative that he imagines he is telling to the "sympathetic soul opposite me" that we are lulled into thinking "real"? As Thomas C. Moser notes, "Although Dowell tells the reader to pretend that they are spending a fortnight together in a cottage by the sea and that he is talking, in a low voice, to his sympathetic auditor, all this is emphatically pretense. Dowell is not talking: he is 'really' writing down this sad story, and over a period of two years."[53] This double frame—a radicalization of the already complicated double frame of *Heart of Darkness*—foregrounds the constructed nature of Dowell's narrative.

We perceive not only *that* Dowell's narrative is constructed, but *how* it is constructed. We watch Dowell weave his narrative as much as we watch the events he is narrating. Despite the disjointed nature of the novel, one thing is constant, and that is Dowell's perspective. Like many modernist novels, *The Good Soldier* presents us with many different, and conflicting, perspectives and points of view. However, unlike *Ulysses* or *The Sound and the Fury*, *The Good Soldier* is told through only one persona. Whereas Joyce or Faulkner included Molly Bloom's or Jason's perspectives to counter Leopold's or Quentin's, Ford filters all perspectives through Dowell:

> At any rate I think I have brought my story up to the date of Maisie Maidan's death. I mean that I have explained everything that went before it from the several points of view that were necessary—from Leonora's, from Edward's, and to some extent, from my own. You have the facts for the trouble of finding them; you have the points of view as far as I could ascertain or put them.[54]

Dowell here admits his own limits and concedes that any story must be told from multiple perspectives, but the narrative refuses to step outside Dowell's consciousness, and the word "I" appears many times to mark the subjective nature, and narratological boundaries, of his telling. Any other perspective is first ingested by Dowell before we are given access to it (and the phrase "points of view" should remind us of the influence of Henry James, especially the heavily focalized *What Maisie Knew* (1897), of which Ford was a devoted fan, and whose protagonist may have inspired Ms. Maidan's name). This is Dowell's chosen method of telling his story, but it also describes most historiographical processes: competing viewpoints and accounts of "what happened" get sorted out by the historian and shaped into one narrative. History has many points of view; *histories* are generally written via one narration, no matter how much they may strive to present various viewpoints (although in the Conclusion I will analyze some recent experiments in history that break this mold). This does not mean that the historian has to take one side of events, as sometimes the historian can leave conclusions up to the reader, as Dowell attempts to do when he tries to put the onus of interpretation on us ("you have the facts"). While a historian with aspirations toward objectivity would attempt to balance out and judge various accounts, with Dowell we can see that there is always going to be a process of vacillation and uncertainty as the historian juggles competing perspectives.

Revisionary Fictions

Historical research involves not just investigating competing accounts, but studying primary documents as well, and in *The Good Soldier* we can read the trip that the quartet takes to Marburg to look at Luther's Protest as a dramatization, or even a parody, of the historical process. Florence fancies herself a historian, "clearing up one of the dark places of the earth, leaving the world a little lighter than she had found it," as Dowell puts it, with a dark echo of Conrad's Marlow. Florence's historical narratives were "done in a way well calculated to arrest a young attention. Did you ever read Mrs. Markham? Well, it was like that."[55] But Dowell then signals that the trip to Marburg would be "a much larger, a much more full dress affair." Unlike Mrs. Markham's potboiling historical tales, which were only loosely based on documented proof and equally served as romances and history, this trip would provide access to "a document which Florence thought would finally give her the chance to educate the whole lot of us together."[56] Florence studies Ranke, Symonds, Motley, and Luther himself in preparation for their journey.[57] But in typical Dowellian fashion, we do not immediately get the trip but rather a long digression (or is it a digression?) regarding how much he likes "catching the two-forty" and what the countryside looks like from the train. Then while Florence "was imparting information so hard," Dowell notices, and then relates to us, the ridiculous incident of one cow throwing another into a river. This scene seems to mock Florence's efforts at relating a historical narrative: Dowell flatly states, "I am not an historian" before finishing his "story" about the flying cow.[58] The narrative here borders on parody: Dowell's childlike enjoyment of the flying cows, his mistake by calling his accent "Pennsylvania

Duitsch" instead of "Dutch," his fuzzy details regarding Florence's narratives.[59] Meanwhile Florence "became positively electric. She told the tired, bored custodian what shutters to open; so that the bright sunlight streamed in palpable shafts into the dim old chamber."[60] Florence is literally shedding light on this primary document that she believes holds the key to Western civilization.

> "And there," she exclaimed with an accent of gaiety, of triumph, and of audacity. She was pointing at a piece of paper, like the half-sheet of a letter with some faint pencil scrawls that might have been a jotting of the amounts we were spending during the day. And I was extremely happy at her gaiety, in her triumph, in her audacity. Captain Ashburnham had his hands upon the glass case. "There it is—the Protest." And then, as we all properly stage-managed our bewilderment, she continued: "Don't you know that is why we were all called Protestants? That is the pencil draft of the Protest they drew up. You can see the signatures of Martin Luther, and Martin Bucer, and Zwingli, and Ludwig the Courageous. . . ."
>
> I may have got some of the names wrong, but I know that Luther and Bucer were there. And her animation continued and I was glad. She was better and she was out of mischief. She continued, looking up into Captain Ashburnham's eyes: "It's because of that piece of paper that you're honest, sober, industrious, provident, and clean-lived. If it weren't for that piece of paper you'd be like the Irish or the Italians or the Poles, but particularly the Irish. . . ."[61]

Florence performs the first job of the historian ably: she tracks down and correctly identifies the primary document. However, everything after that goes horribly wrong. Using the document to abuse the Irish Catholic Leonora and secure her influence over Edward, Florence interprets Luther's words to uphold a bigoted and ultimately nationalist historical vision. (Ford's German heritage and lifelong flirtation with Catholicism would have made him sensitive on both these points.) Physically, the protest seems so powerless, only "faint pencil scrawls," while Florence has come alive with "her gaiety . . . triumph . . . audacity." As with Dowell's narration, there is no "story" that is "there." The story is Florence's—it does not belong to time. Florence's description of Edward is flatly false: "honest, sober, industrious, provident, and clean-lived" describes no one in this novel, least of all Edward.

Thus Florence's research methods are sound enough, but her conclusions—the narrative she weaves using this trace of history—are depicted as ridiculous.[62] Leonora presents a counter-narrative to Dowell after she flees the room: "Don't you see that that's the cause of the whole miserable affair; of the whole sorrow of the world?"[63] Leonora's remark is not meant as a corrective to Florence's; rather, the quick succession of these two conflicting narratives just moments after reading the same primary document demonstrates how much importance lies in the act of historical narration, which inevitably will involve interpretation as much as neutral reporting. (Compare Ford's interest in the narratives that emerge from a document, with Pound's poetics of edited documents.) There is more to this scene than multiple interpretations of one text, however. Leonora storms out of the room as a reaction to Florence's diatribe. She explains herself to Dowell with the question, "don't you know that I'm an Irish Catholic?"[64] This explanation for her actions satisfies Dowell, who states that "[t]hose words gave me the greatest relief that I have ever had in my life," and probably also satisfies most first-time readers.[65] Later, however, the reasons for her actions are revised: she leaves the room not out of Irish Catholic pride but rather from the pain of watching Edward and Florence interact. We find out much later that "[w]ith the answering gaze of Edward into Florence's blue and uplifted eyes, she knew that it had all gone. She knew that that gaze meant that those two had had long conversations of an intimate kind."[66] This is just one example of the novel's use of what we may term "revisionism." Many times Dowell presents us with an event, explains why it happened, and then much later gives us another explanation that is supposed to supplant the first explanation. Motivations for events are constantly being revised. Their trip to Marburg, Leonora's attack on Maisie Maidan, and Florence's death are events that are depicted and explained several times.

Can we see this as metaphorically depicting the broad historical enterprise, the historiographical process in its textual entirety? Certain events—the Fall of Rome, the French Revolution—are continually revised, reexamined, retold. Each new revision is designed to replace earlier ones, to say "*this* is the real reason that *that* happened." Dowell is constantly revising his narrative of events: "What had happened on the day of our jaunt to the ancient city of M----- had been this"[67]; "What in the interval had happened had been this"[68]; "What had happened had been this."[69] Dowell's deployment of complex verb tenses is the result of his narrative's continual revisioning. Of course, we cannot always trust his revisions any more than we can trust his first impressions. While Dowell does seem to advance in knowledge with his revisionary take on events, we should not be completely certain as to his discovery of any final truth. The entire novel works in this revisionary fashion. To say that *The Good Soldier* is nonlinear states the obvious, but to say that it operates via flashbacks or time-shifts is too reductive. *The Good Soldier* is not simply a linear novel hacked to bits and reassembled. Instead, moments are retold like repeated notes in different keys. Throughout much of Part I, Dowell is always about to tell us about what happened when they went to Marburg: "And that enables me to fix exactly the day of our going to the town of M-----. For it was that very day poor Mrs. Maidan died. We found her dead when we got back—pretty awful, that, when you come to figure out what it all means."[70] Pages later, when he writes that "[w]hat had happened on the day of our jaunt to the ancient city of M----- had been this," Dowell's narrative is still hovering

over this event, which readers will already have guessed is of great importance to his story. But Dowell defers the telling and instead keeps repeating
similar phrases, announcing what he is going to tell us.

Any statement by Dowell can soon be qualified: "Upon my word, yes, our
intimacy was like a minuet"[71] turns into "No, by God it is false! It wasn't a
minuet that we stepped; it was a prison—a prison full of screaming hysterics";
"And yet, I swear by the sacred name of my creator that it was true."[72] Even
when Dowell does get around to telling us about an event, he continually
comes back to it to examine its causes. Dowell hints at Florence's suicide several times before he actually describes it at the end of Part II: "She was lying,
quite respectably arranged, unlike Mrs. Maidan, on her bed. She had a little
phial that rightly should have contained nitrate of amyl, in her right hand.
That was on the fourth of August, 1913."[73] Like any good historian, Dowell at
least dates the events he does know (which is an easy task since all major
events occur on August 4).[74] As to why Florence killed herself, Dowell does
not seem certain and gives us several possible explanations. However, he does
not list these in a group for us to choose from, but rather keeps renarrating
what led to Florence's death. The first explanation is with Dowell himself: he
describes striking his servant Julius in a fit of rage, and Florence "got a pretty
idea of my character. It affirmed in her the desperate resolve to conceal from
me the fact that she was not what she would have called 'a pure woman.' She
was afraid that I should murder her."[75] This is the first—and last—instance of
Dowell's temper, so perceptive readers may be credulous as to this initial explanation of Florence's suicide. But soon we are offered another reading: "You
see, the mainspring of her nature must have been vanity. There is no reason
why it shouldn't have been; I guess it is vanity that makes most of us keep
straight, if we do keep straight, in this world."[76] Florence's motive has shifted
from fear to vanity. Finally, we find out that Florence had witnessed Edward
and Nancy together minutes before her suicide. This adds a third motivation
to her actions: jealousy. Her suicide is thus thoroughly overdetermined, but
Dowell keeps all of these motivations in play and narrates them all as if they
were sound theories in their own right. Rather than weigh the value of each
possible cause, he writes small revisionist narratives in which only one of
them at a time is the deciding factor in Florence's death.

This action on Dowell's part, of retelling, may be taken as demonstrating
Dowell's inabilities with his own narration, but I would argue that this notion
is central to Ford's actions as a theorist of narrative. Dowell learns about
"what happened" not by only research (in this case, his interviews with Leonora and Edward), but by writing. He learns about his history by writing a
work of history. Paul B. Armstrong notes how Dowell develops as both a character and narrator through the telling of this story: "If Dowell grows in understanding, he does so by writing. His narration employs language not only
as a means of communication but also as a tool for reflection—an instrument

that makes possible the objectification and analysis of unreflected thoughts and feelings."[77] As Sally Bachner has pointed out, Dowell is no Sherlock Holmes.[78] He lacks the Victorian gift for penetrating reason and deduction, as he tranquilly slept for years while his wife was having an affair in the adjacent room. However, as Armstrong asserts, he does grow and learn, less through investigation than by the process of narration. Rather than investigate Florence's death, he narrates it, at least three times, in an effort to understand her motives. If he does not arrive at a satisfactory answer, for himself or for the reader, that may be less of a shortcoming on his part than an awareness of how much is beyond our comprehension, and hence unrelatable through narrative—"It is all a darkness."[79]

However, Dowell—and Ford—do not end in despair at this conclusion. They soldier on, Dowell finishing his story and Ford finishing over 80 books in his lifetime. *The Good Soldier* may question narrative and despair at our ability to know or relate anything, but it still remains a narrative, and Ford's most successful at that. Ford's insight into the indeterminacy of history does not preclude the practice of historiography; it rather shifts its focus toward the narrative side of writing history. If *The Good Soldier* makes us question the value of narrative as a reliable source of the past, it simultaneously shows the value of narrative as a repetitive process of learning and accessing truths. Ford suggests that it is not through better documentary research—the specialties of the specialists that he so despised—but through more writing and retelling as an alternative form of research into motivations and causes that reveals truths. Just as with Conrad's Decoud in *Nostromo*, Ford questions the writing of history so radically only to ultimately argue for its utter necessity.

Repetition and the Field of History

Any act of writing is an act of repetition: Ricoeur marks the distinction between historiography and the law by the latter's openness to revisions, "which makes the writing of history a perpetual rewriting."[80] Writing is always retelling. *The Good Soldier*, a piece of writing about a man writing, thus dramatizes the textual density of the historical process. (And now the novel itself becomes a text in the chain, as we can include it as a primary source in the history of the novel, a history of the Edwardian era, the history of depictions of adultery, etc.)

Louise Blakeney Williams, however, sees this constant retelling as Ford's vision of cyclical history in *Modernism and the Ideology of History: Literature, Politics, and the Past* (2002):

> Ford, like Pound and Yeats, believed that progressive narrative must be abandoned in favor of a simultaneous or instantaneous style. . . . This date,

the start of the First World War, is the key date of the novel—all the important events occur on it. Thus in "The Saddest Story" and *The Good Soldier* there is no sense of progress. A sense of the contemporaneity of past and present, and of circularity are the controlling structures.[81]

Williams finds in Ford the same interest in cyclical visions of history that we see in Yeats and Joyce. But this is to assume that a written historical record always homologously reflects what it is depicting, that the referent and narrative of history must always be in sync. Williams argues that Ford writes cyclically, and thus believes that history is cyclical. Even if we ignore Williams's collapsing of Ford with his character-narrator Dowell, such a position assumes that Dowell's narrative has mirrored the events that he has tried to recount, which is a dangerous assertion given Dowell's radical unreliability. We should be skeptical about how well any historical record reflects the events it tries to depict, not out of consideration of accuracy—a question of truth— but rather out of shape and representation. In other words, even the most faithful account of the past will involve radical transformations of lived experience into written language. Both teleological and anti-progressivist narratives have taken so many forms, that we should be skeptical about inferring a speculative view of history via the shape of a historical narrative.

We should read *The Good Soldier* as a work about the circularity of historiography, not the circularity of history. The field of history must constantly circle back around key moments or key forces that need more explanation, more retelling. How many volumes on the French Revolution will ever be necessary for humanity to come to a full understanding of it? And how confident are we that the latest version is the most accurate? Thus a circular narrative does not have to imply circular events or forces (in fact, you can easily write a linear narrative about how history is circular), but rather the circular process of depicting and redepicting those events or forces. While *The Good Soldier* is a "historical novel" about the Edwardian or Georgian era, we may instead read it as a "historiographical novel," a novel about the very process of writing history.

Shifting the accent in history from signified to signifier does not signal a flee from history itself, although this Lukácsian critique is still often voiced in contemporary criticism of Ford. Nicholas Brown in *Utopian Generations: The Political Horizon of Twentieth-Century Literature* (2005) argues that *The Good Soldier* is written in "a mode of narration in which history is approached in the mode of the sublime, as the unnamable. Faced with the onslaught of a history that cannot be conceptualized and therefore feels wholly external to them, Ford's characters can only recoil."[82] We have seen, however, that the characters do not recoil but actually turn to history for solace, as a way out of their personal anxieties and crises. But there is another sense in which Dowell specifically is not recoiling from history, and this is in his role as narrator: Dowell writes it all down. True recoiling would be to not commit experience to paper, but Dowell enters into the process of writing narrative history to uncover "what happened." Brown insists, however, that Dowell is avoiding history itself, despite Dowell's supposedly privileged vantage point from which he can watch history unfold:

> this narrative structure exemplifies, in a more intimate register, key features of the historical dialectic in Hegel. Hegel's famous owl of Minerva "spreads its wings only with the falling of the dusk." This means that the significance of an historical period, the synthesis of all the partial truths and the meaning for us of all the contingent events that populate it, is never given with the events themselves, but can only be constructed as a totality from a perspective for whom that period is past.[83]

Brown argues that Dowell has reached a place from which history can be "constructed as a totality" but refuses to confront or accept this reality. Whether or not one believes in what Foucault termed a "suprahistorical perspective" is not quite the issue. Rather, the problem with such a totalization is that it assumes that the "construction" is a final one and will never be *recon*structed. On the contrary, the process of history involves endless rewriting. What Brown interprets as a lack in *The Good Soldier* is actually this very process of endless revisionism, which we can see throughout the history of history. Brown laments that the text "hints" at totalization but that "Dowell's every energy is devoted to keeping totalization at bay."[84] But this is not due to Dowell's avoidances, but rather because the process of historiography never rests, always returning to a historical moment and rewriting it. The total view of an event is never achieved, although we can be cautiously optimistic that we get closer to it with most new advances in historical research. Even within the Hegelian tradition of historiography this is the case, as the "story" told by empirical consciousness gets retold through the dialectical process at the higher level of understanding, and this in turn is retold dialectically at the level of "Spirit."[85] Time for Hegel is part of an eternally recurrent pattern, not in the sense of Vico's historical cycles, but in the cyclical nature of the construction *past-present-future*. What is present now is the past by the time you can articulate it, as the present is dialectically preserved as past as it is negated by time. We can argue that historiography works in the same manner, as texts produced by historians get "negated" by future historians, who also "preserve" past historical interpretations in their work, incorporating their research and arguments, even if only as negative examples. What Brown sees as an "attempt to escape the mediation of history" is actually a deeper confrontation with it than we find in most "historical" novels that would fulfill Brown's definition of history.[86] Most historical novels take their historical content as settled (although there are notable exceptions across all periods). *The Good Soldier* assumes that more research will reveal new historical truths.

Ford's key insights have to do with the very texture of historiography itself, in which returning and retelling are so fundamental. For Ford, this is also ultimately the difference between history and fiction. In an unpublished essay entitled "Historians' Methods" (composed around 1901), another diatribe against scientific historians, Ford writes:

> It is to be remembered that the province of science is to be merely tempo-rary. In the Year 1975 the distinguished Professor So & So formulates a Theory of Grants in aid T.R.E.; in 1980 Mr. Dash will, with remorseless truculence, battle-axe the Theory of Prof. So & So & Prof. So and So will die of grief. In 1999 Sir C. Blank will demolish the proofs of Mr Dash & so on & so on to the end of the chapter. [. . .] A work of art, on the other hand, is final & is totally unaffected by new discoveries. No amount of discovery of the exact facial types of the Virgin Mary will ever discount the beauty & higher truth of Da Vinci's Madonna of the Rocks.[87]

Both history and fiction are discourses that employ narrative, but historiog-raphy is part of a continual chain of revisionism, a constant struggle for prominence. As Louis Mink put it decades later in *Historical Understanding* (1987), the difference "is rather that one historical narrative can *displace* an-other. In the paradigmatic case, an historian's work is always the revision of a received narrative, even though that may not be a text."[88] Historians dialecti-cally "displace" their texts; novelists do not. Joyce's retelling of *The Odyssey* does not render Homer's text less vital, just as Shakespeare's adaptations of Holinshed's *Chronicles* do not stop us from consulting that historical source (we probably consult it all the more in the wake of his plays). The writing of history, by contrast, aims for displacement, attempting to retell the story but this time get it more right.[89] We should not feel compelled to simply believe either in full historical access to the past or a radical relativism about histori-cal truths: when it comes to history, we should simply settle for the best that currently exists, knowing that new work will replace what we think we know. Although *The Good Soldier* is not a work of history—it neither replaces a pre-vious text nor will it be replaced by any rewriting of its content—it intuits this endless process of historiographical displacement, one experienced both by writers and readers of history, by re-visioning the events that Dowell needs to tell and retell.

Returning, Remembering, and Forgetting in *The Return of the Soldier*

West's Modernist Pastoral

Robert Scholes argued in *Paradoxy of Modernism* (2006) that "for all those who felt that some break with the past was necessary, there was still the crucial choice of what part of the Old one was abandoning."[1] Rebecca West made historiography new by turning to a mode almost as old as Western literature itself, the pastoral. Her novel *The Return of the Soldier* depicts Christopher Baldry, a prominent landowner and officer in the army, who returns home from the front suffering from amnesia that erases the last 15 years of his memories. He does not recognize his wife and still believes that he is in a romantic relationship with Margaret Grey, a working-class woman with whom he had a courtship years earlier, but who is now married. He seems content to live in his delusional state, but at the conclusion of the novel Margaret shocks him back into reality by reminding him of his son who died in infancy, restoring Baldry to sanity and returning him to the front.

The novel was a first in many ways: it was West's first novel; it was one of the first novels dealing directly with the Great War, published serially in 1918 in *The Century Illustrated Monthly Magazine* and in book form the next year; it was the first to depict a case of "shell-shock," a condition only recently formulated; and it was one of the first English novels to depict a psychiatrist. Despite these innovative qualities, West occupies an unstable position in the modernist canon.[2] Although she wrote novels, critical studies, biographies, travel books, and histories, like Ford she may have written herself out of the history of modernism. And while *The Return of the Soldier* has become increasingly canonical, her importance in modernist criticism still needs further reinstatement. Her articles for the *New Statesman* and *Bookman* in the 1920s were key defenses of experimental writing (some of which are collected in *The Strange Necessity* [1928] and *Ending in Earnest* [1931]), especially her essay "Uncle Bennett," a clever companion piece to Virginia Woolf's "Mr. Bennett and Mrs. Brown," in which West also takes on the trio of Bennett, Wells, and Galsworthy (and throws in Shaw for good measure). She often up-braided critics for not appreciating the new movements in literature:

> There is now, due to the very slowly emergent consequences of the war, a very clean-cut division between young and old minds. The books which are liked by people under forty are, as a general rule, not the same as the books which are liked by people over forty [who] frequently try to arrest the land-slide by tampering with our critical standards. They overpraise work done in the old manner (which is naturally followed by second-rate and timid minds) and underpraise work done in the new manner (which is naturally followed by first-rate and audacious minds). By "old manner" I mean the style of the last decade or so, unshorn of the mannerisms which those who have come after have detected; by "new manner" I mean the style the pres-ent decade evolves in its attempt to achieve greater precision and harmony than those mannerisms permitted their elders.[3]

In passages like these, West castigates the English literary establishment for failing to recognize the advances both in aesthetics—like T. E. Hulme and T. S. Eliot, she praises a "greater precision" with language—and with the social sensibilities of writers, most likely here Joyce and Lawrence, who pos-sessed the "audacious minds" that made them continually at odds with both critics and censors. But while West was in continuous contact with modern-ism in all its myriad forms, urging older critics to step aside and let the young take the reins of cultural power, she did not share the revolutionary rhetoric of Pound or Wyndham Lewis, and a traditionalist modernism, if we can call it that, is evident in her 1929 contribution to *Tradition and Experiment in Present-Day Literature*, in which she was pitted against T. S. Eliot, defending "Tradition in Criticism," against Eliot's "Experiment in Criticism."[4]

These aspects of her work may have been what drew her to Ford Madox Ford: despite an early aversion to his writings, she was soon in correspond-ence with him.[5] In a review of *The Good Soldier*, she wrote that "it is as impos-sible to miss the light of its extreme beauty and wisdom as it would be to miss the full moon on a clear night" and "this is a much, much better book than any of us deserve."[6] She even found a way to put a positive spin on his chronic wheezing: "There is no end to the pleasant debts one owes to that Mr. Ford Madox Ford who passes among us breathing heavily because of deep dives, of prolonged natations, in perilous seas of faerylands forlorn, now as novelist, now as poet, now as historian, once—and it was then that many of those debts were contracted—as editor."[7] Her biographer Carl Rollyson describes how "Ford and Violet [Hunt] extended an invitation to a prodigy that they hoped to make their protégée" and that her entry into Ford's *English Review* set was her "'coming out' in the literary world."[8] She later described this period in her development as a novelist during a radio broadcast, recently published as "The Novelist's Voice":

> I have, I think, found my voice as a novelist. When I was in my late teens I met Ford Madox Hueffer, who was lying, worthless, and untrustworthy, but was loyal in his dedication to letters, and incapable of treachery to his standards; and I met his close companion Violet Hunt, a forgotten but admirable novelist, a kind and generous and lettered woman. Under their guidance I contemplated a changing fiction which had already, in the hands of Henry James and Joseph Conrad, claimed new rights. It maintained that the novelist had a right to get as far away from plain narrative as a composer gets when he gives up writing piano solos and ventures on symphonies scored for the full orchestra. It was also determined to treat material of the highest seriousness.[9]

Ford and West were the first writers to publish full-length studies of James, whose influence is clearly felt in both *The Good Soldier* and *The Return of the Soldier*.[10] *The Good Soldier* first appeared in the debut issue of Wyndham Lewis's *Blast*, alongside one of West's earliest short stories, "Indissoluble Matrimony." From this close connection to Ford and Lewis, one would think that West was firmly entrenched in the modernist scene, but she wrote to her friend Carrie Townshend: "I have just seen about *Blast* in the *Times Literary Supplement*. It is described as a Manifesto of the Vorticists. Am I a Vorticist? I am sure it can't be good for Anthony [her son] if I am."[11] West's question sardonically expresses her own uncertainty about her relationship to the London avant-garde, and the general neglect of West's early work throughout the century seemed to confirm her doubts. However, one of the possible reasons that *The Return of the Soldier* has received so much more recent critical attention may be because of its unclear but productive relationship to the continually redefined notion we have of modernism. The novel's interest in psychology and nonlinear narrative align it with *The Good Soldier*, while its prose and perspectives seem more *fin de siècle*, possibly echoing middle-period James. Meanwhile it has attracted feminist readings due to its awareness of the gendered aspect of neurosis.

A central problem faced by the novel is that of historical experience, as Christopher Baldry cannot relate his own experiences, and faces a crisis that was generational: part of what the Lost Generation lost was an ability to tell their own story, as when Walter Benjamin asks in "The Storyteller" (1936), "Was it not noticeable at the end of the war that men returned from the battlefield grown silent—not richer, but poorer in communicable experience?"[12] Baldry is an extreme case of this disability, unable to relate even the most basic aspects of his time at war.[13] The narrative itself, instead of depicting the events that Baldry has forgotten, circles around them, highlighting the empty, absent center that is Chris's war memories. As in *The Good Soldier*, we are witnessing a man who has undergone a traumatic experience and is acting out in an effort to come to grips with what has happened. For Dowell, this means endless repetition and returning to key events. Baldry takes the opposite course, as his psyche completely suppresses the memories of the traumatic events and instead retreats into a more comforting past. Both novels highlight important elements of the writing of history: Ford had dramatized the narrative aspect of historiography, how it always involves repetition, rewriting, and returning, while West's work highlights the absence of the past—it is indeed "passed" and we no longer, by definition, have direct access to it, but can only observe its traces, with which we can attempt to construct histories. West's mode exploits this absence, not to retreat from history but to more intimately confront it.[14]

The novel also contains many passages describing landscapes in the kind of language that we dub "pastoral," traces of which we can also find in the Georgian poets included in Edward Marsh's annual anthologies (1912–1922). But *The Return of the Soldier* has a narrative structure that more powerfully appropriates the pastoral tradition, beyond a decorative reliance on bucolic scenes and floral language. West's achievement was to draw upon the pastoral while also making the mode modern. Key to the pastoral, from its classical origins, are the absent, traumatic events or memories that the idyllic imagery of the narrative depicts, as when Virgil in the *Eclogues* describes the lives of shepherds in the country while staying silent about, but simultaneously signaling, the civil wars that were ravaging Rome. Like Conrad in *Nostromo*, West opts to narrate as much by absence as by presence, and she dramatizes the challenges of linguistically depicting historical events like war.[15] In a 1915 review of *The Carnival of Florence*, a popular historical novel by Marjorie Bowen, West writes that "Miss Bowen's method of composition is to shut her eyes, think of a historical period, and double it."[16] Clearly, West is impatient with the historical overloading in the genre and chooses to work by subtraction instead of multiplication, narrating history via ellipses in lieu of direct depiction.

An important discovery by West was how well the pastoral mode addresses so many of the concerns of new ideas in psychology, the war, and literary modernism, and as I will argue later in this chapter, Ford adopted her pastoral insights for his wartime novel *Parade's End*. West's treatment of shell-shock is quite early, possibly the first fictional depiction of a case, thus capturing the formulation in its infancy.[17] But for West, shell-shock is not just a topic for the novel; it informs its narrative structure, and, I would argue, her vision of history. For many writers and critics, the war severely altered our understanding of time, memory, and history, and Baldry is living in what Jay Winter terms "traumatic time": because of his amnesia he is distanced from the war, while his every youthful and uncanny movement signals the lingering presence of his violent memories.[18] West found in the pastoral a supple means of dramatizing Baldry's trauma, while also questioning how experience becomes written testimony: using Cathy Caruth's formulation, we could argue that while Baldry's personal history is blotted out, his damaged psyche allows for an oblique access to the lost past via the malfunctioning psychic mechanisms of the present.[19]

West was not the only writer drawing on the pastoral tradition during the war. Many poets, like Wilfred Owen and Edmund Blunden, experimented with the pastoral, both out of homesickness for English countrysides, as well as for the critical power the mode allowed. In *The Great War and Modern Memory* (1975), Paul Fussell writes that "if the opposite of war is peace, the opposite of experiencing moments of war is proposing moment of pastoral. Since war takes place outdoors and always within nature, its symbolic status is that of the ultimate anti-pastoral."[20] Fussell focuses mainly on poets (and mainly on men) who wrote in the pastoral mode, and presents images of soldiers scribbling out descriptions of a natural world that seemed entirely lost. The homesickness of the trench poets compelled them to write about something else than the hell in which they found themselves, and centuries of English poetic language were there to provide avenues of escape. But the greater challenge that may have induced so many depictions of pastoral scenes was the utterly indescribable nature of trench warfare. Even when poets wanted to depict what they had seen, there was a narratological challenge on an unprecedented scale, and little in the way of established forms or language.

Adopting the pastoral mode allowed West to not only confront contemporary notions of the psyche, but also draw upon a tradition spanning two millennia. There is a specificity to her choice of pastoral tradition, illustrated in William Empson's chapter on Marvell in his classic *Some Versions of Pastoral* (1935), which begins by analyzing the "The Garden," especially the following lines:

> Meanwhile the mind, from pleasure less,
> Withdraws into its happiness:
> The mind, that ocean where each kind
> Does straight its own resemblance find;
> Yet it creates, transcending these,
> Far other worlds, and other seas;
> Annihilating all that's made
> To a green thought in a green shade.[21]

Empson writes:

Either "reducing the whole material world to nothing material, i.e. to a green thought," or "considering the material world as of no value compared to a green thought"; either contemplating everything or shutting everything out. This combines the idea of the conscious mind, including everything because understanding it, and that of the unconscious animal nature, including everything because in harmony with it.[22]

If there are several versions of pastoral, West's is in the tradition of Virgil and Marvell. West uses pastoral scenes to work out the struggles of the conscious with the unconscious mind, to "contemplate everything" while also "shutting everything out." This "everything" is the war, rarely directly depicted but always ghostly present at Baldry Court. Through Baldry's amnesia, West dramatizes the relation between the "conscious mind" and the "unconscious animal nature" that gets released after battle. In the third chapter, Jenny, the narrator, recounts Chris's memories spent with Margaret on Monkey Island (which is the fictional version of where West and H. G. Wells created their own happy memories during their courtship). The description of the landscape and vegetation may sound idyllic and even escapist, but these passages are the negative reflection of the war: "He stood beside the crazy post where the bell hung and watched the white figure take the punt over the black waters, mount the grey steps and assume their greyness, become a green shade in the green darkness of the foliage-darkened lawn, and he exulted in that guarantee."[23] The "green shade" of Marvell's poem appears here not just to echo his lyricism and description of domesticated nature; West is writing in his version of pastoral, as the comforting memories of the lovers' relationship blot out the painful ones that the novel never directly depicts. The verbally dense description of Monkey Island highlights the absent memories that we are only privy to in fragments. Virgil's fields, Marvell's garden, and West's Monkey Island become so richly overdetermined because of the process that Empson highlights: such texts focus on the immediate in all its lushness, while also silently signaling to an absent, powerful force.

Given the popularity of the pastoral during an industrialized war, we may be tempted to see twentieth-century usages as ironizing the mode, since West and other writers were adopting it to talk indirectly about the war and the disillusionment it brought about. But those very dynamics of irony were present in the early formations of the pastoral. In *Pastoral and Ideology: Virgil to Valéry* (1987), Annabel Patterson points out that Virgil's pastoral "referred to something other than itself, and specifically to the historical circumstances in which it was produced—the last phases of the civil war."[24] Virgil's contemporaries would have been struck by the gap between the idyllic world depicted in his poems and the turmoil in urban Rome. Thus the tradition of using the pastoral to hint at war has been there since its conception, but it does not always have this more complex reputation because of its transformations during the Renaissance. Raymond Williams charts these changes in his seminal *The Country and the City* (1975):

So that even in these developments, of classical pastoral and other rural literature, which inaugurate tones and images of an ideal kind, there is almost invariably a tension with other kinds of experience: summer with winter; pleasure with loss; harvest with labour; singing with a journey; past or future with the present. The achievement, if it can be called that, of the Renaissance adaptation of just these classical modes is that, step by step, these living tensions are excised, until there is nothing countervailing, and selected images stand as themselves: not in a living but in an enameled world.[25]

As Williams asserts, by the eighteenth century the pastoral had been largely defanged, drained of its critical nature and used mostly to celebrate power, not interrogate it. Alexander Pope even wrote that "[w]e must use some illusion to render a Pastoral delightful; and this consists in exposing the best side only of a shepherd's life, and in concealing its miseries."[26] Court pastorals brought the countryside—in highly rarefied form—into the urban court, either as a means of containing social unrest, or simply as ironic entertainment. This is the version of pastoral handed down to the twentieth century, which makes all the more remarkable what the 20-year-old West was able to do with it. West's transformation of the pastoral was not just making it new, but simultaneously was rooting it in its older incarnations.[27] Just as T. S. Eliot wrote in *The Use of Poetry and the Use of Criticism* (1933) that "the great poet is, among other things, one who not merely restores a tradition which has been in abeyance, but one who in his poetry re-twines as many straying strands of tradition as possible," West "retwines" two millennia of pastoral tropes.[28] By using pastoral language to portray the Great War, West is updating the mode, not ironizing it.

As Patterson stresses, when Virgil wrote of landscapes and shepherds, he was also writing about military conflict, and one should not take his pastorals as advocating a certain way of life or as merely waxing nostalgic for a Golden Age, and certainly not as a literary abandonment of contemporary events. Virgil's pastorals are partly meditations on violence and war, and they use language about landscapes and *otium* (leisure) to emphasize the chaos and conflict that rages outside the shepherds' small oases of tranquility. Paul Alpers, in *What is Pastoral?* (1996), stresses that "separation and loss are also central in pastoral representations of social injustice. . . . The usual ideas of nostalgia and idyllic retreat wrongly construe the way pastoral deals with such themes."[29] Pastorals dramatize the very human desire to turn away from trauma, while also signaling the inescapable presence of the traumatic source.

Alpers argues that another common misconception that arises when critics deal with the pastoral is the mode's concern with landscape. Landscape is an important element of the pastoral, but we will have "a far truer idea of pastoral if we take its representative anecdote to be herdsmen and their lives, rather than landscape or idealized nature. . . . In their simplicity and vulnerability, shepherds fittingly represent those whose lives are determined by the actions of powerful men or by events and circumstances over which they have no control."[30] West breaks with pastoral tradition in this important aspect. Shepherds were never of the ruling class, and Fussell explains why soldiers were an ideal modernization of classical shepherds: "Strictly speaking, pastoral requires shepherds and their sheep. The war offers both in officers and Other Ranks, especially when the Other Ranks are wearing their issue sheepskin coats with the fur outside."[31] But Christopher Baldry is a landowner, possessing not just Baldry Court but mines in Mexico, which we might guess are the true source of the family's wealth. Upon enlisting, Baldry would have automatically became an officer in His Majesty's Army, and this complicates the pastoral mode (and Alpers might argue that the novel is not pastoral at all). By creating a ruling-class protagonist and using idyllic language to describe feudal estates, West's amends one version of pastoral, forcing a focus on landed society and the changes to that society brought on by war.

Another modernization to the pastoral mode is that of genre. Can we even conceptualize a novel as pastoral? Empson used only one example in his work, *Alice in Wonderland*, but even in that instance he paid little attention to the novel as a form. Alpers explores the pastoral novel in his last chapter, establishing that it is problematic to group novels in with two millennia of pastoral verse:

> Since the novel is the characteristic form of the epoch in which the literary system ceased to be expressed by clearly defined and related genres, it seems neither useful nor plausible to claim for the pastoral novel the literary motivation or generic coherence of older forms.[32]

Alpers may have Bakhtin in mind, for whom the novel subsumes any mode or genre it comes across and is comfortable with coexisting traditions and discourses. We could say a novel bears traces of the pastoral, but could we read a work like *The Return of the Soldier* as *a* pastoral? Alpers continues, "Rather, a piece of fiction can be called pastoral when its author . . . has recourse to usages which are characteristic of older pastorals and which in turn make a tale or novel pastoral in mode." He goes on to analyze several of George Eliot's novels for their pastoral qualities, many of which contain scenes—but only scenes—that seem to operate in the mode.

What is key in analyzing any novel for pastoral influence is thus not to look for instances where the mode breaks down and does not conform to any version of pastoral—no novel will be able, or even possess the ambition, to do so—but rather to see how they are in discourse with the traditions that inform some of their language and structure. West quotes "The Garden," and I will argue that she is channeling the Virgilian conceit of describing bucolic, rural scenes in order to critically comment on urban (or for West, industrial) warfare. The novel opens with Jenny sitting in the nursery of Baldry's dead son:

It was the first lavish day of spring, and the sunlight was pouring through the tall arched windows and the flowered curtains so brightly that in the old days a fat fist would certainly have been raised to point out the new translucent glories of the rosebuds; it was lying in great pools on the blue cork floor and the soft rugs, patterned with strange beasts; and it threw dancing beams, that should have been gravely watched for hours, on the white paint and the blue distempered walls. It fell on the rocking-horse which had been Chris' idea of an appropriate present for his year-old son.[33]

The lyrical description of the first day of spring competes with the absence of Chris's dead son, who is physically indicated only by his rocking-horse. (Woolf would use shoes to a similar effect in *Jacob's Room*.) This is the mode in which the novel works: lush writing surrounding an absent center. Laura Cowan, analyzing the pastoral mode in the novel, notes that "the story is really about absence—and primarily the absence which the war creates."[34] Later, it is Baldry's war memories that are notably absent, but from the beginning there is a family member whose presence is missed.[35] Bucolic imagery was often used as a reminder of harsh winters to come, or devastating plagues recently experienced.[36] Usually, pastoral literature comments on these dichotomies in relation to a community or a region. In this passage, as in the novel as a whole, West shifts this area of concern from landscape to the psyche.

Jenny's description of Baldry Court and the surrounding landscape bursts with imagery reminiscent of previous pastoral poets:

The house lies on the crest of Harrowweald, and from its windows the eye drops to miles of emerald pastureland lying wet and brilliant under a westward line of sleek hills blue with distance and distant woods, while nearer it ranges the suave decorum of the lawn and the Lebanon cedar whose branches are like darkness made palpable, and the minatory gauntnesses of the topmost pines in the wood that breaks downward, its bare boughs a close texture of browns and purples, from the pond on the hill's edge.[37]

In this physical description of the estate—more detailed than any physical description of the characters—we can hear echoes of lyric poets like Marvell or Wordsworth who employed color (West mentions five), distance ("miles," "distant," "nearer"), and floral accuracy ("Lebanon cedar," "pines")—all familiar pastoral techniques and vocabulary. But also notable is the relation of the house to the rest of the landscape. It "lies on the crest," surveying the land with "the eye" that is providing the impressions that form the passage. The house is more than just a vantage point from which we can see the estate: it is what anchors the humans who *own* the land. Williams comments on the relationship of property ownership to the evolution of pastoral modes: "It was that kind of confidence, to make Nature move to an arranged design, that was the real invention of the landlords. And we cannot then separate their decorative from their productive arts; this new self-conscious observer was very specifically the self-conscious owner."[38] The text signals an awareness of this ownership of the land and estate:

> You probably know the beauty of that view; for when Chris rebuilt Baldry Court after his marriage, he handed it over to architects who had not so much the wild eye of the artist as the knowing wink of the manicurist, and between them massaged the dear old place into matters for innumerable photographs in the illustrated papers.[39]

The view is not "natural" in any sense, but rather the result of a labored attempt to appear pleasing to the public, mediated through the magazines.[40] In these two paragraphs, we get the house as object, to be viewed, and as subjective viewpoint, a site from which to view other objects of property. West's pastoralism is thus not the mode of Wordsworth, wandering lonely as a cloud through public, anonymous landscapes. Baldry Court belongs to Chris Baldry, whose "eye" has the proprietary right to survey the landscape and who gains in social prestige by letting other, public eyes look at mediated reproductions of his estate.

After the opening descriptions of Baldry Court, Jenny confesses, "That day its beauty was an affront to me, because like most Englishwomen of my time I was wishing for the return of a soldier."[41] This is the first appearance of the pastoral's inherent irony, employing pleasant imagery and language to invoke trauma or violence. The narrative time of the novel is a brief oasis for Baldry, taking place after the battle that has ravaged his psyche but before the subsequent horrors to come. The "return" of this soldier is doubly the return from battle and also the return *to* battle that closes the narrative (as well as the return to sanity). Jenny says that Chris, away at war, has been in a landscape ravaged by fighting: "By night I saw Chris running across the brown rottenness of No Man's Land, staring back at me because he trod upon a hand."[42] Rather than running through fields of green and trampling on flowers, Chris is in a "brown" space where he walks on dismembered body parts. (Note the possible double meaning of "No Man's Land"—it ostensibly refers to the area between two opposing trenches, where neither side has control. But it hints at the chaos of land that is owned by no man.)

Jenny has not witnessed fighting; rather, "on the war-films I have seen men slip down as softly from the trench parapet, and none but the grimmer philosophers would say that they had reached safety by their fall."[43] All of her thoughts of Chris are her own, not an omniscient viewpoint observing Chris's experiences.[44] This is one of the challenges the novel offers, that of testimony. Since Chris has forgotten his war experiences, Jenny is left only with war films—notoriously propagandistic and misleading—to reconstruct some sort of narrative as to what Chris has undergone, and we should note just how mediated Jenny's access to the war truly is: Debra Rae Cohen, in *Remapping the Home Front* (2002), writes that "[l]ike so many women in wartime, Jenny strains to experience battle vicariously, imaginatively projecting herself into Chris's experience, but she can only filter her imaginings through accounts derived from the popular media. Her mental images of the trenches are borrowed from the 'war-films,' themselves usually secondhand restagings of battle."[45] This triply distanced narrative structure, technically reminiscent of James's short fiction but more in tune with modern media and technology, makes the war hover over every peaceful scene, and this is a key aspect of West's aesthetic. Rather than avoiding the war in the sense that Jameson reads *Nostromo* as avoiding history, both Conrad and West show an urge to depict historical events from a cautious, but also highly mediated distance, as West does with Jenny's war filtering and Conrad had done with his Preface and use of *Fifty Years of Misrule*.[46] The result in the case of *The Return of the Soldier* is a transfer of the tensions of the battlefield onto Baldry Court itself. In this lyrical country-house novel, whose action rarely leaves the estate, the war is inescapable. All of Chris's delusions, idyllic as they may appear, actually stem from some incommunicable horror. Like *Nostromo*, West relies upon negative space and silences to convey historical forces and events, dramatizing not just history itself but our epistemological access to it. As Wyatt Bonikowski writes in *Shell Shock and the Modernist Imagination* (2013), "Because it cannot be grasped as a totality, the war appears in the novel as a series of fragments that cannot be pieced together," and Jenny's distance from the war is in many ways analogous to Baldry's amnesia.[47] In both cases, the real remains beyond the reach of narrative.

History Through the Pastoral

One remarkable aspect of *The Return of the Soldier* is its ability to bring together multiple discourses and traditions: the pastoral, psychological discourse and shell-shock, modernism and Jamesian realism, trauma and history. But West is also commenting on "history" in the sense of the events leading up to her lifetime. Chris's shell-shock temporarily erases any memories he has harbored since 1901. The date is significant: it was the year of the death of Queen Victoria, closing a chapter on a period of consolidation by English landowners that left them in firm control of the countryside but simultaneously at risk of losing national power to industrial interests. Residential settlements in rural areas began in great force after 1900. The anxiety of the British countrymen concerning the incursion of the city into the country had been expressed before the war, most notably by E. M. Forster in *Howards End* (1910). There was also grave political turbulence in the form of Irish nationalism, the suffragist movement, and organized labor.[48] Chris's amnesia serves to "forget" all these forces, nestling his mind safely in the seemingly halcyon days of late Victorianism, although, as Bernard Schweizer points out, the novel then re-enacts the ellipsed years in condensed form: "the orderly, aristocratic, and pastoral setting of Baldry Court comes under stress, first by the intrusion of the working-class woman, Margaret, and then, by the return of the soldier who brings with him the taint of chaos, madness, and death from the war."[49] History is willfully forgotten, but Margaret is the return of such repressed historical memories.

Personal aspects of Baldry's life also inform the choice of 1901. At that time he was not a landowner but a landowner's son, without the worries that come with proprietorship, and Susan Varney points out that Baldry's "amnesia is significantly activated at precisely that point in his history where he had been forced to assume the position of family patriarch—just prior to the death of his father."[50] Correspondingly, his reversion to a time when he was in love with young Margaret Allington erases any involvement with Kitty. With Chris's reversion to an imagined youth, West dramatizes the ability of the unconscious to voice a desire for some "suppressed wish" or goal:

> If madness means liability to wild error about the world, Chris was not mad. It was our peculiar shame that he had rejected us when he had attained to something saner than sanity. His very loss of memory was a triumph over the limitations of language which prevent the mass of men from making explicit statements about their spiritual relationship.[51]

Sentiments that could not have been voiced before the war found their expressions in madness and dislocation. This is one of the many moments of the text that sound to readers, both then and now, as Freudian, and West even felt compelled to refute accusations of her novel being a defense of psychoanalysis. Responding to a letter to *The Observer* in 1928 that she had written a psychoanalytic "Tract," she insisted that "my novel has fundamentally nothing to do with psychoanalysis," while also acknowledging that she spent months researching it.[52] This is clear from her 1917 review of the English translation of *Wit and Its Relation to the Unconscious*, in which Freud is already known for "his work in psychopathology, which has had such an enormously stimulating effect on contemporary thought by its insistence that the dominant factors of the psychic life reside in the unconscious, and that the conscious processes are only imperfect and frequently dissimulative indications of the unconscious processes."[53] West also summarizes Freud's notion of repression, so central to West's novel: "the psyche, like the body, can be overtrained; that if one diets one soul too strictly and makes it perform too many repressions there is a danger of fatiguing a part of it which will throw the psychic mechanism out of gear."[54] Although only a handful of Freud's works were then available in translation, West displays a knowledge of his key ideas, and clearly *The Return of the Soldier* is both immersed in, but also in critical engagement with, psychoanalysis. As we shall see, the presence of the psychologist at the end of the novel marks a complicated stance on West's part, but Baldry's specific symptoms also delineate the novel's relationship to the medical establishment, which was in the process of forming the diagnosis of shell-shock. As Schweizer points out, Baldry "does not seem to conform to the typical patient profile of the shell-shocked soldier during the Great War: he does not have nightmares or hallucinations or suffer from spasms or speech impediments, the common symptoms of shell-shock."[55] This only heightens the focus on Baldry's amnesia, since it is deliberately formulated by West, against the many other possible shell-shock symptoms.

Baldry's reversion both erases unpleasant memories and also unearths repressed desires. Freud explored the relationship between such release and war in "Reflections upon War and Death," written in 1915 (but not translated in English until 1918—it is doubtful West had encountered it before finishing her novel, which was running serially toward the end of the war). He begins by stating that "[c]ivilization is the fruit of renunciation of instinctual satisfaction, and from each newcomer in turn it exacts the same renunciation."[56] We are not fully aware of our desires, according to Freud, because society urges us to suppress or renounce them, and in her review of *Wit and Its Relation to the Unconscious*, West summarizes Freud's notion that "there is an enormous expenditure of psychic energy, most of it wasteful, in response to and revolt against the systems and repressions that humanity lays upon itself in its attempts at civilization."[57] West applied this observation to the hyper-masculine culture of the British landed class, which would never allow the expression of emotion or desire that Baldry truly feels. In a review of R. C. Sherriff's war play *Journey's End* (1928), West compared it to Siegfried Sassoon's *Memoirs of a Fox-Hunting Man* (1928):

> Considering these two works together, one recognizes that they have the same theme; the precipitation of a class bred from its beginnings to eschew profundity, into an experience which only the profoundest thinking could render tolerable, with no words to express their agony but the insipid vocabulary of their education, no gods to guide them save the unhelpful gods of Puritan athleticism.[58]

West could equally be referencing her own first novel. But in *The Return of the Soldier* the war releases some of these repressed, "profound" instincts, and exposes some of society's hidden urges. Freud wrote that "Death will no longer be denied; we are forced to believe in him. . . . . Life has, in truth, become interesting again; it has regained its full significance."[59] War, in bringing death so close to soldiers and non-combatants alike, intensifies life by liberating urges and allowing for a painful process of self-discovery. Since Chris's amnesia brings him back to a time when he was in love with Margaret, the Freudian reading sees this case as a repressed wish that war has unearthed. Chris may not be able to act as witness to what he has seen or experienced, but in a sense he is compensated by his new awareness of his feelings for Margaret.

Empson has found similar ideas in Marvell's "Garden," and it is by examining Freud's ideas alongside Empson's notions of the pastoral that we can see how West is drawing on the pastoral to depict Baldry's amnesia. Empson writes of Marvell's poem that "the first verse comes nearest to stating what seems the essential distinction, with that between powers inherent and powers worked out in practice, being a general and feeling one could be; in this ideal case, so the wit of the thing claims, the power to have been a general is already satisfied in the garden."[60] In Chris's garden he finds "the power to have been" with Margaret all these lost years. Since he has lost his memories, in his deluded mind his powers have not yet "worked out in practice," and he has recaptured the "powers inherent" in his life from 1901. The garden has united Chris's long-suppressed wish to be with Margaret with the ability to actually be with her. Chris's "inherent" desires are thus "worked out in practice" in the garden. Empson continues:

> But self-knowledge is possible in such a state so far as the unruly impulses are digested, ordered, made transparent, not by their being known, at the time, as unruly. Consciousness no longer makes an important distinction; the impulses, since they must be balanced already, neither need it to put them right nor are put wrong by the way it forces across their boundaries. They let themselves be known because they are not altered by being known, because their principle of indeterminacy no longer acts.[61]

It is clear that Chris's "unruly impulses," his love for Margaret, are being worked out in his pastoral scene after having been "made transparent" by his mental disorder. They are not "altered by being known" because shell-shocked Baldry does not know a life apart from Margaret: he does not know Kitty at all and is spared the memories of his mistake. Freud believed that "[w]hat are called mental diseases inevitably impress the layman with the idea of destruction of the life of mind and soul. In reality, the destruction relates only to later accretions and developments. The essence of mental disease lies in a return to earlier conditions of affective life and functioning."[62] Chris's mental disease has done just this, returned to him an earlier, more primal condition where he was free to express his love. This process is a pastoral trope: Empson notes that

> this truth-seeking idea seems fundamental to the European convention of love-poetry; love is always idealized as a source of knowledge not only of the other party but of oneself and of the world . . . because it makes the disparate impulses of the human creature not merely open to the prying of the mind but prepared for its intrusion.[63]

Freud's "instincts" are Empson's "truths." The process of war and love has revealed Chris's instinctual unconscious for all to see, and the "truth" of his repressed feelings for Margaret are unleashed as his psyche is busy repressing battlefield horror.[64]

If one dichotomy set up by the novel is between the green landscapes of England and the gray fields of Flanders, another could be between the realm of a nostalgic past and a brutal present. The pastoral mode serves as both a physical and temporal space of retreat and safety. For much of the novel, it is Monkey Island of 1901 that acts as this oasis: "It was strange that both Chris and she spoke of it as though it were not a place, but a magic state which largely explained the actions performed in it."[65] The "one white hawthorn" becomes for them a symbol of this time and place. (The fact that Chris is not disillusioned at the appearance of middle-aged Margaret shows the power of the disturbed mind that would have seemed unbelievable to readers before the war and the formulation of shell-shock as a diagnosis.) Fussell finds these concepts of ironic oases in the poetry of the war: "the ironist thus has it both ways: he marks the distance between the desirable and the actual and at the same time provides an oasis for his brief occupancy."[66] But the desire of Chris's mind to escape into a safe past is not just a subjective response to battle; it is an absorption of a process undergone by British society in the years before the war. In her modernist novella, West adroitly compressed this development into Chris's mind, and he becomes Empson's pastoral "critic" who is able to have penetrating insights into society from the vantage point of a pastoral landscape. This is a feat that could only have been "achieved" with the increased awareness of mental illness afforded by the psychological effects of trench warfare. And "achieved" may be the apt term, as Jenny states that Chris's "choice" to forget "was the act of genius I had always expected from him."[67]

Chris's amnesia, then, is an attempt to go to a time in his life when these issues were not his concern. Cowan writes that "Chris' affinity with the old Baldry Court . . . suggests that the 'dear old place' built in the eighteenth century before 'modern life brought forth these horrors' had values and integrity," although as both Schweizer and Debra Rae Cohen point out, Baldry's regressive amnesia is hardly an endorsement for nostalgia.[68] Instead, West employs the pastoral to emphasize the distance between green depictions and the gray wastelands across the Channel, not to critique the present and valorize the past, but to show that the war has exposed the contradictions *always* inherent in class society. In this, like Ford in *The Fifth Queen*, she is staging nostalgia rather than endorsing or expressing it. As a young writer, West was impatient with any discourse that tried to find refuge in the past. In a 1929 article, "The Dead Hand," on the state of English criticism, she writes that the reason for its pitiful state "is simply this

English habit of wandering into the past as a refuge from the distressful present. . . . [T]he average English critic stays where he was and takes what used to come when he was a boy."[69] While West was always interested in history, she was often suspicious of its uses.

Another common critical misconception of the novel has to do with the relationship between gender and the war. Feminist critics have done important work on West, rehabilitating her status in the English canon. However, many otherwise excellent critical accounts mistakenly assume an anti-war stance on West's part. Cowan writes that "*The Return of the Soldier* is a feminist interpretation of the war, not because it portrays women in traditionally male roles, but because it questions traditional male and female roles and examines how they contribute to a dysfunctional society whose most malign symptom is war."[70] Phyllis Lassner writes of West's "passive resistance to World War I," and Marina MacKay argues that West's works, including *The Return of the Soldier*, "are directed towards the question . . . : how are women to prevent war?"[71] She concludes that "women take an instrumental role in ensuring the continuation of male violence."[72] But West herself was exactly such a woman exhorting her fellow suffragists to support the war: her feminism did not lead to pacifism, and on the contrary only deepened her commitment to the British war effort. West did not think that imperialism, capitalism, or masculinism caused the war: she thought it was started by a militarized Germany. Rollyson reports that "the opportunity to participate in the war effort energized her," and her writings during the war—some of her best pieces of journalism—are about the explosion of women in the workplace because of the labor shortages caused by mass enlistment.[73] She most clearly articulated her pro-war stance in a positive review of Ford's pamphlet *Between St. Dennis and St. George: A Sketch of Three Civilisations* (1915) tilted "The Novelist in Controversy. A Reply to Mr. Bernard Shaw." Surprised at the seemingly ivory-tower Ford getting involved in propaganda, West writes,

> It is really not quite fair that a man who spends his whole existence in the consideration of beauty, the values of life, and the niceties of language, should be able to stroll out of his garden, look on for a minute at the fight of the controversialists in the highway, and say the right, the illuminating, the decisive thing that settles the whole affair, and leaves them sitting, hot and silly, in the dust. But here, in *Between St. Dennis and St. George: A Sketch of Three Civilisations,* we have Mr. Ford Madox Hueffer . . . picking up that good creature, Mr. George Bernard Shaw, by the scruff of his neck, and shaking him to rights. It seems unfair that he should be so casually right where Mr. Shaw has been so conscientiously wrong.[74]

And as pro-war feminist, West was on the majority side of the split within suffragism over the war, joining Christabel Pankhurst in directing suffragist energies toward supporting the British cause.

So why do some of even West's best critics continue to assume that she disapproved of the war? The critical confusion may lie in her bold confrontation of the horrors of war in her writings, which we may too quickly take to be a condemnation of the war itself, instead of a recognition by West of the high price that society must pay for victory. In a review of Havelock Ellis's *Essays in Wartime* (1916), she writes:

> It is not that he disapproves of the war, not that he is one of those pacifists who believes that the Belgium atrocities were really committed by Viscount Grey disguised as a Uhlan in a false nose and a secret understanding. He perceives clearly that "this war, from our present point of view, is a war of States which use military methods for special ends (often, indeed, ends that have been thoroughly evil) against a State which still cherishes the primitive ideal of warfare as an end in itself"; and that the only way to sicken that State of her ideal is to give her as much war as she asks for. But he destroys every kind of argument by which people pretend that warfare is anything but an offense against humanity, that it is anything more dignified than the frog-marching of an intoxicated Power to the police station.[75]

In this review we see all sides of West's position on the war: her dismissive attitude toward pacifists, her belief in the need to defeat the militarized German state, and finally her recognition of the barbarity of war. West's stance on war remains mostly unaltered by the next world war: in *Black Lamb and Grey Falcon*, she makes her case most explicitly in that text's Epilogue, a clarion call to arms:

> If I wanted my civilization to survive under attack . . . I had to be willing to fight for it. This necessity did not lessen because fighting meant the sacrifice of most of the subtle variations that it has been the happy business of the intellect to impose on the instinctive life. I had to be willing to fight for it even though my own cause could not fail to be repulsive to me, since the essence of civilization was disinclination for violence, and when I defended it habit would make me fear that I was betraying it.[76]

As she makes clear in her review of a 1917 pacifist tract, *War, Peace and the Future*, war can be both terrible and necessary: the author, Ellen Key, "bases her opinion that only to neutrals has it been vouchsafed to perceive the truth that war is a nasty thing, and that men get killed in it. It is impossible to record without bitterness that we also had noted it."[77] Again, West consistently returns to this theme in *Black Lamb*, where she revolts against "the fatuousness of such pacifism as points out the unpleasantness of war as if people had never noticed it before."[78] West was not looking for ways to prevent the war, but rather to win it, and her graphic and intense depictions of the effects of battle on Baldry's psyche need not be a protest against the war itself.

All of which is not to say that making connections between masculinity and militarization are unfounded, as throughout both wars West felt confident enough in her support of Britain to be able to critique many aspects of British society and the culture of war, and the way that patriarchy inevitably leads to violence. Part of what animates the novel may be West's mastery over this tension that we also see in her journalism from the period, and that re-emerge in the next world war with *Black Lamb*, as she is fully aware of the horrors of war but also exhilarated by its surprising revelations, and dedicated to her side's victory.

History and Forgetting

If the novel's pastoral mode is one means of depicting Chris's lost experience, another is the character of Margaret, who enables Chris's new consciousness: as object of affection, she allows Chris to explore his psyche and to discover desires that he has repressed for years. But Margaret as middle-aged woman dramatizes Chris's new, difficult realities. Significantly, her name changes from Allington to Grey: the vibrant colors of the Monkey Island days have metaphorically faded to her current condition. Margaret is ultimately the cause of Chris's return to sanity, as she intuits that much of his evasions are due to his lost child. Chris only realizes his predicament when he is reminded of the death of his young son, and those sad memories return all the memories he has lost.[79] His return marks his severance from his youth, from Margaret, and his idyllic life. The novel ends with a stern morality that is at odds with the bucolic tone of most pastoral literature, and again we see West's impatience with nostalgia or clinging to the past. Jenny concludes that "there is a draught that we must drink or not be fully human," as both the notion of rural England and the landscape of Chris's mind had been too scarred to allow a return to the imagery of idyllic lyrics.[80] (West echoes this line in *Black Lamb and Grey Falcon*, in a similar moment of somber gravity: "Into this world I had been born, and I must resign myself to it. . . . This is my glass, I must drink out of it.")[81] The anxiety and unease created by a disrupted, and notably childless, landowning class also prevents a return to bucolic language. The novel concludes with anti-pastoral images of Chris's "fading happiness" and predicts that he will "go back to that flooded trench in Flanders under that sky more full of flying death than clouds, to that No Man's Land where bullets fall like rain on the rotting faces of the dead. . . ."[82]

It is significant for what we might call West's fictional historiography that the novel begins with forgetting and ends in remembering, as she may be dramatizing two important elements of any writing of history. The novel is "historical" in that it depicts a very specific time and place, and is concerned with subjects that we are accustomed to encountering in works of history: war, class relations, shifting economies. Again, we must guard against the isomorphism of the term. Like Conrad, West would often use "historical" to mean "dated" when used in reference to literature.[83] But it is "historical" in how it stages the process by which a historical event becomes a series of written narratives. The novel is deeply invested in other forms of textuality, and information is obtained from many sources: first there is Chris's letter to Margaret; then his brother Frank's letter to Kitty; in Chapter 3 we have Chris's memories of Monkey Island, and then later Margaret's version of how their relationship ended. Finally, we have the psychologist's take on Baldry's problems, and as Ricoeur has argued, case studies always produce another, interpretive text.

However, we never get the central event—Chris's injury in the war—directly depicted. Instead, it is written around, via letters and testimonies. Just as in *Nostromo*, historical events are left silent, surrounded by a dense network of texts and documents. West praised Ford's technique in *The Good Soldier* "of presenting the story not as it appeared to a divine and omnipresent intelligence, but as it was observed by some intervener not too intimately connected in the plot."[84] While this misreads the extent of Dowell's involvement in the plot of Ford's novel, West's creation of Jenny may have been a response to Dowell—and both Jenny and Dowell are responses to James's short stories and *What Maisie Knew*.[85] All are attempts to highlight the lack of "omnipresent intelligence" in modern narrative. Note how West chooses to conclude the third chapter, in which Jenny has narrated Chris's memories:

> His love was changeless. Lifting her down from the niche, he told her so. And as he spoke her warm body melted to nothingness in his arms. The columns that had stood so hard and black against the quivering tide of moonlight and starlight tottered and dissolved. He was lying in a hateful world where barbed-wire entanglements showed impish knots against a livid sky full of booming noise and splashes of fire and wails for water, and the stretcher bearers were hurting his back intolerably.[86]

Jenny had been recounting Chris's recounting of his memories. In this passage the two recollections become impossible to distinguish. Are these Chris's memories, being told to Jenny? Or are these Jenny's images that she has picked up from the cinema, since she introduces the chapter by saying "this is how I have visualized his meeting with love on his secret island. I think it is the truth."[87] This chapter's double-frame is reminiscent of *Heart of Darkness* and highlights the subjectivity and unreliability of both Jenny and Chris.

Such narrative uncertainty seems far from an ideal basis on which to construct a history, but it is this dense textuality and self-consciousness that makes West's novel attuned to the role that memory and forgetting play in the construction of any historical text, be it an eyewitness account or full historical treatise. Ricoeur writes that "[w]riting, in effect, is the threshold of language that historical knowing has already crossed, in distancing itself from memory to undertake the threefold adventure of archival research, explanation, and representation. History is writing from one end to another."[88] For Ricoeur, research, explanation, and representation are the three "levels" of the historiographical process. In each case there is writing: it is not just at the final stage of a work of history that writing gets done, and this is Ricoeur's attempt to correct White's stress on the aesthetic function of the final narrative in historiography. Ricoeur insists that writing dominates the entire process, not just the last stage when the historian sits down to write a narrative. Eyewitnesses to the fall of Rome, even if they remain anonymous, wrote accounts of their experience, or related them to writers, and Gibbon built his own massive text on such texts. This is the sense that history is "writing through and through"—Gibbon was not the only writer involved in his history of Rome, only the last one (and now his text is a foundational text for other historians: of Rome, of Georgian-era Britain, of English prose).

Eyewitnesses draw upon memory to inform histories, but works of history also help preserve memories and even construct collective memories. Memories produce history, and histories produce memories. One of the reasons that historiography is necessary is because we forget, both on an individual level and collectively. Ricoeur writes, "In this regard memory defines itself, at least in the first instance, as a struggle against forgetting. . . . Herodotus strives to preserve the glory of the Greeks and the Barbarians from oblivion."[89] Without histories, humanity would forget, memories would be lost. As I will explore in my final chapter, West would later write her masterpiece *Black Lamb and Grey Falcon* in part to preserve the memories of Balkan culture before the onslaught of the Nazi war machine. In this sense, forgetting is the enemy of history. "Never forget!" is not so much directed at individuals as at communities: the imperative is to keep coming back to histories to preserve collective memory.

But, Ricoeur maintains, to "never forget" would be "monstrous": we need to forget some things and move on. A culture both remembers and forgets: for us to forget the Holocaust would be a political calamity, but for a Holocaust survivor to forget the Holocaust for days at a time would be a sign of mental health. Nietzsche had championed a type of forgetting in his essay "The Utility and Liability of History" from *Unfashionable Observations* (1876), followed by the second essay of *The Genealogy of Morals* (1887). In the former, he protests that the modern era "suffers from a debilitating historical fever" and that the past "weighs him down or bends him over, hampers his gait as an invisible

and obscene load that he can pretend to disown."[90] He insists that we not educate the young with such a burdensome sense of history. In *The Genealogy of
Morals* he goes even further, arguing for a form of forceful, assertive forgetting that "is rather an active and in the strictest sense positive faculty of repression."[91] Forgetting serves a powerful role in our lives:

> To close the doors and windows of consciousness for a time; to remain
> undisturbed by the noise and struggle of our underworld of utility organs
> working with and against one another; a little quietness, a little *tabula
> rasa* of the consciousness, to make room for new things, above all for the
> nobler functions and functionaries, for regulation, foresight, premedita-
> tion (for our organism is an oligarchy)—that is the purpose of active for-
> getfulness, which is like a doorkeeper, a preserver of psychic order,
> repose, and etiquette: so that it will be immediately obvious how there
> could be no happiness, no cheerfulness, no hope, no pride, no *present*,
> without forgetfulness.[92]

One may sympathize with Baldry's Nietzschean need for "a little quietness"
after serving time at the front, and the *tabula rasa* of his psyche is free of his
memories of marriage and his son's death. For Nietzsche, forgetting frees one
from both haunting memories and also from responsibility, which he describes as a *"memory of the will."* Liberation from memory allows a fuller engagement with life, living in a present free of the past.[93]

We could simply read Nietzsche's essays as anti-history, but Ricoeur asks,
"Could forgetting then no longer be in every respect an enemy of memory,
and could memory have to negotiate with forgetting, groping to find the right
measure in its balance with forgetting?"[94] Could forgetting have a place in the
writing of history? *The Return of the Soldier* is so important as a fictional
dramatization of historiography because it stresses both the importance of
forgetting—Chris's "act of genius" was to forget his war experience, displaying the Nietzschean awareness of the potential active and liberating nature of
forgetting—and also the importance of memories, as West stresses the necessity of remembrance, the "draught that we must drink or not be fully
human."[95] Forgetting is not just escaping from the burden of history, as Nietzsche theorized, but also an essential part of the process of historiography that
is a fuller confrontation with, not retreat from, history. Through memories
and amnesia, and the multiple textual (and cinematic) sources that the novel
incorporates, West formulates her own modernist historiography, one that
attempts to negotiate between the Scylla of amnesia and the Charybdis of
monstrous remembering.

At the heart of this dilemma is the problem of witnessing. Both Baldry and
Ford's Dowell would make poor witnesses for any detective or researcher
trying to figure out what they have experienced. But just as Cathy Caruth
urges us to hear "the moving and sorrowful *voice* that cries out, a voice that is

paradoxically released *through the wound*" in trauma narratives, Baldry can be a powerful witness in a different way.[96] Baldry's breakdown in memory is due to the indescribable nature of trench warfare, which has strained his psyche's capacity for mnemonic processing. Ricoeur, writing of events like the Holocaust, argues that "comprehension is built on the basis of a sense of human resemblance at the level of situations, feelings, thoughts, and actions. But the experience to be transmitted is that of an inhumanity with no common measure with the experience of the average person. It is in this sense that it is a question of limit experiences."[97] Trench warfare, like the Holocaust, is a "limit experience" and has become one of the sites of debate in twentieth century historiography. How does one depict something so far beyond previous examples or accounts of human experience? But Ricoeur shifts the debate slightly: it is not just a case of *representing*—that is, presenting-once-again—the event for which we have an inadequate supply of formal models. There is also what he terms a "crisis of testimony," where even the archival documents suffer from the indescribable nature of their intended referent. "To be received, a testimony must be appropriated, that is, divested as much as possible of the absolute foreignness that horror engenders."[98] The challenge is, as Primo Levi asks, "how to relate one's death?" How, in witnessing, is it possible both to act as witness to the events while also conveying the equally important horrific nature of them? Hannah Arendt wrote that "[i]f I describe these conditions without permitting my indignation to interfere, I have lifted this particular phenomenon out of its context in human society and have thereby robbed it of part of its nature, deprived it of one of its important qualities."[99] Baldry's war experiences are an early example of this ever-present challenge to twentieth-century cultural representation, where the accurate tabulation of atrocities seems to fail the task of memory, and it may be that forgetting is truer to the past than remembrance. An accurate "remembering" of mass atrocities strips historical experience of its horrific specificity, and amnesia and forgetting, somewhat counterintuitively, restore or preserve an adequate sense of horror.

Baldry as witness thus conveys the horror, but the event remains out of reach of memory. Yet his lack of memories stems, Freud might argue, from *too much* memory. Trauma has activated a coping mechanism of forgetting, and while the violent experience remains unknown—as opposed to known and then repressed—it is discoverable through narrative itself.[100] In this sense, amnesia and an overload of memory are not opposite poles but rather a joined condition, and, as we have seen with West's pastoral mode, the absence of memory simultaneously signals the presence of too much memory. Steve Pinkerton states that "Chris's amnesia articulates perfectly the paradox of being locked in a continuous knowing—which is simultaneously an unknowing—of an event that never stops happening yet never really occurs. Amnesia is Chris's way of performing the untellable."[101] This forces the questions: Should Baldry regain mental health by remembering, or by more forgetting? Is there a kind of forgetting that is healthy for someone already suffering from amnesia?

Dr. Gilbert Anderson, the psychiatrist brought to Baldry Estate to cure Chris of his amnesia, seems blithely unaware of these questions that the text seems to pose, which might partly explain the novel's near-parodic depiction of him. Although this is one of the first depictions of an analyst in literature, West does not insert him simply to give a scientific perspective on the events and conditions of the novel, as the psychologist "explains" the story in the conclusion of Alfred Hitchcock's *Psycho*. From the moment we encounter Dr. Anderson, we are encouraged to distrust his authority, as Jenny notes that she "was startled, to begin with, by his unmedical appearance," as she comes upon him kicking a tennis ball around the lawn. However, once he begins to analyze Chris he does seem to make explicit certain themes of the novel: "There's a deep self in one, the essential self, that has its wishes. And if those wishes are suppressed by the superficial self . . . it takes its revenge."[102] The revenge by the psyche is Chris's amnesia, and the doctor then asks, "Well . . . what's the suppressed wish of which it's the manifestation?" He believes that once this is brought to light Chris can be cured, but this is not the way the novel concludes; instead, Margaret realizes that he needs proof of his deceased son to shock him back into sanity. The suppressed wish—Margaret— has been openly visible from the beginning of Chris's ordeal, and it has brought him no closer to sanity. Margaret intuits that "you can't cure him. . . . Make him happy, I mean. All you can do is to make him ordinary."[103] Anderson assents to this, but then it is Margaret who comes up with the plan to cure Chris, and in response "[t]he little man had lost in a moment his glib assurance, his knowingness about the pathways of the soul."[104]

The fact that Dr. Anderson is brought in, and that Chris ends up "cured," only serves to mask the text's relationship to Anderson's character and the psychological discourse for which he is meant to speak. It is not he that cures Chris, but Margaret, and she does so with the knowledge that it is not really a cure at all, but rather a normative gesture at best. Then why does West bring the doctor into her narrative at all? He is neither *deus ex machina* nor object of simple ridicule; rather, he is a means by which West may stage her anxious relationship to the burgeoning field of psychology, a relationship that modern literature at large will grapple with in the ensuing decades. Anderson makes clear his Freudian credentials when he dismisses hypnosis and declares that "I'll do it [cure Chris] by talking to him. Getting him to tell his dreams."[105] While West here is not rejecting his entire field, as psychology's early insights share so much with her own, she is suggesting that it does not go far enough in reading trauma for its own sake and for what it can relate beyond merely a suggestion of how to cure the individual. Anderson's plan is to talk to Chris and eventually unearth the repressed memories, but Margaret succeeds through a different route, shocking him once again. It is not in uncovering a suppressed wish that Chris returns, but rather a repressed horror. In West's world, talking and narratives are not means to an end or a road back to sanity; instead, the narratives *are* the experience, are the absent, horrific history that the mind refuses to directly depict.

Such a dynamic is central to West's aesthetic, as her text is aware of the paradoxical nature of memory and memories and how narrative accesses and depicts them. Sometimes memory is conceived of as something passive, as in Plato's *Theaetetus*, where Socrates sees memory as a block of wax, on which "impressions" could imprint themselves as memories. (Memory in the singular usually refers to the mind's capacity to remember; in the plural it refers to specific images or associations that one can possess or lose.) In this model memory is subject to outside objects and forces. Other representations of the mnemonic process are more active, for example Proust's: memory for his narrator is an aggressive exploration through the past. (While the madeleine may spark the memory, the search for lost time is actively and consciously pursued.) Here the subject has some power over what gets remembered, and through the process of narrating, memories can be unearthed. Ford's Dowell sometimes shares in this mode, as he remembers actively rather than passively. West's presentation of the workings of memory combines the active with the passive model: Baldry has been assaulted by outside forces that force his passive mind into mental instability. More specifically, he has had memories erased, his block of wax wiped clean by the war. This has not been a random process, however, since the effacing from his psyche is overdetermined, and while it is true that trench warfare has obliterated his memories, it is also his repressed desire for Margaret that has forced the forgetting of his life with Kitty. In this aspect, his mind has some power over what gets remembered and what does not, even if it is not the conscious part of his psyche. In this sense, then, Baldry's shell-shock is a method of Nietzschean empowerment, not a diminishing of his human abilities. West may anticipate Deleuze, for whom shock and violence are essential to understanding:

> concepts only ever designate possibilities. They lack the claws of absolute necessity—in other words, of an original violence inflicted upon thought; the claws of a strangeness or an enmity which alone would awaken thought from its natural stupor or eternal possibility. . . . Do not count upon thought to ensure the relative necessity of what it thinks. Rather, count upon the contingency of an encounter with that which forces thought to raise up and educate the absolute necessity of an act of thought or a passion to think. The conditions of a true critique and a true creation are the same: the destruction of an image of thought which presupposes itself and the genesis of the act of thinking in thought itself.[106]

The strange violence of war's encounter is Chris's opportunity for self-knowledge. Nothing in his prewar domestic life compelled him to access the repressed awareness of his unfortunate life choices. Again, the absence of memory is in tension with the presence of newfound wisdom, and Baldry's amnesia is not only a disability forced upon him by historical events, but also a utopian impulse to remake history itself via forgetting.

It may be that forgetting, rather than remembering, can actually be a creative or constructive way of responding to events and memory, and for Deleuze forgetting is not just about Nietzsche's will to escape the accumulation of past knowledge, but rather a means to regain control over linear time. He distinguishes between "empirical memory" and "transcendental memory." The former is a memory of what the senses have once apprehended, and empirical forgetting would then be a severance from that which the senses had transmitted. But

> transcendental memory, by contrast, grasps that which from the outset can only be recalled, even the first time: not a contingent past, but the being of the past as such and the past of every time. In this manner, the forgotten thing appears in person to the memory which essentially apprehends it. It does not address memory without addressing the forgetting within memory. The memorandum here is both unrememberable and immemorial. Forgetting is no longer a contingent incapacity separating us from a memory which is itself contingent.[107]

Just as West would later distinguish event from experience, Deleuze delineates the empirical past from a "transcendental" comprehension of it, and for both thinkers, forgetting has a privileged place. Forgetting for Deleuze is key for a deeper comprehension of one's past and one's being, and West suggests the role of forgetting in creative works of history. What results in West's novel is silence, but certainly not textual minimalism: the modernism of West (and Conrad and Ford) is not the modernism of Schoenberg or Beckett. Again, it is not in the Adornoesque sense that I am finding history in these texts, as West—not the dialectical critic—fills in the silence with overwrought descriptions of houses, landscapes, and gardens, just as Conrad described darkness and bodies of water instead of the "historic" battle waging around his characters, and just as Ford would later construct long passages depicting the workings of consciousness under stress as battle wages around his protagonist. West's lush, maximalist depictions of Monkey Island *are* the histories of the war, in pastoral negative. They are Deleuze's "transcendental forgetting" of the lessons that war forced upon him.

This signals an important development in modernist historiography, which is the basic distrust of historical narratives to represent history, but at the same time an urge to forge ahead with new attempts at narrative. West is skeptical of the ability to directly depict trench warfare (especially via the press or cinema), and instead suggests that any historical narrative must remain at a certain distance from the historical referent and must indicate what is incapable of being directly depicted. As in Conrad, this is not a retreat from history, but rather a suspicion of the self-confidence of orthodox historiography, which believes that it renders history by naming its objects.[108] Conrad's impressionism and West's pastoral distrust this naming and instead surround the historical events in other forms of textuality.

Baldry's dilemma is the double-edged problem of traumatic historical events. We are politically duty-bound to remember, but we should also be able to forget in order to carry on living. The novel hints at two kinds of forgetting: the erasing or effacing of traces in the form of Baldry's amnesia, and what Ricoeur calls "a backup forgetting, a sort of forgetting kept in reserve" that for Nietzsche is more active.[109] Reserve memories are kept apart from active consciousness, but can be actively accessible. Baldry's lack of memories signals the presence of too much memory in the form of psychic trauma, and what he has achieved by the end, by a return of the memories, is also a more healthy forgetting. Now that he has drunk the draught of remembering, he can also forget in the sense that the memories of his dead son and the more fresh memories of trench warfare can be restored to his memory, but in their proper place, which is not at the forefront of consciousness but at the reserve of memory. In this sense, the "return" is both the return of Baldry's lost memories but also their return to their proper place as memory-in-reserve instead of memory as haunting trauma. The irony, of course, is that this very return to sanity will prompt a return to the front and physical danger, an issue that troubled some military psychiatrists like W. H. R. Rivers. West, writing from within the war itself (she finished composing the novel before the Armistice), can only realistically envision a return to battle. Subsequent war writers, with the advantage of hindsight, tried to work out other endings, but the full flowering of war writing only began late into the 1920s with the classic texts by Graves, Blunden, Sassoon, and others. In the meantime, Ford Madox Ford adopted West's key insights—and plot, and character name—for his wartime tetralogy, which came to be known as *Parade's End*.

The Rememoration of *Some Do Not . . .*
(*Parade's End*, Volume 1)

No Enemy and the Wartime Failure of Impressionism

Ford Madox Ford, at age 42, served at the Western Front during the war. He only saw combat for about two months, but he experienced shelling and gas attacks, which inflicted amnesia and caused permanent damage to his lungs. He was a witness to the Battle of the Somme, and much of his output from the 1920s was based upon these experiences. However, the problems of witnessing the war were as much a subject as the experience of war itself. During and after the war Ford struggled with his writing, struck by his inability to relate what he had seen. Like Dowell, he was traumatized by events and struggled to put them into language. While Ford was living through the war, he was always preoccupied with how he would eventually record his encounters with violence, or how West's "events" would become "experiences," how history would becomes histories.

In an essay from 1916, "A Day of Battle," Ford writes about his inability to verbally depict what he has seen at the front:

> I have asked myself continuously why I can write nothing—why I cannot even think anything that to myself seems worth thinking!—about the psychology of that Active Service of which I have seen my share. And why cannot I even evoke pictures of the Somme or the flat lands around Ploegstreert? With the pen, I used to be able to "visualize things"—as it used to be called. [. . .] it used to be my métier—my little department to myself. I could make you see the court of Henry VIII; the underground at Gower Street; places in Cuba; the coronation—anything I had seen, and still better, anything I hadn't seen. Now I could not make you see Messines, Wytschaete, St. Eloi; or La Boisselle, the Bois de Becourt or de Mametz—altho[ugh] I have sat looking at them for hours, for days, for weeks on end.[1]

Ford acknowledges both the visual nature of his earlier writings and also his new inability to reproduce that mode. The war remains out of the reach of a purely visual impressionist aesthetic, fulfilling Conrad's intuited predictions about the future of impressionism.[2] This very difficulty became his dominant subject after the war.[3] Ford struggled with seeing and witnessing, and wrote that his vision of the Somme "only comes back to me as some fragments, confused, comic or even pathetic, as in a cubist picture."[4]

How, then, would Ford write history? His Edwardian, Spirit of the Age aesthetic did not survive the war, as any sort of totalizing vision had become impossible:

> And it came into my head to think that here was the most amazing fact of history. For in the territory beneath the eye, or just hidden by folds in the ground, there must have been—on the two sides—a million men, moving one against the other and impelled by an invisible moral force into a Hell of fear that surely cannot have had a parallel in this world. It was an extraordinary feeling to have in a wide landscape. But there it stopped. [. . .] But as to what had assembled us upon that landscape: I had just to fall back upon the formula: it is the Will of God. Nothing else would take it all in.[5]

The "amazing fact of history" is not just the unprecedented scope of warfare; it is also the inability of the mind to cope with modern war, to put it into language. Ford admits his inability to see anything whole, and his writing here is steeped in conditionals and qualifications. Haslam notes that Ford "uses capitals still at this point—'The Will of God'—in the formula he finds to arrest a conceptual fall. . . . It represents solidity amidst chaos."[6] The appeal to the deity highlights the instability surrounding the narrative viewpoint.

Of course, Ford had already wrestled with such uncertainty through *The Good Soldier*, and while the war is often seen as a major motivating factor behind modernism, critics have more recently theorized it as an accelerating force. It is almost as if the war simply confirmed what writers, painters, and musicians had already intuited about the relationship between the real and our aesthetic depictions of it. Nevertheless, Ford saw the war as a "crack across the table of History," as he would later put it.[7] In a wartime essay titled "Epilogue," he wrote: "If, before the war, one had any function it was that of historian. [. . .] I once had something to go upon. One could approach with composure the Lex Allemannica, the Feudal System, problems of Aerial Flight, the price of wheat or the relations of the Sexes. But now, it seems to me, we have no method of approach to any of these problems."[8] New methods would be needed.

In "A Day of Battle," Ford describes one of the last pleasant days for many of his regiment:

> That is why I told you that this picture remains the most coloured and most moving of the whole war for many of my comrades of that day, for in six days, the majority—the majority, alas!—of them would give their lives in Mametz wood, where more than half the Welch Regiment perished on the 14th July 1916 . . . it was indeed there, on that tranquil river, that they glimpsed civilization, and the gentleness of this bourgeois, friendly, rural, riverside life—for the last time . . .[9]

Ford cannot describe their deaths—not until he began *No More Parades* in 1925 would he attempt to directly depict trench warfare—so instead he opts to write in a pastoral mode, focusing on a day by the "tranquil river." The deaths of the men remain indicated only by the factual statements of the above passage, "But, as for putting them—into words! No: the mind stops dead, and something in the brain stops and shuts down." Patrick Deer, in *Culture in Camouflage* (2009), writes that "the essay is structured around this subversive refusal to narrate the totality of the battlefield, while vividly conveying its fractured points of view. Ford manages in the process to pull off an extraordinary sleight of hand, at once telling that he is not showing, and showing what he's not telling."[10] Ford would return to this theme in *No Enemy* and *Parade's End*. But at this point in his life Ford, usually prolific to a fault, enters the most extended period of writing block in his career.[11] If Dowell's response to trauma was endless repetitive narration, Ford's for several years was silence.[12]

One of the ways that Ford tried to work through his crisis was the manuscript "English Country," a series of essays published in 1919 in the *New Statesman* and later collected as the novel *No Enemy* (1929). It depicts a poet named Gringoire, clearly modeled on Ford, humbly farming and writing after his wartime service. His words are given to us by the "Compiler," a critic who has come to stay at Gringoire's cottage to interview him. As in *The Good Soldier*, we have at least two intertwined narratives, moving at different speeds: there is Gringoire's war experiences, told nonlinearly as fragments of his memory occur to him, and also the linear story of the Compiler and his efforts to record Gringoire's personal history. *No Enemy* is less aggressive in its experimentation than *The Good Soldier*—although it is about the experience of violent conflict, it is a quieter, more meditative work than the novel about romantic entanglements. It does, however, contain radical insights that have important ramifications for Ford's aesthetic and its relationship to the writing of history. The text, like many of Ford's at this time, is self-consciously aware of its own constructed nature, full of footnotes, bracketed asides and even an appendix. Cornelia Cook notes that the novel "calls attention to its own textuality at every opportunity and also alludes widely to other constructions:

not only those of memory, but also of 'history,' myth, propaganda, architecture, cartography, poetry, fiction, political rhetoric and trench engineering."[13] Ford thus emerges from the war fully engaged with the writing of history as much as having lived through it, now intent on finding new forms to describe the modern world.[14]

The Compiler writes in the beginning of the novel that "you hear of the men that went, and you hear of what they did when they were There. But you never hear how It left them. You hear how things were destroyed, but seldom of the painful process of Reconstruction."[15] He later says that "This is therefore a Reconstructionary Tale."[16] The reconstruction ostensibly concerns Gringoire's efforts to move on after the war, as he cooks, gardens, attempts to write, and contemplates the effects of the war on himself and on Europe. But the parallel story—that of the Compiler—is also a Reconstructionary Tale, as he struggles to write down the experiences of the erratic Gringoire and shape them into a coherent narrative. In 1931 Ford wrote that "[t]he world before the war is one thing and must be written about in one manner; the after-war world is quite another and calls for quite different treatment," and *No Enemy* marks a departure from Ford's usual methods in one important aspect.[17] Although, like West's Christopher Baldry, Gringoire is suffering from memory disorders, his condition has more to do with images and visual mental pictures than amnesia:

> "For I may say that before August, 1914, I lived more through my eyes than through any other sense, and in consequence certain corners of the earth had, singularly, the power to stir me." But from the moment when, on the 4th of August, 1914, the Germans crossed the Belgium frontier "near a place called Gemmenich," aspects of the earth no longer existed for him.[18]

Gringoire was a highly visual poet before the war, but during and after he has a hard time seeing—in the full Conradian sense—or remembering things he has seen. Gringoire here is clearly standing in for Ford, who, as a self-described impressionist, "lived through his eyes" more than most writers, and if the goal of impressionism is to make you see, then the war has struck at the heart of Ford's aesthetic. Early impressionism depicted a narrative consciousness that strived to sort through the barrage of images. We might read this mode of impressionism as radically empirical, pushing Hume's logic to its extreme and charting, as Conrad put it in his Preface to *The Nigger of the "Narcissus,"* "an impression conveyed through the senses." But much has changed for Ford after the war, as the impressionism of *No Enemy*, if we can still label it as such, is more about the struggle to *achieve* images than it is a sorting through to find meaning. This may have been what impressionism was all about all along: as Jesse Matz argues in *Literary Impressionism and Modernist Aesthetics* (2001), the impressionist aesthetic "hesitates between two landmark philosophical traditions," empiricism and phenomenology, and its artists "court mediation but worry about its consequences, unsure what ancillary effects come with the impression's perceptual unity."[19] In *No Enemy* the senses have failed, and impressionism must turn to other means to depict experience.[20] Imagery, then, becomes a goal, possibly even a utopian one, instead of a bank of sensory materials.

Throughout the novel Gringoire tries to relate to the Compiler the few moments in the war when he actually *sees*: he describes a flock of swallows after being shelled, and "It was one of the five things of the war that I really see."[21] Note the present tense: it is not that he hadn't seen anything during the war, but rather that he does not now see his memories, even though he is still in nominal possession of them. The data remains, but the pictures cannot be recalled. Since during the war Gringoire was not paying attention to visible objects for their own sake, but for the sake of tactics or safety, he did not retain images: "one recorded less of visible objects, so that fewer visible objects return, and they return less vividly."[22] The Compiler notes that "[h]is eyes must have been at work but not his registering brain. The mind was working otherwise."[23] With moments like this, Ford complicates the impressionist aesthetic, presenting a dissociated psyche, as he, like Conrad in *Nostromo*, grows more suspicious of images as they are given to the eye, and "seeing" becomes something more than just recording (and just as "vision" for Woolf via Lily Briscoe was not purely about sight in *To the Lighthouse*).[24] In his memoir *It Was the Nightingale* (1933), Ford wrote that "You may say that everyone who had taken physical part in the war was then mad. No one could have come through that shattering experience and still view life and mankind with any normal vision."[25] Ford stresses that what was lost during the war was "normal vision," and thus the challenge for writers who experienced the war was to turn pictures into words.

This skepticism of our ability to see would carry through to *Parade's End*, but *No Enemy* is also about the problem this poses for the Compiler/Historian, who must struggle with how to weave a history from these fragmented images.[26] Although we dub *No Enemy* a "novel," it is barely that, and Ford referred to it as a "piece of writing" or a "serious book."[27] While there are two parallel stories, neither has a beginning, middle, or end, and Gringoire's wartime experiences remain fragmented and only yoked together by the efforts of the Compiler, whose own experiences remain equally inconclusive. The narrative of *No Enemy* allows the processes of trauma to inform the narrative, rather than having the narrative attempt to depict the traumatic experience itself. As in *The Return of the Soldier*, the events that have caused Gringoire's shocks remain mostly ellipsed, and we (and the Compiler) must reconstruct Gringoire's experiences through the traces the war has left on his mind and his narrative.

Some Do Not . . . : Ford's Rewriting of West's Pastoral

No Enemy contains many of the same themes that Ford would explore more thoroughly in *Parade's End*: war, trauma, memory, imagery, history. We may read *No Enemy* as the germ of his tetralogy—another instance of rewriting—but I would argue that with *Parade's End* it was not primarily his own work that Ford was rewriting, but rather that of Rebecca West.[28] In a letter from 1918 to her friend Sylvia Lind, West wrote that "I had a weekend with Violet [Hunt] and [Ford Madox] Ford during which Ford explained to me elaborately the imperfection of *The Return of the Soldier* compared to any of his works—a statement with which I profoundly agree but which oughtn't to be made, because it rouses emulation."[29] Ford's remarks may have stung because *The Return of the Soldier* was her first novel and Ford was one of her literary idols. Ann Norton in *Paradoxical Feminism* (2000) has shown how West's first work was influenced by *The Good Soldier*; I would add that an equally strong instance of influence may have been the younger writer's on the elder, and may explain why Ford was so insistent to elevate his own work over a first-time novelist's.[30] My contention is that throughout the twenties Ford rewrote *The Return of the Soldier* as *Parade's End*, especially via the first volume *Some Do Not . . .* (1924), using his personal experiences and the distance of time to come to different conclusions than West.

In 1918, when Ford was lecturing the young Rebecca, he was home from the front for good, unable to write but also in desperate need to relate his experiences. *Some Do Not . . .* is deeply informed by his time during the war, but what has been mostly overlooked are the striking affinities between his work and *The Return of the Soldier*. Both novels deal with shell-shock and amnesia; both are written in a pastoral mode; both depict the collapse of the home front and front line; both use the offspring of the protagonists as a way of suggesting a future for society; and both end with the return of a soldier to the front. Ford, in rewriting *The Return of the Soldier*, did not even bother to change the plot or the first name of the protagonist: in both books the wealthy, landed Christopher, who has a powerful family name but whose estate now makes most of its money from mining, fights and returns home to a bad marriage, suffering from shell-shock in the form of amnesia.

Several critics have noted the obvious similarities, but most have stopped short of arguing for influence or an extended comparison.[31] I would like to argue, conversely, that not only was Ford directly influenced by *The Return of the Soldier*, but that we can read *Parade's End* as a more ambitious, less cohesive, and ultimately more optimistic rewriting of West's first novel. Ford never admitted the influence, and there is no evidence that West was aware of it.[32] But it may be that Ford's interest in writing history, combined with his front-line experiences, found a model with West's novel to apply the epistemological and historiographical lessons from *The Good Soldier* to a depiction of the Great War. The writing of *Parade's End* deepens his confrontation with historiography, not just in the sense of writing about historical events like the war—or, as Paul Armstrong writes, in "painting the broad picture of social change" brought about by the war—but also in meditating on the process of writing history, by finding a work of "history" like *The Return of the Soldier* and trying to rewrite it, thus becoming part of Ricoeur's endless chain of historical rewriting and revision.[33]

Max Saunders suggested that Ford may have been the source for West's protagonist, Christopher Baldry, but Rollyson shows that West had "conceived the plot of her novel" by the middle of 1915, before Ford had been injured at the front.[34] West had read about a factory worker who suffered amnesia after a workplace accident. However, Saunders may be correct in noting how West wove together Baldry's loss of memory with Ford's marital entanglements: even those not close to Ford were aware of his very public problems with Violet Hunt, so it would be difficult to separate Ford's use of his own life for *Parade's End* with West's fictionalization of parts of it. But the similarity of the two novels ultimately goes beyond plot and has to do with modes and conceits, the most prominent being the use of amnesia as not just a plot device but a metaphor for modern memory and history. Christopher Baldry's selective amnesia erases his recent, traumatic memories and transports him to a safer time of his life, whereas Christopher Tietjens's loss goes beyond an obliteration of unpleasant memories. Like Baldry, Tietjens does not remember his actual moments of shock: "The point about it is that I *don't* know what happened and I don't remember what I did. There are three weeks of my life dead. . . . What I remember is being in a C.C.S. and not being able to remember my own name."[35] Unlike Baldry, he has retained his memories of his unpleasant domestic life—his wife Sylvia enjoys tormenting him and constantly alludes to her many affairs—and he has not forgotten that he has been at the front and seen battle. Sylvia's infidelity, the possibility of a bastard son, and his war experience remain on and in his mind, and amnesia offers no respite from his past experiences. (Ford's personal account of amnesia may have informed this, as Ford's temporary loss of memory did not release him from his wartime preoccupation with Hunt; shock does not free Tietjens from Sylvia the way it freed Baldry from Kitty.)

Many of Ford's insights in *Parade's End* can be traced back to West's first novel. One of his ambitions was to demonstrate the inseparability of the home front from the front line. Even before Sylvia arrives at the front in *No More Parades*, we see this inescapable aspect of domestic problems. Tietjens's role as an officer often involves helping soldiers with their domestic squabbles, rather than any sort of military instruction or command.[36] But West's novel was the first to chart this nature of modern warfare, whereby the home and front begin to blur: Baldry's trip home is not an escape from his memories of war, and his "return" to the front will be marked by his painful disillusionment.[37] The supposed differences between the two fronts fade away because of the persistence of memories, which was how West was able to write a war novel that took place in an English country-house. Ford's treatment also exploits this, as we never witness battle in *Some Do Not . . .* : it is also a war story with tranquil England as its setting.

Despite the prewar seeing of Part I of the novel, shock and trauma already mark Tietjens's life. His first breakdown results from worrying about a scandal related to his marriage: Sylvia has hinted that she conceived her son by another man, and Tietjens's friend Macmaster finds him having a nervous breakdown. Tietjens is displaying the same symptoms of shock still shared by many soldiers all over Britain:

> In that way the sudden entrance of Macmaster gave him a really terrible physical shock. He nearly vomited: his brain reeled and the room fell about. He drank a great quantity of whisky in front of Macmaster's goggling eyes; but even at that he couldn't talk, and he dropped into his bed faintly aware of his friend's efforts to loosen his clothes. He had, he knew, carried the suppression of thought in his conscious mind so far that his unconscious self had taken command and had, for the time, paralysed both his body and his mind.[38]

(The concluding line recalls West's language from *The Return of the Soldier,* in which the psychologist explains, "[t]here's a deep self in one, the essential self, that has its wishes. And if those wishes are suppressed by the superficial self [. . .] it takes its revenge."[39]) Ford highlights the links between domestic trauma and shell-shock, as Tietjens's eventual wartime trauma is merely the latest of a series of shocks in his life.[40] Tietjens first has a breakdown at home, in the supposedly safe prewar days, and much of *Some Do Not . . .* charts the domestic social structures that would eventually contribute not just to his wartime trauma but also to the difficulty that society faced in recognizing the disorder and formulating it as a mental condition.[41] (Virginia Woolf simultaneously addressed this in *Mrs. Dalloway* in the struggle between Septimus Smith and his two doctors.) Just as West had lamented that men like Baldry and Tietjens had "no gods to guide them save the unhelpful gods of Puritan athleticism," *Some Do Not . . .* carefully stages the ideology of the English gentleman to show how societal structures contributed to the condition of shell-shock while simultaneously hindering the ability to acknowledge it: "As Tietjens saw the world, you didn't 'talk.' Perhaps you didn't even think about how you felt."[42] This suppression results in his first breakdown, and he almost has a second:

> "By God! I've had a stroke!" and he got out of his chair to test his legs. . . .
> But he hadn't had a stroke. It must then, he thought, be that the pain of his

last consideration must be too great for his mind to register, as certain great physical pains go unperceived. Nerves, like weighing machines, can't register more than a certain amount, then they go out of action. A tramp who had had his leg cut off by a train had told him that he had tried to get up, feeling nothing at all. . . . The pain comes back though. . . .[43]

Domestic scenes like these establish the psychic mechanisms that Ford believed would activate at the front. Despite Ford's belief that the war changed so much about English culture, traumatic repression is one source of continuity from pre- to postwar life.

Ford also appropriated West's radical updating of the pastoral mode. The pastoral enjoyed an ironic vogue during the years after the war, as evidenced by Edmund Blunden's *Undertones of War* (1928). Already in his *No Enemy* manuscript, Ford had included pastoral language to describe the effects of war, as Gringoire describes going to see a play but being preoccupied with battle:

One was in the theater and having been forbidden by the will to think that what surrounded the great walls with their human lining was a vast black map fringed by conflagrations, the poor mind hung faltering.

It fell suddenly back on contemplating the green nook that—on the down behind Albert—it had reserved for itself. Yes, the mind actually did that.[44]

Gringoire's mind flees to the "green nook"—echoes of Marvell—which is simultaneously an attempt to escape from historical experience and memory and also an inverted depiction of that traumatic experience. But Ford's use of the pastoral throughout the twenties owes much to West, who was also drawing upon Marvell's poetry to comment on trauma and the war. Both novels open with detailed, material descriptions of upper-class English life (for West, the country manor-house; for Ford, the first-class traincar) before shifting to bucolic depictions of landscape. Compare the opening pages of her novel with Ford's chapter describing Tietjens's and Valentine's walk through the fields:

This, Tietjens thought, is England! A man and a maid walk through Kentish grass fields: the grass ripe for the scythe. The man honourable, clean, upright; the maid virtuous, clean, vigorous: he of good birth; she of birth quite as good: each filled with a too good breakfast that each could yet capably digest. Each come just from an admirably appointed establishment: a table surrounded by the best people: their promenade sanctioned, as it were, by the Church—two clergy—the State: two Government officials; by mothers, friends, old maids. . . .[45]

As in West's novel, the war is only hinted at, as the "grass ripe for the scythe" foreshadows the carnage to come.[46] *Some Do Not . . .* is, like *The Return of the*

Soldier, a war novel with no direct depictions of war. (The war is only directly described later in the tetralogy, beginning in *No More Parades* and especially in *A Man Could Stand Up*—.) The passage is rich with pastoral language, and also infused with notions of class and power. Here, as in seventeenth-century pastoral plays, the language and allusions represent the economic and political powers of the landed class of England. Ford stresses, through Tietjens's mindset, the characters' good birth, genealogy being the primary means by which wealth, mostly in the form of land, was transferred in the residual aristocratic order in the countryside. The State and Church are there to "sanction" not just their walk through the grass but also the hierarchies in which Tietjens believes. This pastoral trend continues throughout the tetralogy: *Last Post* begins with the "view" that "embraced four counties."[47] Like West with Baldry, Ford has tied Tietjens's notions of the pastoral and privileged perspective with notions of ownership—their idyllic language is actually a meditation on landed power, their innocent walk a confirmation of one class's control over the land and his status as landowner (although Groby, his ancestral home, is in Yorkshire, not Kent).

Critics on Ford differ as to his political intent in employing the pastoral, some seeing it as confirmation of his conservative views, others arguing that he is using it in a more critical spirit. Jonathan Bate and Robert Holton see the novels as expressing a nostalgic desire for a feudal order. Bate writes: "The pastoral works its magic in such a way that the Tory gentleman and the suffragette come together and we glimpse an England that is worth preserving."[48] But Bate may be underestimating the sophistication of the pastoral and its ability, since Virgil, to take place in a garden but be equally concerned with a battlefield, and a comparison with West may help shed light on the debate over the ideological nature of *Parade's End.* We have seen, with West's treatment of the pastoral mode, that hers was not necessarily a new, ironic use of the pastoral but rather a more robust and complex employment of it, and Ford writes his pastoral in a similar spirit. Tietjens's and Valentine's tranquil walk through the mist implies the impending slaughter of England's young men, just as Christopher Baldry's love for Margaret implies recent trauma. The emphasis on the beauty and order of the landscape is an inverted image of the carnage and chaos outside of their small world. Andrzej Gasiorek addresses this most directly: "Both pastoral and the nostalgic longing for it are ironized in *The Last Post,* which does not show feudalism in hibernation but as a shattered ideology."[49] I would agree but argue that we do not even have to view the pastoral mode as ironic—it already is so in its origins and much (but not all) of its use throughout two millennia. Both Ford and West were aware of the irony already inherent in the pastoral and have utilized it to the full extent of its critical power. Their critique of an idyllic order depends upon an awareness of the pastoral's double-edged potential.

While both writers saw the psychologically liberating power of war's destruction, their two works diverge regarding the ramifications of such new freedoms. *The Return of the Soldier* ends with Baldry returning to the front to continue fighting, his "liberated" life with Margaret revealed as an unmaintainable fantasy. West's novel was finished before the war ended, so her work aptly concludes with the return of the soldier to the still-raging war zone. Tietjens escapes from his bad marriage and eventually builds a life with Valentine Wannop, the young suffragist who is the daughter of a friend of Tietjens's father. However, such developments only come much later in the tetralogy. First Ford presents a parting scene at the end of *Some Do Not . . .* that is a far softer and more romantic departure than West grants Baldry in her austere conclusion to *The Return of the Soldier.*[50] I will return to this scene below, but the differences between West's and Ford's treatment of liberation and endings need no more explanation than their composition histories. West could not yet imagine a world not at war, while *Parade's End* was concluded in 1928, which signaled the beginning of the classic, second generation war texts by Graves, Blunden, and others. *Parade's End* is like those works in that it tries not just to depict the war but to envision a world after it, a process Ford had begun in 1923 with his return to both writing and editing (with the newly launched, and soon to fold, *transatlantic review*).

This notion of historical perspective is key to any analysis of Great War fiction. Most of the war texts of the twenties are written in a mode that we might call "historical dramatic irony": often when we read a work of historical fiction or fictionalized memoir the author exploits the fact that the reader knows, historically, how the "story" turned out. Robert Musil's *The Man Without Qualities* (1942) extensively exploits this, taking place in Austria before the Great War with characters preparing to celebrate the emperor's 70 years on the throne. They do not know what every reader knows, that their empire is about to crumble, and that the war will preempt the celebrations. The result is a tone of dramatic irony informed by the assumed historical knowledge of the reader. Paul Ricoeur writes that following a narrative means that every event in a plot has meaning *"after all"*: as we read we are not sure what each piece means to the whole of the work, but once we are finished we can usually look back and see the significance of various actions.[51] Thus the *ending* of the story makes the preceding events make sense. This is teleological but also rational: we follow events, trusting that the ending will make sense of them.[52] With some historical fiction, however, we partially know the "ending" from the outset, and dramatic irony thus dominates the narratives by Musil and Ford. West's *The Return of the Soldier* could not employ this mode, as the war had not yet concluded. Instead, she exploits the opposite: the sense of anxiety and tension as to when (or even if) the war would end. Her intended readership would share in the characters' sense of doom and frustration.

Ford, conversely, depends upon us reading his works with certain historical facts in mind, especially with the opening, prewar chapters. Since the
characters do not know that war is approaching, but we do, much of the language is dramatically ironic as it comments on the war, using the characters'
ignorance as a critical device. Rather than share in the characters' emotions,
we view them from an ironic distance. Macmaster comments to Tietjens,
"You ought to know as well as I do that a war is impossible—at any rate with
this country in it. Simply because [. . .] *We*—the circumspect—yes, the circumspect classes, will pilot the nation through the tight places."[53] Historical
distance allows this scene to depict Macmaster as naïve, his class as misguided. Ford is also able to highlight the utter pastness of this scene, as Macmaster is voicing views only possible before the war. Again, Ford had the
advantage of hindsight when he wrote *Parade's End*, but in both *The Return of
the Soldier* and *Parade's End* the sense of the endings affect the way we read
the work as a whole.

West and Ford create very different fates for their characters: anxiety and
doom for Baldry, irony and rebirth for Tietjens. Even more telling is the fate
of their sons. Baldry's son signifies the presence of death, and his memory
acts as a breaking of illusions and a return to reality and the front—which
puts Baldry Court's only heir in danger. Ford, however, allows Tietjens not
just one but two sons—the ancient manor house of Groby is to have a legitimate heir in young Mark, Tietjens's son by Sylvia (although the parentage is
in doubt), and then Tietjens and Valentine will have a son of their own. So
both land and love are given hope in Ford's tetralogy. This speaks to the heart
of Ford's rewriting of *The Return of the Soldier*. Baldry's attempts at a different
life from the one he leads are abortive; the memory of the death of his son
forces the return of the soldier. Tietjens, however, experiences a rebirth in *A
Man Could Stand Up*— and the world is guaranteed a next generation of male
Tietjenses, both legitimate and bastard. He has a chance to build a new life for
himself with Valentine, and has cast off the old feudal order. This may be
Ford's revision, ultimately optimistic, to West's war novel. Both Christophers
were faced with a crisis and realized what emotions they had been suppress-
ing; only Tietjens, because of his transformation, gets what he truly desires.

Modernism and the "Memory Crisis"

Ford's optimism, if we can read it as such, competes with a radical skepticism
regarding memory and impressions, and also regarding our ability to record
or narrate events. These suspicions threaten the role that the discipline of history plays in modern societies. In his *History of our Own Times*, Ford lamented
that "never in the history of man has the individual been less able to direct the
destinies of people [. . .] for our own times are made up of the most intimate

and most inviolate portion of a man—of his memories."[54] Both West and Ford, then, might be questioning the basis from which the writing of history emerges. Thucydides, in formulating a historiography more scientific than that of his predecessors, used memory—his own and that of other witnesses— to combat the use of myth and tradition in the writing of history. But does the loss of memories thus undermine the "science" of history? Tietjens tells his wife that "[my brain], an irregular piece of it, [is]dead. Or rather pale. Without a proper blood supply. . . . So a great portion of it, in the shape of memory, has gone."[55] *Parade's End*, we might say, is "in the shape of memory," dramatizing the conflict of forgetting and remembering. Ford's own postwar experience informs Tietjens's dilemma: in *It Was the Nightingale*, he wrote:

> It worried me slightly that I could no longer be certain of all the phrases of that ceremonial for the disbanding of a battalion. . . . Nothing in the world was further from my thoughts than writing about the late war. But I suppose the idea was somewhere in my own subconscious, for I said to myself: "If I do not do something about it soon it is possible I shall forget about the details . . ."[56]

Parade's End itself is the solution to Ford's own crisis of memory. His novel about amnesia is, paradoxically, the means to keep his memories alive. Paul Skinner sees this dynamic in much of Ford's postwar work:

> embedded in Ford's experience of war are two profound shocks: one of them, that fierce and inescapable confrontation with the impossibility of writing, with that radical and frightening division of the mind; the other, the horror of forgetting. To remember may bring nightmares; but to forget, for the writer, is infinitely worse than nightmare.[57]

In *Parade's End*, Tietjens struggles with a need to forget and a duty to remember. But as I have argued, his amnesia does not concern wish-fulfillment, as it was for Baldry, since Tietjens is still fully aware of his marriage and unconsummated love for Valentine. Tietjens has forgotten the explosion that has caused his trauma, but not his unpleasant domestic situation. Instead, he has forgotten data, such as names of places, dates, or important political figures. He has forgotten history: "It was not so much that he couldn't use what brain he had as trenchantly as ever: it was that there were whole regions of fact upon which he could no longer call in support of his argument. His knowledge of history was still practically negligible."[58] Tietjens struggles to remember even household names:

> "Met . . . Met . . . It's Met . . ." He wiped his brow with a table-napkin, looked at it with a start, threw it on the floor and pulled out a handkerchief. . . . He muttered: "Mett . . . Metter . . ." His face illuminated itself like the face of a child listening at a shell.

Sylvia screamed with a passion of hatred:
"For God's sake say *Metternich* . . . you're driving me mad!"[59]

Historical data is inaccessible, and further, as Rob Hawkes has argued in *Ford Madox Ford and the Misfit Moderns* (2013), "amnesia has damaged Tietjens' ability to *narrate*. In stark contrast to his confident statements of fact in the opening scenes, his remarks are now instilled with radical doubt."[60] We could thus see Tietjens's lack of historical memory and inability to narrate as intertwined via Ford's long interest in narrative history.

This use of memory and forgetting foregrounds the concern of *Some Do Not . . .* with the social and historical importance of memory. *The Return of the Soldier* was primarily engaging with the problematics of historical testimony; *Some Do Not . . .* shifts toward the implications for society, and how important historical memory is to social practices, institutions, and ideologies.[61] Ford's modernist anxieties surrounding memory may be in response to modernity itself, which for many theorists is defined by amnesia and forgetting. For Ricoeur the problematics of memory and history are philosophical, not historical; that is, they are not tied to a specific culture or era. But Richard Terdiman's *Present Past: Modernity and the Memory Crisis* (1993) sees a "memory crisis" emerge specifically in the modern era (in the broad, post-Enlightenment sense of the term) and argues that our theories of memory themselves should always be historicized. In premodern societies, "objects and people could be said to carry their pasts and their meanings openly."[62] But since the French Revolution, motives and memories become hard to determine because of the shifting structures of society and the economy. Similarly, Paul Connerton, in *How Modernity Forgets* (2009), writes that "modernity has a particular problem with *forgetting* . . . meaning is eroded by a structural transformation in the life-spaces of modernity."[63] Commodification induces amnesia: Marx's theory of the commodity (especially as it appears in Lukács) stresses that the object for sale hides the labor—the history of work—that went into its production, and Terdiman writes that "[e]ssentially, 'reification' is a memory disturbance: *the enigma of the commodity is a memory disorder.*"[64] Reified modern life disrupts the chain of memory that used to bind us to objects in agrarian economies, as signs of labor were more visible in the things that surrounded us. Connerton concludes that "[w]hat is being forgotten in modernity is profound, the human-scale-ness of life, the experience of living and working in a world of social relationships that are known."[65] Amnesia is thus built into daily modern life.[66]

Inevitably, narrative becomes one of the sites through which modernity struggles with issues of memory and forgetting. For Terdiman, the "memory crisis" disrupts the rational chronology of "then" and "now," since we are experiencing the memory "now" even though it's from the past, so the presence of any memory is also the absence of the referent of that memory, which in turn disrupts any notion of linear time, as the past seems to stick around longer that it nominally should. Terdiman shows how literary modernism grapples with this concept, evidenced by the nonlinear experimentation of the early twentieth century. *The Good Soldier* dramatized this "crisis," as Dowell struggled with his memories and how incomplete they were without competing perspectives and testimonies. *Some Do Not . . .* differs in that it has neither the first-person filtering of Ford's earlier novel, nor the fictional device of a writing narrator. Instead, Ford uses a third-person narration that often slips into indirect discourse. (Ford was influenced by Joyce's *Ulysses* in this respect, but of course as a lifelong devotee of Flaubert, Ford was intimate with the rewards of using the third person to express the thoughts of his characters.) In this sense memory and nonlinearity are linked in the novel, as the omniscient aspect of the narration carries us forward through time, while indirect discourse pulls us back as we experience the characters' thoughts and relive their past.

It is this rhythm of forward narrative propulsion thwarted by what Terdiman terms "rememoration" that animates the formal structure of *Parade's End*. A representative scene is from *Some Do Not . . .* when Tietjens and his brother Mark are meeting at the war office. They begin to have a conversation, and Tietjens insists that he is not having an affair with Valentine Wannop. Mark suddenly realizes that his source for gossip, his roommate Ruggles, had been lying: "'Then Ruggles must be a liar.' This neither distressed nor astonished him. For twenty years he and Ruggles had shared a floor of a large and rather gloomy building in Mayfair."[67] Then follows several pages of narration of the past, centering around Mark's shared flat. Eventually we return to the present, and then Valentine arrives to try to say goodbye to Tietjens before he returns to the front. But first she talks to Mark, who brings up her past as a servant, and the next paragraph begins: "That had been the great shock, the turning-point, of Valentine Wannop's life. Her last year before that had been of great tranquility, tinged of course with melancholy because she loved Christopher Tietjens."[68] Again, several pages of past events are recounted, this time through Valentine's memories.

When we return to the "present," however, time has passed, and the novel depicts Tietjens's departure from Valentine in the past tense. We never "see" their goodbyes in the present—the skipped time, now the past, is conveyed to the reader as a remembrance.[69] Their last night together before he returns to the front is depicted as having happened in the past instead of narrated as if it is happening in the present or immediate past. So now not only has the past impinged upon the present, it has obliterated it, rendering each event as rememorated. Narrating as rememoration instead of direct depiction was foregrounded in *The Good Soldier*, and, just as it had important historiographical implications in that novel, here too narrating as remembering opens up a dialogue between fiction and historiography, between the presence of the past in our psyche and the presence of the past in written text. Terdiman writes that "[r]epresentation as rememoration foregrounds the fact that experience *is* always *other* than it *was*: inevitably and constitutively *historical*. Such a construction situates memory as the most consistent agent of the transformations by which the referential world is made into a universe of signs."[70] A case of narrative informed by memory like *Some Do Not . . .* shows how the historical novel in Ford's hands differs from most examples from that genre: events are not simply recounted in the literary past tense in a recognizable historical context, and in a mode often shared by orthodox history. Rather, the very narration itself strives to replicate the process of historical reconstruction, to ingest the historiographical process into its very form. This is the sense in which Ford's tetralogy is not just "historical" in the sense in which it depicts events like the war, suffragism, and so on, but is also invested in the narrative structures and assumptions of the discipline of history.[71]

The heterogeneous formal practices of Ford's tetralogy also suggest critiques and models for the writing of history. Reading *Parade's End*, we witness a slow transmutation of the narrative style itself, a gradual shift from panoramic, omniscient realism to fragmented and elliptical impressionism. As in *Ulysses* or *À la recherche*, the novels are as much about the development of form as they are the development of character or plot. Style has a history within the texts. Genette observes that in Proust's novel there is an "increasing discontinuity of the narrative" as speed slows down as the novel goes on, with longer scenes covering shorter story time.[72] This is compensated by more and more ellipses (blanks, jumps in years). So the text becomes more and more fragmented, but also increasingly slower in the dramatic scenes themselves. A similar dynamic is at work with *Parade's End*, especially if we compare the first few pages—their omniscience, their linearity, the solidity of the world they depict—with what follows. The novels begin realistically, the plot moving, like the train it depicts, "as smoothly [. . .] as British gilt-edged securities."[73] But the formal coherence of the narrative gradually fragments, and when Part II of *Some Do Not . . .* begins we have skipped five years (1912–1917), but then spend a hundred pages on one afternoon. This ellipsed time is not the modernist recoiling from history that Jameson reads in Conrad: Eve Sorum perceptively notes of the skipped years that "[t]he temporal leap does not signal avoidance of the events of war; instead it suggests that this war—a breakdown in the structure of experience—requires memory as a mediator between trauma and narrative. Traumatic events can only be viewed in the narrative structure, *Parade's End* proclaims, through a retrospective lens of memory."[74] As in *Nostromo*, ellipsing history is not the same as avoiding it. *Parade's End* actually interrogates history most radically as it gets away from the realist mode in which the novel (ironically) began, becoming increasingly rememorated instead of narrated from an omniscient viewpoint. Each passing scene strikes us as less and less akin to historical narratives, but this illusion of distance from history should make us re-evaluate how we conceive of historical narration in the first place, and why we assume that "historical realism" is some sort of default mode for historiography. This is another instance in which modernism provides a unique critical vantage point onto the processes of historiography: as a set of aesthetic practices, it dramatizes its textual ontology and is not simply an idiosyncratic or subjectivist method of describing historical events.

Amnesia and the Severance of Social Identity

Parade's End is an epic case of rememoration, a novel series "in the shape of memory." Instead of the writerly concerns of *The Good Soldier*, which focused on ignorance and knowledge, *Parade's End*, and especially *Some Do Not . . .* , dramatize memory and forgetting and their importance to a representation of history. Terdiman writes of amnesia that it "aims to disrupt the linkages of signifier and signified that are sustained in social memory," and Ford's treatment of it highlights the drastic implications that amnesia can have for not just historical but social existence as well.[75]

Even the very means by which Tietjens copes with his amnesia is a meditation on memory and socialization. Before the war, Tietjens had abhorred the *Encyclopedia Britannica*, judging it middlebrow, and was even "tabulating from memory the errors" contained in it.[76] But after his trauma, he has taken to memorizing the encyclopedia to restore his knowledge of history and science. He complains to Sylvia that he could not remember the name of a person from his youth, and "when I knew that I didn't know *that* name, I was as ignorant, as *uninstructed*, as a new-born babe and much more worried about it . . . ."[77] The term "uninstructed" stresses the social importance of memory, since thinkers at least as far back as Locke argued that memory is the basis for social bonds, allowing a transference of collective knowledge so that we do not have, literally, to reinvent the wheel. Memory, both individual and collective, provides the necessary links between subject and society; traumatic amnesia severs these connections. Jay Winter, exploring some of the societal implications of shell-shock, writes:

> A set of assimilable images and experiences, arising from war service, either in combat or near it, radically disturbs the narrative, the life story, of individuals, the stories people tell themselves and others about their lives. Through such stories, we know who we are, or at least we think we do. Shell shock undermines that orientation, that point of reference from which an individual's sense of self unfolds.[78]

Tietjens has had his story disrupted, and thus the fragmented narrative of *Parade's End* is intimately tied to the protagonist's inability to tell his own story. We might see this mnemonic function on a formal level as well: Lukács, in *The Theory of the Novel* (1920), writes that

> [t]he duality of interiority and the outside world can be abolished for the subject if he (the subject) glimpses the organic unity of his whole life through the process by which his living present has grown from the stream of his past life dammed up within his memory. The surmounting of duality—that is to say the successful mastering and integration of the object—makes this experience into an element of authentically epic form.[79]

Memory is key to social identity—it helps alleviate the Kantian subject/object split that the Hegelian Lukács would explore further in *History and Class Consciousness*—and for Lukács the form of the realist novel gives shape to how this process works, dramatizing both the objective world and our subjective views of it, synthesizing the two in one text. Although Lukács maintained that modernism strayed from this task of the novel, *Parade's End* is actually in radical confrontation with this process, as Tietjens's memory malfunctions and we see what vital social roles he loses. He has not just lost data, but his own sense of self.

Tietjens's response to his trauma only increases his attachment to English culture. His memorizing the *Britannica* serves as a sped-up, artificial substitute for the normal cultural processes that instruct us in social memory. Rote memorization carries with it certain dangers, and the attempted cure of memorization is as harmful as amnesia. Ricoeur writes how memorization "is an outrageous denial of forgetfulness and, following this, of the weaknesses inherent in both the preservation of traces and their evocation."[80] Memorization—as opposed to the quotidian processes of memory accumulation—denies important aspects of existence like passion, emotion, and "being-affected"; it "has as its price the neglect of events that astonish and surprise." This is exactly the problem, according to Ford, with an English culture of masculinity that is so controlling of emotions. Through memorization, Tietjens only digs a deeper emotional hole in which to hide his repressed impulses. The very social repressive mechanisms that give rise to shock are here empowered by his will to regain social memory, and memorization only ties him more strongly to the repressive gentlemanly ideology that contributed to his original shock. For West's Christopher Baldry, regaining memory meant a return to functional mental health, even if it simultaneously put him back in harm's way; Tietjens's regaining of memory does not heal his psyche in any meaningful manner, but only further implicates him in the social caste system that precludes any possibility of happiness.

We have seen how Tietjens was "uninstructed," and notably this is the same term that Ricoeur uses when discussing the role of memory in collective historical identity:

At this level of appearance, imposed memory is armed with a history that is itself "authorized," the official history, the history publicly learned and celebrated. A trained memory is, in fact, on the institutional plane an instructed memory; forced memorization is thus enlisted in the service of the remembrance of those events belonging to the common history that are held to be remarkable, even founding, with respect to the common identity. The circumscription of the narrative is thus placed in the service of the circumscription of the identity defining the community. A history taught, a history learned, but also a history celebrated.[81]

The *Britannica* acts as the storage of the "official" history of England and its empire. Before the war Tietjens was "instructed" in being English by the many social institutions that contribute to an individual—family, church, school, state, all the entities that he hails on his walk with Valentine. After his amnesia he is "instructed" by the encyclopedia, relearning about the world around him and the historical past in a distinctly mediated fashion, and in the process participating in the "celebration" of the ruling English ethos. Again, this is a key difference between Ford's work and West's: for Baldry, amnesia offers an escape, even if it is only a fleeting one. But for Tietjens, forgetting does not free him from his domestic entanglements, and only spurs him to reinscribe himself further into a repressive social fabric.

What ultimately saves Tietjens is a different kind of memory, one that we might term "modernist," if such a term can be applied to a human faculty. Tietjens finds consolation in the very concept of nonlinearity that the novel employs to narrate his life. As he and Valentine part at the end of *Some Do Not . . .* , they are finally being honest with how they feel, and he tells her "And I . . . from the first moment . . . I'll tell you . . . if I looked out of a door . . . it was all like sand. . . . But to the half left a little bubbling up of water. That could be trusted. To keep on forever. . . . You, perhaps, won't understand."[82] His fragmented thoughts—and language that is literally elliptical—grasp for what he desires, and what are left out in the ellipses are exactly the feelings that his Englishness wants suppressed. Because of the war and his marriage, the pair can never find an opportunity to be together, and what he wants with his image of the "bubbling up of water" is a sense of stability or constancy with Valentine. But he then argues that they can be together, in a way: "You cut out from this afternoon, just before 4.58 it was when I said to you and you consented . . . I heard the Horse Guards clock. . . . To now. . . . Cut it out; and join time up. . . . It *can* be done. . . . You know they do it surgically; for some illness; cut out a great length of the bowel and join the tube up. . . ."[83] Tietjens wants to do with mental time what Ford is doing with narrative (and what the reader must do to keep up with the narration), as Ford plays bowel surgeon to the fictional time span of his characters, cutting and suturing so that elements are brought together that normally would not be, an act of modernist juxtaposition. Wyatt Bonikowski wisely advises against "reconstructing" the novel so that it resembles a realist epic: such a move "would seem to resist the productive confusion of the impressionistic presentation. In other words, a reading of *Parade's End* puts us in a similar position to that of its characters: reading is a kind of resistance to the disruptive movements of the narrative."[84] As in a cubist painting, there is no Platonic image that has been disrupted: fragmentation is the work itself.

Tietjens's notion of surgery also suggests "cutting out" that which is unhealthy, which may harkens back to his amnesia and how, as for Baldry, it can be a healthy form of forgetting, a rejection of a diseased part. As Valentine cries at his parting, she says that "I'm always crying [. . .] A little bubbling spring that can be trusted to keep on. . . ."[85] Here the lovers desire to embody Deleuze and Guattari's notions of rhizomatic time from *A Thousand Plateaus* (1980): against the collectivizing, universalizing effects of long-term memory, the authors suggest a Nietzschean turn to short-term memory:

> short-term memory is of the rhizome or diagram type, and long-term memory is arborescent and centralized. . . . Short-term memory is in no way subject to a law of contiguity or immediacy to its object; it can act at a distance, come or return a long time after, but always under conditions of discontinuity, rupture, and multiplicity. . . . Short-term memory includes forgetting as a process; it merges not with the instant but instead with the nervous, temporal, and collective rhizome.[86]

Tietjens and Valentine believe they can will memory to be short-term, "rupturing" the impositions of time by forgetting as a means of remembering. The modernist splicing of time can be used to strengthen memory in a healthier manner than the rote memorization of facts—which Deleuze and Guattari might describe disparagingly as "arboreal" or overly centralized—that cements Tietjens to residual Englishness. By cutting up one's mental narrative— or maybe simply by letting the normal processes of memory and forgetting act as they usually do, nonlinearly—one gains power over time and memory.[87] Most tellingly, Valentine's words of farewell to Tietjens are "I will never cut what you said then out of my memory," which, although grammatically awkward, is quite distinct and ultimately more powerful than the standard "I will never forget you."[88] Valentine's words suggest that we do not have to be passive victims of memory and history, but that, like Benjamin, we can "read against the grain" of history and forget in order to remember.

Rather than a distortion of history, Valentine recognizes the already existing gap between historical referent and historical narrative, and that a fragmented narrative can be just as "true" to events as a realist one. Tietjens and Valentine have turned memory and forgetting into something active, not in the sense of rote memorization, but in a more aesthetic will to "cut and suture" time to allow a sense of constancy amidst the flux. As in *The Return of the*

Soldier, the lover is the moral and political compass of the novel, and here Valentine allows Tietjens to experience memory in a libratory way.

"Epic Forgetting": The Necessity of History, the Necessity of Forgetting

Memory thus informs the narrative of *Parade's End*—"the shape of memory"— and forgetting plays a productive role in this process, both through Tietjens's amnesia and his more active "suturing" of unhealthy memories with Valentine. Again we should note the formal affinity between Proust and Ford: Ford saw Proust as a fellow novelist-historian, humbly declaring in his memoir *It Was the Nightingale* that "I wanted the Novelist in fact to appear in his really proud position as historian of his own time. Proust being dead I could see no one who was doing that . . ."[89]

Memory and its strange power links the two writers, especially in light of Walter Benjamin's influential readings of Proust. Benjamin's essay "On Some Motifs in Baudelaire" traces the role of Bergsonian notions of memory in Proust, for whom there is the active search for lost memories—*mémoire volontaire*—and also the less willed *mémoire involontaire*. In the former, Benjamin notes, "Its signal characteristic is that the information it gives about the past retains no race of that past."[90] For example, we can spell words without remembering when we learned to spell them—the past has disappeared from our memory, even through the very act of the remembrance of spelling. Benjamin stresses that the voluntary, conscious drive toward memories—skills, customs, abilities—does not have the same power as involuntary ones when it comes to depicting the past. He argues that when Proust's narrator eats the madeleine, he accesses a more powerful stream of memories, *mémoire involontaire*, first because he had not intended to, but also because of what Terdiman sees as the "disrupting" nature of how memory works. Proust writes that the past is "somewhere beyond the reach of the intellect and its field of operations . . . whether we come upon this object before we die, or whether we never encounter it, depends entirely on chance."[91] For Proust, it is "entirely on chance" whether or not we access this memory, so when his narrator eats the madeleine he has fortuitously stumbled upon a bank of memories and the narrative is "disrupted" as we are sent back into the past. The "search" is an accidental, involuntary one, even if it eventually becomes active. Benjamin suggests that these memories are much more powerful than memories to which we have easy access: "Put in Proustian terms, this means that only what has not been experienced explicitly and consciously, what has not happened to the subject as an isolated experience, can become a component of *mémoire involontaire*."[92] What we have forgotten can be, paradoxically, the most powerful way to access the past.

Benjamin is no doubt interested in this aspect of Proust because of his political interest in the disruptive power of Surrealism and similar schools of art. But Adorno, in a letter to Benjamin, responds to the above passage of the essay:

> Was the moment when Proust tasted the madeleine, the moment which provoked his *mémoire involontaire*, actually unconscious? It seems to me that a dialectical element has dropped out of the theory here, and that is the element of forgetting itself. In a certain sense "forgetting" is the foundation for both these things, for the sphere of experience or *mémoire involontaire*, and for the reflex character of a sudden act of recall that already presupposes the forgetting. Whether an individual human being is capable of having such experiences depends in the last instance upon how that person forgets.[93]

Forgetting is an important "foundation" for memory, as both Benjamin and Ricoeur have argued (and Proust and Ford dramatized), as a memory-in-reserve. The madeleine draws its power from the already completed process of forgetting, and thus we need to forget in order to have a recollection be more powerful later on. If Proust's narrator had not forgotten so much, the taste of the madeleine would not have been so transformative. He had to have forgotten the taste in order to have had the experience of remembering. Adorno continues:

> Is it not the case that the real task here is to bring the entire opposition between sensory experience and experience proper into relation with a dialectical theory of forgetting? Or one could equally say, into relation with a theory of reification. For all reification is a forgetting: objects become purely thing-like the moment they are retained for us without the continued presence of their other aspects: when something of them has been forgotten. This raises the question as to how far this forgetting is one that is capable of shaping experience, which I would almost call epic forgetting, and how far it is a reflex forgetting.[94]

Reification is usually a negative in Marxist discourse, but here Adorno finds a more positive side to it—"epic forgetting"—and he concludes by saying we should start "formulating a distinction between good and bad reification." Adorno conceives of two kinds of forgetting, as Ricoeur would do, and as Proust believed in two kinds of remembering.[95] I would argue that Ford also has multiple understandings of forgetting, and that he is trying to distinguish between Adorno's "good" and the "bad," the epic and the pathological. As there are "bad" memories in the form of repetitive trauma and "good" ones that we need to function as individuals, it would be a mistake to focus too much on either side of this problem, that is, to interpret Tietjens's amnesia as either purely liberating ("good forgetting") or as purely disabling ("bad forgetting").[96]

Tietjens's strengths as an individual relate to his powerful memory, but this is soon revealed to be a weakness, a "bad" sense of memory: "It was in that way his mind worked when he was fit: it picked up little pieces of definite, workmanlike information. When it had enough it classified them: not for any purpose, but because to know things was agreeable and gave a feeling of strength, of having in reserve something that the other fellow would not suspect. . . ."[97] The text does not seem to endorse this way of thinking, despite critics' assertion that *Parade's End* is a deeply nostalgic novel. Valentine castigates the Tietjens and his mental habits, recasting his powerful memory as a hindrance:

> it's the way your mind works. . . . It picks up useless facts as silver after you've polished it picks up sulphur vapour; and tarnishes! It arranges the useless facts in obsolescent patterns and makes Toryism out of them. . . . I've never met a Cambridge Tory man before. I thought they were all in museums and you work them up again out of bones.[98]

Valentine again voices the social critique in the novel itself, and she assails his retrograde way of being and remembering. She attacks not just his way of thinking, but also the structure that underlies the organization of his mental data. Terdiman writes that

> [w]e could say that among the things that memory conserves, perhaps what it conserves par excellence are paradigms, protocols, practices, mechanisms, and techniques *for conserving memory itself.* It would not be hard to argue that a culture's theories do the same: they recall and reproduce the cognitive and epistemological operations their culture has found important.[99]

Tietjens's encyclopedic mind is not just preserving information but an entire way of life, a resilient (if residual) ideology. After amnesia, he lacks not just data, but a sense of order. In this passage describing Tietjens's fitness, he exemplifies the Enlightenment will to knowledge—"to know things was agreeable"—that Foucault criticized in *The Order of Things*:

> Order is, at one and the same time, that which is given in things as their inner law, the hidden network that determines the way they confront one another, and also that which has no existence except in the grid created by a glance, an examination, a language; and it is only in the blank spaces of this grid that order manifests itself in depth as though already there, waiting in silence for the moment of its expression.[100]

Tietjens enjoys putting things into mental order: "Although Tietjens hated golf as he hated any occupation that was of a competitive nature he could engross himself in the mathematics of trajectories when he accompanied Macmaster in one of his expeditions for practice."[101] When he talks with Valentine about local flower and bird names, he mentally translates them into the Linnaean system, one of the clearest examples of the European scientific will to order. For Foucault, during the shift from the early modern period to the modernity of the nineteenth century, "the epistemological field became fragmented" while also establishing increasingly complex levels of classification.[102] This is because of Western culture's new relationship to history. Western culture came to see that there is not just one History; instead, there's a history of production, for example, that is not simply homologous to political history, a history of human evolution, a history of language, and so on. These levels do not advance in synchrony, as Hegel seems to have assumed, and for Foucault the fragmentation of modernity results partly from this rupture in historical epistemology and our inability to place ourselves in a historical setting, despite the gargantuan mechanisms of order that we have at our disposal:

> The human being no longer has any history: or rather, since he speaks, works, and lives, he finds himself interwoven in his own being with histories that are neither subordinate to him nor homogeneous with him. By the fragmentation of the space over which Classical knowledge extended in its continuity, by the folding over of each separated domain upon its own development, the man who appears at the beginning of the nineteenth century is "dehistoricized."[103]

It is in this sense that *Parade's End* tries to work through the implications of literary modernism for historiography, especially given the centrality of "plot" to both history and the novel. Plot is, literally, "the order of things," and in the Hegelian tradition especially, the plot of human history is a divine comedy, moving toward the final chapter of the Absolute.[104] Even non-syllogistic thinkers like Ranke relied upon a rational plot line in their historical narratives. But given the radical interrogation of narrative, subjectivity, and memory by writers like Conrad, Woolf, and Joyce, or by thinkers like Nietzsche, Bergson, and Freud, how could one continue to narrate historical events or epochs?

Ford foregrounds this crisis via Tietjens's nostalgic idealism. Tietjens continually pines for an early period, in his case the early modern era ("What had become of the seventeenth century?"[105]). He is in a sense is an idealist holdout against the process that Foucault has charted, since the prewar Tietjens seemed immune to the epistemological breakdown of the nineteenth century. Of course, this was mostly a mirage, or an almost superhuman will to hold the order of things together that eventually resulted in his shock. The novels chart his disintegration, although not necessarily in Foucault's sense of fragmentation, since with Tietjens we see the wiping clean of historical data and not the disruption of categories. (A more healthy disruption is hinted at during the dogcart ride with Valentine, where his growing love for her, reinforced by the fog and mist, begins to melt his rigid Tory categories: "He had then forty-eight and three-quarter hours! Let them be a holiday! A holiday from himself above all: a holiday from his standards: from his convention with himself. From clear observation: from exact thought: from knocking over all the skittles of the exactitudes of others: from the suppression of emotions. . . . From all the wearinesses that made him intolerable to himself. . . . He felt his limbs lengthen, as if they too had relaxed."[106] As objects lose their visual solidity and blur, his desire to maintain his residual ideologies weaken. Unfortunately, the lovers soon collide with the too-solid automobile driven by General Campion, and Tietjens's holiday from categorical Toryism would have to wait the duration of the war.)

Tietjens as idealist, early modern holdout in a fully modernized world allows Ford a critical perch from which to chart the process of epistemological fragmentation. Foucault concludes that "at a very deep level, there exists a historicity of man which is itself its own history but also the radical dispersion that provides a foundation for all other histories."[107] Because of the multiple histories—economic, biological, linguistic—of which we always partake, what we call "history" becomes overdetermined and has to carry unprecedented weight: "From the nineteenth century, History was to deploy, in a temporal series, the analogies that connect distinct organic structures to one another. . . . History *gives place* to analogical organic structures, just as Order opened the way to *successive* identities and differences."[108] Synchronic orders give way to diachronic histories as means of organizing knowledge, and *Parade's End* dramatizes this shift, but also scrutinizes our ability to represent history at all.[109]

It is at this juncture—modernity's will to history with modernism's suspicion of representational historiography—that Ford's depictions of traumatic amnesia take on such importance for modernist historiography. While under stress, Tietjens says to himself: "*Never think on the subject of a shock at a moment of a shock.* The mind was then too sensitized. Subjects of shock require to be thought all round. If your mind thinks when it is too sensitized its then conclusions will be too strong."[110] This is Tietjens's practical advice to himself under fire, but we could also take it, like the description of Marlow's storytelling in *Heart of Darkness*, as a larger metaphor for modernist narration.[111] For Marlow, "the meaning of an episode was not inside like a kernel but outside, enveloping the tale which brought it out only as a glow brings out a haze."[112] The "haze," we might say, is Tietjens's model of stressful being, as objects or emotions—or history—cannot be directly depicted but must be "thought all round." For Tietjens, this technique is immediately necessary because of the unique nature of trench warfare, but as the novels suggest, there is a key link between battle anxiety and daily anxiety that modernity constantly induces. Shell-shock, in Ford's hands, is both modern and modernist: modern as a formulation that emerges during the war, but modernist in that Ford uses it as a metaphor for the very process of historical representation, the overwhelming modern need for narratives and depictions of history that modernist interrogations have revealed as so contingent and problematic.[113]

It is in this sense that *Parade's End* suggests what a modernist work of history would look like. It is not just "impressionist" in the sense of "giving an impression" of the past, or depicting what it might be like to subjectively experience history.[114] We might say disparagingly that Ford's middling, prewar historical fictions "gave a flavor" of the past, merely imparted imaginative reconstructions of how the senses (hence the metaphor of taste) would record an era different from ours. Likewise, in his more orthodox histories of his own times he strived for "a picture of his own age." Both cases privilege the senses, but by *Parade's End* he had become suspicious of a naïve impressionism's value to the writing of history, as his distrust of empirical methods have forced him even to abandon the earlier impressionist mode that established him as writer. His later work, beginning with the *No Enemy* drafts in the early twenties, is more skeptical of this process, and shell-shock marks the breakdown of impressions, the failure of the senses, as the impression is no longer accessible except as an absence. Isabelle Brasme writes that "the text keeps pointing towards a spectral meaning which is never fully revealed. . . . The centre in Ford's text remains spectral—the reader merely perceives its shadow, its trace, through the superimposition of the various perspectives which . . . never fully coincide."[115] Even a quick visual glance at the pages of *A Man Could Stand Up—* shows the preponderance of grammatical ellipses in Ford's prose; the three or four dots serve several functions, and one is to indicate gaps in perception.[116] The ellipses help Ford stage some central questions: What value does impressionism hold if one has amnesia? If the impression has been wiped clean, what else can an impressionist work with? Any empirical data received by Tietjens in battle are lost forever, except as negative impresses. So the impressionist method of writing history is too credulous: even if we bracket the problematics of interpretation in the recording of impressions, the impressionist technique assumes that the senses will do their duty and report back to the mind what they have discovered. With amnesia, Ford disrupts this chain of signification and instead highlights the distance between any historical event and the historical record. Impressionism—already an unstable and fluctuating method—becomes completely unreliable in *Parade's End* as a means of recording history (although it retains its privileged place in Ford's description of visual phenomena).

What keeps the work from becoming mere skeptical idealism, however, is its drive to work *through* the trauma, to exploit the access to history that shell-shock provides, especially in the social sense that Benjamin and Adorno explored.

While we might say that Ford relaunches Descartes' idealist critique of empiricism (What if you're dreaming? Should you trust your senses then? What if you're drunk? What if you are shell-shocked and have no memories?), Ford is not searching for a pure, Cartesian locale from which to record history, but rather is willing to work through the contingent, which we might say is a hallmark of cultural modernism from its origins (and we should distinguish Ford's late impressionism from his earlier forms).[117]

Traumatic amnesia, and shock in general, become central to a modernist historiography. Paul Sheehan, in *Modernism and the Aesthetics of Violence* (2013), concludes his survey of violence and transgression in modernism with a meditation on depictions of shell-shock: "Much more than just a modern pathology, or an event-specific neurosis, shell shock is a load-bearing metaphor, a platform on which modernism, modernity and shock can meet and interact," and Benjamin's essay on Baudelaire sees shock as central to the modern condition: the poet "placed shock experience at the very center of his art" and there is a "close connection in Baudelaire between the figure of shock and contact with the urban mass."[118] Urban, modern living is a constant state of shock: "Moving through this traffic involves the individual in a series of shocks and collisions. . . . Circumscribing the experience of the shock, [Baudelaire] calls this man 'a *kaleidoscope* endowed with consciousness.'"[119] We should allow the full gravity of Benjamin's argument to sink in: shell-shock is a form of violent trauma, and thus for Benjamin modern living is a constant state of such trauma, and not simply via urban anxieties like noise or traffic. Liesl Olson has charted modernism's relationship to what she terms the "ordinary," best evinced by the routine walks of Leopold Bloom and Clarissa Dalloway.[120] Benjamin's words reminds us, however, that for a period of years such as 1914–1918, or 1938–1945, the "ordinary" does not only evoke such rituals. During trench warfare especially, it becomes impossible to distinguish an event from the everyday: Was the Battle of Passchendaele an "event"? The world wars made mass killing daily, ordinary, routine, "banal."[121] As Benjamin remarks in one of his notes to Baudelaire's "Spleen IV," in modernity "the continuation of the status quo is the disaster," shock is ordinary.[122]

Ford's decision to begin from a place of contingency is a recognition of this perpetual crisis of modernity. As Brecht advised, "don't start from the good old things but the bad new ones."[123] *Parade's End* is, in many ways, a working-through of such a modern crisis, and Ford's imagery has thus come a long way from the Holbein-inspired frozen tableaus of *The Fifth Queen*.[124] Instead of seeking a visual aesthetic of stasis, Ford, channeling cubism, cinema, and *Ulysses*, is reaching toward an aesthetic of fragmentation that places shock at the center of the postwar world and recognizes both the cultural disruptions of modernity but also the need for new forms that self-consciously appropriate such aspects of modern life. For Benjamin, we might say, shock is the result of not being able to process the overwhelming volumes of data of modernity, and in Baudelaire "the sonnet deploys the figure of shock, indeed of catastrophe."[125] Shock, for Benjamin—and, I would argue, for Ford—is not a special state of disability but rather a blanket condition of modernity.[126] Modernism, as a cultural response to the modern condition, struggles to depict the real while also being aware, like Marlow and Tietjens, that things cannot be depicted directly but must be somehow "surrounded" or "thought all round," and that, as Arendt argued, any testament of trauma must do justice to its shocking nature.

Just as we need newspapers and other shock absorbers to deal with modern life, and Tietjens needs mental release valves for his battle anxiety, writers and historians need some way to depict the past that maintains a sense of contingency. Ford's use of shell-shock as a metaphor implies that there is always a distance between the historical object—be it an event in time, or "historical forces" in the Hegel/Marx tradition—and our representation of it. Shell-shock for the individual is the aftereffect of a historical moment that is lost forever but that can be traceable through an examination of traces and symptoms, as in Freudian psychoanalysis, which Ford highlighted in *The Good Soldier*, or in the suggestive power of absence, which West dramatized in *The Return of the Soldier*. *Parade's End* is Ford's most mature formulation of a modernist historiography, one that distrusts the empiricism of direct depiction of objects but still works toward some sort of unearthing of history and human experience.

The consequence of modernity, writes Benjamin, is "the scattered fragments of genuine historical experience."[127] For English readers this translation may remind us of Eliot's "these fragments I have shored against my ruin" from *The Waste Land*, and it is here that Ford's vision of history departs from Eliot's or Pound's. Like those writers, Ford sees the problematics of historical depiction in the modern era, but, like Conrad and West, chooses a different path and does not abandon narrative altogether. In this sense, Benjamin's conclusions more strongly echo the Eliot/Pound constellation than the one I am charting. Benjamin's "On the Concept of History," which desires to "brush history against the grain," uses the image of Klee's *Angelus Novus* to depict the process of history (and historiography? Benjamin, too, might suffer from isomorphism with this conceptualization).[128] The angel is moving forward in time but is facing backward, and thus "[w]here a chain of events appears before *us*, *he* sees one single catastrophe, which keeps piling wreckage upon wreckage and hurls it at his feet."[129] Pound's will to see that "[a]ll ages are contemporaneous," as Wyndham Lewis mockingly described, might, like the angel, see history as "one single catastrophe." If history is singular—in this specific sense—then of course narrative history must be jettisoned as an ideological construct that does violence to both the singularity and fragmentation of history. The fragmented verse of Eliot, Pound, and Yeats, simultaneously saturated in history while also signaling its impossibility in narrative representation, might then echo Benjamin's angelic vision of history. More than simply a choice of genre, these poets—who have been taken as representative of modernism's relationship to historiography—eschew historical narrative in their attempts at historical form.

But as I have been arguing, Conrad, West, and Ford took a different course, and the challenge for them—as it was for twentieth-century historians in the wake of both the Holocaust and structuralism—was to see if historical narrative could be salvaged given modernism's discoveries about representation and its relationship to history. Ford's "solution" was to make these challenges central to the narrative itself, to continually keep the impossibility of depicting history in view while never forgetting the absolute necessity of historical remembering. Unlike West's Great War novel, Ford had the luxuries of hindsight, memory, and leisure time to contemplate the many ramifications of the war to the writing of history. Ironically, West had a low opinion of Ford's memory, as she remembered him in a letter to Ford's biographer Frank MacShane:

> I don't think Ford was a great critic, I don't think it was in his power to be so because of his transforming memory which altered everything. A man can hardly say anything valuable about the great works of literature if he cannot remember a single one of them as they were written. I had the fresh memory of youth when I talked with Ford, and I hardly remember a single occasion when he discussed a great book without it presently emerging that he had a totally false impression of its theme or that he had added or subtracted from the author's list of characters.[130]

Ford's memory was notoriously expansive and unreliable, allowing him to quote long passages from memory that, because of their casually memorized nature, were often taken as suspect. Thus, for many readers and listeners, Ford's very mnemonic capacity undermined veracity, but this dynamic would actually be central to West's *Black Lamb and Grey Falcon*. Nowhere is the conflict of historical writing's utter impossibility and utter necessity more apparent than with her anticipation of the next world war, but also present in that work is an awareness of memory's delicate fragility and menacing tenacity. While Ford was paying homage to the south of France in *Provence* (1934) and *Great Trade Route* (1937)—a pair of volumes that narrate history though travel to give shape to a fragmented and multi-geographic history—West launched the most ambitious effort at narrating history through the techniques of the moderns, urging a world to war.

The Impossible Necessity of *Black Lamb and Grey Falcon*

West's Historical Novel

While a generation of writers were focused on Spain and its civil war, Rebecca West made three trips to Yugoslavia, the first in 1936, on a lecture tour sponsored by the British Council, and the second and third in 1937 and 1938 with her husband. On the later trips she had a more ambitious purpose than merely ambassadorship: she aspired to record the culture and history of the Balkans before the inevitable German advance. West feared that a Nazi invasion would obliterate countless sources of history and collective memory. On one level the resulting volume, *Black Lamb and Grey Falcon*, is a work of witness to this historical moment: having recently read many volumes of Gibbon, she speculates that

> "If a Roman woman had, some years before the sack of Rome, realized why it was going to be sacked and what motives inspired the barbarians and what the Romans, and had written down all she knew and felt about it, the record would have been of value to historians. My situation, though probably not so fatal, is as interesting." Without doubt it was my duty to keep a record of it.[1]

This passage announces several important features of *Black Lamb*: when West stresses that "it was my duty" to construct such a text, she declares that there is an ethical imperative that has driven the writing of her epic work that will shape both her reactions to the region as well as the form of her narrative. As I shall argue, this ethical drive conflicts with the text's realization of the inherent difficulties—West uses the phrase "the impossibility of history"—of her gargantuan undertaking.

The above passage also signals the personal nature of her narrative. *Black Lamb* is to be a work of history of the Balkans in the first person—the first word is "I"—and opens with a description of West's own relationship to the region: "I lay back in the darkness and marveled that I should be feeling about Yugoslavia as if it were my mother country, for this was 1937, and I had never seen the place till 1936."[2] In her Epilogue she writes that

> Nothing in my life had affected me more deeply than this journey through Yugoslavia. This was in part because there was a coincidence between the natural forms and colours of the western and southern parts of Yugoslavia and the innate forms and colours of my imagination.[3]

Passages like this led John Gunther to write her that "it somehow pleased me too that it was not so much a book about Jugoslavia as about Rebecca West."[4] But although she may seem to equate the coming invasion of a nation with her own personal emotions, this rhetorical move is not necessarily narcissistic—and should not be taken one-dimensionally as an invitation for purely biographical criticism—since she argues that the fate of Western Europe has always been tied to the Balkans.[5] She states that she knew nothing of Yugoslavia, "that is to say I know nothing of my own destiny."[6] When she describes the death of the Serbian royal family, she writes that "now I realize that when Alexander and Draga fell from that balcony the whole of the modern world fell with them."[7] Modernity thus began for West on or about June 10, 1903, and the region remained the epicenter of international conflicts that were crucial to the formation of the modern world. Paradoxically, West suggests, the supposedly backward areas of Eastern Europe operated as catalysts for the developments of modernity.

So although the account is highly personal, its ultimate importance is tied to the role the Balkans have played in making modern Europe—"I had come to Yugoslavia because I knew that the past has made the present, and I wanted to see how the process works"—and to the urgent need to record this history before it was engulfed by the Third Reich.[8] Although West had chosen to write her history in the first person, she does this more to stress the importance of Yugoslavia than her own importance. She sees her role as preserver and witness, and not the central subject of her work. However, this self-anointed role bears several problematic consequences, which I will address toward the conclusion of this chapter.

Far more than just an autobiographical account or travelogue, the size, scope, and heterogeneity of *Black Lamb* make it difficult to define generically. As Carl Rollyson writes in his biography, West "interweaves characters, dramatic scenes, dialogue, description, reportage, autobiography, literary criticism, philosophy, theology, and feminism."[9] To this list we might add historiography, biography, botany, art criticism, fashion criticism, and food and wine criticism. Rather than listing genres, however, we might simply label *Black Lamb* a historical novel, one that fully exploits its own Bakhtinian possibilities. Whether it is a work of fiction or what Norman Mailer would later call the "nonfiction novel" is up to debate: there is certainly enough invented and fabricated material to qualify *Black Lamb* as a fictive text.[10] One fictive device West employs is the combination of her second and third trip to Yugoslavia into one. *Black Lamb* contains two instead of three journeys: the central trip that West describes as the present time of the novel, and the first journey, which she took by herself and which she often refers to as a memory.

Black Lamb begins in Croatia and ends in Montenegro. Each region of Yugoslavia is given one chapter, often connected to the next by sections titled "Road." West describes what she sees—people, towns, churches, works of art, and landscapes—and also what she hears from the region's diverse array of inhabitants, who want to talk mostly about the past that they have kept alive in their collective memories. West recounts their stories, both personal and historical, and adds to them her own findings in historical texts and accounts (many included in her bibliography at the end of the volume). Out of her massive amount of data, West had to construct a cohesive narrative, and so she let her itinerary decide the form of her text, although since she was combining various trips she felt free to invent chronologies and sequences. Ford's *Provence* and *Great Trade Route* may have been models, but West had already explored the possibilities of modernist narrative with her essay "Every Third Thought . . ." (1929), a highly interiorized journey through Dijon and Tournus. *Black Lamb* is such a piece writ large; Vesna Goldsworthy notes that it

> marks a shift from "realism" to "modernism" in travel writing. By the time it came to be written, a much wider range of factual material about the Balkans—and other regions of the world—was available. The old remit of the travel writer had been assumed by academics and journalists. West's magnum opus therefore plays a major part in the move to establish a new role for travel writing in a more specialized and compartmentalized world.[11]

West's work occupies a prominent place in the history of the travelogue, in the history of histories of the Balkans, and, I will argue, needs to be regarded as a—if not the—masterpiece of modernist historical narrative. But West's reengagement with literary modernism is never for the sake of style or form alone: her project takes on a sense of urgency because of what the war might usher in (or, from the perspective of West's publication of the text in 1941, had already ushered in). And while she is turning to the modernist experiments for aesthetic models, she simultaneously acknowledges the role that the modern world is playing in the formation of her own form of historiography. West argues that modern, populist authoritarianism destroys whole peoples, and "by that same act it would destroy the political and economic centres of ancient states with pasts that told a long continuous story."[12] By this point in the book, West had spent over a thousand pages painstakingly describing just how rich a "long continuous story" can be told by art, place, and collective memory. Her work is a last-ditch effort to remember what the Nazis will try to make the world forget about the Balkans.

As many critics have noted, *Black Lamb* also draws the reader to the treatment of women, both in the societies she encounters and the histories she consults. West is often enraged by the status of women in Yugoslavia, and brings her decades of immersion in British feminism to bear on what she encounters on her journey.[13] She simultaneously notes the absence of women in most histories, not just in those about the Balkans: "It has always interested me to know what happens after the great moments in history to the women associated by natural ties to the actors. . . . These things are never told."[14] We can see this clearly in her writings on Gibbon, another English historian writing about foreign empires, who appropriately leads off her bibliography at the end of her narrative.[15] Like Gibbon, West is drawn to empires in decay, and she is fascinated—and repulsed—by the "monstrous frailty of empire," any trace of the Turkish or Hungarian influence which at one time or another laid claims to various parts of the Balkans.[16] (West is also quietly preoccupied with her own empire, on the brink of annihilation, as I will soon argue.) In a wartime article for *Vogue*, "What Gibbon Left Out," West imagines meeting Gibbon and what she would say to him. First she gently berates him for leaving out the daily experiences of history:

> Oh, Mr. Gibbon . . . what a lot you left out! You thought to describe the wars of the world and the sufferings they brought, but you are far from rendering an account of them. You tell of the great catastrophes, how great conflicts swung back and forth across Europe through the years. But you do not tell of the little things that fill the days with bitterness. You describe the structure of politics; you omit the substance.[17]

She then accuses him of ignoring the role and experiences of women throughout history: "you never said a word about them, Mr. Gibbon."[18] As Bonnie Kime Scott notes of *Black Lamb*, "More often than not, the stranger elevated to apocalyptic importance is poor or female; in these selections, West shifts the accent of history."[19] Similarly, Janet Montefiore writes that "[h]er book thus deliberately writes back into history the lives and experiences of women, whom she avoids reducing to signifiers because she never forgets their actual, if unknowable, lives and experiences."[20] Like Woolf, and the feminist histories to come in the twentieth century, West attempts to retell the story of European civilization, this time including the role played by women and other marginalized groups.

Feminist revisionism is not the text's central project, however. *Black Lamb* lavishes more attention on male figures from history than female, as well as contemporary men she meets in her travels. We might see West's initial rebuke to Gibbon—that he leaves out "the little things"—as more informing of her work, as she writes in *Black Lamb* that "much of human activity goes unrecorded."[21] West believes the novelist's abilities to render the past are essential to historiography. Her work is so compelling, not only in how it captures the prewar anxiety of Europe, but also because of the narratological battle that is waged throughout the text that has drastic ideological ramifications for the ethical imperatives of feminism and Nazi resistance. *Black Lamb* vacillates between a recognition of what she calls "the impossibility of history"—the seemingly overwhelming difficulties faced by any writer trying to represent a place, a people, a time, a past—and, on the other hand, a passionate obligation to record what she sees and what she hears.[22] Bernard Schweizer notes that "West's worldview cannot help resonating with postmodern concerns about the provisional nature of knowledge and the contingency of dichotomies, while her activism constantly prompted her to formulate prescriptive principles that had a direct bearing on controversial moral, political, and social realities."[23] Although she knows she will fail, she is determined to fail better. She laments, "I understand nothing, nothing at all," but never abandons her gargantuan project.[24] My reading of *Black Lamb and Grey Falcon* will trace the ways in which this battle is fought through her text, as it is her modernist means of resisting the Nazi menace. West explores the ramifications of memory and forgetting for history, how collective memories are kept alive, and how the Third Reich possessed the power to destroy them. Her response to these insights was a struggle to harness the possibilities of narrative—especially in light of the experiments of the modernist novelists whom she had championed for three decades—not only to escape from epistemological and narratological crises, but to save Balkan history from fascist aggression.

Memory and Forgetting

Black Lamb's concern with memory, both individual and cultural, continues the themes of *The Return of the Soldier*, which also dramatized the confluence of subjective and historical memory.[25] On an individual level, it is not only that West is constructing her narrative out of her own personal memories of her trip, but also that she is writing her narrative about her second and third trips to the region, with descriptions of her first 1936 trip included as memories within the 1937 travelogue. Thus the "West" of 1937 remembers 1936, but this is all being constructed by the "West" of 1941. Montefiore notes that "[a]s well as condensing the results of three journeys in successive years into the story of her 1937 visit, she gives herself an implausibly perfect recall of long conversations, which demand almost as great a suspension of disbelief as that required by Nelly Dean, the narrator of *Wuthering Heights*."[26] No matter how powerful West's memory may have been, the size and scope of her work make us question the degree of accuracy of any of her depictions, especially of the long stretches of dialogue that are so long and mannered. (As we have seen, this was a fault that West had found in Ford.) We are reminded of Thucydides, as Montefiore notes: "Their effect is rather like that of debates in Thucydides' *History of the Peloponnesian War*, also loosely based on real speeches, in which the historic actors articulate issues of the conflict with far more self-awareness and clarity than the originals could possibly have done in real life."[27] The reliability of the text is thus a constructed pose, although this very dynamic is one of the central themes of *Black Lamb*.

If the West of 1941 may have lost certain memories to the four subsequent years, she has also acquired many more that cast a shadow over her entire work. West as author, writing in 1941, knows not only that Germany has advanced on and dismantled Yugoslavia, partitioning it between the Axis powers, but also that it is waging war against Great Britain. She writes phrases heavy with dramatic irony into the "characters" of the work, to convey the sense of urgency and anxiety that was so palpable before the war. As Constantine, their friend and guide, darkly intuits, Albania "'will be as a pistol pointed at Yugoslavia.' He shuddered violently and said, '*Ils avancent toujours.*'"[28] *Black Lamb* is one of many historical works to employ this dramatic historical irony, as her first, 1941 readership would have been a nation under attack, and Yugoslavia already completely overrun—no longer even a nation. These two different chronological frameworks are both present in the text, as the narrator of the Epilogue possesses such knowledge, while the "character" of West throughout most of the book does not. Occasionally, the later West intervenes, as when the narrative states of the annexing of Croatia by Hungary that "I do not know of any nastier act than this in history"; her footnote to this line reads, "It must be remembered that this journal was written in 1937."[29] Debra Rae Cohen writes of this method: "West the historian, in other words, is here interrogating West the historical subject; the splitting of the subject foregrounds her manipulations of public and private discourses, and thus her construction of a compound authority."[30] The result is "a multiple 'I' that was both chronicler and subject, historian and housewife."[31] We proceed through the work in a double time frame, as from the opening page West's epigraph announces, "TO MY FRIENDS IN YUGOSLAVIA, WHO ARE NOW ALL DEAD OR ENSLAVED," which forces a double awareness on the reader and endows every scene and sentence with a second, darker meaning. We worry how each church or work of art she recorded fared during the fighting; every character we encounter we could imagine as perished or imprisoned soon after the book was begun.

To further complicate her chronology, the text often contrasts what the West of 1937 experiences with her earlier memories from her first trip: in Skopje in Macedonia, "the quarter was not so vivacious as I had remembered it on my last visit . . . before, these streets had been like a scene in an operetta."[32] Here she asserts that her memory is not reliable, potentially

undercutting her entire project, which is a reconstruction of what she remembers from her journey. Although much of *Black Lamb* is informed by
archival research that West conducted back in England, most key insights
and moments come from her firsthand experience with the people, landscapes, and art of the region. Memory plays such an important role in this
act of witnessing, but West continually doubts her own mnemonic capaci-
ties. Even when she can rely on her memory—"When we came to Neresi it
was as I had remembered it"—she cannot solve the problem of the memories of others that she is trying to record.[33] All human memory is faulty to
some degree, and hampers any historical investigation, but West is more
alarmed by the role that national cultures play in shaping, and sometimes
distorting, collective accounts of the past.[34] In Bosnia they encounter the
sister of Nedyelyko Chabrinovitch, the young Serbian who participated in
the first, failed assassination attempt at Franz Ferdinand. West records the
sister's account for several pages, but the next morning she and her husband
rethink her story and believe that she has given most of it inaccurately. Although they "do not think that she could have lied even if she had wanted
to do so," it is clear that large segments of her story must be fabricated, and
West concludes that "this girl was talking under the influence of a memory
so intense that it as acting on her like a hypnotic drug."[35] Note how West
does not accuse her of suffering from not enough memory, but of *too much*:
like Christopher Baldry, the overload of historical memories, mostly violent, threaten to warp the psyche's ability to faithfully record the past. In the
case of Baldry, this disability "spoke" and witnessed what he had been
through, finding a means to depict an experience that was beyond language,
but in the Balkans, West has a more difficult time reconstructing the histories from her subjects—she is markedly less patient with trauma and its
need to be deciphered. She despairs that she may never be able to fully recover what has already been lost to time. Regarding the assassination of
Ferdinand, she writes, "Leaning from the balcony, I said, 'I shall never be
able to understand how it happened.' It is not that there are too few facts
available, but that there are too many."[36] Like Chabrinovitch's sister, the
"Rebecca West" character herself is suffering from too much memory.

One aspect of memory that *Black Lamb* continually probes is its potential
to be simultaneously fragile and indestructible. Memories are continually
vanishing or corrupted by both time and cultural forces, but often memory
appears immune to time or change. For example, their companion and guide
Constantine recalls his youth as a student in Paris, studying under Henri
Bergson: "That happened to me, nothing can take it away from me. I am a
poor man, I have many enemies, but I was in Paris at that time, which was an
impossible glory, and so Bergson did to me."[37] Any memory of the great philosopher of memory is particularly meta, and West may be using this scene to
show the presence of the past via memories. At the same time, what compels

the need for West's text is the fragility of memory, its ability to be passed over as it becomes past. Were memories so resilient, she would not feel the dread of the approaching German forces so powerfully. West cannot trust the past to the future. She thus constantly doubts the ability of language and narrative to faithfully record the life, culture, and history of Yugoslavia. She wants to record her impressions, but often doubts them; she wants to record the memories of the inhabitants, but she receives them with skepticism and embeds them in multiple layers of uncertainty and subjectivity; she wants to weave these all together into a narrative, while fully aware of the problems such a project entails—as we shall see, she admits that her work might be taken as "nonsense."[38]

History's Impossibilities

A theme to which West continually returns is history's impossibility: "I wondered more and more at the impossibility of learning the truth";[39] "Here is, indeed, another proof of the impossibility of history."[40] West's central metaphor for these impossibilities is the damage of the embroidered cloth that she brings back from Bosnia. The cloth is hand-woven by Bosnian women in Yezero using techniques handed down through several centuries. West later encounters more women embroidering, this time in Macedonia, and meditates on the role that "their embroideries play in the preservation of their ancient culture."[41] She is drawn to these moments where history is conveyed through means other than literary narrative (and we shall see that this renders the need for her own project). West buys some items that, she is told, were embroidered in the nineteenth century. She responds, "How maddening that a person like that should have been swept away by time . . . but her work I shall save, I shall take that home and show it to people, and they will all like it, and I will leave it in my will to someone who will like it, and so it will be rescued from the past."[42] Her plan is to bring back several specimens of clothing to show to her fellow English how glorious a history and culture Bosnia possesses, so the analogy with her own written work should be clear. But Constantine voices doubt: "Of that you cannot be sure . . . the past takes enormous mouthfuls," and at this point in her work we already possess the knowledge, given to us in her Prologue, that the clothes end up destroyed by overzealous Greek washerwomen en route back to England.[43] The fate of the cloths wracks West with guilt: "I had not properly protected the work of these women which should have been kept as a testimony."[44] Again there is an analogy with *Black Lamb*, itself a testimony to Yugoslavia. The crisis here is one of preservation: Will her written work meet the same fate as the Macedonian cloth? Will it, too, not survive the journey into England and into narrative? The text faces not a physical challenge, but rather an epistemological and narratological one: Has it successfully transmitted the testimony and historical traces from the oral and material forms of Balkan culture into English literary discourse?

The metaphor of the cloth is even richer than such an initial interpretation may suggest, because the cloth dramatizes the difficulty of transforming a physical landscape, where West can see what "history meant in flesh and blood," into a textual narrative.[45] Although West relies heavily on the written narrative histories that she lists in her bibliography, she is always suspicious of their reportings. Regarding Serbia's role in the killing of Franz Ferdinand, she writes,

> There is no hypothesis that fits these facts into a recognizable pattern. . . . This is simply guess-work. . . . This makes the mystery more impenetrable by historic method. . . . Among the purple irises I thought of the long shelves of university libraries, their striation under lofty vaults, the reflected light that shines from historians' spectacles, and I laughed.[46]

West is often pessimistic regarding this entire process, as when she refers to bringing the embroideries back to England:

> Here is, indeed, another proof of the impossibility of history. There cannot be taken an inventory of time's contents when some among the most precious are locked away in inaccessible parts and lose their essence when they are moved to any place where they are likely to be examined carefully, when their owners are ignorant of parts of their nature and keep secret such knowledge of them as they have.[47]

West's anxiety over the transference of the items back home—which prove to be justified—also acts as a self-critique embedded in *Black Lamb* regarding its ability to render the "essence" of the Balkans and its history. If West fails, Balkan history keeps its "secret." As in the contemporary debate over the Holocaust Museum, West recognizes the problematics of selection and documentation, as objects or texts dislocated from their original contexts lose their original meaning, and possibly acquire new ones. Like Conrad and Ford, West is skeptical regarding the ability of language and narrative to convey human experience, as essences remain forever out of reach of representation—as both Marlow and West phrase it, such conveyance is "impossible."

West also echoes Marlow when she writes that "[t]he thing I wanted to tell [my husband] could not be told, however, because it was manifold and nothing like what one is accustomed to communicate by words."[48] *Black Lamb* is driven through by a double sense of anxiety, first over the impending war and Nazi conquest, and second regarding West's difficulties in saving Balkan culture from the coming catastrophe by means of language that never seems up to the task of witness or historical narrative. She continually frets that history remains out of the grasp of her means of representation: "Thus is the face of history thickly veiled"[49]; a political murder is "mysterious as history is mysterious"[50]; and "History, it appeared, could be like the delirium of a madman, at once meaningless and yet charged with a dreadful meaning."[51] History resembles what the African jungle was for Marlow, a presence both dreadful and nebulous, powerful and imprecise. (And in both cases we can observe the tendency of Western Europe to see the rest of the world as unknowable.) West employs every narrative technique that she has at her disposal: storytelling, biography, landscape description, art criticism, dialogue; she knows that her tools are limited, "for art is a most uncertain instrument. In writing this book I have been struck again and again by the refusal of destiny to let man see what is happening to him, its mean delight in strewing his path with red herrings."[52] Note the visual nature of this construction: as in Conrad and Ford, imagery is deceptive and a poor guide through the past, and vision is not powerful enough to "see" history in its entirety. West dramatizes this when she finds a sculpture in Bosnia inscrutable, and she concludes that "the best way to see sculpture is not with the eyes but with the finger-tips."[53] But while she may come closer to understanding this sculpture through the sense of touch, she must admit defeat: "My finger-tips could not find the answer. . . . The imagination came to a dead stop."

Nonsense and Supersense

West's responses to these challenges are, first, a frank recognition of ignorance and inability, the Socratic wisdom of knowing that which you do not know:

> It is not pleasant to admit that we know almost nothing, so little that, for lack of knowledge, our actions are wild and foolish. It is not pleasant to be bound to the task of learning all our days, to be under the obligation to go on learning even though it involves making acquaintance with pain, although we know that we must die still in ignorance. To do these things it is necessary to have faith in what is entirely hidden and unknown.[54]

West notes that "numberless people in Great Britain" suffer from this dread of ignorance and respond with bigotry and violence. In contrast, she later notes of the Macedonian peasantry that when they

> loved or sang or worshipped God or watched their sheep, they brought to the business in hand poetic minds that would not believe in appearances and probed them for reality, that possessed as a birthright that quality which Keats believed to be above all others in forming a "Man of Achievement, especially in Literature, and which Shakespeare possessed so enormously."

"Negative Capability," he called it, and it made a man "capable of being in uncertainties, doubts, without any irritable reaching after fact and reason."[55]

West values a distrust of the visible world. This skepticism enables the peasants to "probe" the world for essences, but emerges only because of their "Negative Capability," which allows them a state of uncertainty without undue anxiety or despair. The appeal of this concept for West should be clear, as the quality of Negative Capability would allow her to continue with her ambitious project, even given all the qualifications and objections she raises as self-critique. Keats's words, and the peasants' experience, encourage her to "solve" the problems her narrative faces by writing through it. Her work's enormous length, as much as it is a challenge for the reader, is also the result of West fighting through the challenges she faced in composing it. West was particularly drawn to Keats's theory, because she invokes it again in her manuscript on Mexico, published posthumously as *Survivors in Mexico* (2003):

> We can never find out what the rights and wrongs of the matter really are, and Keats suggests in one of his letters that true greatness consists in getting on with one's work without unduly fretting at this lack of a balance sheet. Negative Capability he called it.[56]

She again brings up Keats in relation to the inscrutability of history—in this case regarding Spain's conquest of Mexico and the role of religion in imperialism—as a means of working through the inescapable problematics of history and knowledge.

But Negative Capability can only take one so far. For West, finding a working solution to the epistemological challenge of history does not necessarily mitigate the narratological or representational ones. Even when West does feel in confident possession of knowledge, as when she desires to convey her experience to her husband, she feels that she lacks the means to represent or depict it. Schweizer analyzes this dynamic in *Black Lamb* and asks if, because of these concerns and anxieties, West is a true precursor of postmodern historiography: "West's proleptic sensibility extends to a kind of protodeconstruction, prefiguring Derrida; it adumbrates a critique of master historical narratives, anticipating Lyotard; and it fosters an aesthetic practice of process."[57] But although she radically questions knowledge and narrative, in a manner that might seem akin to the postmodern, Schweizer argues that

> she looked at these phenomena of chaos, indeterminacy, and confusion much like Montaigne did some four hundred years earlier, seeking solutions to these problems by incessant self-inspection, by tireless inquiry, and by profound speculations about the human condition—approaches that preclude the postmodern decentering of the subject and the rejection of foundational knowledge.[58]

Schweizer judiciously warns against too-eager enlistments of West into a postmodern sensibility because of her commitment to the humanist tradition.[59] However, the choice between humanism and postmodernity ellipses the modernist period and its unique contribution to historical thought. We should be more inclined to see the first half of the twentieth century in its own right, not simply as a transition period for historiography between humanism and postmodern skepticism.[60] Modernism should take its rightful place in the history of histories, and we may appreciate West's "solution" to the problems she encountered in her project. She hints at her method when she suggests that there are different modes of representation: "One can shout at the top of one's voice the information that the 11.15 for Brighton leaves from platform 6, but subtler news has to be whispered, for the reason that to drag knowledge of reality over the threshold of consciousness is an exhausting task, whether it is performed by art or by experience."[61] The common language of travelogues or the standard language of orthodox history would only carry her project so far, for it is the fragility of memory itself, and the nontextual nature of Balkan histories—at least in West's eyes—that give rise to the urgency of the text's creation.

West highlights the lack of adequate historiography of the region because of its oral and folk nature: "The memory of the Nemanyas and their wealth and culture was kept alive among the peasants, partly by the Orthodox Church, which very properly never ceased to remind them that they had once formed a free and Christian state, and also by the national ballads."[62] West observes how many young men "know thousands of lines of folk-poetry about the defeat of the Serbs at Kossovo, and it gives an impression of a great civilization. I know that they tested the patients in the Serbian military hospitals during the war to see how many knew it, and it was something like ninety per cent."[63] In Macedonia she encounters a priest who hears a boy reciting poetry, and the priest exclaims "Verses, tut, tut! It's all right to make up a song in one's head; but to write it down, you can't tell me that's not a waste of time," voicing the Balkan aversion to written, recorded history.[64]

This depiction of Yugoslavia as primarily oral compels West toward some problematic conclusions. She describes how the women who embroider clothes that carry their history within them "are of course not fully conscious of the part their embroideries play in the preservation of their ancient culture."[65] In moments like these, West's ethnocentrism ascribes self-consciousness and textual sophistication to Britain or Western Europe and withholds it from Yugoslavia. She continues, "when an Englishwoman plays a sonata by Purcell she is not likely to feel that she is maintaining English musical tradition," which might suggest an equal scrutiny of Western culture, but usually the text sets up the literary West/West against the oral East. Sometimes this dichotomy is used as a structure with which to critique her own society: she describes a "therapeutic threat in the Western incapacity for appreciating a culture which is not dominated by literature" and writes that "most men who had been brought up within the orbit of Belgrade and Zagreb [urban, cosmopolitan centers] would be infected with Western ideas regarding the importance of material possessions and a written culture."[66] The seemingly critical notion that the West "infects" the Balkans with its need for writing should not distract us from the fact that this suggests a lack of literary ability on the part of Yugoslavia: from her viewpoint, telling history through oral song or architecture is not simply a matter of generic choice. Ironically, if unconsciously, West depicts many moments when she encounters Yugoslavians who want to talk about German, English, and Russian literature, and who remark upon their own literature, which West did not have the linguistic skills to appreciate. (Her French, her husband's German, and Constantine's Serbo-Croat were how she communicated with Yugoslavs she met on her trip.) When she meets a Croat in thrall to Goethe, West tells her not to be ashamed of being a Slav, but does not try to redirect her to any Balkan literature. Were figures like this Croatian woman just "infected" citizens, or examples that disprove West's generalization about literacy in Balkan culture? But more important, West's very act of writing *Black Lamb and Grey Falcon*, by its own logic, should itself be an unwanted intrusion or infection of Western influence, thus canceling out any restorative effect of her project, which at its heart argues that she will speak for those who cannot.

From West's perspective, however, her work is her way of fighting the Nazi threat and salvaging countless stories and cultural concepts from the impending struggle. Her desire to speak "for" Yugoslavia is less Orientalist than interventionist (which carries with it a whole different set of problems, as I will explore later). She stresses the particularities of Western and Yugoslavian historiography and how the latter puts itself at risk by being so enmeshed in the people and places of the Balkans. It is not that English literary narrative history is a *higher* form of historiography than a Serbian church or a Macedonian folk ballad—West's modernist text is too aware of the problems and pitfalls of any narrative that tries to represent the past, and we have seen her scorn at professional historians—but rather that the depositories of Balkan history and collective memory are physical objects: churches, paintings, landscapes, and ultimately the people of the region. According to West, linguistic narratives of the Balkans, both those told by Slavs and foreigners alike, have never been adequate to the past, as she dramatizes in Macedonia:

> The old man stood resting on his scythe. He was proud that we had come to see the palace. It had belonged to Avzi Pasha, he said, and he watched for our faces to lighten. Avzi Pasha, he repeated. But nobody knows anything of him today for there are fewer archives here than there were in Bosnia . . . no clue except some crumpled pieces of paper.[67]

This lack of historical narratives of the Yugoslav past is compensated via the present physicality of Balkan history. Unlike many Orientalizing travelogues, *Black Lamb* always views buildings and landscapes as historical traces: in a typical gesture, West writes of a town square in Dubrovnik, "To the left of the crowd is the Custom House and Mint, in which the history of their forebears for three centuries is written in three stories."[68] Observing a statue in Serbia, she writes that history is "told by the splendid rings on the Tsar Lazar's black and leather hands" and that "[i]t is written here that the lot of man is pitiful."[69] Note West's verbs: it is the physical objects themselves who are narrating Yugoslavia's past.

West most aggressively highlights the physical nature of Balkan histories when she visits the Grachanitsa monastery in Old Serbia (modern-day Kosovo): "It happens that there stands on the plain of Kossovo, some miles south of the actual battle-field, a building which demonstrates what sort of civilization fell with the Serbs. It proves it as no nationalist rhetoric could hope to do."[70] Centuries of Serbian nationalist poetry had struggled to maintain a collective memory of the resistance to the Turkish incursions onto the peninsula, but Turkish rule has obliterated much of Serbia's history: "Our [the West's] forms of historic tragedy have blotted a paragraph here and there, but they have rarely torn out the leaves of a whole volume, letting only a coloured frontispiece remain to tease us. Of Grachanitsa, however, catastrophe has left us nothing but Grachanitsa."[71] The linguistic narratives that were supposed to commemorate Serbia's role in defending Europe from invasion have not lived up to the task of memory. The actual monastery, however, is itself a historical narrative for West, and not just a trace: after exploring Serbia's history, she writes, "All this story is implicit in Grachanitsa, in the lavished treasure of its colours and the vigorous fertility of its form";[72] "Grachanitsa speaks first of all regarding the union of church and state" and "[i]n the church the ardour of these young men becomes comprehensible."[73] Like the Parisian arcades that drew Walter Benjamin, Grachanitsa narrates a history left unspoken in the linguistic registers of Yugoslavia.

Physical traces like the Grachanitsa monastery are vulnerable in a way that a textual history is not. After West discovers some faint traces of the glory of the Bosnian Empire, she asks what happened to its collective memory. It is all gone: "Conquest can swallow all. The Turks consumed Bosnia."[74] Germany will be next to "consume" the region, and just as Constantine warned that "the past takes enormous mouthfuls," Germany will consume the past itself. The visceral and immediate nature of West's prose in describing people and places stress their being in the world, their solidity, but this is what is most at risk as Germany advances, and one of the most anguishing moments in *Black Lamb* comes mere pages before the end, as she relates the first days of the Nazi invasion: "At dawn on April the sixth German planes raided Belgrade and continued the attack for four days. . . . Eight hundred planes flew low over the city and methodically destroyed the Palace, the university, the hospitals, the churches, the schools, and most of the dwelling-houses."[75] The physical depositories of history, the ones she so attentively described and inventoried in her text, were being obliterated while she completed that same work.

Modernism at War

West uses her own failings of memory to signal the weakness of nontextual memories and histories:

> I saw the blue lake of Ochrid, the mosques of Sarajevo, the walled town of Korchula, and it appeared possible that I was unable to find words for what I wanted to say because it was not true. I am never sure of the reality of what I see, if I have seen it only once; I know that until it has firmly established its objective existence by impressing my senses and my memory, I am capable of conscripting it into the service of a private dream.[76]

Here West stages several of her challenges: the problems of language, the problems of memory. But we can also detect her faith in the physical traces of Balkan history, which leads her to rely on the faulty mechanisms of language and memory to catalogue Yugoslavia. She wrote to a friend that the work was an "inventory of a country down to its last vest-button, in a form insane from any ordinary artistic or commercial point of view."[77] Textual narratives may be problematic and to a degree untrustworthy, but they are also portable and easily reproduced, more deftly eluding the long arm of Nazi intelligence. Thus for West written narrative is the only means to keep Balkan memory alive, to capture the "subtler" aspects of history and culture. Not only is West struggling with the impossible and necessary nature of history, she is also aware of the paradox of employing methods that highlight contingency and unreliability while simultaneously striving to have her work make a real and immediate impact among British and American public opinion. To accomplish the seemingly impossible, she would need recourse to aesthetic techniques pioneered by the literary models of her youth, especially those who explored the relationships between memory and narrative.

Proust is the model whose influence some critics have traced, as Montefiore has convincingly demonstrated:

> Such layering of memory through memory recalls Proust, a writer whose work Rebecca West regarded as central to Modernism. Indeed the Prologue and its relationship to the great history that follows it bear a marked likeness to the "*Ouverture*" of *À La Recherche du Temps Perdu*. In both works, an immensely long narrative, loosely based on the author's life, begins with the mediations of a solitary, wakeful narrator at midnight. . . .

And, as in Proust's novel, the narrative starts by moving backwards into scenes from the past, introducing some key figures . . . the Prologue ends with the narrator and reader about to explore the huge undiscovered regions that lie beyond its initial vivid but limited memories. This "looping" of the narrative backwards from the history of the writer's self into the history of a nation, and forward again to her consciousness of the "present," prefigures the method of the whole book.[78]

If we see the character of Rebecca West in *Black Lamb* analogously to Proust's narrator, we notice that both works begin at a later date than most of the action of the text, and on one level the story being told is how the character ends up being the character we are introduced to on the first page.[79] The difference with Proust is one of scope, for West sees herself, representing Western Europe, as suffering from a form of cultural and collective amnesia regarding the Balkans, and must work to unearth those lost memories, at the same time that she is trying to preserve memories that will soon be wiped out by the Nazis. Such a narratological structure also evokes Dante's *Divine Comedy*, which traces how the narrator Dante becomes Dante the author. Like *The Inferno*, *Black Lamb* relates stories and life histories that are in peril of being lost.

Note how West's treatment of memory shifts from *The Return of the Soldier*—also written in the midst of a world war, and also powerful because of the absent presence of war—to the post-Proust *Black Lamb*.[80] Whereas in her earlier novel trauma was a means to depict the undepictable, her later work is in search of lost time in order to avoid trauma and amnesia at all costs. To be sure, West's political compass has altered as well: while she may have given strong support to England in the First World War, in 1941 she was more at the forefront of the war effort, and it may be for this reason that forgetting is so anathema to the sensibilities of the later work. *The Return of the Soldier*, despite facing the horrors of the war, still maintains a measured tone, forgoing impassioned political rhetoric. But the stakes of the Second World War (and possibly the shifting of the Western front from France to London itself) prohibits West from finding any redemptive value in the loss of memory. The text scorns the Benjaminian nicety of forgetting in order for unearthed memories to have such a powerful impact. Western Europe's amnesia is simply and unredeemably regrettable, as is the Balkan cultural amnesia that the Nazis will force upon the region.

While West may fear forgetting, this does not spur her to a willed ignorance of the workings of memory. On the contrary, West has launched, not just a momentous effort at cultural preservation, but also a self-conscious meditation on what a modernist history, informed by contingent and problematic memories, would look like. *Black Lamb and Grey Falcon* deserves to be read as such, and not simply as a work of modernist travel writing. Its participation in experimental modernism becomes apparent when we choose to see it as a narrative of histories: fragmented, highly subjectivized, expressing multiple points of view, and preoccupied with its own form.[81] Its initial epigraphs—one Greek quote, one quote by Shakespeare, and another by Jean Cocteau in French—might recall the opening multilingual salvoes of *The Waste Land*. West knows that her work is a new way of writing travel and history; when she writes that "[a]rt cannot talk plain sense, it must sometimes speak what sounds at first like nonsense, though it is actually supersense" she could be describing any work of modernism, not just her own project.[82] *Black Lamb* refuses to "talk plain sense" and instead draws upon the "insane" revolutions in narration ushered in by the modernist decades. Much like another epic work of modernist history, Pound's *Cantos*, *Black Lamb* employs an aesthetic of both fragmentation and encyclopedic inclusion. As I have argued, however, what distinguishes the two texts is the function of narrative, which in the 1930s Pound was radically deprioritizing. Part of the fascination of *Black Lamb*, by contrast, is to see how far West can stretch the limits of narrative.

West, in her letters, voices an anxiety regarding her radical form and how it will fare as an intervention against Hitler, and the text itself anticipates the challenging ways in which it will be received.[83] *Black Lamb*'s page count is indeed "insane," and even within the text she questions the motives of "this book, which hardly anyone will read by reason of its length."[84] West even stages a joke at her own expense by complaining of the heft of Robert Adams's book of engravings of Roman architecture. The book was left at home as "it weights just over a stone"; West notes that "we couldn't have carried anything so heavy as that in the streets," but her husband suggests that "we could have hired a wheelbarrow and pushed it about from point to point." West objects, "But people would have thought we were mad!"[85] West slyly calls into question the sanity of both the writer and reader of *Black Lamb*.

West's work continually runs the risk of undercutting its own authority, as what is compelling about unreliability in texts like *The Good Soldier*, *The Great Gatsby*, or *The Sound and the Fury* become potentially self-debilitating in a work aimed at geopolitical intervention, not narrative experimentation. Another source of anxiety for West was that she was drawing upon an experimental literary culture whose works generally did not reach a broader audience (a challenge shared by Virginia Woolf, who was simultaneously writing *Three Guineas* in response to fascism in Spain—although Woolf's pacifism in that text is precisely West's target in *Black Lamb*). West's very efforts, in her twenties and thirties criticism, in championing modernist writers was necessary because of their lack of commercial or popular success. She must have been aware, then, of the difficulty of using some of their radicalizations in a work designed for a broader readership. Literary modernism has never been accused of a lack of ambition, but we should appreciate the scope of the project to which West employs some of its techniques. It would not be hyperbole to summarize her goals as nothing less than the preservation of two millennia of cultural memories of an entire multi-nation; the galvanization of the British and American armies into war; and an intervention against the biggest threat to European civilization the world had ever seen. The result is the fascinating transference of literary techniques—that for the most part emerged through small circles in London and Paris, and were beginning to find a safe home in academia—onto a much broader stage.

One of these techniques was the text's radical nonlinearity, with 1937 as its "present tense" and constant Fordian time-shifts back into the past, as in this typical passage:

> The human animal is not competent. That is the meaning of the naked Dalmatian hills. For once they were clothed with woods. These the earliest inhabitants of Dalmatia, the Illyrians and Romans, axed with an innocent carelessness; and the first Slav settlers were reckless too, for they came from the inexhaustible primeval forest of the Balkan Peninsula. Then for three hundred years, from about the time of the Norman Conquest to 1420, the Hungarians struggled with the Venetians for the mastery of this coast, and the nations got no further with their husbandry. Finally the Venetian Republic established its claim, and thereafter showed the carelessness that egoistic people show in dealing with other people's property.[86]

Often, as in this scene, West begins in the present tense—"that *is* the meaning of the naked Dalmatian hills"—and then begins her shift backward in time—"*For once they were* clothed with woods." Then she will tell the story from that point up until the present, bringing the story up to date. This is partly her method to show how "the past has made the present," but also a recognition that a linear chronology would never capture the complexity and richness of Balkan life and history, and that every movement forward in space necessitates a complex journey through time.[87] For example, in her chapter "Rab," a town on the Dalmatian coast, the years through which her narrative passes are 1937, 305, c. 650, 1919, 1937, 1757, 1937, 305, c. 250, 305, 316, c. 450, 480, and finally back to 1937.[88] With her "plot" that constantly moves backward and forward in time, West dramatizes one of her central themes, which is about the radical presence of the past, as memories, either personal or historical, live on past their immediate existence and can have powerful effects on the present: "I was obliged to write a long and complicated history, and to swell that with an account of myself and the people who went with me on my travels, since it was my aim to show the past side by side with the present it created."[89] And while West argued that Macedonia was "the bridge between our age and the past," the complex narrative framework also points, anxiously, to the years to come: West's husband says to her, "No wonder that when you came to Macedonia you were fascinated. You were looking in the magic

crystal and seeing our future."[90] The "future" of the 1937 character of West
was the Nazi rule of 1941.

Black Lamb embeds histories in multiple layers of frames and metacom-
mentaries. Each historical digression is a branch, not just of West's itinerary,
but also of the larger frame of the West of 1941 reconstructing her memories
of receiving the collective memories of Yugoslavia. The text forces us to see
language as not directly depicting memories of the past but rather
re-representing them. For example, while in Bosnia, West recounts the life
and death of Franz Ferdinand. His mini-biography occupies about 30 pages.
But by the end of the recounting, in the chapter entitled "Sarajevo VI," it
begins not with West's narrative voice but rather that of Constantine: "'Do
you see,' said Constantine, 'the last folly of these idiots?' There is a raw edge to
the ends of the bridge, an unhemmed look to the masonry on both sides of the
road."[91] After the long section on Ferdinand, this passage is almost like
waking from a dream, as we are brought back into what we might think of as
the "present tense" of West's narrative (if we accept the present as 1937 instead
of 1941). We might see it as akin to the few moments in *Heart of Darkness*
when Marlow gets interrupted by the first narrator and we are summoned
back to the sailing yacht on the Thames away from Marlow's steamship in
Africa. Constantine's words serve as a reminder that what we have just read
about Ferdinand is partly informed by *his* own knowledge of Balkan history,
and that West's narrative was not giving us unmediated access to the past,
even though that is most likely how we experienced it as readers. To be sure,
West had done research beyond just conversations with Constantine that
would have gone into the Ferdinand biography sections, but on the level of
narrative, Constantine's words highlight the fact that West is re-presenting
his words for the reader, that her mini-biography was a constructed effort
from multiple, and sometimes conflicting, sources.

A related instance is when Constantine relates growing up in Shabats. For
several pages West has him narrate this story, and each paragraph begins with
opening quotation marks, just as most paragraphs of *Heart of Darkness* do.[92]
The paragraph succeeding his story then reverts back to West as narrator: "I
slept, and woke up into a world of mirrors. They stretched away on each side
of the railway, the hedges breathing on them with their narrow images."[93]
Constantine's story, embedded in a double frame, followed immediately by
her sleep, mitigates against any sense of epistemological solidity that we might
hold with this text. Through much of the work we are akin to West as she
awakens on the train, watching as dreamscape and landscape interweave to
produce a protean, translucent world. This hardly seems to be a stable basis on
which to build an epic, interventionist work of history, but again it is the fragile and contingent to which West directs our gaze: if she were to employ the
stability of "realist" history writing, Yugoslavia would emerge as solid and en-
during, even in the face of invasion. The fragility of memory raises the stakes.

Dialogue becomes another site by which West explores the process of transforming history and human experience into narrative form. We must ask why West chose such a stylized, Thucydidian dialogic discourse for her work: Why abandon both the inherited mode of dialogue from Victorian realism, as well as the scientific skepticism of more modern historiography that would not trust such long and obviously fabricated pieces of dialogue? The length of spoken language marks West's sacrifice of what Barthes called the "reality effect" of realist discourse, the network of narratological signifiers that are marshaled to give the illusion of mimetically reproducing reality in language. But this rejection of the reality effect is not present at every level: note how, while describing a dinner in Croatia, she sets up a lengthy discussion, full of long speeches, with just those indices that Barthes sees as the essential components of realism:

> In a restaurant beside the Cathedral people awaited us for lunch: a poet and a playwright. . . . They looked at us absently . . . and, while ordering us an immense meal of which goose-liver and apple sauce were the centerpiece, threw over us the net of an extremely complicated conversation about literature.[94]

The goose-liver and apple sauce serve as markers of the setting, and also as signifiers of West's memory. If she can remember what they ate, we are lured into thinking, she can remember what they said. But when we get to the dialogue, the speeches are too long, and the reality effect fades. We are not allowed to believe that we are eavesdropping on a conversation, and instead are forced to notice how the entire scene is staged. On one level this is in keeping with the text's urge to see itself self-consciously, but it also exploits some of the dynamism of the form of the novel, which, as Bakhtin argued, is able to absorb many different discourses at once. So in the Croatian dinner scene West uses realist setting description alongside the oratorical discourse of antiquity. These narratological components, for Bakhtin, would act as "an active participant in social dialogue," and we come to see West's history as a discourse instead of a window onto the past.[95] West's dialogue allows her to stage this "social dialogue," and in many cases to leave the discussion unfinished, as she permits the various competing perspectives their say and does not always cast one viewpoint as triumphant over the others.

The Croatian dinner scene is central not just for its mixing of styles, but also for the specific content of the discussion. West, her husband, and Constantine are dining with a poet and a playwright, and the playwright declares his enthusiasm for Vaughan the Silurist, and states that "We think . . . that the greatest writers of recent times are Joseph Conrad, Maxim Gorki, and Jack London."[96] This does not go over well with West and her husband: "We blenched. We thought that in fact these people could have no taste, if they would think both Vaughan and Jack London great." But West will not dismiss

Conrad, and soon the conversation turns to his work. West's husband states: "Conrad has no sense of tragedy at all, but only of the inevitable, and for him the inevitable was never the fulfillment of a principle such as the Greek *ananke*, but a *déroulement* of the consequences of an event."[97] The example he uses to illustrate this idea is the story "The Duel" from *A Set of Six* (story written 1906, collection published 1921). West's oratorical style makes us doubt the accuracy of moments like these, so we will never be sure if "The Duel" really did come up in conversation in Croatia in 1937, but as a choice from the works of Conrad it seems apt—and even more conspicuous if chosen years after the actual conversation—as it shares many of the themes of West's project, and thus might be worth a consideration in relation to West's own fictional strategies.

"The Duel" is a historical novella, set in the end of the Napoleonic era, with specific references to major battles as a means of marking time and peppered with real historical figures (such as the Duke of Otranto, and, always slightly offstage, Napoleon himself), all of which combine to capture what Conrad described in his "Author's Note" to *A Set of Six* as the "Spirit of the Epoch." The story concerns two young officers in the army who fight a series of duels throughout their careers. The reason for the first duel is that Lieutenant D'Humbert is under orders to arrest Lieutenant Feraud for fighting a duel with someone else that morning. Feraud is interrupted by D'Humbert at a social call and is promptly outraged that he is disturbed while speaking to a woman of high society, and for the second time that day fights a duel, this time losing as D'Humbert wounds Feraud severely.

Their animosity does not end there, however, and against the backdrop of Napoleonic history—for Lukács in *The Historical Novel*, the moment when Europeans developed a sense of "the feeling first that there is such a thing as history"—these two characters have a history of their own, one that is known only to themselves and that proves a source of great mystery to society at large.[98] There was a "belief which was gaining ground outside that some very serious difference had arisen between these two young men, something serious enough to wear an air of mystery, some fact of the utmost gravity. . . . But what could it be?"[99] None of the other characters is ever able to penetrate to the origins of this conflict: "In mystery it began, in mystery it went on, in mystery it is to end."[100] Even the reader is left wondering at the motives for continual violence.

Lukács wrote that in this era, "[h]ere [were] the concrete possibilities for men to comprehend their own existence as something historically conditioned, for them to see in history something which deeply effects their daily lives and immediately concerns them."[101] D'Humbert and Feraud, witnesses to the rise of Napoleon, the troubled campaign in Spain, and most important, the disastrous assault on Russia, would surely have felt "such a thing as history" if Lukács was correct. But "The Duel" stages a microcosm of the problem of reconstructing "history" as "a history," of moving from referent to signifier. For the duelers, "[t]he feud was in the forgotten past."[102] Only their memories contained any traces of the history of their dispute, as others struggle in vain to uncover the truth of their conflict. This is because, as the narrator states, "truth . . . is not a beautiful shape living in a well, but a shy bird best caught by stratagem."[103] As in Marlow's stories, which are not nuts in a shell but rather mists that create halos around objects, this story concerns the difficulties of uncovering the truth about past events and the challenges in putting such events into representational language. To be sure, "The Duel" is not as marked by what we think of as a modernist style, as is *Heart of Darkness* or *Lord Jim*—it seems more in the twilight of the tradition of Turgenev than the birth of a movement that would include Joyce or Ford. But the meditation on history and the need for oblique means of representation—what Ford called a story that needs to be "thought round" and for West what will at first appear as "nonsense"—marks "The Duel" as one of Conrad's historical experiments.

Conrad wrote in his "Author's Note" to *A Set of Six* that "[t]he truth is that in my mind the story is nothing but a serious and even earnest attempt at a bit of historical fiction."[104] "The Duel" is a historical novella not only in that it takes place in the past with "real" historical indices and characters, but also because it is a rewrite of an actual event that originally appeared in French newspapers in the mid-nineteenth century. The story was soon picked up by other writers, the earliest by Alfred d'Almbert in *Physiologie du duel* (1853), and the first English account was published in *Harper's* in 1858. The last line of that article is "the story is done," but the telling of this story was just beginning.[105] By the time Conrad wrote "The Duel" there were already at least nine versions of the story in print. "The Duel" is thus a proliferative text, part of an endless textual chain of attempts to rewrite a story, the story being about the endless attempts of various characters to ascertain the true origin of the dueling.

Why did Conrad feel the need to throw his version of events onto the growing pile of texts regarding this duel? In the "Author's Note" he writes "that is exactly what I was trying to capture in my small net: the Spirit of the Epoch."[106] The Spirit of the Epoch, the truth of any given historical situation, is the "shy bird best caught by stratagem," and Conrad believed that his style was the "small net" by which truth could be contained and represented. Rebecca West was hunting with a larger net in the Balkans, but she may have brought up "The Duel" because it shares with her work a desire to depict not just the "Spirit" of a time or place but also to stage the difficulties inherent in such an undertaking.

However, the text is not uncritical of "The Duel," although once again, because of the dialogic nature of the scene, it is difficult to see where West the character stands in relation to Conrad and his work. Through indirect discourse we see West's husband argue that in "The Duel" "there is no factor involved that might come into operation, that indeed must come into operation so generally in human affairs that as we identify it we feel as if a new phase of our destiny has been revealed to us."[107] This is in line with West's husband's distinction between *ananke*—the personification of destiny—and *déroulement*, which is the mere workings or mechanisms of time and history. His critique, then, is that events in "The Duel" do not seem like necessary stages in a fated life, but as mere "nexts" as time moves forward.

But the debate takes a turn: "The playwright's wife said that this was true but irrelevant. To her there was a sense of tragedy implied in Conrad's work not by factual statement but by the rhythm of his language."[108] And as a poet, she may be more inclined to appreciate Conrad's form and be more attuned to the "stratagems" of literature necessary to capture any sort of truth. Furthermore, she suggests that form itself is sometimes a transmitter of what the work ostensibly cannot represent. Constantine then takes the debate in another direction entirely:

> He said the sense of inevitability in a work of art should be quite different from the scientific conception of causality, for if art were creative then each stage must be new, must have something over and above what was contained in the previous stages, and the connexion between the first and the last must be creative in the Bergsonian sense.[109]

As a former student of Bergson, Constantine's reference is specific. He is arguing for true Bergsonian creativity, as laid out in the latter's *The Creative Mind* (1923), in which Bergson writes, "we have so much trouble in distinguishing between an evolution and an unfurling, between the radically new and a rearrangement of the pre-existing, in fact, between creation and simple choice."[110] Constantine urges the group to consider creation as something "radically new" and not just what is "next" or what is the old rearranged in new patterns. Note first how West has more than just a passing familiarity with Bergson's ideas: she is not simply associating him with flux and *durée*, but brings up other aspects of Bergson's philosophy. Constantine's reference to Bergson could act as both critique and affirmation of Conrad's story. As critique, it might dismiss the story's sense of inevitability that precludes any sort of radically new creation. But Constantine may be bringing up Bergson to support the poet's claims that Conrad's gifts were not for plotting but rather rhythm and form, and that while "The Duel" may not have a solid "scientific conception of causality," it is an innovative way of writing fiction.

Eventually Constantine turns the conversation toward Tolstoy—that most famous historical novelist of the Napoleonic era—before they begin to discuss Balkan politics. What West's dialogic aesthetic allows are these rich but inconclusive moments where a debate or argument is staged but not resolved, all the while filtered through her admittedly faulty memory. And we should not assume that West's thoughts or opinions, as a character in *Black Lamb*, should be given priority over the others: as in Dante or Proust, the character is in the process of becoming the narrator, but the process is not yet complete. West as narrator possesses more knowledge and life experience than West the character, who is still making her way through an alien world.

The Horror of History

As in *Nostromo*, history in *Black Lamb* is both an oppressive force but also a necessary discourse that allows for textual continuity and the transmission of memory from psyche to narrative. For West, this continuity is an ethical imperative, driving her efforts to "save" the memory of the Balkans from impending destruction. Once more, we must rescue "history" from its own isomorphism if we are to understand *Black Lamb*'s relationship to either meaning of the term.

West often refers to history as a force, or some sort of propulsion from the past: the people of the town of Split are "a harried people of mixed race [that] have been forced by history to run for centuries through the walls and cellars and sewers of ruined palaces."[111] Of the separation of church and state in Macedonia, "[t]he renunciation was forced on it by the troubled character of Byzantine history."[112] A Croatian man they meet

> was simply the product of Dalmatian history; the conquest of Illyria by Rome, of Rome by the barbarians; then three hundred years of conflict between Hungary and Venice; then four hundred years of oppression by Venice, with the war against Turkey running concurrently for most of that time; a few years of hope under France, frustrated by the decay of Napoleon; a hundred years of muddling misgovernment by Austria.[113]

In passages like these, history is a hostile, alien force—alien because it comes from outside the immediate present—that shapes lives, nations, and empires. It appears all-powerful, inescapable, and without pity. At one point she evokes the Greek tragedians, and writes that "[h]istory imposes [agony] on us. There is no use denying the horrible nature of our human destiny."[114] It seems impossible to resist "the horror of history."[115] The tone of these passages is one of resignation, seeing no point in struggling against the onslaught of the inevitable. Nor does history appear to have any rational motive or goal: "History sometimes acts as madly as heredity, and her most unpredictable performances are often her most glorious."[116]

The painful record of collective memories courts her anger: "the quality of Balkan history, and indeed of all history, is disgusting";[117] "It is sometimes very hard to tell the difference between history and the smell of skunk";[118] "Again history emitted its stench, which was here particularly noisome."[119]

History stinks, not because it is old and rotting, as it is not depicted as a corpse, but rather as a skunk, living in the present but hostile to any attempts at capture. West's anger here stems not just from a universal recoiling at the endless cycles of violence that mark just about any history, but also from her realization that her project entails keeping a collective memory of such horrors alive: "This has seemed to me at times an unendurably horrible book to have to write, with its record of pain and violence and bloodshed, carried on for so long by such diverse peoples."[120] She imagines speaking with a typical Balkan peasant, who would respond to her inquiries: "there was fear, there was our enemies without, our rulers within, there was prison, there was torture, there was violent death."[121] Any investigation into the past of this region will inevitably conjure up such morbid emotions and images, risking the fetishization of violence in the resulting textual recreation. To be sure, West is also recording art, language, food, and ritual; all of these cannot compete with the amount of space the text expends on recording the violent stories of the Balkan past. At one point West lapses into simply "Murder. Murder. Murder. Murder."[122]

Much of this violent characterization of the Slavs is West's own ethnocentrism. She writes as part of an inherited discourse that paints southeastern Europe as more chaotic and violent than the Western nations, despite the unprecedented horrors of the Hundred Years War, the Napoleonic wars, and especially the Great War. "Indeed, there is something distinctly non-European in that the Balkans never quite seem to reach the dimensions of the European slaughters" writes Maria Todorova in *Imagining the Balkans* (1997), challenging centuries of anti-Balkan prejudice that continued throughout Western coverage of the Balkan wars of the 1990s.[123] And early in *Black Lamb*, West shows some awareness of this prejudice:

> Violence was, indeed, all I knew of the Balkans: all I knew of the South Slavs. . . . But I must have been wholly mistaken in my acceptance of the popular legend regarding the Balkans, for if the South Slavs had been truly violent they would not have been hated first by the Austrians, who worshipped violence in an imperialist form, and later by the Fascists, who workshop violence in a totalitarian form.[124]

Despite moments like these, and West's genuine affection for the region, she continues to oppose the violent East to the more enlightened West:

> life in Europe has never been orderly for more than a few years at a time and in a limited area; but in the West it has been orderly enough, if only in the homogeneity of its disorder, to allow clever men to lay down principles that they could safely claim to be eternal, since they afforded useful bases for action and thought during some considerable period of time. In the East of Europe it has not been so. Continual and astonishing were its historical convulsions.[125]

The Francophile West was surely familiar with the "historical convulsions" of the long nineteenth century that saw four French revolutions, yet it is the East that retains the image of instability. There is a further irony in that West ascribes violence to the Balkan people, all the while using her own text to urge the Western empires to employ violence on a far greater scale against the Third Reich, the apogee of organized Western violence.

West's interrogations of these Western assumptions only ever remain provisional. While she remains frustrated at the onerous task of constructing a narrative that will preserve memories of violence, and continually doubts the expediency and abilities of her chosen forms, she rarely doubts the ethical nature of her task. As the book proceeds and her arguments against pacifism grow, she asks herself "whether I would be able to suffer from my principles if the need came" and she were forced to fight; but then "I should ask myself with far greater urgency whether I have done everything possible to carry those principles into effect, and how I can attain power to make them absolutely victorious."[126] If history for West is an oppressive, violent, capricious force, it is also a necessity if theorized as a textual chain that enters into discourses of contemporary power, and at West's particular moment she sees the writing of history as her means of intervening in the world. Decoud in *Nostromo* was surrounded by "history" but was not able to sustain his life in "a history," and not only physically perished but was erased from collective memory as well. West is determined not to fail in constructing a history as she makes her way through Balkan history, and she continually argues for the need for her project.

This need implies a lack, of course, and one troubling aspect of *Black Lamb* is West's relationship to British imperialism. When West begins her work by dedicating it to the murdered or imprisoned victims of German fascism, this is not just a rhetorical opening and invitation for sympathy from her readership: it is also a recognition of the beginnings of the destruction of Balkan collective memory, which itself should argue for the necessity of her own work and British and American engagement with the war. The very need for an English writer to come to the Balkans to record their culture suggests a deficiency at the heart of Yugoslavia, paternalistically implying a need for Western assistance. Note the double-edged praise of the Croats:

> They had no compensation for their history, for that never once formed a historic legend of any splendid magnitude. It was a record of individual heroism that no nation could surpass, but it had never shaped itself into an indestructible image of triumph that could be turned to as an escape from present failure.[127]

West praises their courage and heroism but does not believe they ever had the ability to record such qualities, or to craft a narrative that attempted to depict them in language. She asks, "what would England be like if it had not its immense Valhalla of kings and heroes, if it had not its Elizabethan and its Victorian ages?"[128] (Note again Todorova's point that Western Europe somehow eludes a violent reputation despite conquering most of the globe by violent means.)

Unlike Yugoslavia, England and its empire *do* have a national historiography, West argues, and this attitude might direct us to her complicated relationship to empire in the text. She tells her husband that "I hate the corpses of empires, they stink as nothing else. They stink so badly that I cannot believe that even in life they were healthy"; and "[i]t would seem that empire degrades those it uplifts as much as those it holds down in subjection."[129] In her conclusion she states that "I became newly doubtful of empires."[130] Usually in these remarks she is referring to the Roman, Turkish, or Hungarian empires, but what about her own? She writes of the English that "they are on the side of life, they love justice, they hate violence, and they respect the truth. It is not always so when they deal with India or Burma; but that is not their fault, it is the fault of Empire, which makes a man own things outside his power to control."[131] The existence of the British Empire remains mostly silent in the text—conspicuous in a 1,100-page work of imperial discourse that is partly a call to arms appealing to that empire—but in this passage she does critique, if lightly, the English and their treatment of their world.[132] Would this put her on the side of various nationalisms around the world struggling to break away from the British?

It is in her treatment of history, however, that West marks her difference from the forces of anti-colonialism:

> But I saw in British imperialism room for roguery and stupidity as well as magnificence. A conquered people is a helpless people; and if they are of different physical type and another culture from their conquerors they cannot avail themselves of anything like the protection which would otherwise be given them by the current conceptions of justice and humanity.[133]

West here admits some brutality and inequality of the British Empire, but still sees it as a necessary force.[134] For West, the composition of *Black Lamb and Grey Falcon* is one of those moments, an instance where the East stands in need of help from England, even if this means "infecting" the Balkans with imperial conflicts. Critics often characterize her text as an anti-imperial one, just as they take *The Return of the Soldier* for an anti-war novel: Schweizer calls *Black Lamb* an "anti-imperial epic," Cohen refers to her "anti-imperial critique," Zofia Lesinska argues that "the whole economy of her cultural critique is clearly anti-imperialist."[135] But we should be more specific: what West has done with *Black Lamb* is to modernize liberal imperialist discourse through her critique of foreign or past empires. The existence of *Black Lamb* speaks to her belief in the value of the British empire and its cultural ambassadors, and their necessary role in the coming conflict, and she explicitly objects to the

Germans' "gospel which was in essence a call to the destruction of the British Empire and its regeneration in a baser form."[136] To characterize Nazi ambition in such a way is telling, but this belief stretches back well before the war: a decade earlier, in *The Strange Necessity*, West wrote that the Empire "is a political necessity, and a glorious one."[137]

Thus when West urges that "we" go to war, we, in the light of postcolonial theory, might ask just who this "we" would be: the British Empire and its entire military apparatus, which included, for example, large numbers of conscripted troops from the colonies. (The 14th Army, the British forces' largest, had nearly one million men, mostly from Africa and the Indian subcontinent.) This is not to suggest any moral equivalency between British conscription and Nazi extermination, and to simplistically label *Black Lamb* an "imperialist" text would willfully ignore the historical specificities of the situation in 1941, the dire and unique threat that the Nazi regime posed. But what cannot be denied is that the coming world war would be fought with empires—German, British, American, and Soviet—a fact that West's long history of imperial conflicts silently elides. (There is also the related issue of West's reluctance to address the heavy violence that the war was unleashing from within the communities of Yugoslavia. While *Black Lamb* seems to intuit the open reception that many Croats would give to Germany via the Ustase, nowhere does it predict the role played by the Serbian Chetniks in the mass killing of Bosnian Serbs, and she even wrote during the war in favor of the Royalist Chetniks and against Tito's Partisans.[138])

Such ethnocentric views no doubt evidence a late Orientalism, but I would argue that it is more productive to read *Black Lamb* as a key work in the genealogy of liberal, interventionist imperialism. As Uday Singh Mehta explores in *Liberalism and Empire* (1999), "the liberal association with the British Empire was extended and deep."[139] Mehta explores this through nineteenth-century figures like Jeremy Bentham and J. S. Mill, but such attitudes extended into the twentieth century as well, with Tony Blair as its latest prominent spokesperson. Both the Liberal and Labour Parties scarcely distinguished themselves from their Tory opponents when it came to issues of empire: Lloyd George's aggression at the Paris conference in 1919 evinces an unwavering dedication to global British rule.[140] By the start of the Second World War, however, the empire had already lost Ireland (except nominally, which would be resolved by Ireland's neutrality during the war), and the Indian Congress party was ascendant. It was increasingly difficult to maintain either the empire or liberal defenses of it.

The fight against Germany's advances would thus not only bolster the empire but also destroy it, providing imperial actions with a moral legitimacy that it had lost while forever weakening it militarily. West's rallying cry stands as one of the most eloquent calls to arms from within liberal discourse that would soon find more fertile ground in the mid-century United States.

The Epilogue might very well be the greatest essay ever penned in defense of aggressive, liberal interventionism, as when she writes that "[i]t was good to take up one's courage again, which had been laid aside so long, and feel how comfortably it fitted into the hand."[141] This is also what makes her work so dangerous, and is one reason that her ideas are so easily appropriated by Christopher Hitchens (who approvingly conveys the preceding quote) in his effort, via his 2007 Introduction to *Black Lamb*, to marshal her text in the fight against Islamic terrorism. He writes

> West was one of those people, necessary in every epoch, who understands that there are thing worth fighting for, and dying for, and killing for. . . . she knew that the facing of death could be life affirming, and also that certain kinds of life are a version of death. . . . In any time of sniggering relativism and overbred despair, such as we have known and may know again, it is good to know that some enduring values can be affirmed, even if the wrong people sometimes take the right line, and even if people of education and refinement are often a little reluctant to trust their guts.[142]

Here the "wrong people" are clearly the neo-conservatives in George W. Bush's administration who were pushing for war against Iraq in 2003, and the "people of education and refinement" Hitchens's leftist and liberal colleagues, seemingly debilitated by "sniggering relativism." Hitchens surely identified with West's lament at the plains of Kossovo: her line, "I began to weep, for the leftwing people among whom I had lived all my life had in their attitude to foreign politics achieved such a betrayal" is the dominant key of Hitchens's last decade.[143]

Hitchens, despite being disastrously wrong on the Iraq War, actually has a solid case in regards to West's work: far from distorting her original intentions, he successfully links his own views with West's to establish a legitimate, if perilous and potentially toxic, genealogy of liberal imperialist discourse (most clearly embodied in the new forms of Western intervention via Tony Blair and Barack Obama that somehow bridge the gap between liberalism and neo-conservatism). Rather than the older liberal imperialism espoused by Marlow's aunt in *Heart of Darkness*, "weaning those ignorant millions from their horrid ways," West and Hitchens formulate their argument to stress the *preservative* possibilities of Western intervention, West pushing to safeguard Balkan collective memory, Hitchens to defend Iraqi citizens from their own government.[144] When West warns that "posterity might doubt the existence of our contemporary French and English culture if the Nazis destroyed all records of them," she is, analogously, not looking to alter Yugoslavia, but rather call on the British and American forces to maintain and preserve it.[145]

From our vantage point we can easily overlook West's disinclination to face the full nature of the British Empire in the face of the Nazi threat—even

Gandhi eventually endorsed, if tepidly, British efforts against Hitler. (West's intellectual heirs like Hitchens will not be granted such a pass.) Ultimately, West's text is richer than just a polemic, and we should recall what Edward Said found so radical in Conrad's *Heart of Darkness*, and how this also might relate to *Black Lamb*. Said argues in *Culture and Imperialism* (1993) that despite the racism of Conrad's novella, and his reluctance to imagine radically different political worlds, in many places the text works against these ideas:

> Since Conrad *dates* imperialism, shows its contingency, records its illusions and tremendous violence and waste (as in *Nostromo*), he permits his later readers to imagine something other than an Africa carved up into dozens of European colonies, even if, for his own part, he had little notion of what that Africa might be.[146]

Through Conrad's double-frame, which allows a commentary on the Thames and Congo, Europe and Africa, Roman era and the Age of Imperialism, *Heart of Darkness* opens up a conceptual space in which we are given the freedom to formulate other notions of politics and empire. For West, her radical gesture is not in the dating of imperialism—as I have argued, the more historically specific she gets, the more embedded in imperial discourse she becomes—but rather in her recognition that the Balkans *have* a history, and that it is a history worth preserving. Part of what is so offensive in Marlow's description of Africans is the way in which they are described as products of nature instead of products of—and producers of—history. Although West lends some credence to genetic predispositions, it is ultimately to history that she looks to explain present-day Yugoslavia.

West's deep exploration into Balkan history was a radical move in the context of late-imperial racial discourse, especially if we keep in mind that *Black Lamb* is partly a travelogue, and we could even use Carey Snyder's formulation of "ethnographic modernism" to describe West's text. In *British Fiction and Cross-Cultural Encounters: Ethnographic Modernism from Wells to Woolf* (2008), Snyder writes that "whereas professional anthropology increasingly relegated the observer's subjective impressions to the margins of ethnographic accounts in order to create the impression of an objective, authoritarian voice," modernist ethnography "foreground the observer, representing ethnographic encounters as murky, power-laden, and inconclusive."[147] West's commanding voice vacillates between authority and self-doubt, eager for the power to move empires but too conscious of the contingency of narrative to feign objectivity. *Black Lamb* insists in depicting histories of the region as the key to understanding one's experience while there, and, as we have seen, to understanding the importance of the region to modern Europe as a whole. Hers is not an effort to defend the preset quaintness of the region, but rather its rich past, a past at risk from sure destruction. Despite her own cultural limitations, West ultimately believes that Yugoslavia has a past worth preserving.

History's Strange Necessities

We have seen how for Ford, his "solution" to the aporia of necessity and impossibility was his use of traumatic amnesia as an aesthetic paradigm. In the composition of *Black Lamb*, West called upon the aesthetic concerns that she shared with her earlier contemporaries like Conrad, Ford, and Proust to carry the weight of history's impossible necessity. With *Black Lamb*, West answers the rhetorical question that drove her earlier essay "The Strange Necessity": "What is the meaning of this mystery of mysteries? Why does art matter? And why does it matter so much? What is this strange necessity?"[148] West is here referring, not for the need of the artist to express oneself, but for the viewer or reader to see or experience art. In *Black Lamb* she returns to this theme: "As we grow older and see the ends of stories as well as their beginnings, we realize that to the people who take part in them it is almost of greater importance that they should be stories, that they should form a recognizable pattern, than that they should be happy or tragic."[149] She further theorizes it in a historical framework in the Epilogue, which "takes place" in 1941, writing that "all over Europe the sorrowful find comfort in thinking on their history, though it passes from woe to woe."[150] What history ultimately is seems beside the point in moments like these, in which West focuses more on our strange need to shape history into narrative; one quality of the Balkans that attracts West is its people's willingness to confront uncertainty, to try, to borrow from West's later writings, to transform events into experience. Describing a nun in Dalmatia, she writes, "She was among those who will not suffer any event merely to happen, who must examine it with all the force of the soul and trace its consequences, and seek, against all probability, an explanation of the universe that is as kind as human kindness."[151] West is herself undergoing a similar struggle, as she begins her narrative with the killing of King Alexander, lamenting that "I could not understand this event, no matter how often I saw this picture," and thus had to visit the region herself to transform the event into experience.[152]

A key moment for how *Black Lamb* envisions this event-experience transformation is toward the end of the journey, in Montenegro, where they encounter a woman whose life story is possibly the most tragic that West finds. Her life has been ravished by the Balkan civil wars, the Great War, and a long hard existence against natural forces. But although she is living through pain,

> she not only suffered it, she examined it. As the sword swept down on her through the darkness she threw out her hand and caught the blade as it fell, not caring if she cut her fingers so long as she could question its substance, where it had been forged, and who was the wielder.[153]

This woman becomes a heroine for West because of her courage in facing, not just history, but the problems of histories:

Nevertheless she desired neither peace nor gold, but simply knowledge of what her life might mean. The instrument used by the hunter and the nomad was not too blunt to turn to finer uses; it was not dismayed by complexity, and it could regard the more stupendous aurochs that range within the mind and measure the diffuse shadows cast by history.[154]

Like this battered woman, West desires to use whatever "instruments" she possesses to understand the past and how it has shaped her own life, to "measure" the effect of events on modern Europe. West's tools are primarily stories: just at the moment in history when the field of history was starting to question the role of narrative, West made her most elaborate defense of the role of narrative in a history, while ensuring that the historical narrative that resulted was as self-conscious and knowingly mediated as a modernist novel.

West's model of history is thus highly aesthetic and formal, but is always framed as a response to ethical imperatives: "Art is not a plaything, but a necessity, and its essence, form, is not a decorative adjustment, but a cup into which life can be poured and lifted to the lips and be tasted."[155] *Black Lamb* shares the formal ambitions of West's modernist predecessors, but in the service of a project that possesses a more immediate, even urgent, social significance. Many of her references to aesthetics are framed within an ethical construct, as in her (patronizing?) qualms about the aesthetic value of a local church in Dubrovnik:

> The town regarded this horror as a masterpiece. That is to say they admired fake art, naturalist art, which copies nature without interpreting it; which believes that to copy is all we can and need do to nature; which is not conscious that we live in an uncomprehended universe, and that it is urgently necessary for sensitive men to look at each phenomenon in turn and find out what it is and what are its relations to the rest of existence.[156]

Art is "urgently necessary" even in peacetime, and the coming war had heightened this urgency and this necessity. For the West of 1941, the shaping of nature, the interpretation of the "uncomprehended," is about preserving a past in the present against the threats from the future:

> What is art? It is not decoration. It is the re-living of experience. The artist says, "I will make that event happen again, altering its shape, which was disfigured by its contacts with other events, so that its true significance is revealed." . . . It must not be copied, it must be remembered, it must be lived again.[157]

Black Lamb dramatizes the contradiction that would become even more glaring in the wake of the Holocaust: past human experience is almost hopelessly inscrutable, but as a civilization we desperately need to represent it in a comprehendible form. History is both impossible and necessary; the Holocaust is "beyond the limits of representation," but we must "never forget." I have argued that West attempts to mitigate this aporia by means of her unique appropriation of the modernist tradition of James, Conrad, Proust, and Ford. Like these writers, she relies on narrative as a means of depicting human experience. As both a sometimes-modernist writer and as a historian, this choice would not be self-evident: much of the modernist movement was driven by lyric non-narrative verse, and the field of history, increasingly enamored of statistics and more vertical kinds of analyses, was growing suspicious of narrative. As Roland Barthes wrote in *Writing Degree Zero* (1953), "narration is not necessarily a law of the form. A whole period could conceive novels in letters, for instance; and another can evolve a practice of History by means of analyses. Therefore Narration, as a form common to both the Novel and to History, does remain, in general, the choice or the expression of an historical moment."[158] *Black Lamb* is both the choice and a theoretical justification for such choice.

Black Lamb and Grey Falcon anticipates much of the experimental historiography that marked the second half of the twentieth century, but it does not anticipate West's subsequent literary output. *Black Lamb* is her last great experiment.[159] However, many experimental historians, journalists, and essayists have listed *Black Lamb* as formative for their work, as West's choice continues to influence journalists and historians.[160] More important, opting to use narrative to write her epic history marks an intervention in the struggle regarding historical form. I would like to conclude with a summary of just what West achieves by this decision, as it remains a problematic and contested one throughout the twentieth century and into the twenty-first.

Conclusion
History after the Holocaust

As Margaret Stetz has pointed out, Rebecca West's handling of the Nuremberg Trials downplayed the damage done to European Jewry during the Second World War, and throughout the rest of her life West never fully came to terms with the Holocaust and her possible misreading of Nuremberg.[1] The debate regarding what West should have realized in the postwar years is part of a larger discussion on the public acknowledgment of the Holocaust, but West's reluctance to face the full truth is all the more striking given her prophetic depiction of Jews in *Black Lamb and Grey Falcon*. It is almost as if West knew more about the Holocaust before the war than after.

Besides West and her husband, the two most prominent characters in *Black Lamb* are Constantine and his wife Gerda. West changed their names—Stanislav and Elsa Vinaver—to protect their identities after the Germans gained control of Yugoslavia. Gerda and Constantine are an improbable pair: she is a German who detests Jews and Slavs, and he is a Jewish Slav who detests the Nazis. To be sure, Gerda is not a Nazi per se, but West forces her to stand in for the entire German nationalist project. West dislikes Gerda more than anything she encounters in Yugoslavia, and when Constantine informs her that Gerda will be accompanying them to Macedonia, West breaks down: "I stood transfixed with horror. Tears began to run down my cheeks."[2] West's response proves founded, as the trip is something of a disaster, mostly due to Gerda's violent bigotry: around Gypsies she states that "I must smoke here to disinfect myself. When I see these people I feel I am not in Europe."[3] "Disinfect" is a chillingly apt word to represent the ethnic cleansing that was mostly rhetoric in 1937 but official policy by 1941. Gerda berates her husband, "Your Yugoslavia ought to do something with all these horrible people!"[4] Gerda's character soon becomes shorthand for Nazism: "Gerda, in fact, is irresistible. It is therefore of enormous importance to calculate how many Gerdas there are in the world, and whether they are likely to combine for any purpose."[5]

But by the end of the Macedonia chapter, Gerda has become the embodiment, not just of the Nazis, but of evil everywhere. We learn that Gerda "was, after all, the determining element in the Austro-Hungarian Empire all through the nineteenth century."[6] Gerda has thus gone from annoying travel companion to Nazi party rep to transhistorical force of destruction.

West admits that "I love to torment Constantine about Goethe," and as Clare Colquitt points out, "Gerda" is a heterograph for Goethe, appropriate given the way in which the poet seems to invoke West's ire.[7] West's construction of Constantine as a character is the result of the transference of frustrations from Stanislav to "Gerda," letting "Constantine" go mostly unscathed. He is the epitome of cosmopolitanism, a Jewish poet and playwright who studied with Bergson in Paris and is now the Press Bureau Chief for Yugoslavia, in charge of taking around important foreign guests like West. West and her husband mostly adore Constantine, despite his many peccadilloes, and his main drawback seems to be his tolerance toward his own wife. Although well-rounded as a character, Constantine is still called upon to bear the weight of many historical and political forces coursing through Europe before the war. Colquitt writes:

> As chief character in West's travels, Constantine is both hero and victim, Churchill and Chamberlain. In his failure to control his inclinations toward self-sacrifice, Constantine is also symbol, for the martyring impulse to which he abandons himself is symptomatic of that same malaise that West sees operating in the whole of Europe in the late 1930s as country after country capitulates to Hitler and Mussolini.[8]

Constantine as Chamberlain parallels the titular black lamb, which comes from a sacrificial ceremony that West witnesses, and that revolts her because of its perceived affinities to a defeatist peace movement. He is also Jewish and Yugoslavian, both signifiers of trans-ethnic identity, and as there was neither a Jewish nor Yugoslavian state in 1941, he is the culturally overdetermined but simultaneously rootless modern citizen.

Her treatment of other Jews in *Black Lamb* is more revealing given her purpose to record the state of southeastern Europe on the brink of war. Any time she describes Jewish Slavs or any aspects of Judaism, it is with overflowing praise and hyperbolic valoration: Jews "are now the greatest interpreters of modern European creativeness."[9] She describes meeting a Jewish banker in Bosnia: "In his office there lingered something of the best of Turkish life; and in his integrity, in his dismissal of the little, in the seriousness which he brought to the interpretation of his experience, there was preserved the best of what German philosophical training could do for a man of affairs."[10] In both passages, Jews are depicted as the cultural depositories for the greatest of European achievements, and West's praise of Jews are here rhetorical moves designed to counter Nazi propaganda regarding the role that Jews have played in Europe. Against the accusations that Jews have been selfishly draining money out of the economy and vitality out of European genetic stock, West argues that Jews have actually been the group that has preserved the financial stability of the modern economy, and simultaneously embodied the best of European (and even specifically German) culture. In Bosnia, West encounters a Jewish woman who struck West with her beauty: "She lay on a sofa, fluttering up against the downward pull of her injury, as hurt birds do; and she was astonishing in the force of her beauty . . . she had never been frustrated, she had always been rewarded for her beautiful body and her beautiful conduct by beautiful gratitude."[11] West piles on the "beautifuls" to dispute the Nazi geneticist arguments against Jews, and West concludes her description of this woman by admiring "the Jewish care for the continuity of the race."[12] Here "the race" is referring, if not to humanity as a whole, then at least to Europe, the same Europe clamoring for a "solution" to the presence of a large Jewish population.

As both Stetz and Phyllis Lassner have demonstrated, West's philo-Semitism, both before and after the war, was problematic and, as is often the case, carried traces of anti-Semitism.[13] In the case of Black Lamb, West may have hoped that her descriptions of Jewish Slavs would work against the Nazis' influence, but in many sections of the book she shows her despair at what is to come (or for the West of 1941, what has already begun). Bit by an insect, Constantine comes down with a serious fever while they are on their way to Montenegro. West insists that he gets rest, and then "I paused, at a loss for words. I did not know how to say that he was dying of being a Jew in a world where there were certain ideas to which some new star was lending a strange strength."[14] Constantine's routine illness becomes a dark premonition. Many passages in Black Lamb display this sense of dramatic irony, as West the author knows the outcome of Yugoslavia's fate. But there are moments that disturbingly predict a future of which West could not have fully predicted, or even imagined (and that she refused to fully process even after the facts were revealed):

> There came back to me the fear of fire which I had felt earlier in the service, and this was accompanied by a revulsion from the horror of history, and a dread that it might really be witless enough to repeat itself. Fire spreads, and the substances it inflames put up on defense, burn and become ashes. Human beings love to inflict pain on their fellow-creatures, and the species yields to its perverse appetite, allowing vast tragedies to happen and endure for centuries, people to agonize and become extinct.[15]

In 1941 West could not have known the full extent of the concentration camps and the Nazis' Final Solution—few could have guessed at the unprecedented horrors that would become the Holocaust—but Black Lamb is teeming with imagery of violent extinction, and it is hard to encounter passages like these, as well as Gerda's call for a "cleaner" Yugoslavia, and not read the Holocaust anachronistically into the text.

Constantine's illness might be an instance of Yugoslavia providing a symbol of something that West cannot yet put into language, which is one of the major themes of her work. What continually drew West to the Balkans was not just the typical English patronage of a supposedly simple people more in touch with elementary virtues. Instead, West more valued "that quality of visibility that makes the Balkans so especially enchanting."[16] In Western Europe, "because of limitations of language we are debarred from seeing something that is obvious to unsealed eyes."[17] Note her fusion of vision and language: like Wittgenstein's fly in the bottle, thought or truth is constrained by language, which in turns prevents us from seeing the real. But Yugoslavia "writes obscure things plain, which furnishes symbols for what the intellect has not yet formulated."[18] So even if we have not yet established language for depicting an aspect of the real, Balkan culture can provide images that convey the "subtle and penetrating essence" that Conrad's Marlow thought had escaped even the best storytellers. Due to "the Balkan habit of making life fully visible, of gathering up diffused events into an apprehensible symbol," Yugoslavia is able to provide West with truths that resist linguistic form.[19]

Thus one way to read the experimental histories of Conrad, Ford, and West, especially *Black Lamb and Grey Falcon*, are as trial runs for the biggest challenge faced by historians, as the second half of the twentieth century tried to grapple with the collective memory of the Holocaust without preexisting "formulations" of language. I have tried to argue for the importance of modernist historiography in its own right, to take its own place in histories of modernism, the historical novel, and historical writing in general. But these writers can also contribute to a full understanding of how the twentieth century has written about itself, and can provide models for formal innovations in the writing of history. These writers were present at some of the century's worst horrors—Conrad witnessing the abuses of empire, Ford at the Somme, West in the Nazi-threatened Balkans—and thus took for granted the imperative to record what they saw. Their immersion in literary London and Paris, however, forced them to realize the insufficiency of inherited forms. History in *Nostromo* becomes a series of dubious histories; the horrors of trench warfare refuse to cohere in any meaningful testament of witnessing for Ford; history in *Black Lamb* remains "impossible," stubbornly guarding its secrets. But these very dramatizations of the problematics of the historical process are what can be so valuable to theorists of history, as well as creative historians searching for new forms.

While these writers share formal affinities, it should not be surprising that their objects of historical scrutiny are all violent, as the confrontation with modern war or genocide explodes our inherited categories and demands new representational paradigms. Adorno famously pondered if "to write poetry after Auschwitz is barbaric," but it was narrative history that was more shattered by Hitler's efforts at racial extermination. The world wars and the Holocaust were traumatic not just for its victims but for humanity as whole. We and future generations will struggle to comprehend what happened, turning to volumes of history and analysis to try to make sense of it all, but a pressing question has been the role of narrative. The innovations of the *Annales* School marked the radical shift away from the telling of stories, best seen in Fernand Braudel's *Mediterranean* (1949, but begun in 1923), where narratable events were merely "surface disturbances, crests of foam that the tides of history carry on their strong backs."[20] In Braudel's work narrative was relieved of its centuries-old duty of communicating and summarizing past experiences. To extend Braudel's metaphor, stories were not deep enough for *les Annalistes*.

While the *Annales* School had a wide influence, its model of history was not completely hegemonic, however, and non-narrative history never represented the majority of historiographical output.[21] From experimenters like Carlo Ginzburg and the micro-historians, to mainstream popular histories and television documentaries, narrative has maintained its problematic role as conveyer of history. John Burrow argues that narrative does not always have to be simplistic: "The concept of a story is in essence a simple one, but that does not make all narrators either simple-minded or single-minded. Narrative can be capacious as well as directional. What is the 'point' of *War and Peace* or Thucydides?"[22] Likewise, Simon Schama in his experimental *Dead Certainties* (1991) ponders the literal meaning of the Greek *historia* as "inquiry" and concludes, "But to have an *inquiry*, whether into the construction of a legend, or the execution of a crime, is surely to require the telling of stories. And so the asking of questions and the relating of narratives need not, I think, be mutually exclusive forms of historical representation."[23]

Representation itself, however, was under scrutiny as the century progressed. If the traumatic nature of twentieth-century history was one impetus to experiment in historical form, the anti-empirical theories of Roland Barthes, Michel Foucault, Louis Althusser, and Jacques Derrida were another. The set of theorists we have come to call structuralists and post-structuralists compelled many to see historiography as just another "discourse" subject to the same cultural forces as art or literature.[24] In Barthes's essay "The Discourse of History" (1967), he explains why the perceived legitimacy of historiography was being weakened:

> Since it refuses to assume the real as a signified . . . it is understandable that history, at the privileged moment when it attempted to constitute itself as a genre, i.e., in the nineteenth century, should have come to see in the "pure and simple" relation of facts the best proof of these facts, and to institute narration as privileged signifier of the real. . . . Narrative

structure, elaborated in the crucible of fictions (through myths and early epics), becomes both sign and proof of reality. Hence, it will be understood that the effacement (if not the disappearance) of narration in contemporary historical science, which prefers to speak of structures rather than chronologies, implies much more than a simple change of school: a veritable ideological transformation; historical narration is dying because the sign of History is henceforth not so much *the real* as *the intelligible*.[25]

This obituary of historical narrative proved to be premature, but Barthes nicely summarizes the French critical position, deconstructing the seemingly "pure and simple" relationship between what history narrates and that narrative itself, and we are forced to see the difference between "history" as a narrative (signifier) and "history" as "the past" (signified). For Barthes, orthodox history strives, paradoxically, for a sense of transparency in order to hide its own construction.[26]

Once aware of the semiotic or narratological gap between histories and their objects, it became more difficult to read or write history with a sense of epistemological certitude. Because of the attacks by the new theorists, instead of writing "what happened," it seemed as though the historian was primarily writing, producing a textual discourse. Barthes and Derrida touch occasionally on the writing of history, but Althusser was the critic of that generation who most assiduously thought through some of the implications of the new ideas for history. *Reading Capital* (1968) was not just an exercise in how to read Marx's work, but also an argument as to how to read any work of history. Althusser saw *Capital* as Marx's break not only from his Hegelian training but also from the prevailing trends of empiricism, whose fallacy was to believe in "the knowledge of that real object itself as a *real part* of the real object to be known" instead of something *apart* from that object, something that is actually more in the knowing subject than the known object.[27] Althusser ascribed the phrase *"the concept dog cannot bark"* to Spinoza, suggesting that concept is not the same as object, because the former exists only in the knowing subject, while the latter is independent of it.[28] History often conflates the two, seeing as equal the events of the past with a seemingly transparent narrative of it:

> While the production process of a given real object, a given real-concrete totality (e.g., a given historical nation) takes place entirely in the real and is carried out according to the real order of *real* genesis (the order of succession of the moments of *historical* genesis), the production process of the object of knowledge takes place entirely in knowledge and is carried out according to *a different order*, in which the thought categories which "reproduce" the real categories do *not* occupy *the same* place as they do in the

order of real historical genesis, but quite different places assigned them by their function in the production process of the object of knowledge.[29]

Althusser insisted that we must separate the concept of history from history itself, which he sees as the fallacy of both the Hegelian and empirical schools:

> We must have no illusions as to the incredible power of this prejudice, which still dominates us all, which is the basis for contemporary histori-cism and which would have us confuse the object of knowledge with the real object by attributing to the object of knowledge the same "qualities" as the real object of which it is the knowledge. The knowledge of history is no more historical than the knowledge of sugar is sweet.[30]

While Althusser's theorization is mostly epistemological, the implications for narratology were soon apparent, and the most troubling assault on the field of history came from Hayden White's *Metahistory* in 1973. White had absorbed French poststructural theory and thus saw any work of history—"a verbal structure in the form of a narrative prose discourse"—as employing the same techniques as fiction. The historian "performs an essentially *poetic* act, in which he *pre*figures the historical field and constitutes it as a domain upon which to bring to bear the specific theories he will use to explain 'what was *really* happening' in it."[31] White drew attention to the story at the heart of every history.

Over the next three decades, a battle raged between "theorists" and "tradi-tionalists" in academic journals like *History and Theory* and *Rethinking History*, in a sense arguing over what comes first, the referent or the narrative: Is history figured, or, as White asserted, "*pre*figured"?[32] White and his followers encouraged historians to look as much at the narrative as the research of any historical work: they argued that too many historians have simply focused on the research/methodological side of historiography and assumed that good research would lead to good histories.[33]

Such debates have not settled in the same way as they have in English and art history departments. The discipline of history has proved more recalci-trant to "theory." What some might take for a stubbornness, however, we should instead see as an urgent defense of the ethical role that histories play, and that become most apparent when debating representations of the Holo-caust. The seminal debate between Carlo Ginzburg and Hayden White evinces the unease and defensiveness of radical poststructuralism when de-bating events that we must never forget.

But another reason for the more marginal role that "theory" plays in the field of history might be the slippage between debates on epistemology and those on narratology. Too often the critical assumption is that works of realist history give you facts, while experiments in form do not believe in historical certainty. But as *The Good Soldier* has instructed us, these are two related, but ultimately distinct aspects of historical narration.[34] (Ginzburg has proved such an important writer and thinker because of his adherence to a belief in some sort of historical truth that he expresses via narrative experiments.) As Robert A. Rosenstone has insisted, creative historians have not "given up on historical knowing. They simply realize that such knowledge must sometimes be expressed in new ways."[35] A cursory survey of the field of "creative" or "experimental" history reveals techniques and tropes that Conrad, Ford, and West would have found familiar. The works of the historians I will now turn to reflect a desire to move beyond standard formal models. For example, in his Preface to *Mirror in the Shrine* (1988), a history of American encounters with Japan, Rosenstone laments that the field of history "has remained stuck with a model of representation well over a century old," and that "[p]art of my aim is to break with some of the conventions of narrative history, to move beyond the 'realistic' nineteenth-century novel as a paradigm for the historian's 'art.'"[36] Such movement does not automatically imply a disbelief in historical truth.

Creative history has emerged as a legitimate and vibrant field. The 1990s especially saw a growth in works of narrative history that aggressively highlighted their own process of coming to being. Rosenstone, a founder of the journal *Rethinking History*, opens *Mirror in the Shrine* with quotes from Ricoeur and White, and writes that he desires to

> situate my endeavor as one touched by many of the theoretical issues that today stir the realm of criticism. . . . To do this is to raise questions about historical narrative and modes of representation that have been acknowledged by some historians in theory but have yet to touch the way history is conceived or written. My purpose is to raise such questions not in a theoretical way, but within a narrative.[37]

Rosenstone's tone marks a new era of radical self-consciousness in the field of history that we can witness in many subsequent works, and that share with Conrad, Ford, and West a desire for new forms that remain within the scope of narrative. Schama's *Dead Certainties* closes with a brief look at James's *Sense of the Past*, and acknowledges that his own professional challenges echo that of Ralph Pendrel, as they both ponder "the habitually insoluble quandary of the historian: how to live in two worlds at once; how to take the broken, mutilated remains of something or someone from the 'enemy lines' of the documented past and restore it to life or give it a decent interment in our own time and place."[38] Schama's solution seems formally borrowed from a work like *The Good Soldier*: "Both the stories offered here play with the teasing gap separating a lived event and its subsequent narration. . . . Both dissolve the certainties of events into multiple possibilities of alternative narrations."[39] Likewise, Richard

Wunderli's *Peasant Fires* (1992) plays with the distance between narrative and referent: his work begins with an account of the mystical visions of Hans Behem, a medieval German shepherd, but after several pages Wunderli abruptly informs us that "I made up most of that."[40] If we are used to realist historical narratives, we expect a window onto a past reality, but for Wunderli, the "details of the apparition can only exist in our imaginations." The window, as in *To the Lighthouse*, becomes a painting.

Wunderli, like many of his creative contemporaries, stresses the difficulty of achieving a form that could accurately evoke both the past and the process of reconstructing that past:

> The process of making sense out of the past is like describing an image as seen through a series of distorted mirrors: each mirror reflects the image into another distorted mirror as each mirror reshapes "reality." Out of the puzzling set of reflections and refractions, we construct an idealized, coherent picture of what happened. To change the metaphor, we construct a narrative or melody line of events, joined with analytic accents or accompaniment to give the narrative depth and texture. The narrative, then, becomes our past reality. We impose coherence on chaos.[41]

This role of the imagination for both historian and reader is stressed in Greg Dening's *Mr. Bligh's Bad Language* (1992), an account of the famous mutiny on the *Bounty*. Dening's formal model of history is "the space created by the performance consciousness of the presenter in which the audience—or the reader or the viewer—participates in the creative process of representing. It need not distract or disturb. It can enhance the realisation of the representation."[42] As he asserts in his Prologue, "I re-text the already texted past. I have no experience of the past that I re-present other than that past transformed into words, symbolized."[43] Note how for Dening, it is not that historical knowledge is impossible—the epistemological relativism that so many historians fear—but rather that any representation of historical knowledge based on textual traces must be surrounded by an awareness of the process of recreating the past.

What traditionalists might take as relativism, creative historians might insist is simple honesty. James Goodman in *Stories of Scottsboro* (1994) tells the reader that

> I decided whose stories to tell and how to tell them. I chose central themes and some of the contexts in which I would like them to be understood. I decided who should have the first word, and who should have the last. I imposed order—at the very least beginnings, middles, and ends—where there was rarely order, created the illusion of stillness, or comprehensible movement, out of the always seamless, often chaotic flow of consciousness and experience.[44]

Goodman explores the Scottsboro case from multiple angles, possibly modeled on a work like Faulkner's *Sound and the Fury*. Every claim he makes is backed up with historical evidence, but as he announces, he shapes his work into Aristotle's classic definition of a story. Far from any sort of relativism, Goodman instead imparts both the truth of the historical evidence as well as the truth of his narrative construction.

Recent years have produced more works in this line, and there has been an increased turn toward the innovations of experimental fiction. Rosenstone, introducing an anthology titled *Experiments in Rethinking History* (2004), looks back at his early career, writing that "when experimenting with how to write *Mirror in the Shrine*, I worked in a vacuum. There were no models for what I wanted to do and little sympathy from even good friends in the profession, who after reading chapters had difficulty looking me directly in the eye."[45] Even in the twenty-first century, "[p]recious few have yet answered the call to write History that incorporates the techniques or strategies of twentieth-century literature." The few that have generally populate the pages of *Rethinking History*, and one historian included in Rosenstone's anthology, Bryant Simon, wrote that "I decided to take a page or a frame from *Rashomon*, John Dos Passos and Norman Mailer" in the composing of his historical narrative on race relations in 1912 South Carolina.[46] Given these turns toward modernist models, I would like to conclude with two twenty-first-century experiments in historical form that share many affinities with the modernist historians I have been investigating.

Much like the Holocaust Museum, Peter Englund's *The Beauty and the Sorrow: An Intimate History of the First World War* (2011) strives to decrease the distance between the reader and traumatic experience. Englund writes that "distance is frequently the ingredient that makes understanding possible. But distance exacts a price: perhaps inevitably, much of the direct experience is lost."[47] His compensating strategy, again like that of the Museum, is to enforce subjective viewpoints onto the reader: "The reader will follow these twenty individuals, all of them now more or less forgotten, and all of them low in the hierarchies."[48] Instead of the panoramic narrative viewpoints usually offered in histories of war, Englund instead incorporates the lack of knowledge that most participants of the war suffered through. He writes, "I wanted to depict the war as an individual experience, to go beyond the usual historical and sociological categories, and also beyond the usual narrative forms in which, at best, people such as these appear as no more than tiny specks of light, flickering by in the grand historical sweep."[49] Like Ford, Englund transplants Jamesian point of view from the drawing-room to the battlefield.

Sven Lindqvist's *A History of Bombing* (2001) is an even more radical narrative experiment. He opens his book with the following explanatory note:

This book is a labyrinth with twenty-two entrances and no exit. Each entrance opens into a narrative or an argument, which you then follow by going from text to text according to the instruction → the number of the section where the narrative is continued. So from entrance 1 you proceed to section 166 and continue reading section by section until you come to 173, where another → takes you back to entrance 2.

In order to move through time, you also have to move through the book, often forward, but sometimes backward. Wherever you are in the text, events and thoughts from that same period surround you, but they belong to narratives other than the one you happen to be following. That's the intention. That way the text emerges as what it is—one of many possible paths through the chaos of history.

So welcome to the labyrinth! Follow the threads, put together the horrifying puzzle, and, once you have seen my century, build one of your own from other pieces.[50]

What follows is a series of numbered passages that the reader experiences in a variety of orders. As you proceed, you may indeed "build one of your own" histories, although any feeling of empowerment over the narrative of history is undercut by the claustrophobic presence of so much death and carnage. Even while reading milder passages, the reader's eye takes in photographs from other parts of the page, or violent headlines from other sections intrude. The result is a historical text both linear and nonlinear: if we turn pages in the traditional fashion, we can read the passages that are arranged in historical, chronological order (starting with Chinese experiments in rockets in the first millennia); if we follow the arrows, we experience the narrative through a variety of nonlinear paths.

As in Englund's work, perspective and point of view are central themes, but Lindqvist employs a chronological framework that echoes *The Good Soldier*, and a spatial layout that shares much in common with Dada or Constructivist design. Meanwhile, Gertrude Stein's gnomic remark that war "makes things go backward as well as forward" seems to inform the spirit of Lindqvist's entire enterprise, as well as Ford's theory of the novel put forward in *Joseph Conrad: A Personal Remembrance*:

For it became very early evident to us that what was the matter with the Novel, and the British novel in particular, was that it went straight forward, whereas in your gradual making acquaintanceship with your fellows you never do go straight forward. You meet an English gentleman at your golf club. [. . .] To get such a man in fiction you could not begin at his beginning and work his life chronologically to the end. You must first get him in with a strong impression, and then work backwards and forwards over his past. . . . That theory at least we gradually evolved.[51]

Whether a case of influence or coincidence, the modernist affinities with creative works like *A History of Bombing* demonstrate the possibilities of using modernism's methods as formal techniques. Historians will repeatedly return to the past as obsessively as Dowell returns to his trip to Marburg, continuing the efforts to get the story more right, sometimes with Dowell's muted leisure, sometimes with West's urgent sense of necessity. The paucity of language and form, the ethical imperative to remember, and the human need for narratives are aspects of our historical existence that are not likely to go away, and the modernist historiography of Conrad, Ford, and West provide means of struggling with these challenges.

{ NOTES }

Preface

1. Doležel, *Possible Worlds of Fiction and History*, 23.

2. Although Friedländer includes Hayden White in the volume, his introduction makes clear that he objects to White's radical poststructuralism: "The extermination of the Jews of Europe, as the most extreme case of mass criminality, must challenge theoreticians of historical relativism to face the corollaries of positions otherwise too easily dealt with on an abstract level." *Probing the Limits of Representation: Nazism and the "Final Solution,"* 10. Friedländer objects especially to White's notion that the historian's chosen rhetoric shapes the work of history: instead, Friedländer insists, *"it is the reality and significance of modern catastrophes that generate the search for a new voice and not the use of a specific voice which constructs the significance of these catastrophes"* Ibid., 10, Friedländer's emphasis. Ginzburg's essay in the volume, "Just One Witness," pleads for an attempt at historical objectivity based on documents and witnesses, and Martin Jay's "Of Plots, Witnesses, and Judgments," noting that White had actually backed down from some of his most radical assertions when dealing with Nazism, argues for a consensus from serious scholars to achieve some sort of working truth and guidelines regarding depictions of the Holocaust.

3. Dominick LaCapra, in his essay "Representing the Holocaust: Reflections on the Historian's Debate," writes that "I do not think that conventional techniques, which in certain respects are necessary, are ever sufficient, and to some extent the study of the Holocaust may help us to reconsider the requirements of historiography in general." LaCapra, "Representing the Holocaust: Reflections on the Historian's Debate," 110.

4. Roth, *Memory, Trauma, and History: Essays on Living with the Past*, xviii.

5. Ricoeur, *Time and Narrative*, III.188.

6. West, "The Event and Its Image," 187. In 1949 West wrote, "We all know that there are some events which become experience and others which do not: some events which give us information about the universe and ourselves, and some which tell us nothing." *A Train of Powder*, 138.

7. West, "The Event and Its Image," 189.

8. Stonebridge, *The Judicial Imagination*, 26.

9. "Rebecca West and the Nuremberg Trials," 230.

10. West, *A Train of Powder*, 245.

11. West, *The New Meaning of Treason*, 44, 43.

12. Ibid., xxi.

13. West, *Black Lamb*, 374. She returns to the subject later in the text: "after the war we were all running hither and thither, we had many other things to do besides write down

what we had been doing. So the writing of the history of what happened at Sarajevo fell into the hands of a few who were clever enough to look to the future. Now, because there were no papers, because the reports of the trial were then lost to us, there was nothing for serious historians to work upon, and the field was free to anybody." Ibid., 427.

14. Rollyson, *Rebecca West*, 207.

15. Ginzburg, *The Judge and the Historian*, 23.

16. Ricoeur, *Memory, History, Forgetting*, 320.

17. Ibid., 321.

18. Even West's own account that we now read is a rewriting of her original pieces, as Debra Rae Cohen explores. "Rebecca West's Palimpsestic Praxis: Crafting the Intermodern Voice of Witness," especially pp. 158–163.

19. Stonebridge, *The Judicial Imagination*, 24.

20. West, *A Train of Powder*, 246.

21. Stonebridge, *The Judicial Imagination*, 33.

22. Cohen, "Rebecca West's Palimpsestic Praxis: Crafting the Intermodern Voice of Witness," 158.

23. Stetz writes, "Not once does West speak of the suffering of the Jews as targets of organized genocide. The voices of the Jewish dead go unheard in her reporting." Stetz, "Rebecca West and the Nuremberg Trials," 234.

24. Cohen, "Rebecca West's Palimpsestic Praxis: Crafting the Intermodern Voice of Witness," 158.

25. West, *A Train of Powder*, 250.

26. Stonebridge summarizes the critical conversation: "commentary on her Nuremberg writing . . . has tended to either damn her for failing to recognise the horrors of the Holocaust (a charge, as we have seen, that could be leveled at the entire court) or praise her for forging a poetics of memory and loss in the literariness of her prose (a trauma writing *avant la lettre*)." *The Judicial Imagination*, 33. For a praising account, see Ravit Reichman, "Committed to Memory: Rebecca West's Nuremberg," in *The Affective Life of Law*, 103–134.

27. Ochsner, "Understanding the Holocaust through the U.S. Holocaust Memorial Museum," 240.

28. Ibid., 241.

29. Ibid.

30. Barkan, "Introduction," 902.

31. Ibid., 904.

32. Ibid., 908. Charles Ingrao lays out his ongoing work: "The Scholars' Initiative (SI) stemmed from the conviction that native historians and social scientists are best positioned to challenge the tendentious nationalistic narratives that have succeeded so well in dividing the peoples of Central Europe. But to do so, they would need to accomplish two tasks to which most are unaccustomed, and with which they are even uncomfortable. First, they would have to join with scholars from across the successor states to craft a common narrative that exposes and discredits each belligerent's myths about the Yugoslav conflicts, while simultaneously inserting indisputable but inconvenient facts known to their former adversaries. Second, they would need to reach out to the public by engaging media and, when possible, politicians willing to place at least one foot on the common platform that their own scholars have helped construct." "Confronting the Yugoslav Controversies," 950.

33. Ford, *It Was the Nightingale*, 179.

Introduction

1. James, *Literary Criticism*, I.966.

2. Jameson, *Modernist Papers*, 394.

3. Ginzburg, "Microhistory: Two or Three Things That I Know about It," 24.

4. See the Conclusion for more on the *Annales* group, as well as Burguière, *The Annales School*.

5. Oliver Daddow explores this resistance in "The Ideology of Apathy: Historians and Postmodernism." The dual roles of historians, both as researchers and writers, has made the field less amenable to "theory," and as John Tosh noted in *The Pursuit of History* (1984), "[m]any historians who have a flair for working on primary sources find the process of composition excruciatingly laborious and frustrating. The temptation is to continue amassing material so that the time of reckoning can be put off indefinitely." *The Pursuit of History*, 93. When writing is seen as secondary, discourse theory will inevitably have less sway. (Tosh does not include this passage in the later, revised versions of his influential book, now in its fifth edition.) George Iggers writes that the "radical critiques of accepted methods of historical inquiry that have dominated theoretical discussions of history from the 1970s to the present have had an important but nevertheless limited impact on the writing of history." *Historiography in the Twentieth Century: From Scientific Objectivity to the Postmodern Challenge*, 11.

6. Emmanuel Le Roy Ladurie is an important figure in this genealogy, as he included a Preface laying out his research methods that stressed the contingent and constructed nature of his project; subsequent writers like Ginzburg, or for example Amitav Ghosh in *In an Antique Land: History in the Guise of a Traveler's Tale* (1994), weave this self-awareness throughout the historical text itself. See also Giovanni Levi's Preface to *Inheriting Power: The Story of an Exorcist* (1988): "I have for this reason attempted to study intensively a minuscule segment of Piedmont in the 1600s and to reconstruct the biographies of all the inhabitants of the village of Santena who left traces in documents." Levi, *Inheriting Power*, xiv.

7. Ginzburg, "Microhistory: Two or Three Things That I Know about It," 23. Roger Chartier, responding to *The Cheese and the Worms*, wrote that "it is on this reduced scale, and probably only on this scale, that we can understand, without deterministic reduction, the relationship between systems of belief, of values and representations on one side, and social affiliations on the other." "Intellectual History or Sociocultural History? The French Trajectories," 32. Iggers sums up nicely the assumptions and techniques of microhistory: while they "continue to insist that there is a reality external to the historical texts that can be known," "narrative becomes important for the presentation of the historian's findings because it can communicate elements that cannot be conveyed in abstract form and because it shows the process by which the historian arrives at his/her account." *Historiography in the Twentieth Century: From Scientific Objectivity to the Postmodern Challenge*, 109–110.

8. Stone, "The Revival of Narrative: Reflections on a New Old History," 13.

9. Jameson in *Late Marxism* dubs the work of Adorno "modernist," positing that modernism is possibly not just a set of aesthetic practices but "that deeper skepticism about the possibility of representing anything—which is to say, finally, about saying anything at all—that in the face of the palpable fact that sometimes things do get said or represented gives way to a curious exploration of the structures and the preconditions, the electoral

fraud, cheating, rigging in advance, and the tropological framework that enabled such representation in the first place; not excluding a cool analytic assessment of what had to be abandoned *en route*, left unsaid, lied about, or misrepresented." Jameson, *Late Marxism : Adorno, Or, the Persistence of the Dialectic*, 10. Similarly, in *Valences of the Dialectic* (2010) Jameson reads Fernand Braudel's epic historical work *Mediterranean* as "modernist in the way in which the Annales historians waged their fundamental campaign against that central category of narrative, the event, and thus may in some sense be thought to take an anti-narrative position on history writing." *Valences of the Dialectic*, 532. Modernism for Jameson, at least in these contexts, means a certain set of assumptions and practices, and "modernist historiography" may be an apt way to describe what Conrad, Ford, and West were exploring with their historical fictions. However, like I argue, I cannot accept that modernism is perpetually taking "an anti-narrative position."

10. Howe, *A Critic's Notebook*, 185.

11. Ford, *No More Parades*, 3.

12. Lukács, *Historical Novel*, 19.

13. Thucydides, *History of the Peloponnesian War*, 8.

14. For example, Salman Rushdie, Penelope Lively, Julian Barnes, and Gabriel García Márquez all use fiction to narrate historical events in one way or another. Most critics would see these works as examples of postmodern historical novels, but Jonathan White argues that they are writing "modernist historical novels" as they operate in "modernist modes." White is thus employing the term "modernism" as a chosen style rather than the product of the modern era or movement. White, "Politics and the Individual in the Modernist Historical Novel," 209. More recently, Eric Berlatsky writes that postmodernism "critiques narrative's tendency to obscure our access to the past" while simultaneously "it suggests alternative forms as more effective means of accessing the real." *The Real, the True, and the Told*, 15. Berlatsky does not give modernism much attention, but reads Woolf's *Between the Acts* as postmodern. Such a move, more nuanced than Hutcheon's, at least allows for a more complicated picture of twentieth-century historical fiction, although it still mostly maintains the prevailing assumptions about modernism and history.

15. Wesseling, *Writing History as a Prophet*, 73.

16. See also Holmes, *The Historical Imagination*.

17. Wesseling, *Writing History as a Prophet*, 73.

18. Using Renato Poggioli's distinction between the avant-garde and modernism, Wesseling argues that "[t]he historical avant-garde sought to lift the weight of the past by bluntly denying it. . . . Modernist writers, somewhat differently, sought to salvage the bewildering mass of historical information by means of synoptic schemes which divert our attention from processes of historical change to the eternally recurrent." Ibid., 81. Poggioli's distinction between the avant-garde and modernism seems more suited for the Continent than Britain—not even the avant-gardism of Wyndham Lewis "denies" the past.

19. Linda Hutcheon's *A Poetics of Postmodernism: History, Theory, Fiction* (1988) makes this case most aggressively. In an attempt to set up postmodern art and literature as more historical, more playful, and ultimately more insightful than modernism, she creates modernist straw men (mostly men) who were formalist and ahistorical: "There seems to be a new desire to think historically, and to think historically these days is to think critically and contextually. . . . Part of this problematizing return to history is no doubt a

response to the hermetic ahistoric formalism and aestheticism that characterized much of the art and theory of the so-called modernist period. If the past were invoked, it was to deploy its 'presentness' or to enable its transcendence in the search for a more secure and universal value system (be it myth, religion, or psychology). Some writers seemed caught between skepticism and a mystical-aesthetic ideal of historical understanding. ... However, modernism's 'nightmare of history' is precisely what postmodernism has chosen to face straight on." *A Poetics of Postmodernism*, 88. Hutcheon sees postmodern interest in history as "new," which even a cursory survey of modernist texts should be enough to dispel. Again, arguments in this vein shares with New Criticism the formalist assumptions about modernism, seeing works by Joyce or Eliot as "hermetic" despite the proliferation of advertisements in *Ulysses* and dance hall music in *The Waste Land*. Hutcheon does consider Faulkner as a possible argument against her central thesis—surely he is concerned with history?—but is not convinced: "Well, yes and no: paradoxical postmodernism is both oedipally oppositional and filially faithful to modernism. The provisional, indeterminate nature of historical knowledge is certainly not a discovery of postmodernism. Nor is the questioning of the ontological and epistemological status of historical 'fact' or the distrust of seeming neutrality and objectivity of recounting. But the concentration of these problematizations in postmodern art is not something we can ignore." Ibid. Apparently the interest in history that Conrad, Ford, Pound, Eliot, Yeats, Faulkner, Joyce, and Woolf all share *could* be ignored, but such is no longer the case.

20. North, *Reading 1922*, 10. See also Spiropoulou: "Some critics of postmodern fiction perpetuate the canonical appreciation of literary modernism as ahistorical in order to contrast it with postmodernism's pointed revisiting of history and revising of historiographical orthodoxies." Spiropoulou, *Virginia Woolf, Modernity and History*, 4.

21. An example of this is when Hutcheon quotes Jameson (from his essay "Periodizing the 60s"): Jameson argues that one solution to the crisis of historiography is "in the modernist aesthetic itself—in reorganizing its traditional procedures on a different level ... not any longer to produce some vivid representation of history 'as it really happened,' but rather to produce the *concept* of history." Hutcheon concurs but writes that "There is only one word I would change in this: the word 'modernist' seems to me to be less apt than 'postmodernist,' though Jameson would never agree." Hutcheon, *A Poetics of Postmodernism*, 112. This line of criticism uniquely privileges the postmodern instead of seeing so many postmodern concerns already anticipated by the moderns. It turns out, however, that Jameson actually does agree with Hutcheon: in *Valances of the Dialectic* (2009) he extols the postmodern in his brief discussion of the modernist historical novel: "But it is precisely this capacity of the literary text to make Time itself appear, even fitfully, that also constitutes the superiority of the postmodern aesthetic over its modernist predecessor in this respect. For while the latter pursued that mirage of unification which it still shared with philosophy, the former chose to embrace dispersal and multiplicity." Jameson, *Valences of the Dialectic*, 532.

22. Anderson, "From Progress to Catastrophe," 24. Harold Orel, in *The Historical Novel from Scott to Sabatini* (1995), elides the modernist era, and insists that "not a single one of the important novelists born after 1880—those who came to dominate the market in the 1920s—thought it worth their while to write historical romances. ... Their interests lay elsewhere." Orel, *The Historical Novel from Scott to Sabatini*, 163. More recently, Jerome DeGroot spends two pages on the modernist era, one on Virginia Woolf and the

other on H. G. Wells. De Groot, *The Historical Novel*, 43–44. Finally, in his long essay on the genre, Perry Anderson devotes one paragraph to Virginia Woolf. Anderson, "From Progress to Catastrophe," 27.

23. Anderson, "From Progress to Catastrophe," 27.

24. De Groot, *The Historical Novel*, 43.

25. Fleishman, *The English Historical Novel*, 240.

26. For more on the relationship between *Orlando* and history, see Spiropoulou, *Virginia Woolf, Modernity and History*, 75–95. See also Hallett, "Anne Clifford as Orlando."

27. As Marianne Dekoven puts it, "Nothing escapes history, but literary modernism is often discussed as if it did. Depending on their political-aesthetic stance, such discussions either rejoice in modernism's flight from a debased social reality to a realm of rich meaning, aesthetic joy, and pure freedom, or they regret modernism's retreat from accessibility into bristling difficulty, its isolation from the life of society on a rarefied, elitist aesthetic pinnacle." "History as Suppressed Referent in Modernist Fiction," 137. Dekoven is brusque, but her central point strikes me as valid, as this "escape from history" thesis continued to influence literary criticism of modernism.

28. Felski, *Uses of Literature*, 6.

29. Hegel, *Introduction to The Philosophy of History*, 64. Similarly, Robert Berkhofer explains how "[t]he ambiguity of the word *history* is deliberate, for the written history is supposed to reconstruct or portray past events, behaviors, thoughts, etc., as they once occurred. . . . Thus the historian's written history acts as if it were a transparent medium to use a linguistic analogy between the past and the reader's mind, although both historian and reader would deny such an easy equation if raised to their consciousness." Berkhofer, "The Challenge of Poetics to (Normal) Historical Practice," 436.

30. De Certeau writes, "in current usage 'history' connotes both a science and that which it studies—the explication which is *stated*, and the reality of *what has taken place* or what takes place. Other disciplines are not burdened with this ambiguity: French does not refer to 'physics' and 'nature' with the same name. The very term 'history' therefore already suggests a situation of particular proximity between the scientific operation and the reality that it analyzes." *The Writing of History*, 21. Hayden White, in his review of Jameson's *The Political Unconscious*, queries Jameson's use of term "history" and argues that the word "applies to past events, to the record of those events, to the chain of events which make up a temporal process that includes the events of the past and present as well as those of the future, to systematically ordered accounts of the events attested by the record, to explanations of such systematically ordered accounts, and so forth. Throughout all of those possible usages of the term 'history,' however, there runs the thread of the distinction, drawn by Aristotle in the *Poetics*, between what can possibly happen and what actually did happen, between what can be known because it happened and what can only be imagined, and what, therefore, the historian can legitimately assert as a truth of experience and what the poet might wish to entertain as a truth of thought or conceptualization." White, "Getting out of History," 4.

31. de Certeau, *The Writing of History*, xxvii.

32. Ibid., 20.

33. Shanske, *Thucydides and the Philosophical Origins of History*, 9.

34. Lukács, *Historical Novel*, 21.

35. See especially Christopher GoGwilt's *The Invention of the West: Joseph Conrad and the Double-Mapping of Europe and Empire* (1995) and Richard Niland's *Conrad and History* (2010).

36. See Wiesenfarth, *History and Representation in Ford Madox Ford's Writings.*

37. See Schweizer, *Rebecca West: Heroism, Rebellion, and the Female Epic.*

38. There are several collections of West's essays, but there is much more to collect from a writer who wrote contemporary accounts of both suffragism and Margaret Thatcher. In terms of literary experimenters, West promoted Conrad, Lawrence, and Woolf, had qualified endorsement for Joyce (via her 1928 essay *The Strange Necessity*), and was a lifelong adversary of T. S. Eliot.

39. See Skinner, *Ford Madox Ford's Literary Contacts*; Harding, *Ford Madox Ford, Modernist Magazines and Editing*; and Haslam and O'Malley, *Ford Madox Ford and America.*

40. Burrow, *A History of Histories*, 474–475. For David Carr in *Time, Narrative, and History* (1986), storytelling is integral not just to the discipline of history but also "historicity," our lived experience: "we are unable to understand the necessary *social* dimensions of historicity until we go beyond individual experience," and our primary means to do so is narrative. Thus "[h]istorical and fictional narratives will reveal themselves to be not distortions of, denials of, or escapes from reality, but extensions and configurations of its primary features." *Time, Narrative, and History*, 5, 16.

41. Boyd, *On the Origin of Stories*, 131.

42. The Icelandic historian Axel Kristinsson relates Boyd's theories to what he terms the "peculiar" nature of history (Kristinsson, "Af Hverju Er Sagnfræðin Svona Skrítin?" Author's English translation available on his website at axelkrist.com/projects.html).

43. Joyce, *Ulysses*, 28.

44. As Hegel put it, "This application of the principle of freedom to worldly reality ... that is the long process that makes up history itself." *Introduction to The Philosophy of History*, 21.

45. See the section entitled "A Renewed Attempt to Answer the Question: 'Is the Human Race Continually Improving?'" Kant, *Kant's Political Writings*, 177–190.

46. Ranke, *The Secret of World History*, 102.

47. In 1908 Charles Petit-Dutaillis wrote a preface to the works of Bishop William Stubbs, the Oxford historian of the constitutional, history-as-progress school. Petit-Dutaillis chafed against the notion of teleological optimism, arguing that in his age, "when so many illusions have been dissipated, when parliamentary institutions set up by almost every civilized nation have more openly revealed as they developed their inevitable littleness and when the formation of nationalities has turned Europe into an armed camp, history is written with less enthusiasm." Burrow, *A History of Histories*, 422.

48. See Nico Israel, *Spirals.*

49. Jean-Francois Lyotard also addresses the role of narrative in the nineteenth century: "The explicit appeal to narrative in the problematic of knowledge is concomitant with the liberation of the bourgeois classes from the traditional authorities. Narrative knowledge makes a resurgence in the West as a way of solving the problem of legitimating the new authorities." But note that Lyotard's seminal critique of "grand narratives" still allows for the use of narrative itself in historiography, and is thus a markedly different approach than that of Braudel et al. In *The Postmodern Condition* he notes that, despite

the decline of grand narratives, "the little narrative remains the quintessential form of imaginative invention, most particularly in science" in the late twentieth century. Thus storytelling still retains its privileged place in the production of knowledge. Lyotard, *The Postmodern Condition*, 30, 60.

50. Ranke, *The Secret of World History*, 154.

51. Critics of Ranke have unearthed his own subjective and historically determined biases: Iggers argues that Ranke's professional and political position in society was informative of his methodology. Iggers, *Historiography in the Twentieth Century: From Scientific Objectivity to the Postmodern Challenge*, 26. Anthony Grafton writes of Ranke's faith in established sources and how it aided in the growth of Prussian nationalism. Grafton, *The Footnote*, 65.

52. Ranke, *The Secret of World History*, 110.

53. Hegel, *Introduction to The Philosophy of History*, 18.

54. Leon Pompa argues, "For Vico, the peculiar intelligibility of history rests upon insights into our own nature which are accessible to us by virtue of our capacity to reflect upon ourselves in our various social and historical activities, so that we can be aware not merely of the different ways in which we see and react to our world but also of the different conditions which cause us to see and react thus." *Vico*, 167.

55. Dilthey and Bradley's subjectivist historiography continued with the work of Croce and Ortega y Gasset, and eventually R. G. Collingwood.

56. Bradley, *The Presuppositions of Critical History*, 78.

57. Ibid., 101.

58. Ibid., 102.

59. Ibid., 103.

60. It is notable that Eliot focuses more on Bradley's notions of radical subjectivism than on his solutions to this problem. See the note to line 411 of *The Waste Land*, where Eliot quotes Bradley.

61. Rousseau, *The Confessions*, 262, 17.

62. Conrad, *Nostromo*, 244. West, *Black Lamb*, 1128.

63. In *The Whig Interpretation of History* (1931), Herbert Butterfield argues that we must be wary of invoking history with any confidence, and his analysis might speak for these writers: he writes that we must be on guard against history, "as though indeed history, once she had spoken, had put the matter beyond the range of mere human enquiry. Rather we must say to ourselves: 'She will lie to us till the very end of the last cross-examination.' . . . If we must confuse counsel by personifying history at all, it is best to treat her as an old reprobate, whose tricks and juggleries are things to be guarded against." Butterfield, *The Whig Interpretation of History*, 132. This is a far cry from Ranke's belief that a study of history would reveal its "secret," as Butterfield insists that history (conspicuously gendered female) is not just concealed, waiting to be revealed, but rather is actively eluding the grasp of the historian (again imagined as solely male). Modernist experimenters, however, had little faith in Butterfield's objective historian, and instead trusted fictional narratives to convey history and its experiences.

64. Walter Benjamin writes in "The Storyteller" that after the Great War "it is as if something that seemed inalienable to us, the securest among our possessions, were taken from us: the ability to exchange experiences." *Illuminations*, 83. This is a point still highly contested in cultural studies of the Great War, a focal point for debates concerning progress.

The standard view of the war has been that it radically changed the way the modernists saw history, shaking teleological notions. But Jay Winter has persuasively argued that "the rupture of 1914–18 was much less complete than previous scholars have suggested." Winter, *Sites of Memory, Sites of Mourning*, 3. We should thus be on guard against using the war as the central turning-point in a view of history, and in fact Joseph Conrad's approach to the modernist novel in *Nostromo*, published a decade before the war, already exhibits the sense of suspicion and dread we associate with the postwar era. To be sure, the war changed modernism's relationship to the writing of history, or how we write historical narratives. Ford Madox Ford, at the front lines, saw the gap between what he was perceiving and what would eventually be written as "history," and through his work implied that "realist" methods of narrating historical events would no longer be adequate. Instead, then, as serving as witness to historical events—he "witnessed" the Battle of the Somme, if such a witnessing is even possible—his historical narratives exploit the trauma of such experiences, and highlight the gap between event and representation. But, as I will argue, these critical insights had been strongly intuited by Ford during his composition of the radically fragmented *The Good Soldier*, already begun before the outbreak of war.

65. Conrad, *Heart of Darkness*, 17.

66. Watt, *Conrad in the Nineteenth Century*, 175.

67. Watt writes that "[l]ong before *Heart of Darkness* Conrad seems to have been trying to find ways of giving direct narrative expression to the way in which the consciousness elicits meaning from its perceptions. One of the devices that he hit on was to present a sense impression and to withhold naming it or explaining its meaning until later; as readers we witness every step by which the gap between the individual perception and its cause is belatedly closed within the consciousness of the protagonist." Ibid. Jesse Matz, however, has questioned whether this is really how Conrad's impressionism works, demonstrating how impressionism is never simply about empirical absorption of data, as the senses never simply fall into language: as soon as senses are narrated they are interpreted, and there is no "delay" in this process. For Matz, Watt's theory of "delayed decoding" "forces a 'gap' between what it takes to be impression and intellection to emphasize the tenuousness of interpretation, rather than respecting the degree to which explanation and affect coexist in the initial 'impression.' Watt presumes a skeptical orientation, distorting the process in question by placing teleological stress on the final judgment: the 'coding' actually occurs in the fuller nonfigural explanation which follows the impression, not in the impression itself, so what Watt calls 'delayed decoding' might more appropriately be called 'delayed encoding.'" Matz, *Literary Impressionism and Modernist Aesthetics*, 144. For Matz the skepticism of Conrad's impressionism comes *after* we have received the image, in the "explanation."

68. Jameson, *Political Unconscious*, 212.

69. Conrad, *The Nigger of the "Narcissus,"* xlix.

70. Fleishman, *The English Historical Novel*, 211.

71. Genette, *Narrative Discourse*, 284.

72. Ford, *Joseph Conrad*, 195.

73. Conrad, *Nostromo*, 374.

74. Jameson, *Political Unconscious*, 237. Jameson had earlier made a similar point regarding Sartre in *Sartre : The Origins of a Style*, 19–39.

75. Jameson, *Political Unconscious*, 272.

76. Ibid., 278–279.

77. White, *Figural Realism*, 74. White agrees with Jameson's conclusions, but sees in this modernist strategy a positive use for historians, since White is always on the lookout for methods other than narrative to write histories: "And this is why it seems to me that the kinds of antinarrrative nonstories produced by literary modernism offer the only prospect for adequate representations of the kind of 'unnatural' events—including the Holocaust—that mark our era and distinguish it absolutely from all of the history that has come before it." Ibid., 81. So for White these attempts to escape from narrative and history can provide the historian with other tools with which to depict history.

78. White, *Content of the Form*, 173. Joseph Mali uses a similar definition in *Mythistory*: looking mostly at Joyce, he writes, "I define modernism as a cultural movement that consists in the 'recognition of myth,' and I define modern historiography in those terms as well." *Mythistory*, 18.

79. Sayeau, *Against the Event*, 151, 46. For Sayeau, the "everyday" takes precedence over the event in much of modernist writing: writers from Flaubert to Joyce "privileged the everyday over the event—tended to see the world as one that runs on a rhythm defined by banal continuity rather than accentuated series of revolutionary shocks. ... These works manifest a resistance to what we might call the 'metaphysics of the event'—a resistance grounded in a distinctly overdetermined distrust of novelty itself." Ibid., 5.

80. Southgate, *Postmodernism in History*, 164.

81. Curiously, in an earlier essay, "Literary Theory and Historical Writing," Hayden White has argued as much: "it is now possible to recognize that literary modernism did not so much reject narrativity, historicity, or even realism as explore the limits of their peculiarly nineteenth-century forms and expose the mutual complicity of these forms in the dominant discursive practices of high bourgeois culture. In the process, literary modernism revealed new or forgotten potentialities of narrative discourse itself. ... Literary modernism did not repudiate narrative discourse but discovered in it a content, linguistic and tropological, adequate to the representation of dimensions of historical life only implicitly perceived in nineteenth-century realism, both literary and historical." White, *Figural Realism*, 26. These conclusions are at odds with his later statements about modernism's "antinarrrativc nonstories."

82. Woolf, *Between the Acts*, 125.

83. This affinity between Woolf and Benjamin is thoroughly explored in Angeliki Spiropoulou's *Virginia Woolf, Modernity and History: Constellations with Walter Benjamin* (2011), in which she reads Woolf's entire *oeuvre* through a Benjaminian lens: "both writers sought to put into question modern illusions such as the cultural myths of progress, of historical causality, of sanctified tradition and of a dead past, which served to legitimate the present conditions and hence perpetuated structures of oppression. They strove to establish a different relation of the present to the past that overcame binary modes of thought, and would instead redeem forgotten and suppressed aspects of the past for the political urgencies of the present." *Virginia Woolf, Modernity and History*, 24. For Woolf and Benjamin, the result is a focus on marginal historical figures; an insistence that historical texts are always political texts; and a belief that "the past could not be represented 'as it was,' despite the historicist conviction to the contrary, [as] both allowed for the intervention of imaginative, fictional reconstructions and brought to the fore the political demands of the present at play in history writing." Ibid., 47.

84. All this is not to say that the histories produced by the modernists were not highly ideological or even severely problematic. Robert Holton examines the relationship between literature and history in the twentieth century and critiques Conrad and Ford, among others, for the glaring deficiencies in their attempts to do justice to the past. For example, he writes of *Nostromo* that "[n]owhere in the novel are the natives given the opportunity—as the Blancos frequently are—to articulate a political position or to narrate a version of historical events." *Jarring Witnesses*, 59. This is just one of the many useful and valid critiques of modernism's depictions of history, but it is one thing to say that Conrad writes inaccurate history, and another to say that he flees from the very discourse of history. Writing a work of history is not the same as getting it right, which is why I believe Jameson's broader point about Conrad is sound: that his work tries to avoid certain social problems and "solve" them on an aesthetic level. But many professional historians do the same. This is why one must always clarify what we mean by "history": the word too quickly slides into its own referent and becomes something somehow authentic or positive. I am not drawn to modernist histories for examples of non-ideological histories, but instead for meditations on narrative and history, because they so successfully stage the problematics of historiography. We must be able to separate, in any historical analysis of literature, the "what" from the "how" of history, lest we commit the fallacy of isomorphic reductionism.

85. James, *Sense of the Past*, 11.

86. Ibid., 49.

87. Ibid., 32–33.

88. Ibid., 24, 34.

89. "Time Flies," West's "Time Book," exists in holograph form at Yale's Beinecke Library. It involves a man who invents an airplane that can fly through time. Rebecca West Collection, General Collection, Beinecke Rare Book and Manuscript Library, Yale University. (Box 37, Folder 1376.)

90. James, *Sense of the Past*, 87.

91. James was by no means dismissive of the work of the professional historians of his time. For Roslyn Jolly, James's work is marked by a deep engagement in contemporary forms of historiography: "it is precisely this sense of the modern difficulty of uniting the interests of novelist and historian that animates James's idea of the novel as history, and distinguishes it from earlier conceptions which drew on a very different model of historical discourse." *Henry James*, 23.

92. James, *Sense of the Past*, 96.

93. Claude Lévi-Strauss, *The Savage Mind*: hot chronologies "are those of periods where in the eyes of the historian numerous events appear as differential elements; others, on the contrary, where for him (although not of course for the men who lived through them) very little or nothing took place." Lévi-Strauss, *The Savage Mind*, 259. Jolly asserts that James's novel may "be seen as offering resistance to the reality of the war, or to the processes which have brought it about." *Henry James*, 216.

94. For example see Wood, *The Purpose of the Past*. Also Lukacs, *The Future of History*.

95. Conrad, *Notes on Life and Letters*, 17.

96. See Niland: "'The Tale' resulted from Conrad's engagement in propaganda work, and from his correspondence with Ford Madox Ford, stationed in France in 1916, which discussed in detail the difficulties of artistically representing the war." *Conrad and History*, 157.

97. Conrad, *Selected Short Stories*, 225.

98. Ibid., 233.

99. Ibid., 237–238.

100. Ibid., 238.

101. Conrad, *Nostromo*, 451.

102. Vivienne Rundle, in her comparison of the prefaces of Conrad and Henry James, writes that "[s]ince the categories of 'fiction' and 'history' undergo continual dissolution and redefinition within the Conradian oeuvre, the reader is able to position each novel between those two extremes." "Defining Frames: The Prefaces of Henry James and Joseph Conrad," 79. Rundle highlights the theory of textual openness and indeterminacy that Conrad shares with Derrida, but we could also argue that Conrad's preface opens up *Nostromo* to the historiographical process that Paul Ricoeur calls "writing through and through." Since the preface is so inviting to rereadings, it provides a sense of freedom to begin our own writings and rewritings as the text of *Nostromo* enters into the endless chain of textual history.

103. Ford, *Cinque Ports*, 4.

104. Ibid., vi.

105. Ford's own attempts at historical nonfiction stop short of a full deployment of his radical narrative innovations. Before his death in 1939 he was working on what was later published as *A History of Our Own Times*, a work of history that was supposed to cover the years 1870 to Ford's present day. He imagined that this work would reach a popular audience, and accepted his editors' cuts to keep it in line with standard industry practices. He only finished the first volume, which covers 1870–1895. He includes novelistic sketches of historical moments, and Elena Lamberti writes that "according to Ford the new 'imaginative writer' is a type of contemporary historian.... Of course, differing from the Historian, at least on a theoretical level, by so doing the impressionist writer ends by re-creating situations shaped in a carefully conceived narrative discourse, so that both the writer's temperament, and his/her technical skill, play a fundamental role in the rendering of the observation." "Writing History: Ford and the Debate on 'Objective Truth' in the Late 20th Century," 31. However, as much as it might strike us as in some ways a postmodern history, in fact Ford was adhering to the conventions of nineteenth-century realism, and we should see it as sitting safely in the classical, pre-scientific tradition of Western historiography. Unlike some of Ford's other writings, in *A History of Our Own Times* Ford assumes a stable universe; assumes a distinction between objects and a perceiving or writing subject; and assumes the transparency of language as conveying the real. Ford was above all a fiction writer, and it is there, and not in his nonfiction histories, that he actually discovered the most significant insights into the writing of history.

106. Ford, *Critical Essays*, 10.

107. Ford repeats this gesture in *The Great Trade Route* (1937): "I am not an Economist or a Scientific Historian ... or in the least inclined to interfere in the affairs of my kind. What I wrote would raise a howl ... as what I am writing will, from the Economist, the Scientific Historian, and the people who interfere professionally in world affairs. They will say I know nothing about it. But really it is they who know nothing about anything. They have never sat on rocks over the Mediterranean and thought ... and felt. ..." *Great Trade Route*, 396.

108. Attridge, "'We Will Listen to None but Specialists': Ford, the Rise of Specialization and The English Review," 31.

109. Note the similarity to Virginia Woolf's "Mrs. Bennett and Mr. Brown," which targeted Bennett, Galsworthy, and Wells more pointedly than it did Dickens, Thackeray, or the Brontës.

110. Conrad, *Personal Record*, 15.

111. Conrad, *Lord Jim*, 22.

112. James's attitude may have partly been in response to the rise of scientific historiography, as Attridge explains: "Both James and Conrad appear to be defending the validity of other, non-accredited forms of history against this professional research ideal, and their emphasis on the novelist's different means of collecting evidence—impressions, as Conrad puts it—zeroes in on the archival 'fact-grubbing' that characterized the new historical methodology." "'We Will Listen to None but Specialists': Ford, the Rise of Specialization and The English Review," 32. Early modernism, then, was animated by this reaction against new methods of writing history. Similarly, in *Modernism, Media, and Propaganda* (2006), Mark Wollaeger argues that Ford the used impression to offset the fact; that is, to "resist the onset of the posthuman by reinvesting facts with feeling": "The facts of human existence, endlessly reiterated in the daily press, anatomized by technical specialists, and laid out in reference works and actuarial tables, have been split off from experimental immediacy, and by fusing facts and human feeling in the impression, Ford hopes to restore a lost wholeness." Wollaeger relates this to propaganda, his main concern: "This is where the shared dynamic between impressionism and propaganda becomes most apparent. Each aims to restore wholeness and feeling to information, though for quite different reasons." *Modernism, Media, and Propaganda: British Narrative from 1900 to 1945*, 7, 142–143.

113. See for example Alun Munslow's inaugural editorial to *Rethinking History: The Journal of Theory and Practice*, where he describes the orthodoxy of "a sharply defined and conservative *reconstructionist* approach to the past that bears a direct lineage to the nineteenth-century empiricist Anglo-American hermeneutic. For convenience I shall designate this as modernist history." "Editorial," 4.

114. Paul Costello uses the latter term to signify what most cultural critics would call "modernity." Costello, *World Historians and Their Goals*.

115. Bentley, *Modernizing England's Past*, 9.

116. Ibid., 15.

117. Initially the status of science was a debate within English letters, but as war loomed German historians became more of a target for critique, and the debate soon became recast as English empiricism versus German professionalism. Ford's wartime propaganda book, *When Blood Is Their Argument* (1915), lambasts Germany's obsession with pedantic detail and factual accuracy, arguing that they mistake facts for truths. Andrzej Gasiorek argues that Ford's arguments in this text were actually "openly personal interventions that drew attention to the partial, and *interested*, nature of their representations of the historical process." "'In the Mirror of the Arts': Ford's Modernism and the Reconstruction of Post-War Literary Culture," 207.

118. Ford, *Critical Essays*, 10.

119. The phrase later appears in T. S. Eliot's "Tradition and the Individual Talent": "Tradition is a matter of much wider significance. It cannot be inherited, and if you want

it you must obtain it by great labour. It involves, in the first place, the historical sense, which we may call nearly indispensable to anyone who would continue to be a poet beyond his twenty-fifth year; and the historical sense involves a perception, not only of the pastness of the past, but of its presence; the historical sense compels a man to write not merely with his own generation in his bones, but with a feeling that the whole of the literature of Europe from Homer and within it the whole of the literature of his own country has a simultaneous existence and composes a simultaneous order. This historical sense, which is a sense of the timeless as well as of the temporal and of the timeless and of the temporal together, is what makes a writer traditional." *Selected Prose of T. S. Eliot*, 38.

120. Ford, *Critical Essays*, 11.

121. Ibid., 13, 12.

122. In this Ford anticipates Hayden White, but again also anticipates Butterfield. Butterfield uses "whig" in the lower case to imply a method of thought more than a specific political school. The whig tendency is "in many historians to write on the side of Protestants and Whigs, to praise revolutions provided they have been successful, to emphasise certain principles of progress in the past and to produce a story which is the ratification if not the glorification of the present." The whig process "comes into action with increasing effect the moment any given subject has left the hands of the student in research; for the more we are discussing and not merely enquiring, the more we are making inferences instead of researches, then the more whig our history becomes if we have not severely repressed our original error." Once the historian begins "discussing," the historical narrative will take a certain form that is the historian's own, not something "found" in history or historical documents. Butterfield, *The Whig Interpretation of History*, v, 7. Butterfield's essay played a small part in the eventual abandonment of narrative altogether by many historians midway through the century. However, he would not have championed this move: he implies there is a mode of writing history that is free from such impulses, if historians were just careful enough about their work. But for Ford, any attempt at history would be "whig" because you cannot escape the "devil of theorizing." Mid-century structuralists agreed, and abandoned narrative for the most part.

123. Ford, *Critical Essays*, 11.

124. Ford, *Fifth Queen*, 524.

125. MacShane, *Ford Madox Ford: The Critical Heritage*, 32.

126. Wiley, *Novelist of Three Worlds: Ford Madox Ford*, 105.

127. Wrenn, "Henry, Hueffer, Holbein, History and Representation," 169.

128. Ford includes a section of Flaubert's story at the conclusion of his essay "Creative History and the Historic Sense." *Critical Essays*, 13.

129. Sanford Schwartz, in *The Matrix of Modernism* (1985), explains how modernist writers "introduced techniques to heighten the discontinuity between the text and everyday reality. . . . Nineteenth-century novelists tend to use language as a transparent medium for rendering social reality. By contrast, modern novelists such as Joyce tend to foreground the signifying medium itself . . . the modern artist no longer *represents* a pre-existing reality, but *presents* a new set of relations, a 'model' through which to order the world anew." *The Matrix of Modernism*, 102. Schwartz's distinctions may be too schematic given subsequent work on Victorian realism—did any serious nineteenth-century writer believe in the transparency of language?—but Schwartz can help us see that *The Fifth Queen* goes beyond some of realism's practices, as it does not even try to trick the reader

into believing that language is providing unmediated access to reality. Dickens may not have naively believed that he was actually "realistically" presenting London to his readers, but he might have had faith in giving them a narrative space in which they could suspend their disbelief for a period of time and pretend they were seeing London "transparently," in a shared pact between reader and text. Modernism generally resists such arrangements, and in *The Fifth Queen* we are constantly reminded that we are seeing, not the Tudor Court, but representations of the Tudor Court.

130. Louis Marin, in his study *Portraits of the King*, argues that any depiction of a king is involved in the power of that same king: for the early modern period, simply to reproduce his image and record his every major decision establishes him as worthy of power: "To tell the king's history in a narrative is to show it. To show the king's history in his icon is to tell it." *Portrait of the King*, 121. The king does not even need explicit praise—the very repetition of depictions is enough to establish his power. The attention Ford gives to representation may be involved in this nature of royal power.

131. Conrad, *Collected Letters*, II.67.

132. Nield, *A Guide to the Best Historical Novels and Tales*, 10.

133. Although this demarcation can be traced at least as far back as the historical romance writer Clara Reeve, who in the preface to *The Old English Baron* (1780) defined her work as historical romance instead of history, since the latter "represents human nature as it is in real life;—also, too often a melancholy retrospect!" *The Old English Baron*, iv.

134. Harding writes that "[i]n 1902 over 2,000 historical novels were published in England alone." "The Swan Song of Historical Romance: The Fifth Queen Trilogy," 112.

135. Baker, *A Guide to Historical Fiction*, vii.

136. James, *Letters*, IV.208. James might be surprised to see Ford write "I may as well now confess that in drawing Henry VIII in one of my own novels I was rendering the Master in externals." Ford, *Thus to Revisit; Some Reminiscences*, 123.

137. Baker's entry reads: "Brilliant episodes of adventure and daring exploit in the revolutionary broils and the subsequent regeneration of a South American republic, loosely connected into a long story, in which the man of action, Nostromo, a rich Englishman and his admirable wife, an old Garibaldian, brigands, politicians, adventurers and others make a motley crowd of personages. The method realistic, the whole atmosphere and effect ultra-romantic." *A Guide to Historical Fiction*, 239.

138. Ten Eyck, *Ezra Pound's Adams Cantos*, 35.

139. Ibid., 56.

140. Ibid., 57.

141. Pound, *Cantos*, I.12.

142. Ibid., I.51.

143. Ibid., I.63.

144. Longenbach, *Modernist Poetics of History*, 51.

145. Pound, *Selected Prose*, 42.

146. Forster dramatized this feud in *Howards End*: "What? What's that? Your [German] Universities? Oh yes, you have learned men, who collect more facts than do the learned men of England. They collect facts, and facts, and empires of facts. But which of them will rekindle the light within?" Forster, *Howards End*, 24.

147. Ten Eyck, *Ezra Pound's Adams Cantos*, 51, 52.

148. Longenbach, *Modernist Poetics of History*, 116.

149. Pound, *Cantos*, I.40–41.

150. Ibid., VIII.54–61.

151. Ten Eyck writes that "Pound's documentary strategies resulted in his original poetic voice being almost totally subsumed by the sources from which he worked, disappearing with little comment into canto after canto of text-based history." *Ezra Pound's Adams Cantos*, 35.

152. Armstrong, *Modernism*, 10. Interestingly, Jameson says something similar about the postmodern architecture of "historicism": "the random cannibalization of all the styles of the past, the play of random stylistic allusion" is assembled and "randomly and without principle but with gusto cannibalizes all the architectural styles of the past and combines them in overstimulating ensembles. Nostalgia does not strike one as an altogether satisfactory word for such fascination." Jameson, *Postmodernism*, 19.

153. *Time and Western Man*, 6.

154. Ibid., 69.

155. In *Time and Free Will*, Bergson writes that "we can understand that material objects, being exterior to one another and to ourselves, derive both exteriorities from the homogeneity of a medium which inserts intervals between them and sets off their outlines: but states of consciousness, even when successive, permeate one another, and in the simplest of them the whole soul can be reflected. We may therefore surmise that time, conceived under the form of a homogeneous medium, is some spurious concept, due to the trespassing of the idea of space upon the field of pure consciousness." *Time and Free Will, an Essay on the Immediate Data of Consciousness*, 98.

156. Lewis, *Time and Western Man*, 8.

157. Ibid., 171.

158. Ibid., 172.

159. Lewis draws out the political implications of this in *The Art of Being Ruled* (1926).

160. Lewis, *Time and Western Man*, 246.

161. Ibid., 127.

162. In an oblique way, Lewis did recognize the potential of narrative fiction to serve as a kind of history. He wrote that "In Proust . . . we have in a sense a new type of historical practitioner." But again, coming from Lewis this is derogatory, and he goes on to write of Proust's "slight, ailing, feminine body, with deep expansions of bottomless vanity." Proust's attempt at narrative history—if that is what it was—is for Lewis just one more failure of the Bergson school that, given the logic of Lewis's argument, must anachronistically include a narrator like Thucydides as well as contemporaries like Pound or Gertrude Stein. Ibid., 248.

163. Lewis launched other critiques of historiography that predict major debates in the field. Anticipating White, Lewis saw that all history was a type of narrative: "Life is quite exactly for [history-writing] *a drama*. . . . Or it is a *melodrama*—a musical drama. For the historic-mind is that of the sensationalist gallery or pit of tradition." He argued that the historian is never truly objective: "History is an account of the Past, seen through a temperament of certain complexion, and intended to influence its generation in this sense or that." Valid critiques to be sure. But Lewis's reaction to these insights, at least in these critical pieces, is to recoil from narrative history altogether, and to give up on narrative's capacity for working through these challenges. While he may mock Pound's approach to history, he shares with the poet several key assumptions about history and narrative. Ibid., 267, 247.

164. Ten Eyck, *Ezra Pound's Adams Cantos*, 38.

165. Longenbach, *Modernist Poetics of History*, 165.

166. Ibid., 172.

167. Ibid., 208.

168. Ibid., 204, 210.

169. Franco Moretti, in *Signs Taken for Wonders* (1983), analyzes *The Waste Land* and argues that the first impression we get from the poem is that history is only "an accumulation of debris [and] unintelligible." But through the myths of the Holy Grail and fertility gods Eliot hopes to give meaning to these fragments. For Moretti, history becomes devalued: Eliot is not, as some critics assert, trying to idealize a past, but rather trying to downgrade all of human history, past and present, in an effort to privilege myth and faith as the organizing principles of existence. History and causality disappear in Eliot's world, but "existence has regained a symbolic and meaningful aura that seemed irretrievably lost." Meaning thus returns to the world through the system. *Signs Taken for Wonders*, 222, 224.

170. A similar dynamic occurs in Yeats's poetry, as the turbulent events of Ireland during the poet's lifetime compete with ancient Celtic gods and fairies, as when in "The Statues" "Pearse summoned Cuchulain to his side." Louise Blakeney Williams argues that works like this demonstrate how the modernists' early concern with history gave way to a preoccupation with myth: "history first was used by the five Modernists primarily as an aesthetic tool to add atmospheric effect. The lack of specific political, social, or economic content in their early depictions or discussions of the past, moreover, simply contributed to the escapist quality of their work." *Modernism and the Ideology of History: Literature, Politics, and the Past*, 41. But Stan Smith might disagree, as he argues that Pound, Eliot, and Yeats continually referred to history in their poems but then edited out specific references to events in a continual attempt to stand outside history: "one tendency of Modernism, which is to subdue its warring voices to the dominant monologue of the text, creating a pattern of timeless moments unanswerable to history. Yet everywhere the great texts of Modernism struggle against their own domineering tendencies, inscribing in their texture the very resistances and counter-voices they seek to occlude." Smith, *The Origins of Modernism*, 10.

171. I also do not believe that *Nostromo* "suppresses" history in the sense that Marianne Dekoven sees history, in all its forms, suppressed in such works as Melville's *Benito Cerano*, Kafka's "In the Penal Colony" or Woolf's *To the Lighthouse*. In these works "[t]he historical referent is far from fully or successfully neutralized in any of them. On the contrary . . . we are regularly and disturbingly, if subliminally, aware of these referents as we read." I agree with Dekoven on those texts but believe that *Nostromo*, and the works I will consider, operate in a different mode. "History as Suppressed Referent in Modernist Fiction," 150.

172. Jameson does believe that *Nostromo* "renders" history in the Adornoesque sense: "*Nostromo* is thus ultimately, if you like, no longer a political or historical novel, no longer a realistic representation of history; yet in the very movement in which it represents such content and seeks to demonstrate the impossibility of such representation, by wondrous dialectical transfer the historical 'object' itself [capitalism] becomes inscribed in its very form." I am arguing, by contrast, that history as a narrative resides more in the text's "conscious" than its "political unconscious." *Political Unconscious*, 280.

173. Tyrus Miller contrasts Eliot's approach to history, via Eliot's reading of *Ulysses* that stresses how Joyce strings together the chaos of modern life, with Beckett's bleak

minimalist resistance of historical narrative. Miller quotes a 1937 diary entry from Beckett: "I am not interested in a 'unification' of the historical chaos any more than I am in the 'clarification' of the individual chaos, and still less in the anthropomorphisation of the inhuman necessities that provoke the chaos. What I want is the straws, flotsam, etc., names, dates, births and deaths, because that is all I can know." Miller writes, "I take Eliot's and Beckett's antithetical views as ideal types, marking out a field, and as striking signs of the underground historical passage being negotiated." This is insightful, especially into the area that Miller dubs "late modernism," but there are several more marks in the field of the modern that I would like to explore. *Late Modernism: Politics, Fiction, and the Arts between the World Wars*, 17, 18.

174. Ricoeur asks, "can one do history without periodization? . . . Were we to succeed, would this not be to remove from history any horizon of expectation? Even for Lévi-Strauss history cannot withdraw into an idea of an extended space without any horizon of expectation, inasmuch as 'it is only from time to time that history is cumulative—in other words, that the numbers can be added up to form a favorable combination.'" Instead, "Historical knowledge perhaps has never, in fact, stopped dealing with these visions of historical time, when it speaks of cyclical or linear time, stationary time, decline or progress. Will it not then be the task of a memory instructed by history to preserve the trace of this speculative history over the centuries and to integrate it into its symbolic universe? This will be the highest destination of memory, not before but after history." Time is always inscribed in any work of history, but narrative history is uniquely equipped to take an acknowledgment of time into its own form. *Memory, History, Forgetting*, 159, 161.

175. Ricoeur, *Time and Narrative*, I.ix.

176. Ibid., I.xi.

177. Ibid., III.3.

178. Ibid., II.105.

179. Ibid., II.107.

180. Ibid., III.5.

181. Ibid., III.99.

182. Ibid., III.104.

183. Ibid., III.120.

184. Ibid., III.122.

185. Ibid., III.125.

186. Ibid., III.180.

187. Ibid., III.185.

188. Ibid., III.190.

189. Herodotus, *The Histories*, 3.

190. Generally this is also seen as a retreat from politics and current events, but Michael Tratner in *Modernism and Mass Politics: Joyce, Woolf, Eliot, Yeats* (1995) argues that myth was actually an access point to the political world. Noting that political theorists like George Sorel had shown how mass democracy encourages mythic discourse, Tratner argues that "modernism was not . . . a rejection of mass culture, but rather an effort to produce a mass culture, perhaps for the first time, to produce a culture distinctive to the twentieth century. . . . The contest between modernism and realist literary forms was thus not a contest between literature for a coterie and literature for the masses, but rather a contest between different ways of speaking to and from the mass mind, a contest based on

different conceptions of how the masses think." Thus rather than a shift from Victorian liberalism to modernist elitism, we may more accurately describe it as a shift from liberalism to collectivism. *Modernism and Mass Politics*, 2.

191. Although Pericles Lewis writes that in *Ulysses*, "[t]hese characters, while remaining concrete and historical like the characters in any realist novel, cannot be fully understood without reference to the mythical patterns which they are re-enacting. The effect of these mythical patterns is to elevate the characters into almost world-historical figures, but without draining them of their very concrete historical reality." Lewis, *Modernism, Nationalism, and the Novel*, 49. *Ulysses* is clearly obsessed with the recording of historical material, but it is telling that most historically based criticism of *Ulysses* focuses on the *Geschichte* aspect of the term "history." See Vincent Sherry, *James Joyce: Ulysses*, and most recently, Goloubeva, "'That's the Music of the Future': James Joyce's *Ulysses* and the Writing of a Difficult History."

192. Kermode, *Sense of an Ending*, 38.

193. Ricoeur, *Time and Narrative*, II.13.

194. This is born out by George Levine's *The Realistic Imagination: English Fiction from Frankenstein to Lady Chatterley* (1981). In this seminal work Levine proves an awareness of a narratological sophistication on the part of realist texts: "We need to shift our balance in our appraisal of realism. It was not a solidly self-satisfied vision based on a misguided objectivity and faith in representation. . . . Its massive self-confidence implied a radical doubt, its strategies of truth telling, a profound self-consciousness." *The Realistic Imagination*, 20.

195. And of course realism was not naïve to its own narrative structures: besides Levine, see Peter Brooks's analysis of *Great Expectations* in *Reading for the Plot*.

196. Ricoeur, *Time and Narrative*, III.191.

197. Modernism is also preoccupied with time to a degree not shared by the early novel (with the notable exception of Sterne) and Victorian realism. Proust, Mann, Woolf, Joyce, and Ford all obsess over how to depict both how time feels—Bergson's *durée*—but also how this can possibly coexist with cosmic time. We have seen how Ricoeur reads *Mrs. Dalloway* as dramatizing this tension with the chiming of Big Ben. Joyce's *Ulysses* also depends on this interplay of kinds of time. Time speeds up and slows down: during the "Cyclops" episode, pages of verbosity pass between lines of dialogue that are uttered moments apart. So, on the one hand, the novel is phenomenological in that it tries to reproduce what it feels like to experience time. But *Ulysses* also contemplates how we mark time, regardless of how it feels. Despite its prominent phenomenological aspects, it takes place on one specific day in history, and each chapter takes about one hour of the day's time. The chapter lengths vary in page counts, possibly indicating the variable way in which we feel time, but most of them are one hour long, pointing to the ways in which we divide cosmic time up into manageable units. So although the novel posits myth as an organizational principle, there is a competing historical self-awareness implied by the novel's experimental form.

198. Ricoeur, *Memory, History, Forgetting*, 80.

199. Ricoeur writes in a footnote in *Memory, History, Forgetting*, "In this sense, the work marks an advance over my *Time and Narrative*, where the distinction between representation as explanation and narration was not made, on the one hand because the problem of the direct relationship between narrativity and temporality occupied my attention at the expense of the passage through memory, on the other because no detailed

analysis of the procedures for explanation/understanding was proposed. But, at bottom, the notion of the plot and of emplotment remain primordial in this work as in *Time and Narrative*." Ibid., 551n3.

200. Ibid., 138.

201. Ibid., 237.

202. Ibid., 260.

203. White, *Figural Realism*, 41.

Chapter 1

1. Conrad, *Nostromo*, 11, 38.

2. Sherry, *Conrad, the Critical Heritage*, 167.

3. Woolf, "Mr. Conrad's Crisis," 126.

4. Conrad, *Nostromo*, 177, 178.

5. De Certeau has examined the relationship between seventeenth-century princes and their historians: the prince is power, while the historian is "around," or close to power. The historians produced genealogies of the princes, and obviously "this discourse 'legitimizes' the force that power exerts." But the historian also found lessons in the *scenarios* of history: "In this way, it is not satisfied with historical justification of the prince through offering him a genealogical blazon. The prince receives a 'lesson' provided by a technician of political management" on the part of the historian. *The Writing of History*, 7. In this vein, Decoud tells Antonia, "A journalist ought to have his finger on the popular pulse, and this man is one of the leaders of the populace. A journalist ought to know remarkable men—and this man is remarkable in his way." Conrad, *Nostromo*, 146. Decoud's later deconstructions of Nostromo mark a relationship like that de Certeau describes, as does Decoud's ultimate powerlessness: de Certeau writes that the historians "reflect on the power that they lack," 8.

6. Conrad, *Nostromo*, 177.

7. Decoud compares the "young patricians" of Costaguana to those of Rome fighting against Pompey, and compares Montero, unfavorably, with Julius Caesar. Ibid., 133.

8. Demory, "Nostromo: Making History," 317. As Attridge has argued, Conrad's critique of historiography may in fact be more directed at contemporary professional historians than at Victorian ones—that is, the target of the modernists' critiques may not be their nineteenth-century predecessors but rather their contemporaries in academic history—but Demory's central point about how *Nostromo* is so preoccupied with history in all its forms is what I would like to build on in this chapter, especially the distinction between the different semiotic levels of a work of history.

9. Ibid., 338.

10. Erdinast-Vulcan, "Nostromo and the Writing of History," 194. She argues that the novel never fully ventures into a proto-postmodern mode: "it is, after all, an hour-by-hour account of what-really-happened." Ibid., 181. But Conrad's use of ellipses, time shifts, and retrospective impressionism should complicate any such view of the novel.

11. Robin, "Time, History, Narrative in Nostromo," 200.

12. Tellingly, Erdinast-Vulcan's section headings to *Joseph Conrad and the Modern Temper* are "The Failure of Myth," "The Failure of Metaphysics," and "The Failure of Textuality."

13. Reprinted in Sondra Stang's *Ford Madox Ford Reader* (1986). Ford may have written this section while Conrad was too ill to continue the serial installment. However, Xavier Brice argues that Ford did not author the installment, but merely took down Conrad's dictation and inserted the occasional edit. "Ford Madox Ford and the Composition of *Nostromo.*" In either case, Ford had an intimate knowledge of *Nostromo* as he helped Conrad see the novel through one of Conrad's bouts of illness and anxiety. The two writers had a close, but fractious relationship that has been well covered by critics. Ford was introduced to Conrad by Ford's childhood friend Edward Garnett, who was Conrad's literary guide to London. They collaborated on three works: *The Inheritors* (1904), a fable of political intrigue; *Romance* (1905), an attempt at a popular novel; and *The Nature of a Crime*, published after Conrad's death (1924). See Saunders, *Ford Madox Ford: A Dual Life*, I.101–116; Stape, *The Several Lives of Joseph Conrad*, 113–141; Smith, "Opposing Orbits: Ford, Edward Garnett and the Battle for Conrad"; and Koestenbaum, *Double Talk*.

14. Conrad, *Nostromo*, 137.

15. See Christopher GoGwilt: "the contingency of the novel's political invention of 'the Occidental Republic' insists on a disparity between a 'people' and a 'history' which the novel plots as the 'Occidental' limit to political representation." GoGwilt, *The Invention of the West*, 196. Other major postcolonial readings include Chris Bongie's *Exotic Memories*, Stanford: Stanford University Press, 1991; and Stephen Ross's *Conrad and Empire*, Columbia: University of Missouri Press, 2004.

16. For the novel's relationship to Polish and South American history, see Niland, *Conrad and History*, 95–126.

17. Conrad, *Nostromo*, 90.

18. Ibid., 108.

19. Lord, *Solitude Versus Solidarity in the Novels of Joseph Conrad*, 281–282. Demory traces the viewpoints of each character and, via Hayden White, uncovers their methods of "emplotment" in how they arrange historical events in their minds.

20. Erdinast-Vulcan writes that "[t]he evident inadequacy of these historian-figures foregrounds the historical account of the Seperationist Revolution, told by an apparently omniscient, unnamed, and disembodied narrator" that highlights the problems with such a supposedly omniscient narrator. "Nostromo and the Writing of History," 180.

21. Demory, "Nostromo: Making History," 342.

22. Conrad, *Nostromo*, 380.

23. Said, *Beginnings*, 120.

24. Conrad, *Nostromo*, 381.

25. Said, *Beginnings*, 100.

26. White, *Content of the Form*, 20.

27. Unlike fiction, in the field of history, new versions of past events supplant others. This notion (by no means universally accepted) is central to my discussion of *The Good Soldier* in Chapter 2, so I am holding off engaging with it at this point.

28. Moses, *The Novel and the Globalization of Culture*, 75.

29. Ibid., 96.

30. Conrad, *Nostromo*, 112.

31. Ibid., 143.

32. Ibid., 186.

33. Lord, *Solitude versus Solidarity in the Novels of Joseph Conrad*, 280.

34. Doležel, *Possible Worlds of Fiction and History*, 33. Doležel writes that "[f]ictional worlds are imaginary alternatives of the actual world; historical worlds are cognitive models of the actual past. History reconstructs the actual past by constructing models of the past, which have the status of possible worlds." Ibid.

35. Conrad, *Nostromo*, 453.

36. Kermode, *Sense of an Ending*, 38.

37. Conrad, *Nostromo*, 15.

38. Ibid., 13.

39. Ibid., 77.

40. Ibid., 103.

41. Ibid., 104.

42. Ibid., 146.

43. Ibid., 174.

44. Ibid., 175.

45. Woolf, "Mr. Conrad's Crisis," 126.

46. Conrad, *Nostromo*, 381–382.

47. Ibid., 386.

48. Ibid., 203.

49. Ibid., 211.

50. Ibid., 209.

51. There is an echo in General Montero's own self-estimation: "He was able to spell out the print of newspapers, and knew that he had performed 'the greatest military exploit of modern times.'" The newspaper accounts are clearly signaled to the reader as ironic, but Montero takes his own propaganda as truth. Ibid., 96.

52. Ibid., 325.

53. Decoud had suspected as much: "it dawned upon me that perhaps this man's vanity has been satiated by the adulation of the common people and the confidence of his superiors!" And later, "Decoud, incorrigible in his skepticism, reflected, not cynically, but with general satisfaction, that this man was made incorruptible by his enormous vanity, that finest form of egoism which can take on the aspect of every virtue." Ibid., 179, 237.

54. This is another contribution that Conrad makes to the modernist historical novel: while showing the emptiness of orthodox, Great Man history, he is also using a subjective mode of narration to comment on the writing aspect of history, which is especially interesting given Lytton Strachey's similar efforts in *Eminent Victorians* (1918). History is partially told through the subjectivity of Nostromo—his vanity and emptiness are personal to him, and simultaneously important for Conrad's critiques of the discourse of history. Strachey psychologized his subjects, not just to create fuller studies of them, but to suggest something about the period from which they emerged. Conrad's similar plumbing of the depths of Nostromo operates as a dissection of the historiographical process, as this very same man who we see for a charlatan becomes a legendary historical figure via Captain Mitchell's historical tours.

55. Conrad, *Nostromo*, 326.

56. Ibid., 329.

57. Ibid., 413.

58. Erdinast-Vulcan pushes the myth argument further, seeing the conclusion of the novel—Nostromo's death—as a reversion back to myth. When Nostromo is entrusted

with the silver, she argues, he changes: "he relates to the silver as a mystical magic emblem rather than a material thing. When enlisted to the service of the modern myth, the myth of material interests, he becomes infected by it. He, too, becomes an 'interested party' and the silver acquires a different meaning for him." This begins the process of his self-awareness, which for Erdinast-Vulcan is his "figurative" death and marks a triumph, as I have argued, of historiography over mythologizing. She argues that if the novel ended at that point, myth would remained defeated. Nostromo lives on, however, and his real death at its end "reverses the ostensible triumph of the historicist mode in the novel." The legend recounting in the opening section of the novel has come true, and Nostromo dies—literally this time—because of the mythical curse. There is thus a "reinstatement of myth" by the end of the novel. I am not convinced by this argument because of the importance of the middle sections of the novel with Nostromo and Decoud, but it is persuasive and certainly accounts for Nostromo's death scene. Erdinast-Vulcan, *Joseph Conrad and the Modern Temper*, 79, 83, 84.

59. Roland Barthes's essay "Myth Today" argues for a semiotic understanding of myth that stresses its emptiness: "*myths hide nothing.*" The "myth" of Nostromo then hides only his own emptiness. "When [a mythical signified] becomes form, the meaning leaves its contingency behind; it empties itself, it becomes impoverished, history evaporates, only the letter remains." Myths are powerful because they seem full and yet are "emptied" of history: "What is invested in the concept is less reality than a certain knowledge of reality; in passing from the meaning to the form, the image loses some knowledge: the better to receive the knowledge in the concept. In actual fact, the knowledge contained in a mythical concept is confused, made of yielding, shapeless associations. One must firmly stress this open character of the concept; it is not at all an abstract, purified essence; it is a formless, unstable, nebulous condensation, whose unity and coherence are above all due to its function." Barthes, *Mythologies*, 121, 117, 119.

60. Conrad, *Nostromo*, 181.

61. Ibid., 182.

62. Derrida, *Margins of Philosophy*, 316.

63. Ibid., 313.

64. Ibid., 315.

65. Conrad, *Nostromo*, 197.

66. Ibid., 217.

67. Ibid., 207.

68. Ibid., 211.

69. Ibid., 392.

70. Ibid.

71. Ibid., 396.

72. Derrida, *Margins of Philosophy*, 328.

73. Armstrong, *The Challenge of Bewilderment*, 152. Armstrong argues that "Conrad is a political conservative in his belief in the need to preserve institutions in order to sustain the illusions of stability and community. But he is radical and even anarchistic in his skepticism about the justification any social institution can claim." Ibid., 151. See also Cox, *Joseph Conrad, the Modern Imagination*; Miller, *Fiction and Repetition*; and Meisel, *The Myth of the Modern*.

74. Erdinast-Vulcan, *Joseph Conrad and the Modern Temper*, 84.

75. Conrad, *Lord Jim*, 109. Similarly, Decoud's closing phrases to his sister are "all this is life, must be life, since it is so much like a dream." Conrad, *Nostromo*, 197.

76. Conrad, *Nostromo*, 105.

77. Levine, *The Realistic Imagination*, 289.

78. Ricoeur, *Interpretation Theory*, 16.

79. Derrida, *Margins of Philosophy*, 316.

80. Ricoeur, *Interpretation Theory*, 19.

81. Ibid.

82. Conrad, *Nostromo*, 23.

83. Ibid., 18.

84. Ibid., 395.

85. Levenson, *Modernism and the Fate of Individuality*, 64.

86. Ibid., 65. Similarly, Richard Niland writes that "Marlow embodies the urge to historical narrative, while exposing the difficulty of asserting any truth about history." Niland, *Conrad and History*, 77.

87. Conrad, *Nostromo*, 394.

88. Conrad, *Under Western Eyes*, 35.

89. Ibid., 280.

90. Ibid., 243.

91. Ibid., 57.

92. Ibid., 315.

93. Ibid., 317n.

94. Conrad, *Notes on Life and Letters*, 97.

95. Stape, *The Several Lives of Joseph Conrad*, 130.

96. Conrad, *Nostromo*, 14, 18.

97. Niland, *Conrad and History*, 113. GoGwilt puts the café against the backdrop of European intervention: "L'Albergo d'Italia Una becomes the locus for an entirely imaginary projection of European political form." GoGwilt, *The Invention of the West*, 200–201.

98. Conrad, *Nostromo*, 18.

99. Ibid., 21.

100. Ibid., 25.

101. For example: "Giorgio Viola had a great consideration for the English. This feeling, born on the battlefields of Uruguay, was forty years old at the very least. Several of them had poured their blood for the cause of freedom in America, and the first he had ever known he remembered by the name of Samuel; he commanded a negro company under Garibaldi, during the famous siege of Montevideo, and died heroically with his negroes at the fording of the Boyana. He, Giorgio, had reached the rank of ensign-*alférez*-and cooked for the general. Later, in Italy, he, with the rank of lieutenant, rode with the staff and still cooked for the general. He had cooked for him in Lombardy through the whole campaign; on the march to Rome he had lassoed his beef in the Campagna after the American manner; he had been wounded in the defence of the Roman Republic; he was one of the four fugitives who, with the general, carried out of the woods the inanimate body of the general's wife into the farmhouse where she died, exhausted by the hardships of that terrible retreat. He had survived that disastrous time to attend his general in Palermo when the Neapolitan shells from the castle crashed upon the town. He had cooked for him on the field of Volturno after fighting all day. And everywhere he had seen Englishmen in the front rank of the army of freedom. He respected their nation because they

loved Garibaldi. Their very countesses and princesses had kissed the general's hands in London, it was said. He could well believe it; for the nation was noble, and the man was a saint. It was enough to look once at his face to see the divine force of faith in him and his great pity for all that was poor, suffering, and oppressed in this world." Ibid., 26.

102. Niland, *Conrad and History*, 104.

103. Conrad, *Notes on Life and Letters*, 86. Is Conrad using "royal" here ironically to refer to French republicanism?

104. Stape, *The Several Lives of Joseph Conrad*, 138.

105. *Nostromo* has been rewritten, in a sense, by the Colombian author Juan Gabriel Vásquez as *The Secret History of Costaguana* (2011).

Chapter 2

1. Saunders, *Ford Madox Ford: A Dual Life*, I.311. Ford later wrote to Pinker: "Let me whisper into your secretive ear that the novel I am now writing [*The Young Lovell*] is going to be one of the great historical novels of the world." *Ford Madox Ford Reader*, 476. We are not sure if Pinker remembered the earlier letter deprecating historical novels.

2. Ford, *Joseph Conrad*, 186.

3. Ford, *Half Moon*, 133.

4. Ford, *Portrait*, 7.

5. Ford, *Young Lovell*, 15.

6. In an extended analysis of *The Young Lovell* and its visual properties, Sara Haslam writes in *Fragmenting Modernism* that "Lovell sees only in colours that mean something. In addition, everything he sees is distinguishable from its surroundings: no aspect of this world is hidden." Haslam, *Fragmenting Modernism*, 162.

7. Saunders, *Ford Madox Ford: A Dual Life*, I.384; Eliot, *Selected Prose of T. S. Eliot*, 38.

8. Green, *Ford Madox Ford: Prose and Politics*, 36. Compare with Arthur Mizener: "the simple, comforting, and powerful fact that the past—however different from our time in the physical conditions and the social customs of its life—is essentially like the present." "The Historical Romance and Twentieth-Century Sensibility," 569.

9. Ford's 1913 novel *Ladies Whose Bright Eyes*, in which the protagonist from the twentieth century goes back in time to the Middle Ages, may seem the exception to this trend as the language is contemporary. However, the point is still the same: linguistic style is used to emphasize the difference in time periods. The contemporary style of this novel still maintains the "pastness of the past."

10. In *The Critical Attitude* (1911), Ford wrote that "Thomas Cromwell, indeed, gave us Modern England. He gave the country not only the blessings it enjoys, but also its chief problem. He destroyed Catholicism and the rule of the noble; he gave us Protestantism, and a democratic instrument that is nearly as perfect as any that has yet been known." *The Critical Attitude*, 16.

11. Ford's own take on his complex relationship to the Pre-Raphaelites is found in his studies *Rossetti* (1902) and *The Pre-Raphaelite Brotherhood* (1907); and also his memoir *Ancient Lights* (1911). See also Wiesenfarth, "Ford Madox Ford and Pre-Raphaelite Horrors: Or, How Dante Gabriel Rossetti Started the First World War"; Bickley, "Ford and Pre-Raphaelitism"; Saunders, "From Pre-Raphaelism to Impressionism"; Colombino, *Ford Madox Ford and Visual Culture*; Borowitz, "The Paint Beneath the Prose."

12. Hegel, *Introduction to The Philosophy of History*, 55.

13. Ford, *Ancient Lights*, xv. Hegel wrote, "In history, any such principle is a distinct differentiation of Spirit—the particular Spirit of a People. In this particularity, Spirit expresses in concrete ways all the aspects of its consciousness and will, its entire reality: the shared stamp of its religion, its political system, its ethics, its system of law, its customs, as well as its science, art, and technology. These special characteristics are to be understood in the light of the universal character that is the particular principle of a people." Hegel, *Introduction to the Philosophy of History*, 67.

14. Hegel, *Introduction to the Philosophy of History*, 56.

15. This attitude toward a fictional historiography is partly informed by Ford's reaction to modernity. This was arguably Ford's most conservative phase, as his editorials to *The English Review* attest. His defense of art—later the chapter "On the Function of the Arts in the Republic" in *The Critical Attitude*—rests upon the assumption that modern society is now too fractured for any complete picture: "so many small things crave for our attention that it has become almost impossible to see any pattern in the carpet. We may contemplate life steadily enough to-day: it is impossible to see it whole." Arnold's dictum can now be only half-fulfilled, and that half only by the arts: "life is a thing so complicated that only in the mirror of the arts can we have a crystallized view or any vicarious experience at all." The role of history should thus aim to be as artistic as possible, as "[i]t is only the imaginative writer who can supply this, because no collection of facts, and no tabulation of figures, can give us any sense of proportion." Ford, *The Critical Attitude*, 28, 29, 33. Again, as Attridge has argued, this is an attack on specialists, who can only look at isolated parts of society; for Ford, imaginative writers can go beyond specialization. It is no surprise, then, that Ford's historical fiction of the time aims above all to "see it whole," through the use of a uniform style. However, Attridge elsewhere points out regarding Ford's *The Soul of London* that "Although the title . . . proclaims the quest for a unitary essence—a soul, a heart, a spirit—Ford seems less inclined to isolate the nucleus of Englishness than to shatter it" and that what Ford is grappling with is the "irreconcilability of concrete experience with the idea of the whole." Attridge, "Steadily and Whole," 302–303.

16. Green writes of *The Fifth Queen*: "The trilogy is ample, leisurely, spacious and so complexly coherent at a first reading that our return to the text only serves to confirm its virtues. There is no 'instability' or 'turbulence' in the pages of the Tudor novels; no gap between page and reader which must be filled 'productively.' The trilogy establishes 'a single standard of veracity,' as Frank Kermode has put it, excluding any elements which might be uncertain or problematic." The "instability" and "turbulence" that Green notes would be the motivating forces in *The Good Soldier* and *Parade's End*. Green, *Ford Madox Ford: Prose and Politics*, 33.

17. Saunders, "From Pre-Raphaelism to Impressionism," 53, 62.

18. Doggett, "'Those Were Troublesome Times in Ireland, I Understand.'" See also Tóibín, "Outsiders in England and the Art of Being Found Out."

19. Hoffmann, "'Am I No Better Than a Eunuch?'" See also Rose De Angelis, who argues that every relationship in the novel is triangulated, in "Narrative Triangulations."

20. Henstra, "Ford and the Costs of Englishness." See also Patey, "Empire, Ethnology and The Good Soldier."

21. Mickalites, "The Good Soldier and Capital's Interiority Complex."

22. Cobley, *Modernism and the Culture of Efficiency*, 224–245.

23. Samuel Hynes was the first of many to explore the novel's dramatization of a crisis of knowledge. Since variations of the verb "to know" appear over one hundred times

throughout the novel, "knowing" clearly deserves this sort of attention. Hynes, "The Epistemology of The Good Soldier."

24. Moses, *The Novel and the Globalization of Culture*, 85.

25. Ibid.

26. Levenson, *Genealogy of Modernism*, 61.

27. Ford, *The Good Soldier*, 97.

28. Ibid., 147.

29. Ibid., 15.

30. Ibid., 16.

31. Ibid., 18.

32. H. Robert Huntley argues that Ford, in all of his novels, picks a setting in history and then selects a main character from a previous era, i.e., one who represents Raymond Williams's "residual ideology." Huntley writes that "Katharine is the first of Ford's alien protagonists whose archaic ethical and psychological natures throw them into a continual moral and ideological conflict with their age and who—as recognizable historical types—are the direct outgrowth of Ford's reading of history." Huntley, like many critics, reads these novels as evidence of Ford's regressive cultural and political leanings, as Ford clearly favors the feudal Katharine over the more mercantile Cromwell. *The Alien Protagonist of Ford Madox Ford*, 79. Robert Green writes that Ford "saw history as a decline from a distant glory and argued that there had been a progressive decline from feudalism down to the present" and that he "turned back to feudal England as a repository of idealism and communalism." *Ford Madox Ford: Prose and Politics*, 40–41. For Arthur Mizener, "A major motive for turning to the past was to find an image of a golden age, a time when the essential meaning of human experience, its permanent values, had been able to realize themselves in action." *The Saddest Story; a Biography of Ford Madox Ford*, 569. Fleishman argues that "Ford's imagination is poised upon the dichotomy of historical corruption and civilized retirement, and his escapism avoids a personal tone by being expressed in the language and myths of the men of the past. By identifying his own escapism with that of the Renaissance, Ford achieves genuine historical sympathy with another world-weary age." *The English Historical Novel*, 211.

33. Ford, *Fifth Queen*, 55.

34. Ibid., 174.

35. Ibid., 471.

36. Ibid. Critics like Mizener argue that "[i]n this realistic image of the past, Katharine herself is looking back to a yet remoter past which had, she believes, realized an ideal she dreams of re-creating in her own time, and Ford's image of the past thus becomes not an image of justice, but an analogy of the present." *The Saddest Story: A Biography of Ford Madox Ford*, 569. But if the analogy is instead more self-critical, then it is harder to see the text as advocating some sort of regressive social return; instead, it is a warning against uncritical readings of historical texts, for *The Fifth Queen* trilogy is as interesting for what it says about how people use history as it is about history itself.

37. Judie Newman looks at the role of texts within the trilogy: "the plot, though complex, is very carefully engineered to bear witness to the power, in the real world, of letters, which dominate the plot of each volume of the trilogy." Besides the chronicles and histories, there are also the written letters, both official and contraband, that are so important to statecraft in the Renaissance. Newman argues that "Ford is not so much a realist or a romancer here, as a postmodernist ahead of his time, highlighting and satirizing the

desire to step out of time and into myth, exposing the ideal past as a fiction, and drawing attention to the real power of letters, for both good and ill." "Ford Madox Ford's Fifth Queen Trilogy: Mythical Fiction and Political Letters," 405.

38. Ford, *The Good Soldier*, 18. Martin Stannard writes in his notes to this passage that the finding of these statues "thoroughly revised the early history of Greece." Ibid., 18n5.

39. Ford, *The Good Soldier*, 34.

40. Ibid.

41. Ibid.

42. Ibid., 35.

43. Smith, *Ford Madox Ford*, 26.

44. See especially studies of the *Annales* School, most recently Burguière, *The Annales School*. The 1970s especially saw a turn toward popular consciousness, as in Keith Thomas's *Religion and the Decline of Magic: Studies in Popular Beliefs in 16th and 17th Century Europe* (1971) and Peter Burke's *Popular Culture in Early Modern Europe* (1978). In the realm of historical fiction, magic realism has been drawn to "what people thought": the "magic" is often simply the various beliefs that characters, situated in a specific history, adhere to. Mali writes that "a major claim in the historical profession" is "that in order to know who the Egyptians and all other 'barbarians' really were, the historian must know who they thought they were, where they came from, and where they went." Mali, *Mythistory*, 4.

45. Ford, *The Good Soldier*, 11.

46. Ibid., 15.

47. Ibid., 9.

48. For accounts of modernism and *The Good Soldier*, see Hood, "'Constant Reduction'"; and McCarthy, "In Search of Lost Time," which argues that Ford's work should be viewed as part of the Vorticist constellation of writings. For a dissenting view, see DeCoste, "'A Frank Expression of Personality'?"

49. White, *Metahistory*, 7.

50. Ford, *The Good Soldier*, 19.

51. Ibid., 17.

52. Ibid., 15.

53. Moser, *The Life in the Fiction of Ford Madox Ford*, 158.

54. Ford, *The Good Soldier*, 125.

55. Ibid., 35.

56. Ibid.

57. For an analysis of some of Florence's historical diversions, see Poole, "The Real Plot Line of Ford Madox Ford's *The Good Soldier*."

58. Ford, *The Good Soldier*, 36.

59. Smith believes that the "Duitsch" error is Dowell's mistake and not Ford's: "Ford could not have been guilty of this howler, for he of all people would have known that Pennsylvania *Deutsch* is not Holland *Dutch*." Ford's father was born in Germany. Smith, *Ford Madox Ford*, 326.

60. Ford, *The Good Soldier*, 37.

61. Ibid., 38.

62. Carol Jacobs examines some theological implications for history in *The Good Soldier*, in that part of the Protest involved differing interpretations on Christ's phrase "this

is my body." The debate was whether to take this as literal or figurative. Jacobs, *Telling Time*, 88.

63. Ford, *The Good Soldier*, 38.

64. Ibid., 39.

65. Ibid.

66. Ibid., 128–129.

67. Ibid., 56.

68. Ibid., 136.

69. Ibid., 79.

70. Ibid., 53.

71. Ibid., 11.

72. Ibid., 12.

73. Ibid., 75.

74. Whether or not Ford intended to align this date with the start of the Great War remains a textual mystery. See Martin Stannard's "A Note on the Text" in his edition of *The Good Soldier*. Ibid., 187–205.

75. Ibid., 68.

76. Ibid., 84.

77. Armstrong, *The Challenge of Bewilderment*, 198.

78. Bachner, "'The Seeing Eye': Detection, Perception and Erotic Knowledge in *The Good Soldier*," 103–116.

79. Ford, *The Good Soldier*, 15.

80. Ricoeur, *Memory, History, Forgetting*, 320.

81. Williams, *Modernism and the Ideology of History: Literature, Politics, and the Past*, 174.

82. Brown, *Utopian Generations*, 83.

83. Ibid., 92.

84. Ibid., 93.

85. See Sections A, B, and C of Hegel's *Phenomenology of Spirit*.

86. Brown, *Utopian Generations*, 88.

87. Ford, "Historians' Methods." Division of Rare and Manuscript Collections, Cornell University Library. It was previously at Princeton: see James Longenbach's analysis of it in "Ford Madox Ford: The Novelist as Historian."

88. Mink, *Historical Understanding*, 20.

89. We might argue, following Harold Bloom, that writers seek to displace their predecessors, but that is not necessarily saying that they accomplish this.

Chapter 3

1. Scholes, *Paradoxy of Modernism*, 89.

2. Lyn Pykett argues that the critical reputations of these female writers suffer because of their wide-ranging interests and lack of a clear choice of genre. "Writing Around Modernism: May Sinclair and Rebecca West," 103.

3. West, *Ending in Earnest*, 38.

4. Pykett illustrates how gender partly determined how various modernist writers saw themselves in relation to their predecessors: "some innovative experimental novels by

women in the early twentieth century, far from self-consciously seeking to distance themselves from the nineteenth century (and even Victorian) past as did the male writers of the manifestos of modernism, engage in a process of affiliation to and negotiation with nineteenth-century traditions of women's writing." "Writing Around Modernism: May Sinclair and Rebecca West," 109. Stetz echoes this revisionary look at modernism, arguing that West worked "to emphasize not their [modernist writers'] revolutionary, but their evolutionary, character" as she believed that "the modernist movement did share a strong continuity with Western European art of the past." "Rebecca West's Criticism: Alliance, Tradition, and Modernism," 44. Regarding West and Eliot, see West's important essay "What Is T. S. Eliot's Authority as a Critic?" in Rainey, *Modernism*, 714–716.

5. In a scathing review of Ford's novel *The New Humpty-Dumpty*, West wrote, "He began badly by writing, in collaboration with Joseph Conrad, a novel called 'The Inheritors' (probably the most incomprehensible book ever published in Western Europe), of which the very collaboration was irritating, since it left one mystified as to whether Conrad or Hueffer was the man to curse. He followed up that vein by an obscurity of style which made his readers desire to remind him that it is bad manners to whisper, so sotta voce were his jokes and passions. Subsequently he began to dislike his public as much as he had always despised it, and his books became the confidential communing of Mr. Hueffer with his disgruntled soul." "Book Review of 'The New Humpty Dumpty' by Daniel Chaucer," 366. She also wrote an unsigned review of the novel for the *English Review*, Vol. 12 (September) 1912. Ford was no longer editor of the *English Review*. She first contacted him via letter in 1912. West, *Selected Letters*, 16.

6. Ford, *The Good Soldier*, 237, 238. Ann Norton notes the influence of Ford's novel on West: the narrator's remark that "[t]his was the saddest spring" "consciously allies *The Return of the Soldier* with *The Good Soldier*, another book in which women ultimately, and cruelly, control a man's life." Norton, *Paradoxical Feminism: The Novels of Rebecca West*, 12.

7. West, *Strange Necessity*, 229.

8. Rollyson, *Rebecca West*, 51, 53.

9. West, *Essential Rebecca West*, 51.

10. See Wrenn, "The Mad Woman We Love: Ford Madox Ford, Rebecca West, and Henry James."

11. West, *Selected Letters*, 23.

12. Benjamin, *Illuminations*, 84.

13. Adorno echoed this after the Second World War, in his essay "The Position of the Narrator in the Contemporary Novel" (1954): "The identity of experience in the form of a life that is articulated and possesses internal continuity—and that life was the only thing that made the narrator's stance possible—has disintegrated. One need only note how impossible it would be for someone who participated in the war to tell stories about it the way people used to tell stories about their adventures." *Notes to Literature* (Vol. 1), 31.

14. In *Valances of the Dialectic*, Jameson notes this as a quality of many modernist works that deal with the Great War: "it is as if the axial event . . . is mostly visible by its absence, and evoked most intensely there where it is strongly argued against." *Valances of the Dialectic*, 523.

15. Writing under the pseudonym "Lynx" in the illustrated *Lions and Lambs* (1928) by David Low, West wrote that "'Lord Jim' and 'Nostromo' are islands not books. One goes

there to live while one reads them." She stated that Conrad occupied himself "by passing into other times through his study of history." Low and Lynx [aka Rebecca West], *Lions and Lambs*, 25.

16. West, *Young Rebecca*, 297.

17. Shell-shock was first formulated as a mental disorder during the war. As Elaine Showalter has argued in *The Female Malady* (1985), hysteria was considered a mental disease to which only women were subject. When soldiers returned to the front displaying hysteria, the authorities assumed that they were acting like cowardly women. It was only when decorated war heroes also began to show signs of hysteria that the medical wing of the army began to rethink notions of hysteria, and "shell-shock" became the diagnosis for soldiers suffering from inexplicable symptoms. *The Female Malady*, 167–194.

18. See especially Jay Winter in *Remembering War: The Great War Between Memory and History in the Twentieth Century* (2006): "Shell shock placed alongside one line of temporality, in which there was antebellum and postbellum, another sense of time, what some scholars call 'traumatic time.' It is circular or fixed rather than linear. Here the clock doesn't move in a familiar way; at times its hands are set at a particular moment in wartime, a moment which may fade away, or may return, unintentionally triggered by a seemingly innocuous set of circumstances. When that happens, a past identity hijacks or obliterates present identity; and the war resumes again." *Remembering War*, 75. We see this most clearly in Woolf's *Mrs. Dalloway*, where Big Ben's linearity conflicts with the "traumatic time" of Septimus Smith, who "cannot pass," that is cannot get past the past. Nonlinearity—a central trope of literary modernism—also doubles as an homologous reflection of the way the disabled soldier experiences time.

19. Cathy Caruth argues for the power of traumatic narratives like those of shell-shock cases in *Unclaimed Experience: Trauma, Narrative, and History* (1996). Trauma narratives can be the "experience of a survival exceeding the grasp of the one who survives," as the patient's very inability to narrate can itself be a powerful narration. Observing or listening to trauma cases is much like reading a modernist novel; we have to fill in the psychic blanks to understand the damage done and recreate the past. Caruth goes a step further and argues that this method "precisely permit[s] *history* to arise where *immediate understanding* may not." *Unclaimed Experience*, 66, 11. More recently, see Nicole Rizzuto: "I argue that the novel does provide an alternate history of a traumatic period through voices silenced by dominant discourses, but that period is not the Great War. Rather, it is the 'age of empire,' the preceding era in which England's economic and political power as a nation is sustained through imperial and quasi-imperial exploitation abroad and uneven gender and class arrangements at home." "Towards an Ethics of Witnessing," 8.

20. Fussell, *The Great War and Modern Memory*, 231.

21. Marvell, *The Poems of Andrew Marvell*, l. 41–48.

22. Empson, *Some Versions of Pastoral*, 119.

23. West, *Return of the Soldier*, 38.

24. Patterson, *Pastoral and Ideology*, 3.

25. Williams, *The Country and the City*, 18.

26. Pope, *Poems*, 120.

27. Mark Larabee, in *Front Lines of Modernism: Remapping the Great War in British Fiction*, sees West's novel as furthering another tradition: "West follows Romantic-era codes in establishing telling associations between each character's persona and different

kinds of landscapes. She alters the details of the historical setting to build a fictional world whose formation echoes traditional landscape theories. . . . West's novel thus continues an established aesthetic differentiating the beautiful, picturesque, and sublime, while she critiques the status of the sublime as an empowering experience in the context of modern warfare." *Front Lines of Modernism*, 114.

28. Eliot, *The Use of Poetry and the Use of Criticism: Studies in the Relation of Criticism to Poetry in England*, 85.

29. Alpers, *What Is Pastoral?*, 92.

30. Ibid., 22, 24.

31. Fussell, *The Great War and Modern Memory*, 239.

32. Alpers, *What Is Pastoral?*, 376.

33. West, *Return of the Soldier*, 3.

34. Cowan, "Fine Frenzy of Artistic Vision," 287. Cowan argues that West's pastoral scenes on Monkey Island contrast with the more capitalist, modern and industrial renovations of Baldry Court: "Chris' affinity with the old Baldry Court . . . suggests that the 'dear old place' built in the eighteenth century before 'modern life brought forth these horrors' had values and integrity. . . . By having it built in the eighteenth century, West is explicit about its connection with an earlier order." Ibid., 299–300. I do not see the nostalgic elements of the novel that Cowan does, but any analysis of the pastoral in the novel is clearly indebted to her article.

35. Susan Varney notes that the novel "bears witness to a symbolic universe struggling to come to terms with what is, in fact, an unrepresentable trauma. . . . All point to an aesthetic that bears witness to a loss that is itself unrepresentable." "Oedipus and the Modernist Aesthetic: Reconceiving the Social in Rebecca West's *The Return of the Soldier*," 260. See also Gledhill, "Impersonality and Amnesia: A Response to World War I in the Writings of H. D. and Rebecca West."

36. The pastoral mode often subtly hinted at the city as the place from which the narrator has recently escaped; it equally hints at an imminent return to the city. For Virgil, Rome would be code for war and turmoil.

37. West, *Return of the Soldier*, 4.

38. Williams, *The Country and the City*, 124.

39. West, *Return of the Soldier*, 4.

40. Baldry's wife is described in similar fashion: "She looked so like a girl on a magazine cover that one expected to find a large '7d' somewhere attached to her person." Ibid. Stetz sees the influence of Oscar Wilde here: "Thus the House Beautiful, as West recognized, too easily could become an aesthetic obsession and a substitute for more human and humane interests, as it was to the character of Kitty." At the same time, the novel celebrates the very aestheticism it lambasts: "The novel's plot may question the value of seeking after aesthetic effects, but the novel's language paradoxically affirms that value at every turn." "Rebecca West, Aestheticism, and the Legacy of Oscar Wilde," 161.

41. West, *Return of the Soldier*, 5.

42. Ibid.

43. Ibid.

44. Margaret Stetz was the first to stress the importance of Jenny-as-narrator to understanding the novel. See Stetz, "Drinking 'The Wine of Truth': Philosophical Change in West's *The Return of the Soldier*."

45. Cohen, *Remapping the Home Front*, 71. Laura Marcus reports that the film in question is *Battle of the Somme* (1916). Marcus notes that 80 percent of English citizens saw the film during the war. Marcus, "The Great War in Twentieth-Century Cinema," 281. Marcella Soldaini argues that "[t]he distorted images of No Man's Land in Jenny's dreams evoke the feeling of loss, the inability to have a full knowledge of the outside world." "Violated Territories: Monkey Island, Baldry Court and No Man's Land in Rebecca West's *The Return of the Soldier*," 110. Wyatt Bonikowski, meanwhile, explores Jenny's character, noting a shift in her discourse from impartial observer to something more uncertain: "With tropes of trespass and exile, Jenny figures her mediating position not as the synthesizing function she had previously suggested, but as something more threatening and unpredictable. Mediation, moving between spheres, has become a way of getting lost." *Shell Shock and the Modernist Imagination*, 126. And Debra Rae Cohen argues that Jenny crosses so many boundaries: home front/war front, relative/lover, character/narrator; she exists in so many spheres which "exposes the constructed nature of those discourses." *Remapping the Home Front*, 67.

46. Hannah Arendt, writing of the survivors of concentration camps in *The Origins of Totalitarianism*, noted how difficult it was for even the victims to believe their own stories, and how a secondhand source was often necessary to describe the experience of atrocity: "Only the fearful imagination of those who have been aroused by such reports but have not actually been smitten in their own flesh, of those who are consequently free from the bestial, desperate terror which, when confronted by real, present horror, inexorably paralyzes everything that is not mere reaction, can afford to keep thinking about horrors." *Portable Hannah Arendt*, 122. The choice for Jenny as narrator is necessary, then, because she is "aroused" but not "smitten," afforded the luxury of thinking and narrating upon Chris's experiences from which he is too paralyzed with fear and horror to allow to surface up to his consciousness.

47. Bonikowski, *Shell Shock and the Modernist Imagination*, 111.

48. These forces are dramatized by George Dangerfield in his classic *The Strange Death of Liberal England* (1935), which depicts a nation and ruling class in utter crisis. John Stevenson, among other critics, argues that Dangerfield overstates the case of the "Edwardian Crisis." For example, very often labor struggles led to negotiation, not revolt, and helped implement improvements that "consolidated the social fabric." Stevenson, *British Society, 1914–45*, 44.

49. Schweizer, "Modernism and the Referendum on Nostalgia in Rebecca West's *The Return of the Soldier*," 31.

50. Varney, "Oedipus and the Modernist Aesthetic: Reconceiving the Social in Rebecca West's *The Return of the Soldier*," 261.

51. West, *Return of the Soldier*, 65.

52. West, "On 'The Return of the Soldier,'" 68. See Kavka and Bonikowski for the most extended treatments of Freud's theories in *The Return of the Soldier*. Kavka writes of West's "positive characterization" of the therapist, which is contested by many critics and readers. Kavka, "Men in (Shell-)Shock: Masculinity, Trauma, and Psychoanalysis in Rebecca West's *The Return of the Soldier*," 158. See Bonikowski, *Shell Shock and the Modernist Imagination*, 108–110.

53. West, "Humour While You Wait," 2.

54. Ibid.

55. Schweizer, "Modernism and the Referendum on Nostalgia in Rebecca West's *The Return of the Soldier*," 27.

56. Freud, *Character and Culture*, 115.

57. West, "Humour While You Wait," 2.

58. West, *Ending in Earnest*, 77.

59. Freud, *Character and Culture*, 124.

60. Empson, *Some Versions of Pastoral*, 123.

61. Ibid., 124.

62. Freud, *Character and Culture*, 119.

63. Empson, *Some Versions of Pastoral*, 135.

64. Although Eric Leed, in *No Man's Land: Combat and Identity in World War One* (1979), might see West's paradigm as a traditional "drive-discharge model" that posits peace as a time of repression and war a time of instinctual liberation. In fact, Leed argues, "war meant a new and more total pattern of repression to which millions of men, over a period of years, became habituated." *No Man's Land*, 8.

65. West, *Return of the Soldier*, 49.

66. Fussell, *The Great War and Modern Memory*, 239.

67. West, *Return of the Soldier*, 65.

68. Cowan, "Fine Frenzy of Artistic Vision," 299. Debra Rae Cohen writes that "Baldry Court, itself an 'invented' (or reinvented) country house, represents the cultural moment when presence and nostalgia coexist, when the naturalized operations of empire are defamiliarized (at least in part by the advent of the war). While Kitty may respond to the cultural threat of the modern with obsessive denial, Jenny's insider/outsider status allows her unsettling moments of vision." *Remapping the Home Front*, 74. See also Schweizer, "Modernism and the Referendum on Nostalgia in Rebecca West's *The Return of the Soldier*," 34.

69. West, *Ending in Earnest*, 39.

70. Cowan, "Fine Frenzy of Artistic Vision," 289.

71. Lassner, "Rebecca West's Shadowy Other," 44; MacKay, "Lunacy of Men," 126.

72. MacKay, "Lunacy of Men," 134.

73. Rollyson, *Rebecca West*, 59. See West, *Young Rebecca*, Section V.

74. MacShane, *Ford Madox Ford: The Critical Heritage*, 51.

75. West, *Young Rebecca*, 333.

76. West, *Black Lamb*, 1061.

77. West, *Young Rebecca*, 338.

78. West, *Black Lamb*, 774.

79. Freud and others had stressed the importance of childhood in the development of the ego, but a privileging of the powers of childhood is also a pastoral trope, and West harnesses the ability of the pastoral to describe various psychological processes. Empson has noted that "children are connected with [the pastoral] as buds, because of their contact with Nature." *Some Versions of Pastoral*, 128.

80. West, *Return of the Soldier*, 87. Cohen writes that "[t]he very echoing, overdetermined emptiness of Baldry Court—at novel's end a lingering tang of sterility—serves to emphasize the claustrophobia of the conclusion." Cohen, *Remapping the Home Front*, 83.

81. West, *Black Lamb*, 844.

82. West, *Return of the Soldier*, 90.

83. In an article "O.M." (1930), West wrote that "[t]he precise function of *The Forsyte Saga* was historical: it recorded the moment when the middle classes of England, though their wealth and power were founded on capitalism, found themselves forced by their sternly cultivated honesty to admit that there was a great deal of justice in the intellectuals' criticisms of the effects of that system on human happiness as a whole." West uses "precise" as a pejorative, in the sense that Galsworthy's novels serve no other purpose than a documentary one and do not reach the aesthetic heights of the modernist writers that West champions. *The Return of the Soldier* may be as "historical" as Galsworthy's novels, but it also theorizes what it is to write history, an aspect lacking in *The Forsyte Saga*. *Ending in Earnest*, 131.

84. Ford, *The Good Soldier*, 238.

85. In her review she states that this technique was "invented and used successfully by Mr. Henry James, and used not nearly so credibly by Mr. Conrad." Her novel also employs time shifts like those in *The Good Soldier*, but not in the more flamboyant manner of Ford's novel. Chapter 3 and 5 are out of order chronological order, since they flash back to well before the war. Ibid., 224.

86. West, *Return of the Soldier*, 41.

87. Ibid., 33.

88. Ricoeur, *Memory, History, Forgetting*, 138.

89. Ibid., 413.

90. Nietzsche, *Unfashionable Observations*, 86, 88. Nietzsche depicts the overwhelming nature of historical consciousness: "It seems to me that the surfeit of history in a given age is inimical and dangerous to life in five respects: such an excess produces the previously discussed contrast between the internal and the external and thereby weakens his personality; this excess leads an age to imagine that it possesses the rarest virtue, justice, to a higher degree than any other age; this excess undermines the instincts of a people and hinders the maturation of the individual no less than that of the totality; this excess plants the seeds of the ever dangerous belief in the venerable agedness of the human race, the belief that one is a latecomer and epigone; this excess throws an age into the dangerous attitude of self-irony, and from this into the even more dangerous attitude of cynicism." Ibid., 115.

91. Nietzsche, *Genealogy of Morals*, 57.

92. Ibid., 57–58.

93. Hayden White charts the late nineteenth-century resistance to historical excess, with Nietzsche as the most powerful voice of this movement. White, "The Burden of History."

94. See White's *Metahistory*: "human forgetting . . . is required to erase the memory traces that permit a man to linger uncreatively over his own past life." White, *Metahistory*, 349.

95. The earlier essay is more tempered, as Nietzsche argues for a balance between history and forgetting: happiness depends "on whether one knows how to forget things at the proper time just as well as one knows how to remember at the proper time; on whether one senses with a powerful instinct which occasions should be experienced historically, and which ahistorically. This is the proposition the reader is invited to consider: *the ahistorical and the historical are equally necessary for the health of an individual, a people, and a culture.*" Nietzsche, *Unfashionable Observations*, 90.

96. Caruth, *Unclaimed Experience*, 2.

97. Ricoeur, *Memory, History, Forgetting*, 175.

98. Ibid., 176.

99. Arendt, *Portable Hannah Arendt*, 159.

100. Steve Pinkerton argues that "West depicts Chris's condition as less a matter of loss than of excess, echoing Freud and Breuer's emphasis in *Studies on Hysteria* on the presence at the heart of traumatic repetition, and its status as an 'agent' that fosters a sort of continuous present in the subject." "Trauma and Cure in Rebecca West's *The Return of the Soldier*," 4. Pinkerton draws upon Margery Sokoloff's dissertation, in which she refers to Chris's condition as "hyperamnesia."

101. Ibid.

102. West, *Return of the Soldier*, 79.

103. Ibid., 81.

104. Ibid.

105. Ibid., 80.

106. Deleuze, *Difference and Repetition*, 139.

107. Ibid., 140.

108. In a 1930 review West states that a certain biographer "is pre-Strachey in her methods and works not by interpretation but by presentation of the relevant material." *Ending in Earnest*, 170. In her "Foreword to Lytton Strachey" she wrote that "the real secret power of *Eminent Victorians* . . . lies in his preference for personalities over ideas." "Foreword to Lytton Strachey," 686.

109. Ricoeur, *Memory, History, Forgetting*, 414.

Chapter 4

1. Ford, *War Prose*, 36–37.

2. Although Ford did write letters to Conrad full of impressionistic renderings of battle, especially the sound of shells. These writings found their way into *A Man Could Stand Up—*. See O'Malley, "Listening for Class in Ford Madox Ford's *Parade's End*."

3. Sara Haslam writes that "[a]s well as possessing a function within the action and the development of the novel, theories of picture-making and capitalising figure in Ford's non-fictional writing on the subject of the war. In 1916 he was wrestling with what he then deemed to be an insurmountable problem: how to write about what surrounded him." *Fragmenting Modernism*, 93.

4. Ford, *War Prose*, 32.

5. Ibid., 38.

6. Haslam, *Fragmenting Modernism*, 93.

7. Ford, *A Man Could Stand Up—*, 17.

8. Ford, *War Prose*, 59.

9. Ibid., 34.

10. Deer, *Culture in Camouflage*, 16.

11. Deer, on the other hand, argues that "Day of Battle" is informed not by trauma, but resistance: "Ford's very ambivalence can be read instead as an act of resistance. The essay reveals that this is a deliberate silence, actively produced." Ibid., 17.

12. "Silence" for Ford meant only two books a year. Much of it was based on previously written material.

13. Cook, "Constructions and Reconstructions: *No Enemy*," 191.

14. Cook writes, "This continually reconstructed 'reality' effectively challenges both the 'history' constructed as 'progress' by Victorian liberalism, then constructed as determined advance by modern materialism, and wartime constructions of contemporary events as Apocalyptic. *No Enemy* exposes ways in which public 'history' is constructed by juxtaposing them with the record of personal, experienced history. It replaces chronological narratives of progress with multi-layered descriptions of wartime landscapes, with reflections on events and their representation, and with narrative patterns of repetition and anachrony which display the endless possibilities for reconstruction in our knowledge and expression." Ibid., 197. Similarly, James Longenbach, in his brief analysis of *No Enemy*, writes that "[s]tudded with footnotes, capped with an appendix, and convoluted with digressions, the text of *No Enemy* is designed to force the reader to question the reliability of its account of historical events." "Ford Madox Ford: The Novelist as Historian," 158. Most recently, see Larabee's probing reading in *Front Lines of Modernism*, 38–54.

15. Ford, *No Enemy*, 9.

16. Ibid., 18.

17. Saunders, *Ford Madox Ford : A Dual Life*, II.epigraph.

18. Ford, *No Enemy*, 18.

19. Matz, *Literary Impressionism and Modernist Aesthetics*, 26,33.

20. As Parkes writes, "Crystallizing in extreme form the shocks of modernity, Ford suggests that the terrors of the new mechanized warfare may be experienced only as fragmentary, mediated after-effect: the actual war stays off the page, as if it has disappeared into a black hole." *A Sense of Shock*, 140.

21. Ford, *No Enemy*, 44.

22. Ibid., 48.

23. Ibid., 56.

24. See Laura Colombino, *Ford Madox Ford: Vision, Visuality and Writing* (2008), which analyzes Ford's works through the lens of modernist visual aesthetics: "Ford's significant involvement with painting is tackled here from a very specific angle (by no means the only possible one): that of the logic of the gaze, the desiring eye or 'scopic drive,' that is, the visual implications of the ego's traffic with the unconscious." *Ford Madox Ford: Vision, Visuality and Writing*, 16.

25. Ford, *It Was the Nightingale*, 63–64.

26. See Patrick Deer, who detects "a powerful skepticism for the commanding perspective" in *Parade's End*. Deer, *Culture in Camouflage*, 50. Jonathan Boulter writes that "[b]y presenting the past as a series of static images—rather than narratives—the narrator tacitly acknowledges the relation between trauma and stasis, the relation between the desire to transcend the trauma of the past and the equal desire to keep that trauma fixed in a continual and paradoxically static past." Ford "thematizes the notion that the conflation of trauma and narrative (specifically autobiography)—the attempt to contain personal trauma and mourning within the epistemological bounds of narrative—can only produce the symptomology of trauma rather than the overcoming of trauma itself. It is precisely within this symptomology, however, that Ford's nuanced relation to trauma is made manifest. Trauma perhaps cannot be contained, narrated, or framed within discourse; an indivisible remainder will always exceed the boundaries of narrative." Boulter, "'After . . . Armageddon': Trauma and History in Ford Madox Ford's *No Enemy*," 77–78.

27. Saunders, *Ford Madox Ford : A Dual Life*, II.80–81.

28. *Parade's End* is composed of four volumes: *Some Do Not . . .* (1924); *No More Parades* (1925); *A Man Could Stand Up—* (1926); and *Last Post* (1928). Note the inclusion of punctuation in the first and third titles.

29. West, *Selected Letters*, 40.

30. Norton, *Paradoxical Feminism: The Novels of Rebecca West*.

31. Jane Marcus's editorial comments for the short story "Indissoluble Matrimony" note that *A Return of the Soldier*, "like Ford's Tietjens novel *No More Parades*, is a study of shell shock and the effects of the First World War on the relations between the sexes." West, *Young Rebecca*, 266. Celia Malone Kingsbury includes a brief comparison of the two works and how they depict shell shock, observing that "[b]oth Christopher Tietjens in *Parade's End* and Christopher Baldry in *The Return of the Soldier* lose memories of events and facts acquired prior to the war, and both memory losses are appropriate to the characters' circumstances." *The Peculiar Sanity of War*, 122. Max Saunders's biography of Ford brings up West's novel, which "illustrates how another novelist can use the idea of shell-shock to explore the psychology of war: the way the journey to France does not only alienate the solider from his homeland, but from the land of the living, taking him into an underworld of trenches and dug-outs, or a 'No-Man's Land' with the company mainly of corpses." *Ford Madox Ford: A Dual Life*, II.256. Angus Wrenn's conclusions are representative of the criticism on these two novels: "And of course the shell-shock theme [of *The Return of the Soldier*] parallels Ford's own life in the trenches at this time and his eventual writing of *Some Do Not. . . .* It is not suggested that West directly influenced Ford, but what is striking is the way that both exploit shell-shock and amnesia in terms of their association with marital infidelity." Wrenn, "The Mad Woman We Love: Ford Madox Ford, Rebecca West, and Henry James," 174.

32. Although, in a 1962 letter to a researcher doing work on May Sinclair, West described how Ford may have incorporated some of Sinclair's life into his fiction but "Ford probably did not recognize it, for gratitude was not his strong suit." West, *Selected Letters*, 387.

33. Armstrong, *The Challenge of Bewilderment*, 226.

34. Saunders, *Ford Madox Ford : A Dual Life*, II.29; Rollyson, *Rebecca West*, 63, 69.

35. Ford, *Some Do Not . . .*, 208.

36. And see *It Was the Nightingale*: "My own observation of active warfare has led me to a singular conclusion. . . . What preyed most on the mind of the majority of not professionally military men who went through it was what was happening at home. Wounds, rain, fear, and other horrors are terrible but relatively simple matters; you either endure them or you do not. But you have no way by which, by taking thought, you may avoid them. [. . .] But what is happening at home, within the four walls, and the immediate little circle of the individual—that is the unceasing strain!" Ford, *It Was the Nightingale*, 216.

37. Misha Kavka argues that one of West's goals with her novel was to show how the wartime trauma was linked to issues on the home front: "the novel refuses a theory of trauma which remains enclosed within the context of war neurosis." "Men in (Shell-) Shock: Masculinity, Trauma, and Psychoanalysis in Rebecca West's *The Return of the Soldier*," 159.

38. Ford, *Some Do Not . . .*, 101.

39. West, *Return of the Soldier*, 79.

40. David Trotter writes that Ford "relativizes anxiety" in *Parade's End* by showing the similarities between the two. Trotter, "The British Novel and the War," 52.

41. The classic account of this is of course Elaine Showalter's chapter "Male Hysteria: W.H.R. Rivers and the Lessons of Shell Shock." *The Female Malady*, 167–194.

42. Ford, *Some Do Not . . .*, 8.

43. Ibid., 152–153.

44. Ford, *No Enemy*, 220.

45. Ford, *Some Do Not . . .*, 131.

46. Bruce Thornton argues that the novel is not actually pastoral but georgic, a mode in which labor and farming are stressed instead of the pastoral's emphasis on leisure and shepherding: "Rather than a pastoral resolution he has already rejected, Ford in *The Last Post* gives us Tietjens attempting to provide for himself and Valentine and their unborn child a self-sufficient life whose meaning comes from the work they do to protect that self-sufficiency. It is the emphasis on Christopher's labor as a small farmer and antique furniture dealer that distances the novel from the ideal freedom and leisure of pastoral, and places it in the georgic mode." Thornton, "Pastoral or Georgic?," 61.

47. Ford, *Last Post*, 9. Andrew Radford explains the political and economic implications of their knowledge of the landscape: "[Flowers' names] are arranged so that overlooked flora become fundamental to Tietjens's definition of landscape as the topography of class . . . his account is less a vivid impression of what he sees than a linguistic exercise in the way a traditional vocabulary arranges itself . . . feudal culture has evolved the language of landscape, where the master-tenant relationship has kept Tietjens and his 'great landowning class' dominant." "The Gentleman's Estate in Ford's *Parade's End*," 314.

48. Bate, "Arcadia and Armageddon: Three English Novelists and the First World War," 156.

49. Gasiorek, "The Politics of Cultural Nostalgia: History and Tradition in Ford Madox Ford's *Parade's End*," 66. Gasiorek's essay is the best political reading done on Ford's work, putting Ford's ideas in the context of "Tory Radicalism," as opposed to the mainstream Tory ideologies of the time. Gasiorek writes that *Parade's End* "dramatized Ford's struggle with and scrutiny of the cultural and political beliefs he himself espoused, and it does so by questioning the legitimacy of the very tradition in which those beliefs were formed and articulated. The result is a deeply ambivalent text, which criticizes the pre- and post-war 'condition of England' but also portrays the search for social renewal through a return to the politics of a long-dead Toryism as a utopian fantasy." Ibid., 53.

50. Although see the "original ending" to *Some Do Not . . .* that Ford excised, in which Tietjens sees Sylvia for one last domestic squabble. *Some Do Not . . .*, 407–420.

51. Ricoeur, *Time and Narrative*, I.150.

52. In historical fiction there is always a "present" toward which the historical events are marching. They will not always reach the novelist's present, but they are always moving towards it. Thus the present is always built into historical works, as their future (and the novelist's present) casts an ironic shadow over the historical past.

53. Ford, *Some Do Not . . .*, 27.

54. Ford, *History of Our Own Times*, 15.

55. Ford, *Some Do Not . . .*, 207.

56. Ford, *It Was the Nightingale*, 162.

57. Skinner, "The Painful Processes of Reconstruction: History in *No Enemy* and *Last Post*," 72.

58. Ford, *Some Do Not . . .*, 221.

59. Ibid., 205.

60. Hawkes, *Ford Madox Ford and the Misfit Moderns*, 152.

61. There is an analogy with Ford's own methods, at least in how he conceives them: in *It Was the Nightingale*, he writes that "unless I know the history back to the remotest times of any place of which I am going to write I cannot begin the work." Ford, *It Was the Nightingale*, 224.

62. Terdiman, *Present Past*, 6.

63. Connerton, *How Modernity Forgets*, 3. For Connerton, "a major source of forgetting . . . is associated with processes that separate social life from locality and from human dimensions: superhuman speed, megacities that are so enormous as to be unmemorable, consumerism disconnected from the labour process, the short lifespan of urban architecture, the disappearance of walkable cities." Ibid., 5.

64. Terdiman, *Present Past*, 12.

65. Connerton, *How Modernity Forgets*, 5.

66. Jameson echoes these concerns in *Postmodernism*: "For a society that wants to forget about class, therefore, reification in this consumer-packaging sense is very functional indeed; consumerism as a culture involves much more than this, but this kind of 'effacement' is surely the indispensible precondition on which the rest can be constructed." We feel powerless in front of the commodity since we cannot see its history; consumerism is then "a compensation for an economic impotence which is also an utter lack of political power." For Jameson, postmodern culture, which may seem transparent, is actually opaque: not because of any sense of murky depths, but rather because of the amnesia of reification. *Postmodernism*, 315–316.

67. Ford, *Some Do Not . . .*, 250.

68. Ibid., 279.

69. For more on time-shifts in *Parade's End*, see Fowles, *Ford Madox Ford*, 73–75; and Trainor, "Third Republic French Philosophy and Ford's Evolving Moral Topologies."

70. Terdiman, *Present Past*, 70.

71. Armstrong writes that Ford questions the separation between the self and society that most nineteenth-century historical novels took as their starting point: *Parade's End* "explores how society and history are paradoxically part of the self and yet alien from it at the same time—part of its lived situation, which it is thrown into and also helps to create, but also an irreducible otherness that may be experienced as an anonymous force from without." *The Challenge of Bewilderment*, 226.

72. Genette, *Narrative Discourse*, 93.

73. Ford, *Some Do Not . . .*, 3.

74. Sorum, "Mourning and Moving On," 158.

75. Terdiman, *Present Past*, 108.

76. Ford, *Some Do Not . . .*, 13.

77. Ibid., 210, Ford's emphasis.

78. Winter, *Remembering War*, 52. See also Leed: "Continuity often seems to be the *sine qua non* of identity. An experience which severs the thick 'tissues of connectivity' that weld separate events into a self is most often viewed as a *loss* of identity. Concepts of identity modeled on the process of maturation and cognitive development often presume something which war effaces: the notion that there is only one self and one sphere of existence." *No Man's Land*, 3.

79. Lukács, *Theory of the Novel*, 127.

80. Ricoeur, *Memory, History, Forgetting*, 66.

81. Ibid., 85.

82. Ford, *Some Do Not . . .*, 346.

83. Ibid.

84. Bonikowski, *Shell Shock and the Modernist Imagination*, 72.

85. Ford, *Some Do Not . . .*, 349.

86. Deleuze and Guattari, *A Thousand Plateaus: Capitalism and Schizophrenia*, 17.

87. For Deleuze and Guattari, such splicing "enabl[es] one to blow apart strata, cut roots, and make new connections. Thus, there are very diverse map-tracing, rhizome-root assemblages, with variable coefficients of deterritorialization. . . . The coordinates are determined not by theoretical analyses implying universals but by a pragmatics composing multiplicities or aggregates of intensities." Ibid., 16.

88. Ford, *Some Do Not . . .*, 350.

89. Ford, *It Was the Nightingale*, 199. Ford considered a plan to translate Proust's work, "more as a distraction than as a way of making a living" writes Saunders, although he quotes Ford as saying that translating the entire work "wd. bore me to tears." Saunders, *Ford Madox Ford : A Dual Life*, II.99.

90. Benjamin, *Selected Writings IV*, 315.

91. Ibid.

92. Ibid., 317.

93. Adorno and Benjamin, *The Complete Correspondence, 1928–1940*, 320.

94. Ibid., 321.

95. De Certeau comments on this as well: "writing *is* repetition, the very labor of difference. It is the memory of a forgotten separation. To take up one of Walter Benjamin's remarks concerning Proust, we might say that writing assumes the 'form' of memory and not its 'contents': it is the endless effect of loss and debt, but it neither preserves nor restores an initial content, as this is forever lost (forgotten) and represented only by substitutes which are inverted and transformed according to the law set up by a founding exclusion. Scriptural practice is itself a work of memory. But all 'content' that would claim to assign to it a place or a truth is nothing more than a production of a symptom of that practice—a fiction." *The Writing of History*, 323.

96. For example, Eve Sorum argues that Tietjens "stands as a representative soldier whose loss of memory encapsulates what Ford saw as a central problem for postwar Britain, the nation's difficulty moving past a trauma that it could not quite—in fact, refused to—remember." By *Last Post* the mute Mark Tietjens is "the horrific embodiment of silence" that followed the war, as the nation willed a form of social amnesia. Sorum's argument is essential to any understanding of cultural memory in Ford's work, and I would like to further her findings by examining the "good" alongside "bad" forgetting. Sorum, "Mourning and Moving On," 155, 161.

97. Ford, *Some Do Not . . .*, 90.

98. Ibid., 169. Valentine goes on to say that, while she suffered from "dreadful anxiety," she also found methods of psychic release: "if I hadn't let off steam I should have had to jump out and run beside the cart. . . ." Valentine has healthy techniques of dealing with stress to which Tietjens does not have access. Ibid., 170. This is highly gendered, as later Captain Mackenzie laments, "Why isn't one a beastly girl and privileged to shriek?" Ford, *No More Parades*, 23.

99. Terdiman, *Present Past*, 15.

100. Foucault, *Order of Things*, xx.

101. Ford, *Some Do Not . . .*, 84.

102. Foucault, *Order of Things*, 346.

103. Ibid., 368.

104. Although the French title of Foucault's work was *Les mots et les choses*, Foucault approved the English title, and the English-language Preface indicates that *The Order of Things* "was, in fact, M. Foucault's original preference." Ibid., viii.

105. Ford, *A Man Could Stand Up—*, 87.

106. Ford, *Some Do Not . . .*, 162.

107. Foucault, *Order of Things*, 370.

108. Ibid., 219.

109. For Terdiman, the disruptions of modernity revealed that a collective past is and always was a construction: "These developments defined a situation of great stress. A social formation depends for its stability on a relatively stable understanding of its past, consequently on a generalized assent to the structures and cultural discourses produced out of that past to regulate the present." *Present Past*, 31.

110. Ford, *No More Parades*, 38.

111. Compare to Siegfried Sassoon in *Sherston's Progress*, who also stresses the delay in shock: "Shell-shock. How many a brief bombardment had its long-delayed after-effect in the minds of these survivors, many of whom had looked at their companions and laughed while inferno did its best to destroy them. Not then was their evil hour, but now; now, in the sweating suffocation of nightmare, in paralysis of limbs, in the stammering of dislocated speech." *The Complete Memoirs of George Sherston*, 557.

112. Conrad, *Heart of Darkness*, 5.

113. Christopher GoGwilt, in *Passages of Literature: Genealogies of Modernism in Conrad, Rhys, and Pramoedya* (2011), sees forgetting as central to Ford's project of modernist criticism: "It is the very distortion of Ford's memory, and the insistence on his own presence at the scene of writing, that helps establish the mythology of an English modernism translating into English the ideals of a French modernism modeled on a Flaubert or Mallarmé." Ford's memory, faulty and creative, "effects a temporal-historical distortion that evokes an economy of modernist collaboration tied to a history of modern European economic and political exploitation." *Passage of Literature*, 73, 79.

114. See Lamberti: "On the one hand, Ford acknowledges the importance of the creative act of the historian who selects his documents (what Conrad calls 'second-hand impressions') and renders them in a form that should aim at turning 'the dry bones' into 'the picture of an era' (Ford therefore, seems to suggest a new form of historical discourse, that we could add to Hayden White's metahistory tassonomy); on the other hand the novelist, whose goal is that of showing the true spirit of his own time, selects his impressions (that, following Conrad, we could so call 'first-hand impressions'), traces a picture of his own age and gives historical relevance to poetry." "Writing History: Ford and the Debate on 'Objective Truth' in the Late 20th Century," 38.

115. Brasme, "Between Impressionism and Modernism: *Some Do Not . . .*, a Poetics of the Entre-Deux," 193.

116. The 2012 Carcanet editions allow close scrutiny of Ford's experiments with ellipses; in her "A Note on the Text" to *A Man Could Stand Up—*, Sara Haslam writes, "The

most impressive characteristic of the [typescript], on first view, is the unpredictable nature of its punctuation. The minimum number of suspension dots in what is unquestionably Ford's favourite kind of punctuation, for example, is three, but the maximum is eight." Ford, *A Man Could Stand Up—*, lxxii. Isabelle Brasme explores Ford's use of ellipses in "'A Caricature of His Own Voice.'"

117. For Parkes, this "deconstructive turn in Ford's historicism" occurs in his writings of the thirties. I see the earlier *No Enemy* as the key breakthrough text, although agree that by "shifting attention from singular heroes to larger social entities and movements, Ford initiates a change in the meaning of his impression, whereby the lexicon of individual shocks or (in Max Saunders's alternative formulation) passions gives way to one of public quakes and tremors." *A Sense of Shock*, 180, 179.

118. Sheehan, *Modernism and the Aesthetics of Violence*, 169; Benjamin, *Selected Writings IV*, 319, 320.

119. Benjamin, *Selected Writings IV*, 328. See Adorno's *Minima Moralia*: "Life has changed into a timeless succession of shocks, interspaced with empty, paralyzed intervals. But nothing, perhaps, is more ominous for the future than the fact that, quite literally, these things will soon be past thinking on, for each trauma of the returning combatants, each shock not inwardly absorbed, is a ferment of future destruction." *Minima Moralia*, 54.

120. Olson, *Modernism and the Ordinary*, 45–56, 66–76.

121. Although we must consider Steven Pinker's counterintuitive findings in *The Better Angels of Our Nature: Why Violence Has Declined* (2011) that the twentieth century was actually the least violent in history. For Pinker, twentieth-century violence has been spectacular but ultimately peaceful compared to all previous eras. Pinker, *The Better Angels of Our Nature*. The modernist draw to violence, then, might be more fetishization than documentation.

122. Benjamin, *Gesammelte Schriften Bd.1*, I.1:1139.

123. Benjamin, *Understanding Brecht*, 121.

124. Haslam elegantly writes that "[i]t is as though Ford has had to become the Historian of another time in order to learn more fully how to become a better, more thorough, historian of his own time." *Fragmenting Modernism*, 48. Alexandra Becquet analyzes "the kaleidoscopic nature of Ford's pictures, a quality which Benjamin considers to be responsible for the Baudelairian stroller's experience of shock. Indeed, kaleidoscopic images are shifting: the superimposition of two images produces a third and/or a visual blend which in its turn generates an unsettling endless refraction. Ford's images are therefore characterized by the same constant metamorphosis Benjamin places at the root of the shock cinema creates." "Modernity, Shock and Cinema: The Visual Aesthetics of Ford Madox Ford's *Parade's End*," 196.

125. Benjamin, *Selected Writings IV*, 324. Jameson, in *Marxism and Form* (1971), explores the affinities between Benjamin's theories of shock and Freud's. For Freud, trauma was the result of "incompletely assimilated shock" because the normal defenses against shock were broken down. Jameson argues that Benjamin historicizes this process: "In Benjamin's hands, this becomes an instrument of historical description, a way of showing how in modern society, perhaps on account of the increasing number of shocks of all kinds to which the organism is now subjected, these defense mechanisms are no longer personal ones: a whole series of mechanical substitutes intervenes between consciousness

and its objects, shielding us perhaps, yet at the same time depriving us of any way of as-similating what happens to us or of transforming our sensations into any genuinely per-sonal experience." While modernity provides constant shock, it also finds means of ab-sorbing it: the daily newspaper for Benjamin is one of the mechanisms that blunt the daily shock of modernity. Jameson, *Marxism and Form*, 63.

126. However, Franco Moretti, in *Signs Taken for Wonders* (1983), critiques Benjamin's notion of shock as somehow permanent in modernity: "the question we have to ask is whether the category of the traumatic and exceptional event is really the most appropriate for the analysis of the experiences of urban life." Moretti argues that urban life is so pre-dictable, in the sense that cities are planned and designed for the unexpected, that urban-ity itself is what absorbs the shock of the new. *Signs Taken for Wonders*, 116.

127. Benjamin, *Selected Writings IV*, 336.

128. Ibid., 392.

129. Ibid. And see again Adorno's *Minima Moralia*: "The recent past always presents itself as if destroyed by catastrophes. The expression of history in things is no other than of past torment." *Minima Moralia*, 49.

130. MacShane, *The Life and Work of Ford Madox Ford*, 260.

Chapter 5

1. West, *Black Lamb*, 1089.

2. Ibid., 1.

3. Ibid., 1088.

4. West, *Selected Letters*, 174–175.

5. Marina MacKay addresses this: "Largely, her reputation is reliant on a version of feminist history that West herself would likely have rejected, insofar as it privileges the private over the public status of the work. For example, there is critical consensus that this book is an epic achievement, nevertheless West's admirers describe *Black Lamb and Grey Falcon* in almost apologetic terms." "Immortal Goodness: Ideas of Resurrection in Re-becca West's *Black Lamb and Grey Falcon*," 178. MacKay urges critics to be more attentive to the historical specifics of its composition and setting, as she does in a follow-up article in which she again explores the critical debates surrounding West and the excessive atten-tion to biography and femininity: "Although I necessarily hesitate to endorse it—after all, it is thanks to feminist scholarship that West is even in print—there is perhaps a need for criticism to acknowledge the ways in which West located her feminism, as she argued women must, within a broader network of political engagement." "Lunacy of Men," 127.

6. West, *Black Lamb*, 21.

7. Ibid., 11.

8. Ibid., 54.

9. Rollyson, *Rebecca West*, 209.

10. See especially Montefiore, *Men and Women Writers of the 1930s*, 204–210.

11. Goldsworthy, "*Black Lamb and Grey Falcon*: Rebecca West's Journey Through the Balkans," 2. See also Paul Fussell's *Abroad*: West's "image of Fiume as 'hacked by treaties into a surrealist form' suggests a relation between the literal frontier scene between the wars and the methods of the art and writing of those years aiming at a critical, and even satirical, refraction of modern actuality." Fussell, *Abroad*, 36. Loretta Stec notes West's

glorification of the Balkans: "Travel narratives and utopian literature share a number of features, including the creation of an alternative world against which one's own is measured, and the use of a traveler or guide to explain the other world. … Much of the volume describes the riches of the South Slav cultures as a counterpoint to the cultures of Western European nations degraded by fascism, capitalism, and other aspects of modernity." "Dystopian Modernism vs Utopian Feminism: Burdekin, Woolf, and West Respond to the Rise of Fascism," 189–190. For a situating of West's treatment of the Balkans in the tradition of Western representations of Yugoslavia, see Hammond, *The Debated Lands*, 149–151.

12. West, *Black Lamb*, 1114.

13. However, Stec persuasively argues that West mostly shelved her feminism during the war years as part of the drive to defend Britain from fascist invasion: "West wished to mitigate the subjection of the woman to the man but not abolish it. Rather she argues that the woman needs to stop carrying the plough in order to protect her womb, an 'instrument of the race,' or nation; she nostalgically argues for a return to essentialist definitions and roles of gender that subordinate women in sex-gender systems more subtle than the one this episode implies. West concludes in *Black Lamb* that women must heroically submit to male domination for the sake of national security while nations must actively and heroically resist domination by other powers." "Female Sacrifice: Gender and Nostalgic Nationalism in Rebecca West's *Black Lamb and Grey Falcon*," 139.

14. West, *Black Lamb*, 418.

15. Ibid., 1154. Although West is not afraid to critique Gibbon's work: of Pope Gelasius, she writes that "Gibbon's description of him as a villainous Army contractor is nonsense," and I do not believe she is using "nonsense" in the same charged way that she uses it to describe her own work. Ibid., 811.

16. West, *Black Lamb*, 379.

17. West, "What Gibbon Left Out," 123.

18. Ibid., 124.

19. Scott, *Refiguring Modernism*, 162.

20. Montefiore, *Men and Women Writers of the 1930s*, 189. See also Lesinska, *Perspectives of Four Women Writers on the Second World War*, 142–146.

21. West, *Black Lamb*, 156.

22. Ibid., 785.

23. Schweizer, "Rebecca West's Philosophy of History," 230.

24. West, *Black Lamb*, 696.

25. And, possibly, a continuance of her interest in amnesia: Goldsworthy writes that "[f]aced with the beginning of another war, *Black Lamb and Grey Falcon* confronts a different kind of amnesia—Britain's deliberate pretence that the war can be avoided if a couple of East European states are sacrificed—at a similarly high personal cost to Rebecca West." "*Black Lamb and Grey Falcon*: Rebecca West's Journey through the Balkans," 7.

26. Montefiore, *Men and Women Writers of the 1930s*, 202–203.

27. Ibid., 203.

28. West, *Black Lamb*, 1029.

29. Ibid., 54. Another such intervention is visible in the last photograph included in the original Viking edition of 1941. Unlike the other photographs, taken mostly of churches and landscapes in the late 1930s, the last one shows King Peter II taking the Oath of

Accession in March of 1941, signaling resistance to Hitler's demand that Yugoslavia join the Axis powers. The photo thus postdates the events of the main text.

30. Cohen, "Rebecca West's Palimpsestic Praxis: Crafting the Intermodern Voice of Witness," 154.

31. Ibid., 159.

32. West, *Black Lamb*, 648.

33. Ibid., 687.

34. Montefiore highlights the fact that West has her own, mostly unacknowledged, heritage of collective memory: "two main kinds of historical narrative can easily be distinguished: one the one hand the 'collective narrative' of European history, told from the perspective of an explicit liberalism to which the writer's allegiance is made plain from the start, and on the other, the personal narrative of West and her husband on their journey, also seen from the perspective of left-liberalism." Montefiore draws upon the work of Maurice Halbwach, whose theory of "collective memory" sees how group memory gives individuals a "frame of reference" from which to form their own individual memories. *Men and Women Writers of the 1930s*, 189.

35. West, *Black Lamb*, 426.

36. Ibid., 350.

37. Ibid., 457.

38. Ibid., 1128.

39. Ibid., 170.

40. Ibid., 785.

41. Ibid.

42. Ibid., 435.

43. Ibid.

44. Ibid., 22.

45. Ibid., 103.

46. Ibid., 770.

47. Ibid., 785.

48. Ibid., 23.

49. Ibid., 372.

50. Ibid., 381.

51. Ibid., 1114.

52. Ibid., 1128.

53. Ibid., 409.

54. Ibid., 380.

55. Ibid., 482.

56. West, *Survivors in Mexico*, 93.

57. Schweizer, "Rebecca West's Philosophy of History," 226.

58. Ibid.

59. See for example Lesinska, who argues that "[t]he audaciously eclectic form of West's text creates a space for alternative temporalities. In Bhabha's formulation, alternative temporalities can be identified with such conceptualizations of history which challenge the grandiose narrative celebrating the progress of Western civilization and its concomitant justification of imperialism and celebration of capitalist modernization." Lesinska launches a sophisticated analysis of West's narrative but does not acknowledge

that all of West's efforts are marshaled to defend a mostly traditional European human-
ism and, more specifically, British liberalism. *Perspectives of Four Women Writers on the
Second World War*, 145. And as Montefiore notes in her discussion of West and Lyotard,
"Rebecca West's historical vision strongly invokes the 'grand narrative' of Christianity."
Men and Women Writers of the 1930s, 194.

60. Schweizer does note that "[o]f course, most of West's work was written before the
onset of postmodernism properly speaking, and so any attribution of postmodern qualities to West's work has to be additionally qualified by saying that her worldview and artistic practice express an avant-garde or protoform of the postmodern critique." "Rebecca
West's Philosophy of History," 224.

61. West, *Black Lamb*, 644.

62. Ibid., 519.

63. Ibid., 494.

64. Ibid., 726.

65. Ibid., 785.

66. Ibid., 741.

67. Ibid., 685.

68. Ibid., 234.

69. Ibid., 516.

70. Ibid., 846.

71. Ibid.

72. Ibid., 861.

73. Ibid., 863.

74. Ibid., 444.

75. Ibid., 1146.

76. Ibid., 23.

77. Rollyson, *Rebecca West*, 207.

78. Montefiore, *Men and Women Writers of the 1930s*, 77.

79. See also Rollyson: "In her prologue, Rebecca, like Proust, explores each phase of
her feelings by delving further and further into the past and then reeling it back into the
present. Her prologue is comparable to the 'overture' in *Remembrance of Things Past*, in
which Proust's method, themes and characters are encapsulated." *Rebecca West*, 209.

80. In *1900*, West gently rebukes Proust for "soft soaping" the Dreyfus Case in his
novels, by which she means that he has "water[ed] it down" to spare the reader "the insen-
sate brutality and meanness of human destiny" of history. *1900*, 145–146.

81. Although Schweizer argues that West's fragmented style is actually the product of
her choice of epic genre: "the heterogeneous expansiveness of *Black Lamb and Grey
Falcon* reflects one of epic's inherent qualities." *Rebecca West: Heroism, Rebellion, and the
Female Epic*, 83.

82. West, *Black Lamb*, 1128. Interestingly, the term "nonsense" had been used by
Ludwig Wittgenstein in his *Tractatus Logico-Philosophicus* (1918), to designate whatever
cannot be depicted in logic or language: "If I cannot say a priori what elementary propo-
sitions there are, then the attempt to do so must lead to obvious nonsense. The limits of
my language mean the limits of my world." Wittgenstein, *Major Works*, 5.5571, 5.6.
West's usage of the term also anticipates Julia Kristeva's *The Sense and Non-Sense of
Revolt* (2001).

83. Although for the most part readers were quick to see *Black Lamb's* value as a work of history: B. W. Huebsch, her American publisher and one of its earliest readers, wrote to her on November 30, 1939, that "[i]t seems to me you have created a new and fascinating method of presenting history." Rebecca West Collection, General Collection, Beinecke Rare Book and Manuscript Library, Yale University. (Box 10, Folder 404.) Rollyson reports this letter as from Harold Guinzberg, also at Viking, but the letter is from Huebsch. Rollyson, *Rebecca West*, 200.

84. West, *Black Lamb*, 773.

85. Ibid., 140.

86. Ibid., 116.

87. Ibid., 54.

88. Ibid., 128–137.

89. Ibid., 1089.

90. Ibid., 765, 805.

91. Ibid., 362.

92. Ibid., 450–454.

93. Ibid., 454–455.

94. Ibid., 58.

95. Bakhtin, *The Dialogic Imagination*, 276.

96. West, *Black Lamb*, 58.

97. Ibid., 59.

98. Lukács, *Historical Novel*, 23.

99. Conrad, "The Duel," 352.

100. Ibid., 408.

101. Lukács, *Historical Novel*, 24.

102. Conrad, "The Duel," 354.

103. Ibid., 362.

104. Conrad, *Collected Works*, x.

105. Conrad, "The Duel," 418.

106. Conrad, *Collected Works*, xi.

107. West, *Black Lamb*, 59.

108. Ibid.

109. Ibid.

110. Bergson, *Creative Mind*, 10.

111. West, *Black Lamb*, 138.

112. Ibid., 640.

113. Ibid., 119.

114. Ibid., 148.

115. Ibid., 643.

116. Ibid., 162.

117. Ibid., 488.

118. Ibid., 127.

119. Ibid., 492.

120. Ibid., 1126.

121. Ibid., 55.

122. Ibid., 152.

123. Todorova, *Imagining the Balkans*, 6. In her work Todorova asks, "How could a geographical appellation be transformed into one of the most powerful pejorative designations in history, international relations, political science, and, nowadays, general intellectual discourse? This question has more than a narrow academic relevance. It is the story of (1) innocent inaccuracies stemming from imperfect geographical knowledge transmitted through tradition; (2) the later saturation of the geographical appellation with political, social, cultural and ideological overtones, and the beginning of the pejorative use of 'Balkan' around World War I; and (3) the complete dissociation of the designation from its object, and the subsequent reverse and retroactive ascription of the ideological loaded designation to the region, particularly after 1989." Ibid., 7.

124. West, *Black Lamb*, 21.

125. Ibid., 640.

126. Ibid., 913.

127. Ibid., 55.

128. Ibid., 56.

129. Ibid., 280, 284.

130. Ibid., 1089.

131. Ibid., 1060.

132. Most treatments of *Black Lamb* do not pay much attention to British imperialism, but see Milena Todorova Radeva's dissertation, "Philanthropy, the Welfare State, and Early Twentieth-Century Literature," 91–95.

133. West, *Black Lamb*, 1091.

134. Richard Tillinghast argues that what drew West to Yugoslavia in the first place was its similarities to Great Britain: "Perhaps part of the reason she felt at home with the notion of a 'united kingdom' was that she herself was a citizen of such a state. With an Anglo-Irish father, a Scottish mother, she herself was, for lack of a better term, British." "Rebecca West and the Tragedy of Yugoslavia," 15.

135. Schweizer, *Rebecca West: Heroism, Rebellion, and the Female Epic*, 89; Cohen, "Rebecca West's Palimpsestic Praxis: Crafting the Intermodern Voice of Witness," 152; Lesinska, *Perspectives of Four Women Writers on the Second World War*, 141.

136. West, *Black Lamb*, 1116.

137. West, *Strange Necessity*, 140.

138. West's satirical story "Madame Sara's Magic Crystal" was only published posthumously in 1992. It lambasts Tito's Partisans and Britain's willingness to back Tito over Draža Mihailović and the Serbian Chetniks. She wrote that, at the urging of the Foreign Office, she withheld publication, "thus giving guarantee of my willingness to sacrifice myself to the needs of the country." West, *The Only Poet and Short Stories*, 167. *Black Lamb*, and its pro-Serbian bias, resurfaced to prominence during the NATO operations in the Balkans. David Farley, in *Modernist Travel Writing* (2011), argues that West's pro-Serbian views reached the Clinton administration via Robert Kaplan's *Balkan Ghosts*, and may have delayed US action against Slobodan Milosevic's regime. *Modernist Travel Writing*, 161.

139. Mehta, *Liberalism and Empire*, 4.

140. The imperial memos of Leonard Woolf are revealing as to the state of liberal views on empire during the 1920s and 1930s: as Luke Reader explores, "Woolf's work for the LPACIQ [Labour Party Advisory Committee on International Questions] actually

Notes to Pages 175–179

presented a renewed model of imperial rule. Although Woolf opposed empire for its inherent tendency towards economic exploitation, his work nevertheless presumed that the development of colonial space remained contingent upon British experts on imperial policy successfully enacting methods of human management." These views were not shared by Leonard Woolf's wife, who died a pacifist and fierce critic of empire. Reader, "'Not Yet Able to Stand by Themselves': Leonard Woolf, Socialist Imperialism, and Discourses of Race, 1925–1941," 104.

141. West, *Black Lamb*, 1125.

142. Ibid., Introduction, xli.

143. Ibid., 913.

144. Conrad, *Heart of Darkness*, 12.

145. West, *Black Lamb*, 164.

146. Said, *Culture and Imperialism*, 26.

147. Snyder describes ethnographic modernism as "literary texts that emulate modern ethnographies, in which metropolitan observers voyage into foreign cultures, regarded as exotic, primitive, or traditional." *British Fiction and Cross-Cultural Encounters*, 2,7.

148. West, *Strange Necessity*, 58.

149. West, *Black Lamb*, 55.

150. Ibid., 1149.

151. Ibid., 160.

152. Ibid., 17.

153. Ibid., 1012.

154. Ibid., 1013.

155. Ibid., 55.

156. Ibid., 265.

157. Ibid., 1127.

158. Barthes, *Writing Degree Zero*, 29.

159. Although *Black Lamb* was certainly not her last work of history: her last published work, *1900*, is a series of historical essays on the year 1900, as West explores the political, social, and cultural features of that year, interweaving her own childhood memories to add personal color. She also wrote the historical novel *The Birds Fall Down*— a retelling of a real series of events that Ford Madox Ford related to West many years previous—drafting it in 1944 but not completing it until 1962. (Ford had heard the story from his sister Juliet Soskice, whose husband was a Russian involved in politics and espionage.) It depicts the years leading up to the Russian Revolution, tracing the activities of terrorist groups and tsarist counterespionage activity. West thus continued her immersion in history throughout her life, but *Black Lamb* represents her last attempt to find radical new forms with which to depict the past. See Christensen, "The Azev Affair and *The Birds Fall Down*."

160. Christopher Hitchens, who penned the Introduction to the 2007 Penguin edition of *Black Lamb*, has cited her as an influence; Geoff Dyer, the novelist-historian, has mentioned West many times in essays and interviews; Åsne Seierstad and Anne Coleman are other examples of recent explicit acknowledgments; the title of Tony White's *Another Fool in the Balkans: In the Footsteps of Rebecca West* (2006) speaks for itself.

Conclusion

1. Stetz, "Rebecca West and the Nuremberg Trials," 235.

2. West, *Black Lamb*, 623.

3. Ibid., 660.

4. Ibid., 662.

5. Ibid., 801.

6. Ibid., 803.

7. Ibid., 806. Colquitt, "A Call to Arms," 83. Rollyson reports that West attacked the German polymath to annoy Stanislav: "At dinner Rebecca provoked Stanislav by denying Goethe's greatness. She admired his brilliance, but she could see he was poisoned with German thought. Stanislav said Goethe had opened up the classical world, Rome, and the very meaning of culture not only to Germans but to all of Europe. Rebecca rejected Goethe as an impostor and extolled Gibbon." *Rebecca West*, 191.

8. Colquitt, "A Call to Arms," 79.

9. West, *Black Lamb*, 1083.

10. Ibid., 322.

11. Ibid., 398.

12. Ibid., 400.

13. See Lassner, "Rebecca West's Shadowy Other." Also see Lassner and Trubowitz, *Antisemitism and Philosemitism in the Twentieth and Twenty-First Centuries.*

14. West, *Black Lamb*, 991.

15. Ibid., 643.

16. Ibid., 202.

17. Ibid., 61.

18. Ibid., 914.

19. Ibid., 1038.

20. Braudel, *The Mediterranean and the Mediterranean World in the Age of Philip II*, 21. For critics like Ricoeur and Jameson, however, narrative was latent in the work of *les annalistes*. Jameson writes in "Marxism and Historicism" that structure "can always be grasped and rewritten in terms of something like a narrative or teleological vision of history" and thus "the structural attempt to reduce the multiplicity of empirical moments of the past or of other cultures to some fundamental typology or system would seem to be a failure, insofar as the surface categories of such narrative history find themselves smuggled back into the typology to lend it a generally disguised content." *Ideologies of Theory*, 2: *Syntax of History*:169.

21. Burrow argues that the popularity of the *Annales* School was due to "the decline of France, earlier than that of Britain or Germany, as a great power, and disillusionment with the notoriously centralizing tendencies of the French state inherited from Richelieu, Louis XIV and the Revolution." Americans, on the other hand, have drawn more on narrative historiography, especially foundational narratives, to explain how they have come to be the world's superpower. Burrow, *A History of Histories*, 468.

22. Ibid., 474.

23. Schama, *Dead Certainties*, 325.

24. In "Nietzsche, Genealogy, History," Foucault wrote that Nietzsche "always questioned the form of history that reintroduces (and always assumes) a suprahistorical perspective: a history whose function is to compose the finally reduced diversity of time into

a totality fully closed upon itself; a history that always encourages subjective recognitions and attributes a form of reconciliation to all the displacements of the past; a history whose perspective on all that precedes it implies the end of time, a completed development. The historian's history finds its support outside of time and pretends to base its judgments on an apocalyptic objectivity. This is only possible, however, because of its belief in eternal truth, the immortality of the soul, and the nature of consciousness as always identical to itself." Furthermore, "[h]istorians take unusual pains to erase the elements in their work which reveal their grounding in a particular time and place, their preferences in a controversy. . . . Nietzsche's version of history sense is explicit in its perspective and acknowledges its system of injustice. Its perception is slanted, being a deliberate appraisal, affirmation, or negation." *The Foucault Reader*, 86,90.

25. Barthes, *The Rustle of Language*, 140.

26. This was not always the case with history: Herodotus, the problematic founder of the discipline of history, used the term *historia* to mean "inquiry." Herodotus passed on local histories—what we might now consider folklore—but did not necessarily believe in the factual basis of the stories he was recounting. As much as Thucydides is looked to as providing the "scientific" aspects of history, Herodotus did have a sophisticated understanding of the relationship between the events of the past and the narratives we tell about them. See Burrow, *A History of Histories*, xiii.

27. Althusser, *Reading Capital*, 37.

28. Ibid., 105. Althusser's views are usually seen as antithetical to those of Lukács, but in *History and Class Consciousness*, Lukács stresses the necessary role of mediation in any theory of epistemology: "Mediation would not be possible were it not for the fact that the empirical existence of objects is itself mediated and only appears to be unmediated in so far as the awareness of mediation is lacking so that the objects are torn from the complex of their true determinants and placed in artificial isolation." *History and Class Consciousness*, 163.

29. Althusser, *Reading Capital*, 41.

30. Ibid., 106. Althusser musters these arguments for his more central one in *Reading Capital*, which is that Marx was not narrating a historical, linear narrative of capitalism but rather proposing a structural model for it. Jameson, in "Marxism and Historicism," writes that "such synchronic models do not discredit History in any absolute sense as an object of study and representation, but rather determine a new and original form of historiography, a structural permutation in the latter's narrative form or trope." *Ideologies of Theory*, 2: *Syntax of History*: 155.

31. White, *Metahistory*, ix, x. White summarizes his arguments in his Preface: "1) there can be no 'proper history' which is not at the same time 'philosophy of history'; 2) the possible modes of historiography are the same as the possible modes of speculative philosophy of history; 3) these modes, in turn, are in reality *formalizations* of poetic insights that analytically precede them and that sanction the particular theories used to give historical accounts the aspect of an 'explanation'; 4) there are no apodictically certain theoretical grounds on which one can legitimately claim an authority for any one of the modes over the others as being more 'realistic'; 5) as a consequence of this, we are indentured to a *choice* among contending interpretive strategies in any effort to reflect on history-in-general; 6) as a corollary of this, the best grounds for choosing one perspective on history rather than another are ultimately aesthetic and moral rather than epistemological; and,